KANGAROO

DREAMING

KANGAROO

An Australian Wildlife Odyssey

DREAMING

Edward Kanze

Sierra Club Books
SAN FRANCISCO

The Sierra Club, founded in 1892 by John Muir, has devoted itself to the study and protection of the Earth's scenic and ecological resources—mountains, wetlands, woodlands, wild shores and rivers, deserts and plains. The publishing program of the Sierra Club offers books to the public as a nonprofit educational service in the hope that they may enlarge the public's understanding of the Club's basic concerns. The point of view expressed in each book, however, does not necessarily represent that of the Club. The Sierra Club has some sixty chapters coast to coast, in Canada, Hawaii, and Alaska. For information about how you may participate in its programs to preserve wilderness and the quality of life, please address inquiries to Sierra Club, 85 Second Street, San Francisco, CA 94105.

www.Sierra.org/books

Published by Sierra Club Books in conjunction with Crown Publishers. Member of the Crown Publishing Group.

Random House, Inc. New York, Toronto, London, Sydney, Auckland

www.randomhouse.com

SIERRA CLUB, SIERRA CLUB BOOKS and Sierra Club design logos are registered trademarks of the Sierra Club.

Printed in the United States of America on acid-free paper containing a minimum of 50 percent recovered waste paper, of which at least 10 percent of the fiber content is postconsumer waste.

DESIGN BY LYNNE AMFT

Library of Congress Cataloging-in-Publication Data

Kanze, Edward.
    Kangaroo dreaming : an Australian wildlife odyssey / by Edward Kanze.—1st ed.
      p.   cm.
    1. Natural history—Australia—Anecdotes.   2. Adventure and
adventurers—Australia—Anecdotes.   3. Kanze, Edward.   I. Title.
QH197 .K34 2000
508.94—dc21   00-030102

ISBN 0-609-60796-0

10 9 8 7 6 5 4 3 2

For Peg, Keith, Beris, and John

Contents

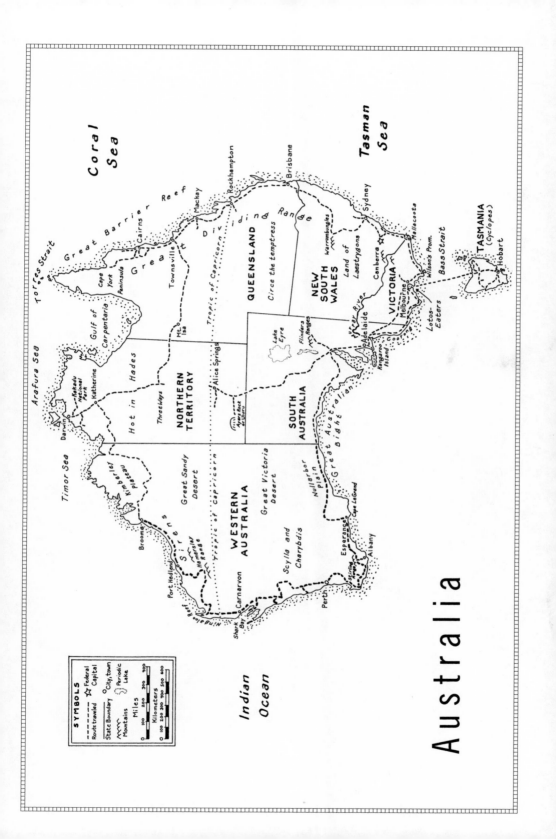

Preface

ON A RIVER in Australia's torrid Northern Territory, my wife, Debbie, and I drifted in a fourteen-foot boat. Below us, estuarine crocodiles cruised like enemy submarines. The largest reptiles alive, these aquatic T-rexes grow to twenty-four feet. They have prodigious appetites, and the place swarmed with them.

Trembling like eucalyptus leaves, we looked toward the banks. In the grass, crocodiles sprawled, several of them longer than our boat. Around us the eyes of other crocs bulged above water the color of lentil soup. They watched us with interest, and as it sank in that we were being scrutinized like a menu, our stomachs knotted. Yet fear of the unknown, I find, is worse than that of the known. It was the monsters we couldn't see, the ones lurking beneath us, that most rattled our equanimity.

The river and the boat-rental office in which we had signed our lives away lay at the end of thirty-five miles of dirt road rife with potholes. The evening before, a sinewy man in a sweat-stained T-shirt had fetched a clipboard from a shack and worked out the deal. As the money changed hands the following morning, he grinned like a piano keyboard. "Get in," he said. We got in. Another flash of teeth and gaps. Grunting, the man grabbed our bow. With a sickening hiss of metal against sand, the boat slid backward, straight into the channel. The man watched from the bank for several minutes, smirking like a Roman who had just tossed his lions a couple of tasty Christians.

On the surface, all was serene. The St. Mary's River lay smooth as glass, reflecting clouds. Amber rays of sunlight slanted out of the northeast, gilding palms that grew along the banks. Cool air brought the tang of brackish water and fish. The time was seven-thirty in the morning.

Rising cautiously to my feet, I pulled the starter. The outboard roared to life. *Thank heaven.* Fifteen minutes earlier, we watched two fishermen set off in another rental boat. The man in the stern yanked the cord again and again. The thin-skinned vessel drifted in a basin roiling with crocodiles.

I imagined us in the same situation, miles upstream. What would we do? Swimming for shore in the St. Mary's would be like skydiving without a parachute—exciting, but fatal.

As the motor purred reassuringly, I nosed the boat upstream. In the bow, Debbie sat quietly, her face drawn tight against her bones.

For better and for worse, we knew that *Crocodylus porosus,* the estuarine crocodile, has catholic tastes. Exceeded in ferocity only by the dinosaurs of old, and native to India, southeast Asia, Australia, and New Guinea, it seizes, perforates, drowns, and devours a smorgasbord of prey: water buffalo, beef cattle, lizards, dogs, kangaroos, men, women, and children. The reptile is cunning, an expert at ambush. A favorite modus operandi is to ease softly into a river or waterhole at the first clump of hooves or footsteps, then lie submerged where the path meets the shore. If a cow, kangaroo, or tourist is foolish enough to enter the river for drink or dunking, the monster is ready. It erupts from its hiding place like a missile from a submarine. Crunch go the jaws.

Gazing into an uncertain future that morning, I saw the journey we were making around Australia in a new light. Ours was no ordinary jaunt around the tourist circuit. It was an adventure of Homeric proportions—a wildlife odyssey. We had traveled to Australia to gain firsthand knowledge of the plants, animals, and people that make the continent unique. And we were finding that monsters, temptresses, and misanthropic reptiles lay frequently in our path.

If anyone could be blamed for our predicament, it was Ralph Waldo Emerson. Early in the year preceding our departure, I read Robert Richardson's *Emerson: The Mind on Fire.* The book triggered a feeding frenzy. I bolted Emerson's essays morning, noon, and night. As I did, the same ideas that had goaded Henry Thoreau into forsaking a soft bed in his parents' house for the cold comforts of Walden Pond fortified my resolve to see Australia, at once. In *Nature,* Emerson wrote:

> To the body and mind which have been cramped by noxious work or company, nature is medicinal and restores their tone. The tradesman, the attorney comes out of the din and craft of the street and sees the sky and the woods, and is a man again. In their eternal calm, he finds himself. The health of the eye seems to demand a horizon. We are never tired, so long as we can see far enough.

I was tired. During the year leading up to our departure, I saw beyond the walls of my office only rarely. Noxious work afflicted me, left me pale and withered, eyes glued to a computer screen, or to pen and paper, hindquarters stuck to a chair. I was in my late thirties. Friends thought my desire to give up everything for a year in the Australian bush was madness. College kids do things like that. I hadn't been a college kid in eighteen years. Yet my instincts told me to go, and without delay. "Trust thyself," advised the mentor of Thoreau and Burroughs. "Every heart vibrates to that iron string."

Debbie caught the bug, too. A year of Ralph at breakfast, Waldo at lunch, and Emerson at dinner infected her with a serious case of self-reliance. She was weary of office work. The ringing of telephones was driving her mad. Emerson spoke to both of us. The cool man with the fiery mind advised frank action. Only later would circumstances show that the sage's wisdom had its limits. In the river full of crocodiles, for example, our iron strings played Retreat.

"In self-trust all the virtues are comprehended," wrote Emerson, who probably never gazed on a reptile big enough to eat him. "Free should the scholar be—free and brave." Free we were. No jobs, no commitments, no itinerary. As for brave, only events would tell.

Every wanderer may secretly fancy his journey an odyssey, and travel has a way of testing the mettle of us all. Nevertheless, the parallels between our rambles in Australia and Odysseus's trials are uncanny. The Greek, no hero when it came to eschewing comforts, traveled by the best, fastest, and most comfortable means available to him—a boat supplied with sails, sailors, oars, oarsmen, and numerous goatskins of wine. We acted in kind. After traversing the Pacific on a jumbo jet equipped with cabin crew and a bar, we explored "that great America on the other side of the sphere," as Herman Melville called Australia, in a sixteen-year-old Toyota.

Regarding a woman's presence in this odyssey, consider the following points. The original Homeric journey took place before the advent of feminism. A man could abandon his wife for ten years in those days, never write home, and return with a reasonable chance that dinner would be waiting on the table. Times had changed. My odyssey was Debbie's, too. She had no more interest in staying home, pressing olives, and shrinking violets than I had in leaving her to fend off suitors. We had no son or daughter, no Telemachus, to defend her virtue, nor the means to host a decade-long house party. Debbie, too, longed for adventure. And perhaps, having read of Circe and Calypso, of Clinton and Lewinsky, and of wandering men and Trojans, she knew it would be tempting fate to send her husband off without a chaperone.

Our two greatest concerns upon arriving in Australia, lotos-eaters and Cyclopes notwithstanding, were intoxicated drivers and snakes. We could, and did, greatly reduce our risk of harm by the former by driving cautiously and staying off roads after dark. This stratagem also helped prevent fatal encounters with kangaroos, which are more thick-headed around automobiles than are deer in our own part of the world.

As for snakes, our extensive experience with them in North America gave confidence that even the deadly ones would do their best to avoid us. Nonetheless, we would be wary. "Serpents are so numerous in Australia," wrote the nineteenth-century explorer Carl Lumholtz, that "it is of course necessary to keep a sharp look-out and not get too close to them. They may be met everywhere—on the ground, in the trees, in the water, nay, even in the houses. . . . The bushman's precaution of always examining his bed before retiring to rest I deem worthy of imitation." We'd look before we slept.

In light of such hazards, why choose Australia?

Years before our departure, I had a recurrent dream. I was alone and confused on a grassy hillside at twilight. The air was cool, the grass green. This was a foreign place, yet I felt at home. Suddenly I became aware of movement. Figures were creeping toward me from the shadows. They were animals, neither walking nor hopping but rocking awkwardly back and forth on short arms and long legs. The motion reminded me of contraptions I'd seen pumping oil from wells in Texas. The animals had long faces, big dark eyes, and tall ears.

Kangaroos.

The kangaroos seemed to be waiting for me to do something.

Three times during the 1980s, I traveled from the United States to New Zealand. In that country of islands, a thousand miles distant from Australia, I roamed far and wide, studied the habits of extraordinary animals, and collected material for a book. In New Zealand I picked up Australian radio broadcasts and stood on bluffs overlooking the Tasman Sea, nearly convincing myself I could make out the Kangaroo Continent, dark and low on the horizon. People said to me, "If you're going that far, you might as well go to Australia." I chose not to. Like Thoreau, who opted to travel widely in Concord, I craved sharp focus, not a blur of thrills. I concentrated on New Zealand and let Australia wait.

Perhaps the kangaroos were waiting for me to come to Australia.

My longest visit to Colorado-sized New Zealand spanned two months. Australia, the size of the U.S.A. minus Alaska, would require a longer stay. To visit its farthest reaches, to wander from the Kimberley region of the northwest to Tasmania in the southeast, to explore the tropical rain forests of northeastern Queensland and the skyscraping jarrah and karri forests two thousand miles away in Western Australia, I would need months, if not years. So Australia remained on the back burner. I cooked New Zealand into a book. Meanwhile the dream of kangaroos came back again and again.

As years came and went, my knowledge of Australia grew by increments. I ferreted out and devoured reports penned by a Who's Who of writers—James Cook, Joseph Banks, Charles Darwin, Anthony Trollope, Mark Twain, Elspeth Huxley, Bruce Chatwin, Jan Morris, Tony Horwitz, Paul Theroux, and others. Alan Moorehead's books piled up at my bedside. I read Robert Hughes's *The Fatal Shore* and learned that Australia was populated first by Aborigines who arrived on foot when New Guinea was linked by a land bridge, and second by the cream of English society—Luddites, malcontents, miscreants, and other people smart and cheeky enough to steal a few silver spoons from the wealthy rather than starve. At the time, the Industrial Revolution blackened English skies, making a few rich and hundreds of thousands poor. While the ruck of England stayed behind and worked itself to the grave, rebels and adventurers fled or were exported in chains along with a few hardened criminals. Together they filled the Australian gene pool with the qualities epitomized in Hollywood films by Errol Flynn, a Tasmanian.

As Robin Hood and Captain Blood, Flynn was saucy, wickedly intelligent, and fearless. He answered to neither god nor government, but to his own sense of decency. (His off-screen decency was another matter.) The more I learned about Australia, the better I understood why so many renegade thinkers from the northern half of the globe had been drawn there.

Jonathan Swift, fascinated by accounts of the great southern continent brought back to England by William Dampier, set the early chapters of his best-known work, *Travels to Several Remote Parts of the World by Lemuel Gulliver* (1726), in Australia's West. Much later, D. H. Lawrence, seeking refuge from a homeland he found increasingly confining and small-minded, came to Australia for a visit and toyed with the idea of emigrating. From Norway and Germany came the zoologists Carl Lumholtz and Bernard Grzimek, and from the United States the nature writers John Muir and Edward Abbey. Muir arrived across the Indian Ocean by tramp steamer, Abbey by jet over the Pacific. Abbey loved the place, and often threatened to return there and settle. "Time to light out," he wrote in his journal a few months before his death, "for the last good country: Dinkum Aussieland." Muir loved Australia, too. "Wish I could spend a yr. here," he scribbled in a notebook after his first day ashore.

Penelope—er, Debbie —and I decided to follow Lawrence, Muir, and Abbey. We had no intention of treading reverently in their footsteps, but resolved to make our own fresh prints. Late one northern-hemisphere autumn, we committed ourselves to going. This was our plan: we would have no plan. We agreed to follow our noses. If that meant boating among crocodiles or crossing unforgiving deserts, so be it. Beneath our seeming madness lay Emersonian method. "Culture is not the trimming and turf-ing of gardens," wrote the Transcendentalist sage, "but the showing [of] the true harmony of the unshorn landscape with horrid thickets and bold mountains and the balance of the land and sea." We would spend little time in the trimmed, turfed cities of Australia. They have been written about at length by others. Urban Australia presents the visitor chiefly with a transplanted Euro-American culture, spiced by local flavor. Nor would we attempt to immerse ourselves in Aboriginal culture. Daisy Bates, Bruce Chatwin, and competent anthropologists had done that before us. They were better students of Australia's native life than we, and we were better naturalists.

Our design was simple. We would roam the length and breadth of the country, making firsthand acquaintance with animals known, if only vaguely, to children and adults all over the globe—kangaroos, wallabies, koalas, wombats, duck-billed platypuses, echidnas, Tasmanian devils, kookaburras, and emus. In locating these archetypal Australians, we would trek through forests, pick our way through shrublands the Australians call "mallee," wade through grasslands, and trudge through deserts, getting to know flora as well as fauna. If all went well, if we managed to survive the ozone hole, bush fires, quicksand, drunk drivers, snakes, crocodiles, and venomous sea creatures, we would slog through enough horrid thickets and scale enough bold mountains to discern their harmony. Rather than ornamental boomerangs, we would bring home ideas and stories.

This, then, is a nature and adventure story, a book about how we roamed the world's oldest continent, bounding after kangaroos, waddling after wombats, and cruising among crocodiles. It is also an account of people met along the way. While in the "bush," as Australians call their back country, we passed 131 nights in a tent and two in the open, lying with snakes and scorpions under an indigo firmament shot through with glittering stars. In the process we met a broad cross-section of antipodean wildlife and *Homo sapiens australis*. The reader will meet both in these pages.

North, west, and south—south, west, and north—
They lead and follow Fate—
The stoutest hearts that venture forth—
The swagman and his mate.
A restless, homeless class they are
Who tramp in border land.
They take their rest 'neath moon and star—
Their bed the desert sand,
On sunset tracks they ride and tramp,
Till speech has almost died,
And still they drift from camp to camp
In silence side by side.
They think and dream, as all men do;
Perchance their dreams are great—
Each other's thoughts are sacred to
The swagman and his mate.

—Henry Lawson,
from "The Swagman and His Mate"

KANGAROO
DREAMING

I

Leaving Troy

AT THE BEGINNING of the *Odyssey,* Homer's hero was missing. Odysseus had long been away, skulking inside wooden horses and hacking at Trojans. As far as his wife, Penelope, his son, Telemachus, or the other folks in Ithaca knew, the great warrior had vanished into the maw of fate.

For us the situation was similar. In 1990, Debbie fell under the spell of a naturalist and writer with an erratic income. In 1992, on Leap Day, she married him. A few weeks later, seeking a change of scene and refuge from the high cost of living in New York and Connecticut, we fled to hot, humid, hurricane-battered Mississippi. There, in a city called Ocean Springs, we vanished, at least as far as our northern friends were concerned. Almost all who knew us imagined us waging war with oppressive heat, plagues of mosquitoes, and Neanderthals. In fact, Ocean Springs and its citizens welcomed us warmly, and the town proved a hotbed of artistic and intellectual activity, an Athens of the South.

Hardly had Odysseus fled Troy and set a course for home than he made a watering stop at Ismarus, land of the Cicones. "I sacked the city and slew them," he says in T. E. Lawrence's lively prose translation of the *Odyssey.* The Greeks also made off with the Cicones' wine. Enraged by the Greeks' mischief, Zeus whipped up terrible storms. The Greek fleet was nearly wrecked, bringing Homer perilously close to losing a good story.

As for Debbie and me, we stopped on the way to Australia in New Zealand. We did not slay the New Zealanders, who greeted us kindly, and what wine we took we paid for. Our good behavior earned its reward. A week later, Zeus gave us a smooth flight to Melbourne.

But I leap ahead of the story. Before we could flee Ocean Springs, we needed to equip ourselves with knowledge and muster provisions. Of the two, provisioning proved easier. Calling on the miracle of mail order, and finding a latter-day Athena in our Visa card, we bought an expedition-grade tent to house us for nine months and more, wide-brimmed hats to guard our necks and noses from the harsh antipodean sun, rain suits (for hiking in the downpours we might encounter in Tasmania and New Zealand), heavy socks, a candle lantern by which we might read in our tent during long winter nights, and 150 rolls of film to photograph all the kangaroos we aimed to see.

Each of us would carry his allotted limit of luggage, but no more. This was an Odyssey on a shoestring. No plunder would fatten our wallets along the way. We would pack two suitcases each, stow these in the hold of the airplane, and take two carry-on bags apiece. Into these receptacles we crammed the newly purchased items, plus the following: three cameras, eight lenses, two tripods, two tripod heads, three strobes, a miscellany of other photographic gear, a mountaineering stove, fuel bottles, a pot to cook in, a cup each to drink from, eating utensils, matches, candles, a first-aid kit, a coil of rope, a pocket knife, a whetstone, walking sticks, sleeping bags, thin foam mattresses, a traveling library of natural history books, a few paperback novels, toiletries, and all the clothing we would need to keep us comfortable in conditions ranging from arctic to equatorial. Trying to force it all in became a challenge, a test of the tensile strength of the suitcases. A few things were jettisoned, among them a razor and razor blades. From this Odyssey I would return home as Odysseus did, bearded, bedraggled, a stranger.

Hauling the gear to the airline check-in counter without appearing that we were smuggling uranium ore proved an exercise in Laurel-and-Hardiness. I lifted the bags one by one onto the scale, sweat beading on my forehead. Having exported myself before, I knew that if I arrived early and checked in matter-of-factly, the outrageous weight of my bags might be ignored. The ploy worked. Smiles, a tapping of keys, and seat assignments followed. Soon we were slinking away with boarding passes.

Headstrong, Odysseus launched into his journey with little idea of the perils and prospects ahead. We learned from his mistake. Although we left the exact nature of our travels to serendipity, we did a little homework before embarking. The idea was to prepare ourselves for the Lotos-Eaters, Cyclopes, Sirens, and seductresses we might meet along the way. As it happened, much of the information we gathered about Australia was already familiar to us, reinforcing Emerson's notion that we can learn only what we already know.

We discovered, or rediscovered, that Australia was simultaneously an island, a continent, and a country. All three, or all one, depending on your viewpoint, represent an area roughly the size of the United States of America minus Alaska. Like the U.S.A., Australia comprises individual states, six of them, plus two mainland territories and a miscellany of islands. The best known of the states, and the first to have been settled by Europeans, is New South Wales. It occupies several hundred miles of Australia's eastern coast, reaches far inland, and covers an area about half the size of Alaska.

To give another comparison, New South Wales equals the acreage of all of America's New England states plus New York, Pennsylvania, Ohio, Indiana, and Illinois. Rain forests blanket the northeastern mountains, ski resorts operate in the south, and the west is flat, dry, and hot. The capital of the state is Sydney, a bright, bustling place covering an area about the size of Los Angeles. Its 3.5 million people constitute the majority of New South Wales's population. The other 2.2 million live mostly in smaller towns and cities, with a few hardy ranchers, farmers, and park rangers spread thinly over the outback.

Victoria, Australia's second most populous state, lies in the relatively cool southeast. Within its boundaries occur plains and deserts, several modest mountain ranges, and a scenic coastline that bends around the southeast corner of the continent from the New South Wales border in the east to the South Australian frontier in the west. In area, Victoria equals America's New England states, with two New Jerseys added. It is slightly smaller than the United Kingdom, although the U.K. holds nearly fourteen times the population. Among Victoria's cities, Melbourne (pronounced "Melbin" by its natives), at 3 million, is the largest.

One hundred fifty miles across the tempestuous Bass Strait, an overnight ferry ride from Melbourne, lies the island of Tasmania, formerly known as Van Diemen's Land. The smallest and least populous of Australia's states, Tasmania approaches the size of Scotland and is slightly larger than West Virginia. Farther south than the rest of Australia, it is surrounded by water that remains chilly in summer and turns frigid in winter. Tasmania is Australia's coolest state, and also its wettest and most forested. Much of the land resembles New Zealand—mountainous, heavily wooded with Antarctic beech, frequently shrouded by rain and fog, and ringed by quiet coastal villages and a sawtooth coastline. The capital, and the largest town on the island, is Hobart.

Back on the mainland, directly to the north of New South Wales and beyond, lies Queensland (pronounced as if two words), the second-largest of Australia's states. More than double the area of New South Wales, larger than Alaska, two and a half times the size of Texas, and seven times bigger than the U.K., Queensland stretches from Brisbane, near the New South Wales border, more than a thousand miles north to the tip of the Cape York Peninsula. It also sprawls westward along the southern reaches of the Gulf of Carpentaria, deep into the continent's dry interior. Brisbane (pronounced BRIZ-bin), the capital, has about 1.3 million residents, almost half the state's population.

Running across Australia like a waistline, the Tropic of Capricorn divides Queensland in two, slices off the southernmost quarter of the Northern Territory, and cuts the largest Australian state, Western Australia, into nearly equal halves. Western Australia, often called "W.A.," is the country's Alaska—not in climate, which tends toward the hot and dry, but in the sense that it is remote from the rest of the country (separated by harsh deserts), immense (more than ten times the size of the United Kingdom, or larger than all of the United States east of the Mississippi), beautiful beyond imagining, and governed by politicians who seem bent on running it like a fire sale. Given its vastness, W.A.'s population of 1.5 million is minuscule by northern hemisphere standards. Practically everyone lives in Perth, while a few rugged individuals scatter among small towns, outback ranches, mining communities, and dairy farms.

East of W.A., snug against more than a third of its interior boundary, lies South Australia, the third largest state. South Australia covers four times the area of the U.K. and could swallow Texas and Colorado, with room left over for dessert. The capital, Adelaide, hums with the movements of a million residents, about the same number of people as live in Dallas. Climate varies. The southern coastal region collects enough rain to quench Adelaide's thirst and to allow ranches, a bit of heavy industry, and vineyards to thrive. The Barossa Valley and McLaren Vale, both found here, produce some of the finest wines in any hemisphere.

The state's interior is a different story. Barren, rocky, sun-scorched places called "gibber plains" spread to the horizon. Look at a map and you'll find Lake Eyre. On any other continent such a basin would hold an inland sea. Here it lies empty nearly all of the time, like a crater on the moon. Lake Eyre fills only a few times a century. Australia is the world's driest continent, by far. Nowhere is the scarcity of moisture more apparent than in the northern, geologically ancient reaches of South Australia.

Two territories fill out Australia's boundaries. One is immense, the other tiny. The big one lies directly north of South Australia and is known as the Northern Territory, or simply "the Territory." Its boundaries circumscribe an area five and a half times the size of the U.K., with only 1/332 the population. If the Northern Territory were placed over the northwestern United States, it would cover Washington, Oregon, Montana, Idaho, and Wyoming, and lap slightly over the Canadian border. Less than 200,000 people live there, the lion's share of whom divide between Darwin, the capital city in the tropical north, and Alice Springs, the administrative center of the south.

Last comes the Australian Capital Territory, or "A.C.T." A district of nine hundred square miles, thirteen times the size of America's District of Columbia, the A.C.T. surrounds the built-to-order, steel-and-glass city of Canberra. The construction of the federal capital began in 1923. In a neutral location tucked within the Great Dividing Range between Sydney and Melbourne, streets were laid out and cornerstones placed, all according to a plan laid out by Walter Burley Griffin, a Chicago architect. Griffin was dismissed from the project before it reached completion, but the city kept growing. Today its nearly 300,000 inhabitants are mostly bureaucrats and workers in service industries, all suckling directly and indirectly on the taxpayer's milk of kindness. Canberra is an Aboriginal word, sometimes translated as "woman's breasts."

Superficially, Australia resembles the United States. The distance from sea to shining sea is similar, about 2,700 miles from the Pacific coast of Queensland to the Indian Ocean beaches of Western Australia. In important respects, Australia and the U.S.A. form mirror images of each other. Both have long east-west axes, relatively shorter spans from north to south, and immense peninsulas reaching toward the Equator—Florida, dangling into the Caribbean, and the Cape York Peninsula, thrusting toward New Guinea.

For all the similarities, however, the differences between Australia and the U.S.A. are profound. Australia's mainland stretches from latitude 9 degrees South, in the islands of the Torres Strait, to 39 degrees South at Victoria's Wilson's Promontory. It straddles the Tropic of Capricorn and lies uncomfortably close, on summer days, to the planet's midriff. The U.S.A., by contrast, sits in cool, comfortable temperate latitudes, ranging from the forty-ninth parallel along the Canadian border of the Far West to nearly twenty-four degrees at Key West. The Tropic of Cancer misses North America entirely, threading the needle between Florida and Cuba.

If you took the forty-eight states and pushed them southward to the vicinity of Mexico, the result would be a place something like Australia. The sun would be stronger, the temperature hotter, the landscape far more dry. Like Mexico, Australia finds itself squarely under one of the bands of persistent high pressure that ring the globe in the vicinity of 30 degrees North and South. In these zones, dry air pushes down toward the earth's surface, bringing little rain and soaking up what wisps of moisture are present. Thus are born the world's great deserts. Winds blowing from the oceans surrounding Australia moderate the effect, but overall the country is hot and parched, a place of deserts and near deserts, with lush forests restricted mainly to cool Tasmania, humid stretches of coast, and a few high mountains.

Peaks are scarce in Australia, and not very imposing. Kosciusko, the highest, rises to only 7,310 feet. The Great Dividing Range, which parallels the eastern shore, is not especially great, except in beauty. South Australia's Flinders Ranges, Western Australia's Kimberley Plateau and Hamersley Range, and the Dividing Range form scattered bulges, but Australia otherwise resembles a pizza. A few lumps lie sprinkled over the middle like sausage and mushrooms, while the crust drops steeply along the sides.

Australia's unpredictable climate would confound Debbie and me, just as Zeus, Poseidon, and Aeolus exasperated Odysseus. Our fickle god was El Niño. This periodic quirk of global wind patterns, occurring on a changeable cycle of two to eight years, allows the balmy waters that normally pool around Australia to pour eastward across the Pacific. When the oceans around the country cool, evaporation rates plummet and droughts begin. And persist. When showers come, they arrive erratically. Some places go eight years without rain, then are savaged by cloudbursts. "Australia," writes the Australian biologist Tim Flannery, "is the only continent on Earth where the overwhelming influence on climate is a non-annual climatic change." Odysseus would have blamed it on Zeus.

Aside from its mercurial weather, Australia is a stable place. Its landscapes are often described as "ancient," "timeless," and "unchanging," and with good reason. The continent's rocks, for the most part, are very, very old. Among them are some of the earliest formations on Earth, many bearing traces of the planet's first stirrings of life. There have been no significant upheavals in recent geologic memory, nor any catastrophic periods of volcanism save for a stray eruption here and there. Recent ice ages have treated Australia gently. In nearby New Zealand, by contrast, tectonic shifting forces the Indian Plate against the Pacific Plate, creating active volcanoes on the North Island and towering mountains on the South.

About 53 million years before ancestral Aborigines ignited the continent's first campfire, the block of land that includes present-day Australia pulled away from Antarctica. For the future home of Aborigines and Englishmen, the result was a jagged southern coastline, rocky and forbidding. Much of the coast looks as if the separation occurred yesterday. Cliffs front against the sea like raw wounds. Along with South America and Africa, Australia once formed part of an ancient supercontinent that geologists call Gondwana. India, also part of Gondwana, careened away about 140 million years ago. It smashed into Asia and pushed up the mountains known today as the Himalayas. Earlier still, about 180 million years ago, Gondwana was married to a northern supercontinent that geologists call Laurasia.

At the time Australia pulled away from Antarctica, the two continents were watered by warm rains and covered in part by rain forest. Before long in geologic time, however, Australia drifted into the high-pressure zone around 30 degrees South, and Antarctica slid into the high latitudes, where barometric readings also soar toward the upper reaches of the scale. Deserts spread over the divorced continents—a frigid polar desert, in Antarctica's case.

For the Gondwanan plants and animals of Australia, the move to the dry subtropics proved more fortunate than the fate met by similar flora and fauna in Antarctica. The move was made slowly, allowing opportunities for adaptation. Simultaneously, the planet cooled, a situation that hurried Antarctica's wildlife toward oblivion but moderated climatic change in Australia. In fact, as planetary temperatures declined, Australia drifted toward the Equator at a rate that approximated the rate of cooling. The cooling and warming canceled each other out, and the island continent, with its placid geology and freedom from recent glaciations, enjoyed a relatively stable climate. This lucky happenstance helped to rescue ancient Gondwanan plants and animals that were dying out elsewhere.

Australia's northward journey came to an end, or at least to its present location, when its tectonic plate collided with the block of crust underlying Eurasia and Indonesia. Although rocks below the ocean's surface collided, the lands above water never touched. The failure of a land bridge to develop between Eurasia and Australia had important implications for wildlife. Animals that could span the remaining gap by flying or swimming had a relatively easy time getting across in either direction. The same held true for plants whose seeds could drift on the wind, float in the sea (and remain viable), or survive passage in the digestive tracts of bats and birds. But an unbridgeable barrier remained for organisms unable to manage the crossing. Biologists call the hurdle Wallace's Line.

The namesake of the biological divide separating Eurasia from the Australian region was Alfred Russell Wallace. Wallace is most often remembered as the naturalist who arrived at a theory of evolution at the same time as Charles Darwin. A gentleman and good sport, Wallace secured the admiration of posterity by allowing Darwin to publish first. In another spirit, however, Wallace later undercut his own reputation. A frequenter of séances, he asserted that reputable mediums could provide authentic dialogue with the dead.

Today, Wallace is best remembered as the first biologist to describe the zoological rift that divides the Australian region from the rest of the world. T. H. Huxley, a colleague and staunch admirer of Darwin and Wallace, dubbed the division "Wallace's Line."

Wallace happened upon his line while exploring the Malay Archipelago. The peculiar animals of Australia were well known by this time, but it was Wallace who pointed out that while a great many of them occurred over much of Australia, New Guinea, and adjacent islands, they vanished abruptly along a division that ran east of the Philippines, bent south and west, and threaded the needle between Bali and Lombok. Kangaroos bounded up to one side of the divide but did not cross. Tigers, tapirs, elephants, orangutans, monkeys, pheasants, and woodpeckers edged up to the other, yet something held them back. It was water. Deep and stormy, an ancient channel separates Bali from Lombok, keeping tigers out of the outback and kangaroos out of Asia.

Our odyssey would spin us around the Australian side of Wallace's Line, where marsupials, or pouched animals, still abound. Among them, two of the world's three egg-laying animals, the duck-billed platypus and the short-beaked echidna, cavort in creeks and roam the countryside, lapping up ants. Wallace's writings provided a good idea of the beasts we might discover:

> The Marsupials are wonderfully developed in Australia, where they exist in the most diversified forms. . . . Some are carnivorous, some herbivorous; some arboreal, others terrestrial. There are insect-eaters, root-gnawers, fruit-eaters, honey-eaters, leaf or grass-feeders. Some resemble wolves, others marmots, weasels, squirrels, flying squirrels, dormice, or jerboas. They are classified in six distinct families . . . and subserve most of the purposes in the economy of nature fulfilled in other parts of the world by very different groups. . . . [They] are members of one stock and have no real affinity with the Old-World forms which they often outwardly resemble.

These were the creatures we wanted to know.

While the strangeness of Australia's fauna is well known, the factors that endowed the region with such odd life-forms are not. In fact, scientists still grope for explanations. One of the most colorful was published in London in 1793 by a Captain John Hunter. Hunter proposed that Australia's animals resulted from a continent-wide orgy, "a promiscuous intercourse between the different sexes of all these different animals." The theory of "random promiscuity," as it came to be known, found adherents in England. One of its defenders, the historian Ann Moyal reports, was Charles Darwin's grandfather.

By 1859, the year Darwin's *Origin of Species* saw print, scientists in England, continental Europe, and America had reached the conclusion that Australia was a repository of backward, incompletely evolved creatures that had died out elsewhere as modern, superior animals evolved. "It may be doubted," wrote Charles Darwin, " . . . whether the Australian marsupials, which are divided into groups . . . feebly representing our carnivorous, ruminant, and rodent mammals, could successfully compete with these well-developed orders." He concludes, "In the Australian mammals, we see the process of diversification in an early and incomplete state of development."

After the publication of his theory, Darwin became a celebrity and wielded great influence. He had critics, of course, especially among dogmatic Christians, but many took his words as revelation. Darwin's thoughts on Australian animals, refined and expanded in *The Descent of Man* (1871), dominated thinking on the subject for a hundred years. He opines:

> The Marsupials stand in many important characters below the placental mammals. They appeared at an early geological period, and their range was formerly more extensive than at present. Hence the Placentata [the placental mammals, meaning all mammals except for the platypus, two species of echidna, and marsupials] are generally supposed to have been derived from the Implacentata or Marsupials. . . . The Monotremata are plainly allied to the Marsupials, forming a third, and still lower division in the great mammalian series. They are represented at the present day solely by the [platypus] and Echidna; and these two forms may be safely considered relics. . . . The Monotremata are eminently interesting as leading in several important points of structure towards the class of reptiles.

In Darwin's eyes, the mammals of Australia represented outmoded relics of the past.

Exhibiting the "foolish consistency" that Emerson called "the hobgoblin of little minds," scientists entered the twentieth century nearly unanimous in believing that platypuses, kangaroos, and their kin represented inchoate counterparts of superior, more advanced animals that live elsewhere. Yet there were dissenters. Richard Owen, a commanding figure among nineteenth-century biologists and the man who coined the term *dinosaur*, expressed a different view. "I have always connected with the long droughts in Australia," Owen wrote to a colleague, ". . . the singular peculiarity of organisation which prevails among the Mammalian quadrupeds of Australia. . . . In order that quadrupeds should be fitted to exist in a great continent like Australia . . . those quadrupeds must posses an organisation suited to such peculiar climatic conditions." Owen left open the possibility that marsupials and monotremes represented not throwbacks but life-forms exquisitely suited to life on a continent unlike any other.

Twentieth-century advances in paleontology and physiology prove that Owen was on to something. In 1992, for example, a 55-million-year-old tooth was extracted from Australian rock. It belonged to an early placental mammal called a condylarth. The notion that Australia's animals had never competed with the more recently evolved placental mammals suddenly looked as if it might be incorrect. Physiologists also stirred the pot. At Harvard University, scientists measured the energy consumption of kangaroos bounding at varying speeds and compared them with the energy expenditures of placental mammals such as deer. The results showed that while a deer uses more and more energy the faster it runs, a kangaroo reaches a plateau of energy use, then moves faster and faster with little additional cost. The kangaroo accomplishes the feat with an efficient body design that harnesses the mechanical energy of its motion to pump air in and out of the lungs, and that recycles, in the manner of a pogo stick, much of the energy of one bound into the springing power of the next. Efficient in their use of energy, kangaroos and other marsupials may hold a competitive edge over placental mammals in the low-moisture, low-energy, low-fertility ecosystems in which they live.

Tim Flannery, director of the South Australian Museum in Adelaide, takes the case a step further, suggesting that the stupidity for which marsupials are sometimes ridiculed may bring important benefits. "It may indeed pay to be dumb in Australia," Flannery writes. Marsupials, he notes, have smaller brains and are probably less intelligent than placentals, yet this apparent deficiency may prove a hidden advantage. Compared with the ecosystems of Africa, Eurasia, and the Americas, Australian environments are low in nutrients and energy. In such a context, a smaller, less energy-hungry brain offers an advantage over a big brain that demands abundant fuel. Killing off males after mating may offer benefits, too. Flannery points out that three groups of marsupial predators, in the manner of spiders, sacrifice the lives of males shortly after breeding.

We will never know what the first humans to arrive in Australia made of its singular bestiary. Early visitors and settlers communicated without written languages. We have no clear record of their lifestyles, let alone of their perceptions of kangaroos and wombats. Further, the peopling of Australia represents one of anthropology's great mysteries. The country may have been settled 30,000 or 40,000 years ago, as some experts believe, or, if recent claims regarding the antiquity of markings on a Northern Territory rock prove credible, humans may have been around far longer, perhaps 100,000 years or more. To complicate the issue, uncertainty surrounds not only the *when,* but the *who.*

At least two distinct groups of people have shared Australia during the last few tens of thousands of years. Bones from Lake Mungo, an archaeological site in New South Wales, provide the earliest unequivocal evidence of the ancestors of modern Aborigines. Skeletons found there belong to a lithe, gracefully built people with the high, bulging foreheads of modern humans, Aborigines included. The site dates to about 30,000 years ago. Other bones, only about 9,000 years old, complicate the matter. These were dug from Kow Swamp, a site along the Murray River in Victoria. The Kow Swamp people had heavy bones, stocky frames, swept-back foreheads, overhung brows, and massive jawbones. They probably looked something like Europe's Neanderthals. Who were they? Nobody can say.

However and whenever the Great South Land was colonized, people were flourishing there when explorers from other parts of the world arrived to "discover" them. The Aborigines, or Aboriginals, as the English called them, spoke more than three hundred languages and occupied every corner of the country, from the desert interior to the cool plains and forests of Tasmania, and from the tropical rain forests of the northeast to the arid mountains of the west. The Aborigines wore clothing and lived in houses in some places, and wandered naked in others. All hunted, many fished, and cultural practices, depending on the place, included infanticide, tribal warfare, the creation of rock paintings, and beliefs in a formative period called the Dreaming, or Dream Time. Readers wanting to immerse themselves in Aboriginal studies would do well by starting with Geoffrey Blainey's *Triumph of the Nomads* and Bruce Chatwin's *The Songlines.* The body of literature on Australia's Aboriginal heritage is vast.

Had Odysseus cruised Australia's coast, he would have spied smoke mushrooming into the sky and attributed it to fire-breathing monsters. In fact, the smoke emanated from bush fires set by humans. The popular perception of Aborigines in recent years gives us the noble savage—a saintly people living in thoughtful harmony with wildlife and the land. The view appears more reasonable than its predecessor, that of the natives as brutes deserving of extermination, but it probably comes no closer to the truth. Between the blackball and the whitewash seems to lie the heart of the matter, and ecological historians such as Tim Flannery and Stephen J. Pyne are bringing us the story. They tell of Aborigines who are ordinary humans, fully as crafty and controlling as the Europeans, a people who used not guns, axes, and bulldozers to turn the continent's ecology upside down, but fire.

"Humans brought chronic fire, inextinguishable fire; they were uniquely a fire creature for whom fire was a universal tool," writes Pyne in *Burning Bush: A Fire History of Australia.* Pyne shows how Aborigines used fire to manipulate Australia's flora and fauna to their own ends on a continental scale. In *The Future Eaters,* Tim Flannery picks up the theme and takes it a step further, explaining how the disruption of ecosystems by Aboriginal fire, along with the hunting that came with it, probably drove an array of native mammals to extinction in the same way that New Zealand's original Polynesian settlers exterminated a dozen species of giant flightless birds, and the first Americans may have barbecued to oblivion the mammoth and mastodon. A new picture emerges of the first contacts between Europeans and Aborigines. This one shows equals meeting equals, despite the European superiority in weaponry.

Before I'd done much background reading, I believed that, Aborigines aside, Australia was explored and settled almost singlehandedly by the English. I was wrong. The French were involved, too. So were the Dutch, the Spanish, and the Portuguese. Who came first? The best candidates are a fifteenth-century Chinese explorer named Ch'eng-ho and Arab traders who maintained a base in the islands known today as Indonesia.

The first hard evidence that Northern Hemisphere explorers reached Australia appears in an atlas published in Flanders in 1578. Inside lies a map on which is drawn the coast of an unexplored southern continent. The convolutions match the eastern and northern coasts of Australia with remarkable fidelity. On the title page, an illustration shows four animals, one in each corner—a horse, a camel, a lion, and a large, furred animal with a pouch on its breast. From the pouch poke the heads of two young. Where did sixteenth-century French cartographers come up with an accurate chart of the Australian seacoast and a knowledge of kangaroos or kangaroo-like marsupials? The most likely explanation is that they based their work on accounts and charts carried to Lisbon by Portuguese traders.

The first *documented* visit by Europeans to Australia is credited to the Dutch mariner William Jansz. In March 1606, more than a century after Columbus sailed to the Americas, Jansz guided his ship *Duyfken* into the Gulf of Carpentaria. Following the western shore of the Cape York Peninsula southward, Jansz saw little that interested him and turned

around at Cape Keer-Weer. Before quitting the area, however, the crew
disembarked to fill water barrels at Port Musgrave. A skirmish broke out,
the first recorded in Australia between the Age of Sail and Age of Stone.
We know nothing of the Aboriginal side of the story. From the Dutch we
learn that a sailor died of a spear wound.

As far as Jansz could tell, Australia joined to New Guinea. This point
of geography was soon cleared up by Luis Vaez de Torres, flying the Spanish colors. In August 1606, Torres sailed through the narrow gap between
Australia's Cape York Peninsula and New Guinea's southernmost bulge.
The channel's discovery remained secret from other maritime powers
until the British raided Manila 150 years later. The passage is known today
as the Torres Strait.

In the first half of the seventeenth century, following Jansz and Torres,
came a succession of Dutch explorers. One of the early ones was Dirck
Hartochsz (often Anglicized as "Dirk Hartog"), who explored the Western Australia coast in his ship *Eendracht* in 1616. Another was Abel Jans-
zoon Tasman. Tasman is remembered as the first European to visit New
Zealand, and for lending his name to the Tasman Sea. He also played an
important role in Australia's exploration. In 1642, during his first reconnaissance of the region, Tasman sailed past the Australian mainland without managing to see it, but eventually blundered on a substantial island off
the southeast coast. He named the place Van Diemen's Land, after his boss,
Anthoonij van Diemen. Two hundred ten years later, the old name was
dropped and the island became Tasmania. Abel Tasman returned to Australia in 1644 and scouted the northern coast.

The most colorful of Australia's early explorers was the English ship's
captain, naturalist, writer, confidence man, and pirate William Dampier.
A New Voyage Around the World (1697), written by Dampier, tells the story
of a visit to Australia's northwest coast. Describing strange animals, a land
unthinkably empty compared to Europe, and natives who, "setting aside
their human shape . . . differ but little from Brutes," Dampier's book
stirred enormous interest in the faraway country. The Aborigines, as the
Englishman saw them, were ugly and lazy. Sadly, such descriptions
encouraged the perception of Australia's natives as a people without rights
or feelings. Dampier returned to Australia in 1699.

William Dampier's writings caught the interest of Jonathan Swift, who
parodied them in *Gulliver's Travels* and *A Tale of a Tub*. The lesser known
work, published a year after the appearance of Dampier's second book,

A Voyage to New Holland, involves a Pope named Lord Peter who buys "a large continent (purgatory) lately said to have been discovered in Terra Australis Incognita." The story advances, and before long it has been decided "by a general doom, [that] all transgressors of the law are to be transported" there. Ironically, Swift's joke may well have inspired the English penal colony that Australia would soon become.

Europeans flitted to and from the coasts of Australia through much of the eighteenth century. Only after James Cook, collecting a salary of five shillings a day, shoved off on the 25th of August, 1768, bound for the Great South Land, did the European history of Australia lurch forward in earnest.

Cook scouted the coasts of New Zealand, then set sail for Australia. The first land he spied, on the 20th of April, 1770, was the Victoria coast. For twenty-seven days, Cook and crew followed the rocky shores of Victoria and New South Wales. Near the present site of Sydney, *Endeavour* entered a capacious harbor. Cook named it Botany Bay, commemorating the success of his ship's naturalist, Joseph Banks, in gathering plant specimens there. The company lingered a week. The sailors scrubbed *Endeavour's* hull and decks, mended sails, and ventured ashore to fetch firewood and water. Cook found no giants thirsting for the blood of Englishmen, but sailing north along the coast of modern-day Queensland, he met something equally treacherous—the Great Barrier Reef.

On the twelfth of June the ship struck coral. Four planks in *Endeavour's* hull gave way, and three more were damaged. But one man's luck is another's gain. While Cook supervised forty-eight days of repairs, Banks reconnoitered the countryside. His journal provides the world's first clear written description of a kangaroo:

> Quadrupeds we saw but few, and were able to catch few of them that we did see. The largest was called by the natives kangaroo. It is different from any European and indeed any animal I have heard of or read of except the Gerbua of Egypt, which is not larger than a rat when this is as large as a middling lamb; the largest we shot weighed 84 lb. It may however be easily known from all other animals by the singular property of running or rather hopping upon only its hinder legs carrying its fore bent close to its breast. . . .

After Cook, Banks, and company returned home, plans for a penal colony at Botany Bay were soon in the making. Australia's Aborigines, who had long enjoyed a monopoly over the continent's natural resources, were about to suffer the rudest of awakenings.

It was only a matter of time before a naturalist, living and working in a former English colony called New York, would start dreaming of kangaroos, and only a matter of years before this presumptive Odysseus met a Penelope harboring similar notions, and then only a matter of months before the two would announce a plan to wander the Kangaroo Continent and see the fabled animals for themselves.

The day the scheme leaped out of the pouch in which it had been secretly developing, the Mississippi community in which we then lived burst open in joy. Christian, the soft-spoken Parisian who ran the French bakery on Washington Avenue, ran into the street wearing a white apron. "Australia!" he cried, having heard the news. "Wonderful!" A boyish smile came over his thin face. "Will you see the ornithorhynx?" Christian meant the platypus, and we told him we aimed to see many. "Ah, the ornithorhynx. You are so lucky," he muttered, marching away with a smile. And so it went all day. Betty, a volunteer at the art museum where Debbie coordinated educational programs, loaned us Australian books and tapes given to her by a daughter living in Sydney. Linda, the woman who delivered our mail, told me that the one place in the world she'd really like to see was Australia. By day's end, the word had spread to every corner of town. Cars passed, windows rolled down, and arms waved. "Australia! Have a great trip!" We felt like characters in a Jimmy Stewart movie.

In the end we received so many invitations for wining, dining, and talking about our impending odyssey that it began to feel as if the journey were a fait accompli. Yet inside, behind our jaunty façades, we trembled. Dangers loomed. We would soon be blundering around a country in which being eaten by a reptile or digested by a fish is a serious risk. This was no tour we were going on, no comfortable, orchestrated excursion in hotels and buses. With our modest funds we would buy an old car, repair it when it broke down, and drive it on the wrong side of the road. Most of the time we would sleep on the ground among all the venomous snakes we'd read about. Our food would come not from a hotel kitchen or caterer, but from supplies we would purchase in grocery stores. Food was costly in Australia, we'd been told. There would be no steaks and cheesecake, no poached salmon and truffles. Ours was a beans-and-rice Odyssey, with little cash to spare.

Among all the variables that swirled in our heads, one thing was certain: despite our reading, we had an enormous amount to learn. "You know so much more of a country when you haven't seen it than when you have," quipped Mark Twain as he arrived in Australia on the 15th of September, 1895. We knew what he meant. Our brave talk would soon mean little. Our ignorance would come tumbling down on us the moment we stepped off the gangway.

When to go, and where to begin? For Odysseus, these matters were decided by fate. His homeward journey began at Troy at the end of a brutal war. Our journey could begin anytime, anywhere. We could touch down in Sydney, as most tourists do, or catch a flight to Cairns, near the Great Barrier Reef. Melbourne, in civilized Victoria, also offered a good starting point, as did Perth, in the west.

In the end we picked Melbourne. A major city seemed a wise place to begin. We could gather maps and information, round up supplies, and make initial contacts with the natives. Melbourne rather than Sydney, because we had decided, after studying climate charts and estimating how long our money could be stretched, to begin our journey at the tail end of summer and end it nine months later. Autumn would arrive swiftly. If we wanted to explore Tasmania, the coolest, wettest part of the country, we would have to hurry—either that or see the island through a veil of cold, wet rain. The point of origin for ferries to Tasmania, Melbourne was the logical place to start.

So off we went. The wind howled out of the north the morning of our departure, the thermometer read 19 degrees Fahrenheit, and the Gulf of Mexico rose and fell in violent waves. Aeolus and Poseidon were angry. Had there been an oracle handy, we might have arranged a consultation. As it was, we steeled our nerves, hoisted packs, lifted suitcases, and sailed over the horizon.

2

Among the Lotos-Eaters

A STORM OF divine origin battered the Greek fleet after its departure from the land of the Cicones, threatening the *Odyssey* with abridgment. But Odysseus, son of Laertes, inventor of the Trojan Horse, pressed on. Nine days of sailing brought no land in sight. But on the tenth, a green country rose above the horizon. It was the land of the Lotos–Eaters, a group of prototypical flower children who did little but loll about lotos ponds all day, feasting on leaves that drugged them into a pleasant languor.

Flying toward Melbourne at 30,000 feet, Debbie and I had little idea of the adventures that lay ahead. But our guard was up. By all accounts, Australians were lotos-eaters, people of legendary bonhomie who loved food and drink and had lost all desire to live anywhere else. Forewarned by Homer, we steeled ourselves to resist temptation.

Westward we flew, a quiltwork of clouds spreading beneath us. Vapor, plowed by winds, eventually broke into furrows, and in them we spied land. It was colored a pale green and rose and fell like the sea. Soon there were buildings, some covered by red roofs, others by shiny tin, and beyond, a dark band of forest. Kangaroos live down there, I thought to myself, and so do wallabies, wombats, and more than seven hundred species of birds.

As the jet banked, I glimpsed a city, as bright and shiny as if it had been built yesterday. I was reminded of the giddy moment in the film *The Wizard of Oz* when Judy Garland, playing Dorothy Gale, emerges from a forest accompanied by a scarecrow, a tin man, a lion, and a terrier. In the distance rises the green, gleaming Emerald City, home of the vaunted wizard. The connection reverberated deeply here. Over the rainbow from the rest of the world, Australia is often called "Oz."

Wheels scuffed tarmac, then thundered. I nearly choked on excitement. When people and luggage blocked the aisle, I entertained brief, Odyssean thoughts of hacking my way to the exit. Liberation came soon, fortunately, and we burst into the dry Australian air.

No one waited to greet us, nor did anyone back home pace beside a telephone, eager for news of our arrival. No brass bands played, no animals were sacrificed in our honor, and the gods kept silent. We collected our luggage, negotiated safe passage through Australian customs, and made our way to a bus.

"We're not in Kansas anymore," I said to Debbie, mining the Oz analogy for another scoop of ore. The bus driver greeted us warmly, answered our questions, and loaded our heavy bags in the bus's gaping belly. "Right," he said, closing the bay. "Let's have a look at Australia, shall we?"

A black-and-white bird, a bit larger than a sparrow, walked across a lawn near the bus stop. It was the sort of harmless, agreeable-looking animal that one immediately feels a fondness for. "A magpie-lark," announced the expedition's ornithologist, fishing Graham Pizzey's *Field Guide to the Birds of Australia* from her pack. "Also known as the pewee." This was a big moment for a pair of wildlife enthusiasts freshly arrived on the continent. The magpie-lark represented the first of more than four hundred species of birds we would identify before the journey was done.

Soon we were off. The bus barreled out of the airport, the driver putting our nerves on edge by keeping to the left-hand lane. Toward Melbourne we sped, the tall buildings growing nearer and higher until we were among them, rattling down streets fronted by shops and marquees that created a convincing facsimile of England. Mark Twain found Melbourne "a stately city architecturally as well as in magnitude," and so did we. The city was immense, a world in itself, and its stone and brick buildings made a handsome sight.

Streets led on and on, through neighborhoods with butcher shops hawking legs of lamb and greengrocers tending bins of fruit and vegetables. Following streets that John Muir, visiting in 1903, found "well paved," lined with "grand substantial buildings," and bustling with "people apparently healthy [and] good-natured," we at last reached the core. The people we saw there looked as amiable and healthy as the Australians of Muir's time. Judging by complexions, which ranged from

Northern European alabaster to Mediterranean bronze to Aboriginal and African black, the denizens of Melbourne hailed from the far corners of the world.

The bus disgorged us in a parking area beside Flinders Street Station, Melbourne's answer to the great railway stations of Europe. Grand and forbidding in an appealing sort of way, the edifice reeked of the old British Empire. It swallowed us, luggage, strained muscles, and all. A few minutes later we sat on a train speeding toward Sandringham.

The train whisked us out of the city and into the suburbs. Houses and backyards occupied by children, women taking down laundry, and dogs and cats flickered by like images in a silent movie. The homes were low and plain, mostly one- and two-story affairs, some of brick, others of wood. Nearly all had a relaxed, unbuttoned look about them, an appearance that harmonized with impressions of Australia I'd formed at a distance—that of a country devoted to the pursuit of happiness and not preoccupied with its image. Whenever a road came into view, we saw men in suits and women in dresses, racing home in Japanese cars. It was rush hour.

Trees paraded past the window, and the ones with peeling trunks and pendulous, gray-green leaves I guessed to be eucalypts, members of the genus *Eucalyptus*. Pressing faces against the glass, we peered among the limbs in hopes of spying a kookaburra or parrot. All we found were house sparrows, starlings, and pigeons.

Piling out of the train and onto the platform with an expedition's worth of luggage, we made quite a scene. People stared. Inside the station, white-haired women with translucent skin flecked with liver spots stole glances at us, and when we caught them at it, they smiled politely. The air was steamy. Overdressed after crossing the Tasman Sea from cool New Zealand, we peeled off sweaters and outer shirts and wiped the first Australian sweat from our brows.

Debbie and I took turns stepping out the door to watch for a white Land Cruiser. It belonged to a woman about whom we knew a great deal, yet who was a complete stranger. Her name was Beris Caine. A retired industrial psychologist, she lived not far from the shore of Port Philip Bay in a suburb called Beaumaris. Beris was a wildlife enthusiast, a keen watcher of birds and student of botany, a person for whom all things were of interest, from the sex life of the platypus to the intimate anatomy of flowers. Rounding up the names and phone numbers of contacts before we left the U.S.A., we had picked her from among several people in Melbourne who might help us launch our odyssey on the right foot.

Soon the Land Cruiser materialized. We greeted the handsome, dark-haired, sixty-eight-year-old behind the wheel with an American "hello." "G'day, Debbie and Ed," Beris Caine said jauntily. "Welcome to Australia."

When we showed Beris our piles of gear, she flinched. The back of the vehicle was loaded high with boxes bound for an "op shop," or second-hand store. After a pause, Beris professed confidence we would fit. In due course the miracle was performed, and ten minutes later we were climbing out in Beris's driveway and offered a cup of tea.

"What's that noise?" asked Debbie. Terrible squeals and screeches came from the backyard.

"Rainbow lorikeets," replied Beris. She spoke in the tone an American or European would use in saying "sparrows."

Debbie and I looked at each other in disbelief. Studying field guides to Australian birds before leaving home, we had singled out the rainbow lorikeet, a parrot of many colors, as the bird we wanted to see more than any other. Was it possible we had stumbled upon the Grail so early?

We crept around the house. Three of the most vividly colored birds we had ever set eyes on fluttered around an upturned whiskey bottle, its cap pierced by a hole through which sugar-water oozed. Rainbow lorikeets!

One of the parrots dangled with its sky-blue head toward the ground and chartreuse tail up. A crimson and yellow breast bulged like a ripening tomato. Glaring malevolently at its competitors through blood-red eyes, the lorikeet opened a red-orange bill and screeched at terrifying volume. Thus we had our first earful of a paradox that would follow us around Australia: the most beautiful parrots make the most hideous of sounds. As we drew near, the lorikeets flashed orange-red wing linings and flapped into the trees.

After tea, buttered bread fresh from the oven, and bowls of homemade soup, Beris gave us a house tour. The place consisted of a single story, stretching from Beris's bedroom on one end to a sunny dining room and library on the other. It was outside the library that the lorikeets flew and feasted. There were books everywhere, and coffee cups and wineglasses, a piano, a spinning wheel, and craft projects in varying stages of completion. Shelves in the dining room were lined with hundreds of volumes on Australia's flora and fauna, the finest natural history library we could have hoped to find in our first days in the country. Beris showed us to a guest room and insisted that we help ourselves to tea, coffee, food, drink, books, and showers.

A little while later we regrouped for a walk. Beris led the way, following one street, then another, passing small, comfortable homes immersed in flowering perennials. We hurried across a busy highway, traversed a grassy strip, and disappeared through a gap in a wall of shrubs. On the far side we found silence, sunshine, and the scalloped waters of Port Philip Bay.

For an hour we ambled, strolling along wet sand at times, picking up shells, at other points leaving the shore to follow paths that climbed along a bluff. We saw an array of birds. Crested terns and Pacific gulls flew and landed, pied cormorants swam and sunbathed, and a Nankeen kestrel (a kind of falcon) hovered overhead in a cobalt blue sky.

On the way home, as we skirted a brushy area, Beris stopped to point out a chattering sound. We listened for several minutes, waiting for the maker to appear. It proved to be a superb fairy-wren, a male whose head, back, breast, and tail were colored a blue as dazzling as the lorikeet's. The tail was comically long, making the bird appear unbalanced on the branch. Good heavens! We had hardly arrived in Australia, and here was another bird on our list of must-sees. Nine months lay ahead. Could we keep up the pace?

We watched the fairy-wren cock its tail, perhaps asserting dominion over territory. Each male presides over a tribe that includes the female that bears his young and a retinue of lackeys. Incest and inbreeding are rampant. So is philandering. The male darts out of his territory, plucks up flowers he never gives to his mate, and flirts his way into as many affairs as he can manage. Meanwhile the female cuckolds him back home, sharing her favors with traveling men.

In 1922, during a stay of several months in Australia, D. H. Lawrence came to know fairy-wrens. Their prodigious tails struck the author of *Women in Love* as "preposterous."

During his stay in Australia, Lawrence wrote his novel *Kangaroo* in a seaside cottage in Thirroul, near Sydney. In it he wrote of birds, including "one brown, one with a sky-blue patch on his head, like a patch of sky." Lawrence observed that the wren "seemed to have no deep natural fear, as creatures in Europe have, . . . only sometimes a grey metaphysical dread." The metaphysical dread was in Lawrence's head, I think, but otherwise his description serves nicely.

The next morning, our first in Australia, commenced at Beris's. Soon we were packing for a picnic lunch with friends she was eager for us to meet, Peg and Keith MacLeod. A plan had been hatched to drive out to the MacLeods' place in an outer suburb, pick them up, and set off for a place called the Healesville Sanctuary. At Healesville we would haul out provisions, enjoy a meal alfresco, and spend the afternoon roaming among live animal displays. We would see our first platypus, Beris predicted, and a good many other indigenous animals as well.

Beware the lotos-eaters. Danger flashed on my radar screen as I helped to gather supplies. "In your bedroom," Beris instructed, "you'll find wine behind the curtains covering the walls. Pick out a bottle of red. And we'd better have a white as well." As she spoke, Beris was wrapping a bottle of chilled champagne in a towel. "We'll have some champers, too," she said. Into the Land Cruiser went the bottles, thermoses of tea and coffee, and enough fresh bread, sliced meats, jams, chutneys, cheeses, and fruit to keep a small army victualed for a week. Little did I know that the MacLeods would up the ante. We would have to watch our step. If we weren't careful among these lotos-eaters, we might abandon our journey and spend nine indulgent months in Melbourne.

An hour's drive past bustling shopping plazas and dusty industrial complexes brought us into the country, where we turned onto a dirt track. It led to a house set among trees. A tall man and a woman of modest stature, both gray of hair, waved and smiled as we drove to the door. "G'day!" and "Welcome!" they cried. I have no clear memory of who said what to whom in the commotion that followed. Goodwill flowed from these people like Ciconean wine. Slender and sharp-featured, Keith examined us through wire-rimmed glasses. He was seventy-four. Like her husband, Peg, seventy-one, looked youthful for her years. She had a cherubic face and kind, intelligent eyes. "Come in, come in," she said, making no mention that we had arrived an hour later than scheduled. We clumped up a wooden stairway onto a deck. "Have you seen a grey butcherbird?" asked Keith, pointing to a limb.

The butcherbird had a hooked bill and feathers that looked as if someone had rolled it in charcoal. "As you might guess," Keith continued in a voice that sounded as much English as Australian, "the butcherbird is a predator."

"We feed them bits of mince," added Peg, in speech more distinctly Australian. We learned later that Peg had grown up on a farm in the interior, while Keith was raised on the coast.

After a round of tea and a peek at the house, we were off. Keith took the wheel of Beris's four-wheel-drive. We thundered up a narrow dirt road into the hills, hurtling around blind corners at frightening speed. I shudder to think what would have happened had we met an oncoming car, tractor, or truck. Eventually the rough track spilled us onto pavement, which we followed the rest of the way to Healesville.

During the drive, our hosts kept up a lively discourse on botany and zoology. Keith, a retired abalone diver, schoolteacher, and businessman, and Peg, a businesswoman, school principal, and teacher, matched Beris in their knowledge of natural history. All three were widely traveled. At times they had roamed together, joined by Beris's late husband, John Caine. The trio made perfect company. We had come to Australia to study wildlife and hobnob with locals, and here were the most generous and able of teachers.

As trees flew by at sixty miles an hour, we heard them identified and discussed. Most were eucalypts, members of the genus that dominates Australia's woody flora. Others were wattles, genus *Acacia,* and she-oaks, genus *Casuarina.* Beris explained that eucalypts belonged to the family Myrtaceae, while Peg contributed information on the diverse and interesting Proteaceae, a mostly African family that also includes such trademark Australian plants as banskias, grevilleas, hakeas, dryandras, bottlebrushes, and the macadamia tree. Proteas produce robust flowers on stiff woody stems. Birds and mammals are their chief pollinators, which probably accounts for the sturdiness of their stems and blossoms. Keith told us about acacias. The majority of species, he said, about six hundred of the world's eight hundred, are Australian. Debbie and I had seen American acacias during travels in Texas and Arizona.

The trees crept closer to each other as we sped along, and eventually formed a forest. The landscape buckled. Climbing higher, we came to a place where the trees had been thinned. "Fire," said someone, pointing to places where the trunks were charred. A discussion ensued about the frequency of bushfires, some of them catastrophic. Keith told of a recent fire that had blazed perilously close to the MacLeods' house in Officer, and Beris told us of the great bushfires that punctuate Victoria's history— Black Thursday in 1851, Red Tuesday in 1898, and Black Friday in 1939. On Black Friday, Melbourne temperatures soared to 114 degrees Fahrenheit in early afternoon. Fires sprang up, some caused by natural events, others by arson. Heat and winds encouraged the flames, which coalesced and spread. When the nightmare was over, millions of acres of forest had been incinerated and seventy-one people killed. "Fires are part of the natural scheme of things," said Peg, "but they're a bit worrying when your home, barns, or livestock lie in the path of danger."

The discussion ended when a crow-sized UFO of gray and brown flew across the road with powerful wing strokes and landed in a gum tree. Its plump body and spearlike bill told us it was a kingfisher, none other than a laughing kookaburra, the "merry merry king of the bush" of children's-song fame. Looking regal and important, the kookaburra found comfortable footing, shook kinks from its wings, and wiggled a rusty tail.

The fits of apparent jocularity to which the kookaburra is prone earn it nicknames such as "laughing jackass" and "woop-woop pigeon." The vocalizations are reserved for encounters with other kookaburras, and it was our bad luck that the others had flown. Although the bird's laugh sounds funny to human ears, the sound asserts a serious territorial claim. At great volume the kookaburra chortles, raises its tail, and bares its bottom. Translated roughly, the display means "Up yours!" The taunt often produces a chorus from a neighboring tribe, and the result, our companions told us, is a performance that must be heard to be believed.

Much as the kangaroo serves as the mammalian emblem of Australia, the laughing kookaburra acts as unofficial national bird. It seizes the job with gusto—rousing people from bed in the morning, laughing during inappropriate moments at outdoor weddings, and disrupting the dreariness of funerals. It is a bird that makes a strong impression on anyone who sees it. "An ugly, healthy, ubiquitous brute of a bird," wrote Anthony Trollope of the kookaburra, which he found in the gum forests of Victoria. Mark Twain was kinder. "In the Zoological Gardens of Adelaide," he wrote in *Following the Equator,* "I saw the only laughing jackass that ever showed any disposition to be courteous to me. This one opened his head wide and laughed like a demon, or like a maniac who was consumed with humorous scorn over a cheap and degraded pun." Twain gives us a meeting between great comedians, one in a suit, one in feathers.

As Melbourne slipped farther behind us, the forest grew lush. My eyes began to embrace the beauty of our surroundings with an enthusiasm they had not been able to muster an hour earlier. Signs of fire were absent. The trees, mostly the eucalypt known as mountain ash, grew straight and tall like utility poles, and wisps of bark lay composting at their feet.

Visitors from the north tend to look unfavorably upon the Australian bush, at least at first. D. H. Lawrence found the eucalypt woods "so phantom-like, so ghostly, with its tall pale trees and many dead trees, like corpses, mostly charred by bush fires . . . and the foliage so dark, like grey-green iron." Lawrence complained that the bush was "deathly still" and the birds "swamped in silence." I wonder if he needed a hearing aid. Everywhere we went, lorikeets, crimson rosellas, and king parrots screeched in the treetops. Lawrence had a point, however, about the way things looked. The leaves of eucalypts look thin and austere to eyes accustomed to oaks and maples, and the tattered trunks appear gaunt and lifeless. Initially, European, American, and Asian visitors are often repelled by the Australian bush. Australians, on the other hand, find their forests beautiful. Many would find our own woods wanting. The difference, of course, lies in the brain of the beholder. As Emerson put it, "The ruin or blank that we see when we look at nature, is in our own eye."

Our eyes warmed to the eucalypts. Given time, we learned to love these ragged soldiers, these conquerors of a land harsher than any other in the terms it demands for survival. John Muir had blazed a path for us. During a stop in Australia beginning in December 1903 and stretching into January 1904, the Scotland-born, Wisconsin-raised naturalist took a chiefly intellectual interest in the local flora until traveling out to Healesville and beyond. Away from the city, Muir's botanical notes take an enthusiastic turn. "A charming place in the heart of forest primeval," he says, describing the country home of a friend. Muir wrote admiringly of blackwood acacia trees and "glorious ferns."

Regarding ferns, Debbie and I were in complete agreement with Muir. Many of the ones we saw along the road stood thirty feet high, and their fronds spread like lacy umbrellas. Conservative of trunk but extravagant of foliage, the tree-ferns reminded me of parasol-toting Victorians out for a Sunday stroll.

Our visit to Healesville forms only a blur in my memory. We dove into our picnic, of course, and as I sipped red wine while nibbling on bread painted with chutney, watching colorful birds flit through the branches above, I thought to myself that if this was lotos-eating, I was a convert. The breads, relishes, and meats were superb and the conversation witty and thoughtful. I felt like a character in a Hemingway novel, enjoying a bit of good living in some quiet corner of the Pyrenees. Yet the carefree life had its cost. By the time we reached the live animal exhibits, my head and vision swirled in a lotos-eating haze.

Of the hours that followed I remember only two things clearly: that we strolled along narrow forest paths, identifying an array of birds new to us (rufous fantail, white-naped honeyeater, and bell-miner, among others), and that we lingered inside a building in which the cycle of day and night had been cunningly reversed. Here we watched the world's weirdest mammal, a creature of the night, swim and dive as if it were midnight.

When stuffed specimens were first shipped back to England in the late 1700s, the platypus was seen by the scientific establishment as a taxidermist's practical joke. Someone, it seemed, had removed the bill from a duck, stitched it to the carcass of an animal like a muskrat, then attached the webbed feet of a frog. Yet the platypus, it turned out, was real, as genuine, albeit as unlikely, as a giraffe.

Among writers commenting on the platypus, none is more original and perceptive than Mark Twain:

> Nature's fondness for dabbling in the erratic was most notably exhibited in that curious combination of bird, fish, amphibian, burrower, crawler, quadruped, and christian, called the *ornithorhynchus* [or platypus]—grotesquest of all animals, king of the animalculae of the world for versatility of character and make-up.

Twain wasn't finished. He rarely was. "You can call [the platypus] anything you want to, and be right," says Twain, quoting a fictitious naturalist. The platypus is simultaneously a fish, land animal, amphibian, "hybernean," duck, quadruped, seal, mammal, and "manifestly a Christian, for it keeps the sabbath when there is anybody around, and when there isn't, doesn't." In the end Twain concludes that the animal "has all the tastes there are, except refined ones; it has all the habits there are, except good ones."

We watched two platypuses swim circles around an artificial pond. Through sheets of glass holding back cool water, we saw them plunge to the bottom, their brown fur glittering with sequins of air. The animals prodded the bottom with rubbery nose-pieces, vacuuming up food in the sludge. The bills looked vaguely like a duck's, but were wider.

We were thankful our companions had brought us to Healesville. At the same time, the sight of platypuses swimming in a tank left us nonplussed. We had traveled to Australia to see wild animals on their terms, not through polished glass. Our approach would be Emersonian—direct, visceral experience was our goal. And so, despite all the wonderful things we saw that day, we returned to Beris Caine's delighted by our new friends but disappointed with the duckbill. We wouldn't feel we had truly seen a platypus until we found one on our own.

The following day, Valentine's Day, brought another movable feast. In the same agreeable company we visited Coolart, an old cattle and sheep ranch that was transformed at the turn of the century by Frederick Sheppard Grimwade into a country estate. The place had since become a wildlife sanctuary.

When the weather cooperates, a day spent outdoors among sympathetic friends races along at extraordinary speed. So it went at Coolart. Hardly had we arrived, strolled, and lunched than it was time to leave. But twenty-one new species of Australian birds on our expanding list proved that our time on the property was fruitful. We loved the willy wagtail, a wide-ranging bird of the Australian countryside that forever pirouettes on fenceposts, its tail held high. The wagtail aims to frighten insects into motion, and the ploy must work splendidly well, for wagtails are everywhere. The spotted pardalote was gorgeous. A compact bird smaller than a fairy-wren, it flashed among the twigs of a tree, gleaning insects from the bark. The male, showier than the female, sported tangerine-colored underwear, an equally gaudy patch of feathers on the throat, and a head, nape, and wings made dazzling by bold white stars set against a black field.

We saw several honeyeaters, too. Australian honeyeaters belong to a large, diverse family of birds responsible for pollinating hundreds of the continent's plants. Of those we found with our binoculars at Coolart, two stand out. The New Holland honeyeater was a sleek, rakish bird with bold black and white stripes and touches of gold on the wings. We would see hundreds of them in the weeks ahead. Less common, the eastern spinebill was red-eyed, white-throated, and cinnamon-bellied. Its bill was sharp and curved like a cobbler's awl.

And there were more—a crimson-headed, lemon-bellied parrot called the eastern rosella, a grey fantail, a yellow robin, hoary-headed grebes, four kinds of ducks, cormorants, a reed-warbler, a welcome swallow, and, adding Old World charm, a European goldfinch with a tricolor face. There was also a dark, crowlike bird that the four of us, scrutinizing bird

books, identified as a little raven. Crows and ravens are so closely associated with the northern hemisphere that they look out of place in Australia. Ironically, the birds may be more at home on the Kangaroo
Continent than anywhere else. Studies of living and fossil members of the
group show that the birds evolved Down Under, spread to Asia, Europe,
and the Americas, and then died out in their ancestral homeland. Only
millions of years later did crows and ravens return to Australia, where
today there are five species.

Lunch at Coolart was like lunch at Healesville—magnificent, a blissful
hour of lotos-eating. Lest we fail to detect peril in the situation, Keith
gave a warning. "You'd better be careful, you two," he said. "We tend to
grab hold of visitors and not let them go." I looked at Debbie, and she at
me. Peg and Beris were laughing. We might never break free of this threesome. At the moment I couldn't have produced a reason why I might
want to. The bonhomie was contagious, the eating grand, the wine far
more savory than the cheap stuff we'd be buying with our own spare
coins.

For better and for worse, the *Spirit of Tasmania* came to our rescue. It
sailed from the port of Melbourne, and tickets were already booked and
paid for. If this wasn't incentive enough, we looked the prospect of per-
petual lotos-eating in the eye and found the iron core of our resolve.
Adventure beckoned. Only the stomach-churning waters of the Bass
Strait separated us from an island of farms and wilderness. Tasmania—
home of sheep, cows, wild platypuses, and the famous Tasmanian devil.
Keith and Peg stored our surplus gear. Beris delivered us to the wharf.
What would we find across the Strait? On this point Homer was clear. We
had better watch out for Cyclopes.

3

We Meet the Cyclopes

THE WANDERER NEVER knows when he may blunder into a Cyclops.
Australia, and Tasmania in particular, is overrun with them. If we define
the term broadly, it can include not only one-eyed misanthropic giants,
but also people who behave like them, and single-holed mammals, too.

The order Monotremata (literally, the "one-holers") consists of the
world's three egg-laying mammals. The star of the group, the duck-billed
platypus, occurs only in Australia. Lesser known are the short-beaked
echidna, or spiny anteater, of Australia and New Guinea and the long-
beaked echidna, a New Guinea specialty that roamed Australia in Aboriginal times. Each member of the trio excretes, egests, mates, and, in the
case of the female, lays eggs through a wonderfully versatile orifice called
the cloaca. Latin for "sewer," *cloaca* is an unkind name for a vital body part.
Reptiles have cloacae. So do amphibians. Fish have them, and so do most
marsupials and shrews.

As *The Spirit of Tasmania* carried us toward Devonport one bright February morning, we scanned the forested massif behind it with excitement
and dread. Adventures loomed for us in the island's wild interior. With
luck we'd encounter our first free-roaming kangaroos and walk through
some of the best preserved temperate rain forest in the world. I also had a
familial interest in the place. A great-granduncle on my mother's side, a
man named Thomas Quigley, had lived on Tasmania from 1920 to 1930.
A clergyman, he had served as rector of an Anglican church in Hobart. I
knew little of Quigley save for the fact of his sojourn on the island, yet
the connection was enough to provoke fascination. As a boy, I was excited
to learn that Tasmania in the late eighteenth and nineteenth centuries had

been a Devil's Island of the South Pacific, a place where the most recalcitrant and loathsome of England's convicts were disposed of, like trash
carted to a landfill. Penal settlements on the island welcomed the new-
comers to cold cells, iron bars, lukewarm gruel, backbreaking work, and
brutal lashings. Tasmania was also the home of the Tasmanian wolf or
tiger, perhaps the strangest marsupial of all. Although this predatory
cousin of kangaroos succumbed to extinction in the 1930s, one of its
close relations has not: the Tasmanian devil. The devil is a nocturnal marsupial that crawls out of holes in the ground, screams like a demon, and
devours the flesh and bones of corpses.

Dread arose because we were mindful of the lessons of Homer. Hardly
had Odysseus and his men broken free of the lotos-eaters than they
downed an imprudent volume of Ciconean wine and blundered ashore
on a coast populated by Cyclopes. Terror followed. Shouldering a
goatskin of wine with which to continue their bacchanal, Odysseus and a
dozen men walked into the cave of an absent shepherd. Inside they found
plump cheeses drying on racks, vats full of whey and milk, and pens
crowded with succulent lambs and kids. As any reader of the *Odyssey*
knows, the Greeks had liberal ideas about personal property. The sailors
made ready to raid the larder. The boss nixed the plan, however, assuring
his companions that the shepherd would be compelled to offer gifts of
food and wine according to ancient rules of hospitality. They waited for
the owner's return.

The idea backfired. One-eyed, oversized, and vile of disposition, the
shepherd clumped into the cave and sealed it closed with a boulder. Then
he spied the Greeks. A demand to know who they were prompted a
speech from Odysseus, but words only raised the giant's ire. With a powerful hand he reached down, grabbed two men, and knocked their heads
on the ground. Brains spilled out. As the rest of the party watched in horror, the Cyclops pulled the bodies to pieces, ate them, and promptly fell
asleep.

What to do? The Greeks had no cellular phone. Even if they had
owned one, it wouldn't have worked in a cave. No human weapon would
have any effect. All they could do was wait.

Soon the Cyclops rose, masticated two more Greeks, and stepped outside for some air. While he was gone, Odysseus and Co. took a log, sharp-
ened one end, and hardened the point in a fire. When the monster came
back and swallowed two more of the party, Homer's hero spoke. He gave

the Cyclops a false name, telling the brute that he was "No Man." He also gave the misanthrope three goblets of wine. The name would play a part later, but the intoxicant had its desired effect at once. The Cyclops slept. Sparing no detail, Homer tells us that the giant roused at one point and vomited, spilling a revolting slurry of bile, wine, and partially digested Greeks.

While the monster slumbered, the voyagers leaped into action. They heated the pointed log once more in the coals, then rammed it into the Cyclops's eye, twirling the weapon to heighten the damage. The eyeball boiled like an egg. Waking, the giant roared and raged. Neighboring Cyclopes called out to know if their comrade had been harmed, and in response, the monster cried that he had been attacked by "No Man." Taking this to mean all was well, the others went away.

Blind and furious, the Cyclops sat in the cave's mouth, daring the Greeks to slip past. Odysseus hatched another scheme. Lashing sheep together in groups of three, the captives hid in the belly fur, one to a troika, and rode to freedom. Odysseus came last, clinging to the short hairs of the monster's prize ram. The Greeks sailed away, shouting unkind taunts about the visually impaired.

With Odysseus's travails in the back of our minds, Debbie and I stepped ashore. At first, all went smoothly. A bus piloted by a friendly driver hauled us and our gear southward, following the Bass Highway to Deloraine, then turned east through hilly grazing country to Launceston. Anthony Trollope visited Launceston in the nineteenth century and found it "a clean, well-built town." It hadn't changed much. When we visited, the metropolis boasted a population of more than 60,000 and contained numerous historic buildings, two McDonald's restaurants (a third was on the way), and a neoclassical establishment that called itself the Aquarius Roman Baths. We asked for a peek at the baths and were ushered into a hot, clammy place that combined the serenity of an African water hole with a sensual feast worthy of Caligula's Rome—six fat and well-heeled women with gray hair, soaking in a tile-lined wallow called the Tepidarium.

After we climbed off the bus, a telephone call sealed our fates. A couple who lived on a farm about forty minutes by car from the city invited us to come and stay. Our understanding was that we would stay two nights, although our hosts made clear we were welcome to linger a week. The appeal of the visit was great. We would see the Tasmanian countryside, not an easy thing to accomplish without a car and carrying so much equipment. Our hosts promised that we would find a platypus swimming in their pond.

At the appointed hour, the pair appeared, driving the most compact of cars. Blood drained from their faces as they ogled our pile of gear. He was Mario, originally from Italy, and she Ruth, from England. (Not wanting to hurt feelings, I scramble identities.) The introductions were curt, the handshakes perfunctory. It seemed odd. Our hosts paid little heed to our short introductions, and Mario cut Debbie off in mid-sentence to suggest we get under way. At the time we attributed their manner to the weather and time of day. It was late afternoon, and unusually hot for Tasmania. Mario and Ruth seemed weary and eager to be home.

The farm was reached by a series of roads that grew narrower and bumpier until trees engulfed the car. We lurched to a stop inside an old wooden shed. Mario's white, bony fingers pulled the key from the ignition. Had our imaginations been active, we might have seen the disappearance of the key into a pocket as the equivalent of a Cyclops plugging a cave with a boulder.

From the car we were led not to the house for a cup of tea, as is de rigueur in Australia, but to a pile of logs. Mario handed me an ax. "You can split, no?" he asked, eyebrows lifting in challenge. To Debbie he turned and explained, "We pile the wood over there, just so. No?"

For more than an hour, with a growing sense we'd been shanghaied, I cleaved while Debbie stacked. Ruth vanished into the house, and Mario was not long in following. "They're probably preparing a big meal," we thought to ourselves. Eventually a back injury that I'd aggravated before leaving home forced me to lay down the ax.

Between the woodshed and the house, hidden by a vegetable garden and a thicket of ornamental plantings, ran a lane. On the right-hand side, as we strolled toward the door, grew tall grass. Beyond the grass lay a pond, shallow and muddy. Mario and Ruth called the pond a "dam," an Australian term for a man-made impoundment. In the grass we spied the head of a large snake. The scales were steel-gray, and the body, what little we could see of it, gleamed coppery brown. Mario had said in an authoritative huff that the reptile was a tiger snake, one of Australia's most feared reptiles. After we acquired a good reptile book, we identified the snake correctly. It was a copperhead—not the copperhead that inhabits forests in eastern North America, but the far more lethal Australian copperhead,

Austrelaps superbus. Copperheads are only about a sixth as venomous as tiger snakes, but their modified salivary secretions are still nasty enough to wreak havoc on the human nervous system. The venom causes a whole-sale death of blood cells and inflicts serious damage to flesh. The copper-head lay half hidden by grass. Although we would have liked a better view, we steered safely around it.

Inside, Mario and Ruth were sipping tea. Might we join them? Cups were produced. The bathroom? Down the hall. In the loo, rules were posted. The sink must be washed and toweled dry after each use. The toilet must be scrubbed after each bowel movement, brush provided. The shower stall must be cleaned and dried with a squeegee after each ablution. And after a shit or shower, the fan must be run for five minutes. I shud-dered. We had no Ciconean wine along, and sheep were in short supply.

Between the tea and the supper that followed, we slipped outside into the cooling air. There our discomfort was eased by the sight of a small mammal, plump and thickly furred, rising to the surface of the pond. It floated for a few minutes, making circles with its rubbery bill. Then the apparition arched its back, raised its round bottom, and dove. Dear Athena—it was a platypus!

This was no coddled specimen, like the portly platypuses we'd seen at Healesville. It was the real McCoy, as sleek and frisky as an otter.

There was no telling whether the platypus was male or female, whether it had a nest with a pair of leathery eggs inside, or if it carried the highly specific tick, *Ixodes ornithorhynchi,* that feeds only on the platypus's hemoglobin-rich blood. All we could see were its ups and downs. During the ups, the bill masticated treasures retrieved during the dives. The diet of the animal consists chiefly of small, wiggly things from the bottoms of ponds, lakes, and streams—insect nymphs, mostly, and also a seafood salad of crayfish, freshwater shrimp, assorted invertebrate larvae, and horsehair worms. To locate food, the platypus uses receptors on its bill to sense elec-trical impulses generated by the muscle movements of its prey. Adult platypuses have no teeth, so the chewing we witnessed was accomplished with horny pads.

However peculiar, the platypus possesses charisma. David Fleay, the Australian naturalist who was the first to breed platypuses in captivity, once made a catalog of prominent world figures who in one way or another had a soft spot for the duckbill. His list is long. On it are Queen Elizabeth II, who during a 1954 visit to Australia, had Fleay deliver a live platypus to her bathtub so she could make home movies of it; Winston Churchill, who kept a stuffed platypus on his desk; and an array of others, including H. G. Wells, Elspeth Huxley, Zane Grey, Lawrence Rockefeller, Gilbert Grosvenor, J. B. Priestley, Joy Adamson, Lloyd Bridges, and Rupert Murdoch.

Among non-Aboriginal platyphiles, the first may have been David Collins, who published an account of wild duckbills in his *Account of the English Colony in New South Wales (1798–1802)*. Collins describes "an amphibious mammal, of the mole species" that is "considerably larger than the land mole." Soon he gets to the body part that separates his subject from all other mammals. "The most extraordinary circumstance observed in its structure was, its having, instead of the mouth of an animal, the upper and lower mandibles of a duck," Collins writes. The platypus is thus "enabled to supply itself with food, like that bird, in muddy places, or on the banks of the lakes, in which its webbed feet enabled it to swim, while on shore its long and sharp claws were employed in burrowing; nature thus providing for it in its double or amphibious character. These little animals had been frequently noticed rising to the surface of the water, and blowing like a turtle."

All that Collins describes quickly becomes apparent on watching a platypus. Yet there is more to the mammal than meets the eye. The male, for example, is venomous. He makes poison not in modified salivary glands, as the copperhead does, but in glands on his hind legs. To this day no one has been able to determine what purpose, if any, platypus venom serves. Hollow, clawlike spurs deliver the jolt, and venom is produced only during the breeding season. The handling of a male in breeding trim can be risky.

Fleay writes of a fisherman who caught a platypus on a hook and line. While trying to ease the struggling creature off a hook, the man was spurred several times on the wrist. "Within five to ten minutes," reports Fleay, "severe agony up the arm became so intense that the victim vomited and his hand and arm bloated to an extraordinary extent as far as the elbow. The fisherman escaped without permanent injury, but the pain and swelling lingered for a week."

Another cryptic trait is the platypus's habit of laying eggs. By remarkable coincidence, a young Cambridge University zoologist named William Hay Caldwell, working in Queensland, discovered the platypus's mode of reproduction at virtually the same hour that William Haacke, curator of the South Australian Museum, extracted an eggshell from the pouch of a short-beaked echidna. Overnight, the notion that all mammals give live birth wriggled unceremoniously out the window.

Debbie and I pulled away from the venom-jabbing, egg-dropping, bill-brandishing mammal and shuffled indoors. Supper consisted of glasses of water and vegetables cooked to the consistency of toothpaste. "Beans must not squeak," announced Mario, who tended to speak imperiously.

Ruth concurred. "It's important to cook beans properly," she said. And so went the conversation, as one-sided as that between Odysseus and the Cyclops.

To liven things up, Debbie and I asked questions and garnered curt answers. The couple had six children, all grown. They had met when Mario was a young civil engineer in Venice, and Ruth was a girl on holiday with her parents. Thirty years ago, politics, familial and otherwise, had driven them to Tasmania. Ruth was dark-haired and boyish, perhaps fifty-eight, with a light overlay of wrinkles. Mario, slight, white-haired, and prunish, seemed a decade older. Where, we wondered, were the six children? None were around to help with the farm.

After dinner, Debbie and I excused ourselves and stepped out to enjoy the last hour of sunlight. Our stroll began with the *hoo-hoo-hoo-ha-ha-ha-*ing of rival clans of kookaburras. The birds bared bottoms at each other from adjacent eucalypts and filled the air with laughter. In trees near the house, we spied a fan-tailed cuckoo, a bird with an orange-brown belly and an eye-catching black-and-white tail. Farther away, a drab gray bird, slightly smaller than the cuckoo and unfamiliar to us, darted across a paddock. We looked up the second bird in a field guide. It was a grey shrike-thrush. In time, the shrike-thrush would prove a faithful companion to us all over the continent, a species we could always pick out when the identifying got tough. On this first meeting, the bird sang snatches of melody in a full, yet soft, whistle. *Joe, Joe, Joe Witty,* the bird seemed to say.

Circling toward a pondside cabin in which Ruth assigned us a bed, we heard new sounds—a cacophony of clicks, clucks, and grunts. Who were the callers? The noise came from a paddock. We scanned with binoculars and soon had an answer. Chickenlike birds, tarnished copper of back and gray of belly, ran after each other on yellow-green legs. Their eyes were as red as cherries. These were Tasmanian native hens, flightless relations of moorhens and gallinules.

Thumbing through a bird book, we learned that native hens graze in pastures, mostly on tender young shoots. Many farmers despise them. The

reproductive habits of the birds are scandalous. Sex ratios in most populations are six males to four females, and mating typically occurs in
ménages-à-trois. Males help rear the chicks, even when the young are not
their own. At first this largesse confounded biologists. Then genetic studies revealed that the males in any given threesome are almost always brothers. Helping raise a stranger's offspring would qualify as altruism, a rare
thing in nature. Rearing nieces and nephews that share a significant portion of your genes, however, qualifies as plain old self-interest.

Were we mad, or were some of the native hens singing antiphonally?
There was a game of sonic ping-pong going on, with clicks and clucks in
one quarter setting off similar sounds in another. We consulted the books.
Indeed, Tasmanian native hens are known to "see-saw" back and forth in
two-part disharmony.

"We have good news," announced Ruth the next morning at breakfast. "Our neighbor, Egbert, has agreed to bring his truck to the high paddock. Mario has cut up a tree, and we'll bring the logs back for splitting."

"Yes," added Mario, his eyes shifting uneasily in a skull the size of cantaloupe. "This came up unexpectedly. It is very generous of Egbert to
come on a Sunday morning. We go."

We went. It was 7:00 A.M. Until eleven we hauled chunks of wood fit
for a Cyclops to lift, up into the high bed of Egbert's flatbed. Egbert was
an antique, a grizzled draft horse of a man who kept pace with Debbie
and me as we wrestled massive logs onto a platform nearly as high as my
throat. Mario worked intermittently, picking up smaller logs, pausing
often to pontificate. Ruth stayed at home.

Feeling that we'd been had, Debbie and I slowed the pace of our labor.
This led to further ejaculations from Mario. "You might try that big one,
no?" he said with wrinkled brow. "We must make use of Egbert's truck
while we can." Eventually the job was done. Heaped high with leaden,
fine-grained eucalyptus, the truck rumbled off with the old man at the
wheel. Mario waved halfheartedly from the rear.

We limped back to the house by a roundabout route and, during the
interval, hatched a plan. This was Sunday. We would resist Mario and
Ruth's attempts to bully us into staying until the following Saturday, as
they had been trying to do ever since we arrived. We would also ignore
their cries of inconvenience regarding our transport back to Launceston.
A bus ran several times daily from a nearby village. Surely our hosts would
carry us that far. As for the timing of our exit, we decided to do the

decent thing—stay one more day, donate another day of labor, and depart on Tuesday morning.

Despite their pushiness, we felt sorry for Ruth and Mario. They were as pathetic as Odysseus's blinded Cyclops. Perhaps fed up with the bathroom rules and labor-camp treatment we had been receiving, their children stayed away. Alone, the pair played at farming. They seemed to be struggling, with little interest, energy, or know-how. It would have been easy to do the Odyssean thing, to put out their eyes with fire-hardened sticks, but out of pity we resisted the temptation.

Our plan went over like a roach in chowder. Civility, for a moment, nearly gave way to a shouting match. Yet the message got through. Mario invited us to spend the afternoon roaming and relaxing, and Ruth, who suddenly switched on charm, beckoned us into the living room. There she demonstrated the method she and Mario used to make important decisions—reading the sticks of the *I Ching*.

The remainder of our stay passed without incident. There were quiet meals, a few more glasses of water, and an eight-hour work day under a hot sun. Debbie and I weeded a plantation of trees near the pond. The chief merit of the job was that it allowed us to keep an eye on the platypus while keeping clear of our hosts. Why the animal hunted by day we had no idea, for duckbills as a rule are nocturnal. Perhaps food resources were poor here, and to satisfy its appetites the platypus had to work a longer-than-normal schedule. Or maybe Tasmanian duckbills, having to make do with the long days and short nights of the island's summers, have no choice but to swim when the sun shines. Whatever the reason, we watched the animal with delight.

At the bus stop the following morning, Mario dumped us without lending a hand with our luggage. He marched in and out of a hardware store, then drove off with no wave or good-bye.

During the ride back to Launceston, Debbie and I decided that to safeguard our lives, liberty, and happiness, it would be best to abandon our plan to buy a car when we returned to Melbourne. Instead we would gain freedom of movement by finding one straightaway.

For three days we shopped. After leaping Olympian hurdles that included a sleazy used-car dealer, a dishonest mechanic in cahoots with him, and the intricacies of finding, paying for, licensing, and insuring an automobile in a country other than our own, we drove off in a 1980 Toyota Corolla station wagon.

Ten miles out of the dealer's yard, the car's fuel gauge quit working. A door lock broke, and the steering began to feel sloppy. Worried that the troubles might prove the tip of a mechanical iceberg, I proposed returning to Launceston for a confrontation. Debbie vetoed the idea. She begged me to put Mario, Ruth, the dealer, and the mechanic far behind us.

One hundred twenty-five highway miles lie between Launceston and Hobart, a city Mark Twain called "the neatest town that the sun shines on" and Elspeth Huxley called a "bungaloid sprawl." At sixty miles an hour we covered the distance quickly. We passed through grazing country that rolled gently, the paddocks dotted with cattle and sheep. In the sky we glimpsed a wedge-tailed eagle, soaring in the blue, and took in the pretty sight of pink-and-gray cockatoos, commonly known as galahs (ga-LAHs), flapping overhead in a whirl of color. When a park appeared, we stopped for a picnic.

In the trees, green rosella parrots squawked and leered as we nibbled fruit and cheese. The name *rosella*, applied to several Australian parrots, originates from the Sydney suburb of Parramatta, formerly known as Rose Hill. Early settlers found parrots living there and dubbed them "Rose Hillers," a name corrupted over time to "rosella."

During the break, Debbie read aloud from a Launceston newspaper. A great white shark, one of larger than average size, had been seen cruising up and down Tasmania's eastern coast. Swimming was being discouraged at several beaches. Seals, a mainstay on the great white's menu, inhabit Tasmania's coastline in great numbers. Sharks feed on them, and since great whites lack the brains or desire to distinguish people from seals, swimming among them is risky.

Grzimek's Animal Life Encyclopedia informed us that great white sharks sometimes exceed 6,000 pounds and grow to more than thirty-eight feet in length. They are "reputedly the most dangerous of all sharks," and "enter coastal regions, where they can be a great danger to swimmers." There was more. "One great white four and a half meters long bit a man in two," reports Grzimek, "and a six-meter-long specimen can swallow a man whole. . . . They are known to attack small boats and thus bring the occupants into a dangerous situation." Swimming and boating along the Tasmanian coast were not in our plans.

Eventually the road expanded to form a six-lane motorway. It carried us out of the hills into a wide basin filled by Hobart and its suburbs. To our left, the Derwent River flowed past a Cadbury chocolate factory. To our right, red-roofed houses and sprawling shopping centers edged up gentle slopes.

Much water had poured down the Derwent since December 2, 1642, the day Abel Tasman anchored near the site of modern-day Hobart. The Dutch explorer sent a landing party ashore, and the men returned excited. They had seen, according to Tasman, "high, yet level land with greens (unplanted being forthcoming from God in nature), fruit-bearing timber in abundance, and a running water [and] place many empty valleys. . . . The land is widely provided with trees, which stand so, that men may pass everywhere, and see far from them, so that on land always, one could get sight of the people or wild animals. . . ."

At the time the island was home to Aborigines long isolated from their mainland cousins. They were different enough in material culture and appearance from other Aborigines that their close kinship has only recently been established. The first humans arrived in Tasmania some 35,000 years ago. Low sea levels during the last ice age created a land link to the continent, and people could simply walk across. When the ice melted, the Bass Strait filled and the people living on the island were cut off.

When people are confined to a small area, strange things happen. For Tasmanians, the isolation that followed the ice age led to a loss of the ability to ignite fires. The islanders also stopped eating fish. This was a curious development in a land of rivers and seashore. At about the same time, around 3,500 years ago, bone tools ceased to be made. This may have been the worst of the losses, for bone needles were vital to the manufacture of clothing, and the island's climate is cool.

To the French explorer Marc-Joseph Marion du Fresne, who visited the island in 1772, the Tasmanians seemed little advanced from apes. They used only crude stone implements and lacked the boomerangs, spear-throwers, hafted axes, and intricate bone tools of mainlanders.

No one can say for certain why Tasmania became technologically impoverished. Tim Flannery theorizes that several factors were at work, all associated with the small size of the island's population. The specialization of toolmakers was impossible in such a limited society, Flannery proposes, and occasional mass poisoning by red tides made the eating of fish too dangerous to chance. Compounding these hazards, the warming of Tasmania at the end of the glacial period converted most of the island's buttongrass plains to rain forest. This was a disaster. The plains had supported large numbers of wallabies, and wallabies provided the islanders with a resource that can be difficult to obtain in Australia: protein.

Encounters between Tasmanians and Europeans, the first outsiders to arrive in 35,000 years, often proved violent. Du Fresne, three months before New Zealand's Maoris butchered and devoured him, shipped two sailors ashore dressed only in their birthday suits. The idea was to make peace. Something backfired. One side hurled stones, the other musket-balls. When the melee subsided, one Tasmanian was dead and several lay bleeding.

In time, Europeans wiped out the Tasmanians down to the last man, woman, and child, save for a few offshore islanders. Genocide is the word that best describes the government-sanctioned slaughter. A woman named Truganni, said to be the last full-blooded Tasmanian, died in 1876.

Yet not all encounters were hostile. In 1802, for example, barely a year before the founding of the first English settlement at Hobart, the French explorer Nicholas Baudin sought intercourse with the natives and enjoyed pleasing results. Smiles, laughter, and gifts flew back and forth, according to the account of the ship's zoologist, François Peron. A pretty young woman named Ouray Ouray, black and naked, took a shine to an officer and flirted with him. Everyone seemed to relish the encounter, and the groups parted with warm farewells.

The story has an amusing sequel. Later a group of natives urged Peron and a shipmate to strip, "perhaps to assure themselves," the zoologist wrote, "of our sex." The two men declined. A young sailor stepped boldly forward and offered to bare his essentials. He peeled, and then, to his chagrin, he "suddenly exhibited such striking proof of his virility that they all uttered loud cries of surprise mingled with loud roars of laughter." Peron's analysis strikes a low blow. "They had the air of applauding the condition," he wrote, "as if they were men in whom it is not very common. Several of them showed with a sort of scorn their soft and flaccid organs and shook them briskly with an expression of regret and desire which seemed to indicate that they did not experience it as often as we did."

One of the few vivid pictures of Tasmania's natives before history fell cruelly upon them comes to us from the English explorer Matthew Flinders. Hearing voices along the shore near the mouth of the Derwent, Flinders rowed ashore to investigate. There he found two women and a man. The women fled, but Flinders managed to dispel the fears of the man sufficiently to engage him in a dialogue of pantomime. "The quickness with which he comprehended our signs spoke in favor of his intelligence," wrote Flinders. "He had also marks raised upon the skin, and his face was blackened and hair ruddled as is sometimes practised by them. The hair was either close cropped, or naturally short; but it had not the appearance of being woolly."

History's glimpse of the Tasmanians is fleeting. English settlers, convicts, soldiers, and bureaucrats soon began a slaughter. Muskets and cannons felled men, women, and children. In the interior, English shepherds captured and castrated native men, and wives were sometimes forced to wear their husbands' heads around their necks like pendants. The carnage and torture was sanctioned and sometimes carried out by the British authorities.

In 1825, bounties of five pounds were placed on the heads of Tasmanian adults, and two pounds on the heads of children. The island's population at the time of contact is uncertain, but educated guesses put it at around 5,000. By 1830, less than sixty years after du Fresne's original encounter, the number had dropped to about three hundred. Seventeen years later a census recorded forty-seven. By Christmas Day of 1876, when the English governor and his colonists were talking piously of peace on Earth and goodwill toward men, the last full-blooded Tasmanian lay dead.

Debbie and I rolled into Hobart in high spirits, not thinking then of the tragedies that darken the island's history. The afternoon was bright and clear. Green hills rumpled down to meet blue waters, and a waning sun in the northwestern sky cast every object in golden light. We pulled out a road map. A woman named Betty Nicholson, who lived in a suburb called New Town, was expecting us for dinner.

We pulled up beside a picket fence on which a wooden sign painted with the number 52 was nailed. A bushy palisade of trees beyond the fence concealed the house from the street. There was a gate. Through it we padded, carrying a loaf of bread.

A concrete walk led to the door of a low, sprawling house. Verandas surrounded the place, paint peeled on wooden trim, and trees, shrubs, and vines threatened to bury the structure in jungle. A gray-haired woman hurried toward us down a long hallway. "Hello, Betty?" I said.

"No," muttered the woman, hurrying past us and out the gate.

A second woman emerged, hobbling into the sunlight from a doorway that suggested the mouth of a cave. She was round of figure and stout of leg, and coffee-and-milk-colored skin stretched over her Polynesian features. Beneath billows of gray hair she bared her teeth in a warm smile. "Hello, Betty?" I inquired.

"No, no, Betty's inside," said the most musical of voices. The accent was English, but the intonation hinted at palm trees and warm ocean breezes. "You must be the two Americans. Betty is waiting for you." The woman introduced herself as Dorothy, shook our hands with soft palms, and led us inside.

Through the doorway we walked, down a shadowy hallway that smelled of mold, and into a room with maroon walls stained black in places by soot. A kitchen, perhaps. The temperature was high. At a table heaped with papers, books, and jars of jam, marmalade, and honey sat a woman of indeterminate age. She wore a tattered, sleeveless T-shirt, and a straw hat with a wide brim blocked our view of her eyes. "Betty?"

"Good, good," said Betty Nicholson briskly. "You're here. You must be exhausted. Please sit down and have some tea." Behind Betty loomed a fireplace. Its mouth opened halfway up the wall, and in the gaping maw, a blaze spat and crackled, scenting the room with smoke.

Tea and toast followed. Betty welcomed us kindly, offering use of a comfortable bedroom for as long as we cared to stay. "Come and go as you like. Please use my house as a base," said a woman who was still little more to us than a name on a slip of paper. In the bedroom we found a fireplace, firewood already laid in it, awaiting the touch of a match. There was an enormous bed buried in quilts, a pair of single beds, two ancient wardrobes, and a wooden wheelchair with a seat made of cane.

Back in the kitchen, Dorothy stirred a pot while Betty soliloquized on the glories of the hearth. "For atmosphere," she said on this Tasmanian summer day, "there's nothing like a fire to provide a bit of cheer."

Dorothy dished up bowls of stew while Betty recruited me to fetch a load of firewood. I did as instructed. Stepping through a side door, I entered an alcove. There I found a old leather baby carriage, as black as bat wings. It looked like a contraption that might have ferried Queen Victoria around as an infant. The carriage showed heavy wear. I wheeled it outside, filled it with eucalyptus wood that I found stacked along a wall, and pushed the load to Betty.

During the meal, Dorothy satisfied our curiosity. She was a a Fijian, although for years she had lived in Whangerei, on New Zealand's North Island. A daughter lived in Hobart, but her place was too small to house

Dorothy when she visited. Betty rented Dorothy a room, and the two women had become friends.

The pair listened with great interest to our plans for a wildlife odyssey. "Have you seen a kangaroo or a wallaby?" Betty wanted to know. We lamented that we had not. Dorothy giggled. "I hope you won't mind me telling you," Betty continued, "that you've just eaten one. Dorothy made this wonderful stew from a wallaby tail."

And so we met our first kangaroo.

Hobart was a handsome city of old brick buildings and bustling streets. The downtown reminded me of England, with rows of compact shops, sidewalks overhung with marquees, and well-dressed businessmen and professional women walking swiftly, deep in conversation. At the Salamanca Market, an open-air bazaar, we bought vegetables and bread.

Around the corner from the Salamanca, we discovered Battery Point, the neighborhood where Errol Flynn lived as a boy. The steeple of St. George's Church, consecrated in 1838 and a near-replica of St. Pancras's Church in London, towered over the old houses and narrow streets.

Thomas Quigley, a great-granduncle on my mother's side of the family, served at St. George's as rector from 1920 to 1930. He was a formidable man, to judge by the look of him. The current rector, a Reverend Bill Jolly, escorted us inside the church despite the fact that we arrived after closing time. He showed us a line-up of rector's portraits dating back to the early days, and among them was my distant relation. Irish by birth, Thomas Quigley came to Australia in the teens, married a Sydney woman, and served at St. George's for a decade before returning to the northern hemisphere. His features were more Teutonic than Celtic, suggesting Vikings on the family tree. His expression was one of commanding righteousness.

Before we departed, Bill Jolly, a kind man with a sad face, spoke of the Reverend Quigley's oldest son. Tom Quigley the younger, he said, was seventy-six, retired, and lived in a suburb of Sydney. We would look him up.

Hobart appealed in a serene, outpost-of-the-Empire sort of way. Yet, after a couple of days, its flavor began to seem little more than a variation on the denatured taste of Euro-American cities everywhere. Modern urban environments are spiced with the culture of the countries that support them, but the underlying ingredients are the same: bricks, stone, concrete, steel, glass, asphalt, humans, starlings, English sparrows, and pigeons, combining in a limited number of variations. We hungered for the real Tasmania—savage wilderness and rugged coastline, mountains and plains, wombats and wallabies. And so, in a series of journeys radiating out from our base at Betty Nicholson's, we left the city to explore the countryside.

Our first sortie brought us to Port Arthur, an old penal settlement east of Hobart on the Tasman Peninsula. We found it a creepy place, a prison with a gruesome history, burned and ransacked to an empty shell, then transmogrified into a pricey tourist attraction. A sentry at the gate wanted twenty-six Australian dollars for the two of us. Appalled, we drove away. Following a dirt road until it ended, we arrived at the summit of a high cliff. Below, waves thundered against rocks. A dead wombat that had blundered over the edge lay stinking, its flesh sunken, fur clotted, teeth bared toward the sun.

At four-thirty, admission at Port Arthur fell by half, and we returned. No one, unfortunately, bothered to tell us that the museum closed at five. By the time we made our way from the parking area in a high meadow to the inner workings, the exhibit halls were bolted shut. Our thirteen dollars brought us only views of bland, manicured lawns, a few impressive specimen trees, and plaques that made light of the place's somber history. We didn't like this place, which was undoubtedly upholding a tradition. To salvage something positive from the visit, we spent a half hour watching a white-faced heron stalk fish along a rocky bay.

Our next foray brought us away from Hobart, Betty, and Dorothy for nine nights. We began by driving south to Kettering, an hour from Hobart, and catching a car ferry to Bruny Island. Rolling off the boat in late morning, we were soon shuddering our way along the island's corrugated roads.

After traversing the isthmus of sand that links the island's halves, we came to a fork. Turning left on a whim, we followed a road that zigged and zagged into low hills, then descended to the shore of a bay. A cold wind stirred the water to a rough chop. The road continued beside the sea, passed through a hamlet with a post office *cum* grocery, and ended at the Adventure Bay Caravan Park. There we pitched our tent in a light rain and spent the first of 131 Australian nights sleeping—or trying to—on the ground.

Roger Aldridge, the brusque but helpful man who ran the campground with his wife, Jo, explained the origin of the bay's name. Tobias Furneaux, captain of HMS *Adventure* on Cook's second expedition to the

South Pacific, christened the waters in honor of his ship. Furneaux and crew spent five nights anchored there, seeing no Aborigines but declaring them, on the basis of their traces, "very Ignorant and wretched." Cook sailed into Adventure Bay soon afterward. He carried with him a young ship's master named William Bligh. Four years later Cook was back again. This time he found the terrain around the bay "for the most part of a good height, diversified with hill and Valley and everywhere of greenish hue [and] well-wooded." There were "several sorts of birds," Cook added, all scarce and shy. "A sort of opossum, about twice the size of a large rat" was also spotted, as were two groups of friendly natives.

We found that although the landscape had changed little since Cook's day, the natives hailed from a different tribe. They slept in nylon tents, like our own, or camped in travel trailers, which they called "caravans." Among a dozen such portable abodes, we settled down to a cold, damp sleep. All night, waves crashed like cymbals against the shore.

"What's that sound?" Debbie bolted awake before me. Outside the tent, it sounded like the aftermath of a college fraternity party, which is to say, people were violently puking. Nonplussed, I withdrew deeper into my warm cocoon. Debbie dressed hurriedly and crawled outside. Moments later I heard her triumphant cry, "Yellow wattlebirds!" They sounded like retching Delta Upsilon boys to me. I snoozed another hour.

The day passed quietly. When it was raining, we retreated indoors to Jo Aldridge's café and drank coffee brewed in a French press. Roger Aldridge bustled in and out between carpentry projects, soaked by a cold drizzle. He told us about Bligh.

The notorious captain of HMS *Bounty* visited Adventure Bay, said Roger, four times in all. One stay in 1788 began the twenty-first of July and ended the fourth of September, only a few months before Fletcher Christian mutinied and set his captain adrift. We were camped, Roger said, in more or less the exact place where Bligh, Christian, and others of the crew came ashore in longboats.

Bligh saw "several eagles, some beautiful-plumaged herons, and a great variety of paroquets" at Adventure Bay but made no mention of wattlebirds. His 1788 party found "A.D. 1773" cut in a tree, a memento of Furneaux's visit. Lest the crew grow lazy ashore, Bligh kept them busy. They planted Indian corn, plantain trees, pumpkins, grapevines, and a variety of fruit trees, including apples, oranges, lemons, plums, peaches, cherries, and apricots. A few Aborigines turned up to investigate. Their

voices reminded Bligh of "the cackling of geese." He gave them gifts. The
Bruny islanders showed little interest. When *Bounty* was restocked with
drinking water and edible greens, Bligh commanded Christian to weigh
anchor. The ship sailed off to its famous destiny.

Each time the winds eased and the rain slacked off, we darted outside
to hunt for wildlife. The blustery shore was barren. In the grassy paddocks
and eucalypt forest that ringed the campground, we found a flame robin
with a breast visible a hundred yards off, tree martins, dusky woodswallows, and a troupe of parrots that were so large we first took them for
hawks. Making a great ruckus, the birds were big and black, with out-
landish crests, red eyes, and swaths of yellow painted across their tails.
They were ripping bark from a dead tree. Graham Pizzey's *Field Guide to
the Birds of Australia* resolved the mystery. These were yellow-tailed black
cockatoos, parrots whose calling is to pry bark from dead and diseased
gum trees and feast on the grubs and termites underneath.

While Debbie steamed herself in the campground shower, I snooped
outside. I was hoping to find and photograph Tasmanian native hens. In
the morning several of them had run clucking among the tents and caravans. I was skunked on hens, but I found something equally good: a splendid fairy-wren, singing on a fencepost. There were woodswallows, too,
snatching insects from the air, and a friendly lamb tethered to a tree. On
my way back to the café in a light rain, I met an old woman walking
beside two bristly terriers.

"Bloody rabbits all over the place," she said. I hadn't noticed, or asked.
She pointed a crooked finger at a chicken coop, one end of which was
badly undermined by warrens. "See this little one?" she said, nodding to
the more sprightly of the dogs. "He's five years old. Last year he killed
eighty rabbits." The woman's red, wrinkled face flushed with pride.
"Now this one's fourteen. She's retired from the business, but in her
day . . ." I was left to complete the sentence on my own as the woman
hobbled away.

In any other country, one would recoil from a bloodthirsty woman and
murderous dogs. But in Australia, one pays them tribute. The reason is
rabbits. They arrived from England on Christmas Day, 1859. Set loose on
a farm near Geelong, Victoria, they were swarming all over the continent
by the end of the century. European rabbits are burrowing animals that
riddle landscapes with holes. Voracious eaters and prolific breeders, they
wreak unspeakable havoc on native plants, and in so doing they contribute

to the demise of other animals. Rabbits remain terrible pests all over Australia. The introduction of diseases such as myxomatosis and rabbit calcivirus have reduced the numbers somewhat, but bunnies still make big trouble for ranchers, vegetable farmers, and the indigenous animals we had come to see.

The last minutes of light found us leaning against a wire fence, straining for a glimpse of a white goshawk we had spied earlier in the day. The bird failed to appear, but in tall grass on the far side of the wire, something moved. We switched on a torch, as Australians call a flashlight. *Nothing.* The light illuminated only a clump of grass a little taller and thicker than the grass around it. Something moved again, a dozen yards to the left. We strained our eyes and made out a shape, wide at the bottom, narrow at the top, with two erect and prodigious ears. The animal stood about four feet tall. What could it be? Debbie switched on the light. In the feeble glow cast by the bulb, our first wild, uncooked kangaroo took shape like a hologram.

It was a wallaby, a Bennett's, the species whose flesh we had sampled at Betty's. Before excitement could sink in, a convention of the animals was under way. From a dozen places high on the slope, wallabies pogo-sticked down to damp spots where the grass grew thick and tall. Six of the animals were albinos. In the silvery glow of a crescent moon, they cut ghostly figures.

Had we arrived in Australia centuries earlier, the kangaroos would have baffled us just as they flabbergasted Dutch, French, and English explorers. The first recorded response of a European to a kangaroo comes from François Pelsaert, sailing on the Dutch ship *Batavia* in 1629. Pelsaert wrote of seeing "large numbers of a species of cats, which are very strange creatures; they are about the size of a hare, their head resembling the head of a civet-cat; the forepaws are very short . . . [and] its two hind legs [are very long] and it walks on these only, on the flat of the heavy part of the leg. . . . Its tail is very long, like that of a long-tailed monkey."

Arriving a century and a half after Pelsaert, the botanist Joseph Banks, sailing with Cook, reacted to kangaroos with a similar groping for vocabulary. "In gathering plants to-day," Banks wrote in 1770, "I had the good fortune to see the beast so much talked of, though but imperfectly; he was not only like a greyhound in size and running, but had a tail as long as a greyhound's; what to liken him to I could not tell, nothing that I have seen at all resembles him."

A sneeze gave us away. The wallabies froze. We heard a loud thumping of feet, like the alarm response of rabbits on steroids. A moment later the animals were bounding up the hill, fading into the darkness.

We had seen them well. The marsupials had thick, shaggy coats, and their color (except for the albinos) was gray-brown, tinged here and there with rust. Bennett's wallabies never reach the size of the eastern grey kangaroos Banks described, but males average forty-three pounds and sometimes approach sixty. Females weigh about thirty-one pounds, well more than the average beagle.

The motion of the wallabies fascinated me. Starting off, an animal would lean forward, push off with its enormous hind feet and legs, and, using its tail as a counterweight, bound over the ground with a forward tilt. Unless a wallaby was creeping slowly, its forelegs hung limply and ineffectually, like the undersized arms of *Tyrannosaurus rex*.

Eventually we tired. Cold air poured down the hillside and drove us toward the tent. Yet we had cause for celebration. This was our first wedding anniversary, although we had been married four years. (Send cards on February 29.) We toasted the occasion with red wine sipped out of plastic coffee cups, rejoicing in togetherness and the fact that years of dreaming had at last brought us close to kangaroos.

More rain fell the next day, leaving us to curse the fact that we'd spent five sunny days in Hobart. We made the best of things, drinking Jo's delicious coffee, scribbling notes in journals, dashing out between showers to search for wildlife. After nightfall we drove back to the isthmus.

Penguins materialized, as Jo had predicted they would. Like wind-up toys they waddled out of the sea and climbed the dunes, where their nesting burrows lay. I had seen wild penguins during earlier journeys in New Zealand, but these were the first for my bird-loving Penelope, and she was captivated. By moonlight we watched a sleek, blue-and-white adult regurgitate a mouthful of fish into the maw of a fuzzy nestling. There may be better ways to spend an evening, but we couldn't think of one.

Just before leaving Bruny, Debbie and I made a side trip to the island's northern half to search for a rare bird. The forty-spotted pardalote, a tiny creature that picks flea-sized sucking insects and their sugary excretions from leaves and twigs, occurs only on Flinders Island in the Bass Strait, and in five places in eastern Tasmania. One would hardly expect a bird that feeds on insect shit to be a fussy eater, yet the forty-spotted pardalote survives on just that. It thrives only if presented with a single species of tree, *Eucalyptus viminalis,* and the tree's attendant retinue of insects. Humans admonish their children that fussy eating habits will lead to grief. The pardalote, finicky to the point of peril, proves the point by edging toward extinction.

We drove slowly, up a winding road. In a gully where the appropriate tree abounded, I parked the car. Together Debbie and I scoured the branches with binoculars. At first we saw nothing. Then, directly above us, we spied little birds, nervous and flighty, picking bugs from the leaves. The birds stayed still too briefly for us to count their spots, but their shape, size, dirty white undersides, and faded yellow cheek patches gave them away as forty-spotted pardalotes.

During the ferry ride back to Kettering, the *where-where-where* cry of the forty-spotted pardalote echoed in our heads. Ignoring it, we plotted our next move. There were alluring places to see along the coast—Maria Island, a national park north and east of Hobart, and Recherche Bay, a half-day's drive to the south—yet our instincts argued for the center. Tasmania's greatest claims to fame are its wild, mountainous interior and vast, shadowy rainforests. We had not set foot in either. As a white-breasted sea eagle soared over our heads and the gunmetal-blue waters of the D'Entrecasteaux Channel rocked the ship, we gazed toward green slopes rising in the west and decided to set off inland.

An uneventful drive brought us south along the coast through Weaver and Gordon, then northward along the lower reaches of the Huon River to Huonville. This was orchard country, and apples appeared everywhere—in baskets by the roadside, dangling like Christmas ornaments from trees, and bouncing past us when they rolled off the backs of trucks. At Huonville we bought groceries, then followed the west bank of the river to Geeveston. Beyond loomed dark forest. The road turned to coarse gravel, grew narrower and narrower, and wove between immense trees. At first most of them were eucalypts, but the higher and wilder the country grew, the more we noticed rain-forest species such as sassafras (no relation to its North American namesake), myrtle, and leatherwood.

As darkness descended, the Toyota labored over a pass into Hartz Mountains National Park. The place was empty. There were no people, no rangers, no buildings, and, of paramount concern, no campground. Could we pitch the tent? We searched for a promising spot. Rocks covered every bit of ground. Even the parking area, paved with sharp stones, offered a bed of nails. With our station wagon piled high with gear, only one option remained. We would have to cocoon inside sleeping bags and sleep in the front seats.

In the morning we wriggled out like born-again butterflies. I was dismayed to find that my back, aggravated by our Cyclopean labors on the farm, had not suffered the bucket seat gladly. My spine felt as rigid as a broomstick. When I tried to flex it, the pain was blinding. This posed a problem. We had come to climb Hartz Peak, a 4,100-foot crag of dolerite formed during the breakup of Gondwana and carved to its present shape by ice, winds, and erosion. Shrubby trees grew on talus between the mountain and the car, and they gave a view to the summit. Under the first clear sky in days, the climb looked inviting. Yet each step I took hurt like the thrust of a lance. I could no more satisfy my thirst for the summit than Tantalus could quench his longing for water.

So we shuffled. We made it as far as Lake Osborne, Lake Esperance, and Ladies' Tarn, glorified names for shallow troughs gouged from the rock by glaciers. At an ant's pace, we enjoyed good looks at birds, most notably an elegant-looking songbird with a white throat, red eye, and head streaked with gray. It was an olive whistler.

Back at the parking area, a man sat half in and half out of the blue sedan next to ours. He was ripping off hiking boots as if hurrying to catch a train. Rainer, an architect, came from Stuttgart. He was taking a leave of absence to see the world, and had been roaming for eight months. I asked Rainer what he had seen along the way. As if answering a foolish question, he rattled off the names of mountains. How did Hartz Peak compare with the others? Rainer had just returned from the summit. "It was easy," he said bitterly, as if being easy were despicable. "Five hours according to the sign—that's ridiculous!" A snort. "I did it in three and a half hours with no trouble."

When I told Rainer I had back trouble and would not complete the climb, he gazed at me in horror. "Ach," he cried. "This is an easy walk. Anyone seventy years old could do it as quickly as I did." About forty, the German had a mustache that, when he spoke, bristled like a pincushion.

Rainer suffered, it seemed, from a psychological condition common to most of the young travelers we were meeting. We called it the "Tas-mania." The presenting symptom is a determination to reach the tops of the maximum number of the island's peaks in the minimum amount of time. Perhaps I baited Rainer. I said, "It would take us more than five hours. We like to study things along the way—wildflowers, trees, lizards, birds."

"I cannot see birds," said Rainer, taking the defensive. "I do not have binoculars."

"Yes, you can." It was my turn. "We just saw a very beautiful and interesting bird called the olive whistler. It was perched in a tree along the track, just a meter or two from where we stood. It was too close for binoculars to focus on. We saw it only because we were moving slowly."

Rainer turned away, saying nothing, and busied himself in his car. A few minutes later he turned to face me, keys in his hand. "This was just a little one," he said. "I climbed the highest mountain in Southeast Asia—Gunong Kinabalu, in Borneo. Four thousand one hundred meters!"

Borneo is a wild place. Scaling its tallest peak cannot be an easy thing. "How long did it take? Several days? A week?"

"Two days," said Rainer. "I hike very fast." Seconds later, gravel flew into the air as the architect and his car raced toward the next conquest.

What do Rainer and people like him see as they travel? Why do guidebooks, park rangers, and fellow travelers often encourage one to march up every barren summit and windswept ridge? I was, and remain, baffled. Alpine ecologists might come away enthralled by such places, but others take home little more than bragging rights and postcard-style photos. Pretty views provide quick thrills, like the titillation of catching someone undressing near a lighted window. But I craved a deeper intimacy—one that would give me contact, close and genuine, with the living things that made Tasmania different from any other spot on the planet.

A confession: I have been as guilty as anyone of rushing from one pretty spot to the next. When my travels follow such a path, however, the journey is little more satisfying than watching television or pasting postcards in an album. At its most superficial, travel is consumptive, a mere gathering of experiences to mull over and brag about later. Yet it can be far richer. An odyssey can be a slow unfolding, like the blossoming of a flower, an opening up to new viewpoints and visceral encounters. We chose the "slow, unhonored, and unpaid task of observation," as Emerson called it. Neither of us envied Rainer the notches on his stick.

Our next stop was Mount Field National Park. Getting there required a long drive back to Hobart, followed by a lengthier haul up the Derwent Valley. The park entrance lay a few miles west of the village of Westerway. We arrived in early evening, an hour before nightfall.

Our first act on arriving at Mount Field was to flag down an off-duty park ranger. His name was John Megalos. He was lean and mustachioed, about forty, dark-haired and tanned. On learning we were naturalists and occasional park rangers from America, John unlocked the office door, switched on the lights, and spent an hour educating us about the park's geology, flora, and fauna. "You'll have to go here, and here, and here," he said, pointing to the map. He looked disappointed when we told him we'd be staying only a couple of days.

Set in the bottom of a valley, the campground at Mount Field lay under a dark and ponderous forest. The trees were immense, broad of bole and reaching heights of two hundred feet and more. We pitched our tent among them, feeling like ants. As the dusk came in like fog, our eyes were drawn to a broad expanse of lawn.

A faint residue of the day persisted there. In it we made out the shapes of animals long of tail, immense of hind leg, and dainty of forepaw. They were kangaroos, species unknown.

Approaching, we saw that there were two kinds—large, woolly Bennett's wallabies, and small, dark Tasmanian pademelons. We spent three nights in the campground, and by the third the job of distinguishing wallabies from pademelons was easy. The wallabies were more massive, their tails thick and plush like velvet bell-ropes. I wanted to grab one and tug, although the gesture would hardly have been appreciated. The pademelons, by contrast, were delicately built and had skinny tails, like rats.

The wallabies tolerated a close approach. We watched as they grazed on clumps of grass, listened to their chewing, and detected the sour smell of the droppings that trailed behind them like raisins. The animals moved slowly, yet their stout tails and sturdy hindquarters suggested power and speed. I decided to try an experiment. Wondering how fast a wallaby could move, I walked straight at one. At first it hobbled away, rocking back and forth on its front and rear legs. Then I put on a burst of speed. The wallaby rocketed off, bounding at astonishing speed. I ran and ran and continued running until I fell to the ground, gasping for air, my back throbbing. The kangaroo accelerated without apparent effort, its hind feet touching the lawn without a sound.

Back at the campsite, I buttered bread and heated a can of asparagus soup. Immediately we had visitors—brush-tailed opossums, three gray, one black. The black one had a pink nose.

Although Australian opossums borrow their name from the American variety, the animals look very different from each other and are only distantly related. While the American version looks ragged and ratlike, the

Australian wears a handsome coat of fur, has a plump torso suggestive of a scaled-down koala, and has a cherub's face topped with Mickey Mouse ears. The possums that joined our dinner showed no fear. They paced beneath the table. They brushed against our ankles. Eventually, one leaped up and put a hind foot squarely in Debbie's soup. She cheered. The asparagus had the texture of old rope, and it floated in a soup stock that tasted like boiled socks.

About the time we were ready to sleep, a brown mammal about the size of a squirrel came plodding into the dim glow of our candle. The creature had a pointed face, more toothy than a rodent's. Round white spots daubed its flanks, as if it were dressed in a clown suit. The tail was slender and brown. We thumbed through our copy of Ronald Strahan's *Complete Book of Australian Mammals.*

The visitor proved to be an eastern quoll, a cousin of the Tasmanian devil. Quolls are sometimes called "native cats," although they are no more closely allied to felines than humans are to wallabies. To us they looked like giant shrews. There are about forty species in the family, ranging from the badger-sized Tasmanian devil to dunnarts, antechinuses, phascogales, planigales, ningauis, and the kultarr. Several of the smaller species could be mistaken for mice—and were, by early settlers. The eastern quoll feeds mainly on insects but is also known to take birds, bandicoots, rabbits, and rats. Females give birth to up to thirty young, yet have only six teats in the pouch. It seems a harsh arrangement. The first half-dozen newborns to reach the nipples survive, while the rest wither and die.

We were thrilled. Marsupial carnivores are notoriously difficult to locate, and this one had saved us the trouble of a hunt. Eastern quolls are rare and possibly extinct on the mainland. On Tasmania, where the introduced dingo and red fox have not invaded, the native predators flourish.

We used our first full day at Mount Field to explore the forest that stretched beyond the campground. There we found streams roaring down gorges, punctuated now and again by great curtains of falling water. There were humid ravines crowded with tree ferns, birds everywhere (most conspicuously, crowlike grey currawongs that screeched like parrots amid the foliage), and enough variety of leaf and bole to keep us botanizing for hours. The tallest of the titans, the swamp gums and stringybarks, stood so high that gazing into their crowns required painful contortions. Both species had trunks as thick around as grain silos, and tatters of bark lay in heaps at the bases of the swamp gums. I cannot overstate the massiveness of the trees. The grandest stood nearly three hundred feet from base to topmost twig. They reminded me of the Saturn V rockets that blasted astronauts toward the moon, and, like them, seemed in a hurry to reach the sky. I found myself musing on life's conquest of the universe. Will organisms from Earth conquer space in rocketships, or will they simply grow there, radiating inch by leafy inch into the cosmos, creating a salubrious climate as they go? Just as the arms race put humans in space, a similar competition, one in which the stakes are carbon dioxide and sunshine, drives trees ever farther into the stratosphere. Forests, it seems, play a never-ending game of "Can You Top This?" and their answer to the question is *yes, yes, yes.*

On the second day, we drove into high country. Following the Lake Dobson Road, we climbed through forest, traversed the windy openness of Wombat Moor, and arrived on the shore of Lake Dobson. Summer had not yet ended in the valley, but a cold blast of wind that struck us as we climbed from the car foretold the coming of winter.

Black currawongs, crowlike birds with yellow eyes and slight hooks at the tips of their bills, watched from dwarf forest that bordered the parking area. We were near tree line. Among towering, palmlike plants called pandanni (members of the heath family, although they looked like giant club mosses), the trail carried us up and out to bare rock and tundra. The air was cold and stinging. We pressed on until midafternoon, trudging ever higher until a shelter appeared at a place called Tarn Shelf. Enjoying a respite from the wind, we sipped water and nibbled on fruit and crackers.

We trudged back to the car under a gray sky, feeling chilled and pensive. Savage mountains and wild, empty valleys loomed in every direction. In puddles along the trail we heard the chatter of frogs. The sound was comforting, a good thing. As the mountain air made mischief with the muscles of my back, I was desperately in need of cheer.

From Mount Field, we drove straight into Southwest National Park, renowned for its vast temperate rain forest. The soils of the park are rich by Australian standards and drenched by almost constant rain. All the way from South America, three-quarters of a world away, gales blow in daily, unimpeded by any landmass.

Tasmania's southwest is wet, windy, and cold, hostile to human endeavor. Yet plants thrive. Many belong to the genus *Nothofagus,* a primitive group with a long history. Also known as Antarctic beech, *Nothofagus* was among the world's first flowering plants. The group probably evolved in South America, then spread across Gondwana 80 or 90 million years ago. Antarctic beeches range today through New Guinea, New Caledonia, New Zealand, Australia, and South America. Africa, formerly part of Gondwana, lacks them, suggesting that the birthplace of our own species snapped off the supercontinent earlier than its neighbors.

While crossing the Humboldt Pass, we stopped to explore a buttongrass plain—a vestige of the great expanses of buttongrass that covered Tasmania during postglacial times. The plains provided hunting grounds for thylacines (the marsupial wolf, or tiger) and Aborigines. The tall grass looked inviting, and, tired of driving, we charged into it like kids set loose from school.

As soon as my feet disappeared into the verdure, I thought about tiger snakes. I had read that they abound on buttongrass plains. Walking slowly, prodding the ground ahead with a walking staff, would be prudent. I knew of a man bitten on the right index finger by a tiger snake. He died two hours later. I also knew that tiger snakes were prolific breeders. One female earned a place in the herpetological record by giving birth to 109 young.

Slowly we advanced. A green bird, big-headed and possessing a long tail, flushed from the high grass. It stroked the air with brisk wingbeats and vanished back into the vegetation a hundred feet ahead. We advanced toward the place. The bird popped up again, then dove down. This sequence was repeated twice more. Every time, the bird disappeared without giving us the long look we wanted. Yet there was little question of identity. Size, shape, color, and habitat told us that we had stumbled on one of the most difficult Australian birds to locate in the wild, the rare, secretive ground parrot.

Had we waded through the buttongrass a century earlier, we might have seen dozens of ground parrots, as well as the most singular of modern marsupials, the thylacine. Perhaps a thylacine, tail trailing stiffly behind it, would have streaked past us, running down a wallaby. We would have seen its stripes. Thylacines combined the sartorial good looks of zebras with the hypnotic grandeur of top predators such as lions and leopards. They were called "tigers" because of their stripes, or "wolves" by virtue of their lupine form and habits. Yet the similarities to these better-known animals were shallow. The female carried young in a pouch, and thylacines of both genders had the bony skulls and compact brains that characterize marsupials.

An adult thylacine (the name means "marsupial dog") weighed about fifty pounds and looked something like a Doberman pinscher. Stiff and stout at the base, the tail never wagged the way dog tails do. Once humans arrived in Australia, there was little cause for wagging. The introduction of the dingo from Asia during Aboriginal times meant peril. Dingoes were faster and more aggressive than thylacines, capable of killing their young and outcompeting them for prey. By about 3,000 years ago, thylacines persisted only in Tasmania, a place dingoes did not reach. There the marsupial predator survived until the last of its kind, an animal filmed and photographed extensively, died in the Hobart Zoo in 1936.

Thylacine sightings are occasionally reported today, yet almost certainly represent wishful thinking. Well-funded scientific expeditions to remote corners of Tasmania have produced no convincing signs of the animal's existence, and no road-killed animal has turned up to sway the skeptic. Thylacines roamed open plains, indulging a taste for wallabies and sheep. If they still lived, people would see them, farmers would defend livestock against their muttonous appetites, and every zoo in the world would clamor for the privilege of exhibiting them.

The thylacine declined in Tasmania with shocking speed. Sheep ranchers made war on the predators, abetted by Tasmania's small size. Top carnivores require vast areas to maintain breeding populations, so the thylacine was probably at risk of extinction long before Europeans arrived. A bounty was placed on the animals in 1830. It was rescinded in 1909, but by then thousands had been slaughtered. Ironically, the thylacine's increasing rarity stirred international interest. Zoos and museums demanded to have specimens, live and stuffed. Individuals that might have repopulated the species died in the name of appreciation.

Much of the little we know about thylacine behavior was learned during the first quarter of the twentieth century by zookeepers in Berlin, London, and New York. In cages, marsupial wolves paced restlessly. They opened their jaws nearly 180 degrees, far wider than any dog. German biologists considered the thylacine profoundly stupid and coined a term, *Beuteltierstumpfsinn,* to describe the dimwittedness of the animal and its marsupial cousins. The zookeepers, however, may have been the real dimwits. The trusting nature, "persistent stupidity," and vacant stare of the Tasmanian tigers watched by the German zoologist Ludwig Heck in Berlin may have had less to do with the animal's intellectual shortcomings than with its response to violent capture, transportation across oceans, and life not on a buttongrass plain but behind iron bars on a concrete slab. Certainly the thylacine had its talents. It could jump six or seven feet in the air from a standing position, and it was cunning enough to feed on fast-moving self-defense experts such as the Bennett's wallaby.

Off we drove, sorry to have missed the thylacine by sixty years, but glad to have seen the ground parrot. That night was our first in Southwest National Park. We camped at the terminus of the Scott's Peak Road, a twenty-five-mile strip of rock and dirt that dead-ended in dense forest. Rain fell heavily on the cold, gray afternoon of our arrival, and it was still spattering on our tent when we awoke. My back felt as if someone had taken a welding torch and fused all the vertebrae.

In the morning we returned to a junction, then swung westward on the Gordon River Road. A thoroughfare to nowhere, the route provided the only means of penetrating the southwest by car. It owes its existence to giant hydroelectric dams that increased the island's electric production ten times between World War II and 1975. Oceans of concrete moved down the road, as well as crews of workers, miles of steel reinforcing rods, house-sized turbines, and assorted paraphernalia. The highway cuts across one of the planet's last great regions of wilderness. Not surprisingly, some people view it as a gift from God, others as the Devil's handiwork.

Through dripping rain forest, we skirted mountains rising on the left and right. At midday the sun slipped free of clouds and flooded the land with light. Our first stop was a campground at a place called Ted's Beach. There was little of note here—a few rocky campsites, a building of sinks and toilets, a view out to a sheet of blue water ruffled white by wind. The air blew fresh, clear, and cool.

Although a road map designated the body of water before us as Lake Pedder, environmentalists would scoff. The original Lake Pedder was hailed by many as Tasmania's most pristine and picturesque body of water. In 1972, however, a hydroelectric dam was built downstream. It drowned Pedder and its sandy beaches beneath a vast reservoir.

In Launceston, we had met a man named Bob Brown who advocated the reservoir's draining and the resurrection of the original lake. Pedder would regain its beauty in twenty years, he told us, if the plug was pulled at the dam. A week after meeting Brown, we picked up a newspaper to find he had made history. Running as a representative of Australia's Green Party, Bob Brown had won a seat in the Australian Senate.

Little interested in seeing the reservoir, but keen on savoring the last minutes of daylight, we pitched our tent and drove off. We hurried through Strathgordon, a town that flourished during the days of dam construction but is now almost a ghost town, plunged back into the bush, and eventually ran out of pavement at the Gordon Dam. Dark and lifeless compared to the riot of vegetation beside it, the edifice reminded me of an illustration in Edith Hamilton's *Mythology*. The woodcut shows Hades carrying Persephone off to the Underworld. Grim cliffs, barren of moss or flower, loom on either side, and a heartbreaking blackness fills the depths. As a child, the illustration gave me a chill every time I saw it. I felt similarly here. In the dying light, the stark concrete and the shadowy, bottomless gorge inspired despair.

Between the dam and our sleeping bags lay ten miles of winding road. In twilight, nocturnal animals would be emerging. Among them we hoped to find a Tasmanian devil.

Halfway back to camp, a dark, hairy thing ran into the road and squared to face us. A devil? We lurched to a halt. Picking up a flashlight, I leaped from the car.

The animal stood as high and wide as a bulldog, yet there was nothing doglike about it. It looked more like a koala that someone had sat in front of a television and fattened on beer and hot dogs. The face was broad and bristly. In it were set forward-facing eyes, and between them a handsome nose bulged round and black. Cute in a stuffed-animal sort of way, the animal stood frozen, blinking in our headlights. "A wombat!" cried Debbie.

The wombat's body language said that it was royally pissed off. It stood defiantly in the road, as if it had every intention of blocking the car's progress. It stared at its feet. Then the wombat did something that shattered our notion of the animal as a placid-tempered herbivore. It huffed, puffed, and charged. Bolting toward us, the marsupial cannonball shot close enough to Debbie's legs to extract a bite. Fortunately, it declined this opportunity. Huffing again, the wombat retreated to the road's edge. We felt relieved. This was no elephant. But the wombat had formidable incisors, and it was clearly unhappy with our presence.

Finally the wombat struck a photogenic pose—body in profile, face angled in our direction, with not a single object to distract the eye in the background. I grabbed a camera and snapped on a flash. As I was focusing, the animal turned and crashed into the bush.

I slept little that night. Nightmares involving killer wombats were not the problem. I was a victim of demonic possession—the Southwest's cold, damp air had penetrated my back, and the results were monstrous. I walked like Quasimodo and struggled to undress. Every time I dozed off, pain jolted me awake. In the morning I crawled out of the tent haggard and twisted.

There was only one thing to do. Our Hobart friend Betty Nicholson was a "physio," or physiotherapist. She had offered to work on my back. I had declined, feeling unable to afford the expense of treatment and unwilling to accept the service gratis. At this point, however, there was little to do but accept and see what magic Betty could work.

Three sessions of ultrasound, electric shocks, massage, and Betty's supreme optimism put me right. The ancient black box that she used to send jolts of current to electrodes pasted on my back looked like a relic from Frankenstein's castle. Yet it worked. After one treatment I could walk without pain. After two I could bend. After three I was ready to resume the journey.

Over the next three days, Debbie and I drove a route that traced a fishhook on the map. We returned to the turnoff for the Gordon River Road, but this time continued on through a range of mountains to Lake St. Clair National Park. We spent one night at the lake, sleeping in a campground in which Bennett's wallabies outnumbered people. The next day we pushed on, northward and to the west, until we reached Lake Burbury late in the afternoon. There we pitched the tent in a deserted campground.

Perhaps the hydroelectric generators nearby filled the air with negative ions, for here our odyssey nearly ended. After more than a month of round-the-clock companionship, including several nights squeezed together on rocky ground inside a cold, damp tent, Debbie was sick of my presence, and I of hers. Our conversations had deteriorated to pained sighs and monosyllables. We were tigers in a cage, ready to rip each other to pieces over the slightest provocation. Somehow Debbie managed to prepare a meal, and I to eat my share and scrub the dishes. We wriggled into our sleeping bags without speaking a sentence.

The following day, after a cheerless breakfast, we traversed the curve of the fishhook. Crossing the mountains to Queenstown, we detoured west to Strahan on Macquarie Harbor, drove north via Rosebery to an unnamed junction, and veered east toward Cradle Mountain. Along the last stretch we found a young wombat. It lay dead in the road, fresh blood still trickling from its nose. The carnage of wildlife on Australian highways appalled us. As in America, people hurry from place to place at literally breakneck speed. We saw little regard for mammals, birds, reptiles, amphibians, and other creatures too slow or unwary to get out of the way.

Aside from eruptions of marital friction, the long drive was notable for two sightings. One was a road-killed reptile, a tiger snake, fat and black and still twitching after the car ahead of us had crushed its midsection. "Tiger snakes," writes the herpetologist Harold Cogger, "are probably the best known of Australian snakes, having been responsible for a significant proportion of snake-bite deaths in this country." This one had shiny round scales that looked like sequins. Wary even of dying snakes, I searched for a stick to move the animal to the shoulder. When I returned, the snake lay still. I lifted it respectfully and placed it on a catafalque of yellow flowers.

The other newsworthy sighting occurred at Lake St. Clair. Walking in a forest of eucalypts, *Nothofagus,* sassafras, and tree ferns, we were rounding a bend in a footpath. Suddenly, out of the undergrowth and wobbling from side to side as if drunk, a beast straight out of Wonderland appeared—a pincushion moving under its own steam. The pins were golden, about as thick as the average knitting needle, and they projected from a coat of black hair. The creature had no tail, at least as far as we could see. Out of what seemed to be the forward end poked a snout, dark, leathery, and about two inches long. When we came upon the animal, it was running its nose along a rotting log. Edging closer, we saw a tongue delicately lapping up ants.

We had blundered onto another of the world's egg-laying mammals. This was a short-beaked echidna. It was smaller than we expected. If I'd been foolish enough to pick it up, I could have cupped it in the upturned palms of my hands. It was, I believe, a juvenile.

Whether young or old, the echidna, if a male, would never see its testicles. They remain undescended for life. For this indignity the animal is compensated by a prodigious grooved penis, with four red knobs bulging from the tip. The penis has a sexual function only, for an echidna urinates from its cloaca. During the breeding season, males bustle after females like railroad cars trailing a locomotive. Little is known about its sexual habits, but mating surely requires delicacy. A captive female echidna was once observed marching up the back of a male, straight over the top, and down the far side until her bottom pressed against his face. Not a subtle move, but the male took the hint and copulation followed.

The echidna paid attention to us only when I approached closely with a camera. Then, ducking like a shy child, it tucked its face into the leaf litter. After counting to ten, or seeming to, the animal resumed ant-hunting as if nothing had disturbed it. Was it fearless? Nearsighted? Stupid? We wondered. Echidna vision is poor and may have little practical use. A blind echidna discovered by a researcher in Queensland was found again in perfect health, a year and a half later.

As for courage, echidnas often hold their ground and commence digging at the first sight of a human. They keep going until the soil caves in around them, and they vanish. It seemed that we had happened upon one of an idiosyncratic, tolerant minority.

Our echidna was perhaps conserving energy. Living according to frugal energy budgets, the species gets by on one-third of the oxygen consumed by placental mammals of comparable size. It was also possible the echidna was taking the encounter philosophically. Thirty percent of the animal's brain, the so-called "silent area," has no known function. Scientists postulate that this gray zone functions in decision-making, in considering the consequences of actions, and in the development of memory and personality. By proportion, the corresponding region in the human brain is smaller.

Inside an echidna's head the scientist finds a labyrinth of wrinkles. This may be significant. A highly convoluted brain surface generally corresponds with great intelligence. Is the echidna a wandering philosopher that roams Australia in deep thought? No one can say.

Cradle Valley National Park and a campground just outside it provided us with rain, ice, high winds, occasional sunshine, and home for four nights. Snow fell heavily in the high country, creating pretty scenes of white and green but spoiling our hopes of an overnight trip into the mountains. Scott-Kilvert Hut, the cabin in which we had planned to pass the night, stood on a windy saddle too dangerous to climb without mountaineering gear. The jagged dolerite of Cradle Mountain rose on one side, Mount Emmett on the other. Between them the hut was bolted to 175-million-year-old igneous rock, stuff formed when Australia and Antarctica were parting. Its name honored the memory of a schoolteacher and student who, one summer day in 1965, were caught nearby in a storm and died of exposure for want of shelter.

The weather reminded us that Tasmania can be a hostile place. On warm days, stepping on tiger snakes and copperheads is always a risk. When the sky turns gray and windy, the risk increases. Hypothermia and frostbite are serious threats, even in summer.

No more grueling journey has ever been recorded than the crossing of the island in 1822 by Alexander Pearce and seven fellow convicts. They stole away from a work party at the Macquarie Harbor penal settlement, commandeered a boat, crossed the bay, and struck into the interior. Two men mutinied and fled. The others pressed on.

One by one, starving and cold, the fugitives bashed each other over the head and cannibalized their flesh. In the end the party contracted to two: Pearce and a companion named Greenhill. Neither man allowed himself to sleep, fearing the other's intentions. Finally Greenhill dozed, and Pearce attacked. "I run up, and took the axe from under his head, and struck him with it, and killed him. I then took part of his arm and thigh, and went on for several days." Robert Hughes tells the story in his book *The Fatal Shore*. Pearce was eventually captured and returned to prison, where he recounted the grisly specifics. A year later he escaped again, this time with a man named Cox. Pearce killed Cox, too, dined on his flesh, and was captured soon thereafter. This time he was hanged.

A couple of days earlier, Debbie and I were eyeing each other much like Pearce and Greenhill. But now, despite cold and rain, warmth returned to our partnership. Perhaps it was the echidna that turned the tide. In our wildest dreams we had never anticipated meeting Australia's egg-laying mammals so early in our journey. But we had, and good luck brought deep satisfaction. Also, thanks to Betty, my back felt grand.

A few minutes after making camp, and before we continued up the Cradle Mountain road in search of supper and beer, another bit of good fortune intruded. It was a mammal that may well be the most handsome in Australia—a spotted-tailed quoll, or tiger-cat. Far larger than the eastern quoll we'd seen at Mount Field, this beast looked like the formidable predator that it was. It padded blithely into the barbecue area behind the campground picnic shelter, confident, afraid of no one. Its body was the size of a large housecat's, yet elongated and covered by a woolly coat. The fur was a rich chocolate brown, daubed with bold white polka dots. Spots ran all the way down the back and the tail. Although the quoll's body looked soft enough to cuddle, its toothy, blunt face, suggesting murder and mayhem, discouraged the idea.

The quoll showed an interest in only one thing—licking grease from the tops of gas-heated grills. It was a joy to watch the animal move. As lithe as an otter, it flowed up one side of a cooking station and down the other, pausing just long enough to clean the sticky surface. We had close looks at the teeth, which were numerous and sharp. The male uses them to grab the back of a female's neck. Their lovemaking marathons sometimes last eight hours.

When not licking up fat or copulating, spotted-tailed quolls roam forests in Tasmania, Victoria, New South Wales, and Queensland. To nourish themselves, they eviscerate birds, small mammals, reptiles, and insects. Quolls are much less common than they used to be. Foxes and housecats kill them for dinner and sport.

The quoll moved off. So did we, for the lodge up the road offered significant temptations: food, beer, and that ungainly, oversized, badgerlike cousin of the quoll known as *Sarcophilus harrisii,* the Tasmanian devil. We had learned that the lodge's bartender put out table scraps every night. Among the animals he attracted, said the campground manager, were wild Tasmanian devils.

So we ate, drank, and joined a dozen other visitors on a dark porch, waiting. Among them was a tall, distinguished-looking black man with a voice like Bing Crosby's. He was about sixty years old, judging by his wrinkles, and he was dressed in a checkered shirt and flannel trousers. "Very exciting, eh?" he said to me, smiling warmly. I nodded, speechless at first. It suddenly struck me. The man was the first Australian Aborigine I had set eyes on since arriving in Australia thirty days earlier.

As we waited, I was reminded of the scene in *King Kong* when Fay Wray stands lashed between wooden posts, anticipating the debut of her co-star. Here, a ruddy leg of mutton took the place of blond virgin. The meat was tethered on a wire beneath a wooden platform. Above, the bartender spread salad greens.

Possums appeared, plump and gray, and devoured the veggies greedily. Bennett's wallabies came, too, arriving on silent hops and clearing the platform's edge. Beneath the table, shielded from the light, the mutton leg dangled in partial shadow.

Minutes passed. We found the suspense excruciating. After twenty minutes, half the crowd gave up and retired to the bar. Then the wire began to jerk. It swung back and forth. All eyes strained to see what was doing the pulling.

Soon a collective *oooh* rose from the gallery. Spotlighted theatrically, the devil himself had the mutton in his teeth and pulled against the tether. He looked like a miniature black bear, broad and big-headed, as dark as the night. In size he suggested an overfed Scottish terrier. A slash of white ran over his rump, another across his throat.

Without a growl or whirl of dust, the devil vanished. At the moment we lost sight of him, he clutched a piece of flesh in his white, pointed teeth.

A few minutes later the beast reappeared. It bared its cutlery and charged up to a possum that, putting herbivorous tendencies aside, had decided to sample the mutton. Faced with certain injury, the possum fled. The devil of Tasmania lorded over his arboreal cousins, it seemed, like a barbarian king of old.

Early European settlers of the island found it difficult to love a mammal that slept in holes in the ground (often in the company of half-eaten corpses), emerged after dark to feed on the dead, and filled the nights with its demonic screams. The first zoologist to study them kept two chained to each other in a barrel. As one might predict, they behaved like a husband and wife thrown together in a car and a tent: to wit, like devils.

Contrary to reputation, however, the devil is a candidate for sainthood. It bothers no one, is "engagingly affectionate, playful, and mischievous," according to a biologist who lived with them, and keeps Tasmania free of stinking corpses. The devil commits no greater sin than making off with an occasional chicken or barnyard duck. Generally necrophagous though it may be, a typical Tasmanian devil makes the average poodle seem dirty and unkempt.

We spent three days at Cradle Mountain. One evening we watched a platypus paddle across the glassy surface of Lake Dove, slicing through upside-down mountains. We read, dozed, strolled, watched devils behind the pub, and wrote in our journals. Torrential rain often drove us into the campground cooking shelter, where we sipped tea and passed the hours happily.

One Cradle Mountain walk brought us through a dark, dripping forest of Antarctic beech and into a meadow littered with green, fibrous cubes, each about an inch across. Our guess about the cubes was confirmed by a ranger. They were wombat scats. From the meadow we followed a faint track to a gnarled, shaggy Methuselah of a tree. It was a pencil pine, a Tasmanian endemic, rooted there, said a park ranger, for about 2,000 years.

Stiff, short leaves wrapped around the twigs, forming cylinders approximating the diameter of pencils. We also saw a close relation of the pencil pine called the King Billy pine. This tree's leaves bristled from the twigs like thorns. The identity of King Billy himself is unknown. The most appealing theory, and perhaps the most unlikely, is that he was the chief of Tasmania's vanished Aborigines.

That afternoon I passed a memorable hour dancing with a wombat. I spied it far off in a meadow. Eager to take photographs, I decided to see how close the animal would let me approach. It was a large one, about fifty or sixty pounds, although giant wombats that lived until the end of the last ice age grew larger. The animal threw suspicious glances at me now and again. Otherwise it went about its business, which consisted of snipping off grasses with its paired upper and lower incisors.

For every mouthful of grass a wombat swallows, a gastrointestinal odyssey lies ahead. The path begins in a churning whirlpool, the stomach, and from there leads to a twelve-foot-long colon and hindgut in which the grass slowly ferments. A similar digestive tract is found in koalas and horses. Forty or fifty hours after the start, what's left of the pulp emerges dried and neatly cubed from the animal's bulbous rump.

I kept a long way from the wombat at first, slowly closing the distance between us every time it bolted. In a soft voice I told the animal who I was and where I had come from and how much I admired a marsupial that could force its way through brush like a bulldozer and, when given no alternative, crush intruding dogs against the walls of its burrow. The ruse worked. The wombat grew to trust me. We wandered side by side, shuffling through tall grass colored pumpkin-orange by the westering sun. At times I stood close enough to stroke the animal's fur. Each time I resisted the urge. I was grateful for the intimacy and would not violate it.

The wombat would feed for hours, perhaps all night. By morning it would retire to a burrow, one of several it occupied in a time-share arrangement with neighbors. Wombats sleep like old men. They turn occasionally, and when the need strikes them they yawn, snore, gnash their teeth, fart, and belch.

Early Europeans in Australia thought the wombat was a kind of badger. The first written description dates to 1798. A man named John Price first described the creature the Aborigines called "Whom-batt." The animal stood "about 20 inches high," Price wrote, "with short legs and a thick body with a large head, round ears, and very small eyes. [It is] very fat and has the appearance of a badger." The explorer Matthew Flinders expressed culinary interest. Wombat, he found, "resembles lean mutton in taste, and to us was acceptable food."

Today, common wombats are absent from much of their precolonial range. Not many people eat them, but human development appropriates prime habitat, and farmers make war on the animals with traps and poison. Wombats can riddle a pasture with holes, turning it into a mine-field for cattle, and they are experts at demolishing rabbitproof fences. Rabbits themselves are also a problem, eating many of the plants that sustain wombats.

When the light grew dim, I left my furry friend to rejoin Debbie, who was watching birds high on the hill. A storm was coming on, and we hurried back to our campsite.

In the morning we found our nylon home floating in several inches of water. Pulling on warm clothes and raincoats, we emerged in a cutting sleet to find the tent fly covered in ice. Packing up was miserable. We completed the job in a frenzy, loaded the car with our sodden gear, and sped out of the park.

Both Debbie and I felt a growing urgency. There were two more Tasmanian parks we wanted to visit, Mount William and Asbestos Range. There were dozens of birds yet to see, more devils to meet, and one more wombat to encounter. Yet March had arrived. Autumn was all but upon us. To reach the red, dry center of Australia, and to get there before the days waned sharply and the nights grew long and dark, we would need time and the winds on our side.

Odysseus sailed away from the island of the Cyclops shouting taunts at the monster he had blinded. When *Spirit of Tasmania* steamed out of Devonport four days after we drove out of Cradle Valley, Debbie and I stood silently at the rail. Why press our luck? A yellow-nosed albatross cruised overhead like a jumbo jet, then swept over gray-green sea. The Bass Strait parted before the bow. Beyond it, unseen, loomed the mainland.

4

Aeolus Throws a Boomerang

ONE-EYED MAN-EATERS BEHIND them, Odysseus and Co. advanced to the next challenge. It began at Aeolia, home of Aeolus, lord of the winds. Joan Crawford had nothing on Aeolus. He commanded that his daughters marry his sons and insisted they take meals together as a united and happy family. In light of such dysfunction, it is no wonder winds blow violently one moment, softly the next, and, when needed to fill sails, collapse into doldrums.

Never bashful about accepting favors, Odysseus enjoyed a month of Aeolus's breezy hospitality. Then, eager to get on with the journey, he requested help in the form of favorable winds. Aeolus obliged, enclosing ill winds inside the skin of a nine-year-old bull and giving the sack to Odysseus. Ahead of a steady blow, the Greeks sailed for nine days and nights. Odysseus remained awake, we are told, out of romantic anticipation for Penelope. On the tenth morning, however, as the green, familiar hills of Ithaca rose above the horizon, he fell asleep. Odysseus's shipmates had been eyeing the wind bag and its silver cord. They suspected it contained treasures. So, as Odysseus dozed, the bundle was opened. Out rushed the ill winds. They blew the fleet all the way back to Aeolia.

As Debbie and I plotted a second departure from Melbourne, the path ahead presented an Odyssean parallel. The winds would throw us a boomerang, too, launching our car and its contents west along the Victoria and South Australia coasts, north to Ayers Rock, Alice Springs, and the central deserts, and then all the way back to Melbourne. The strange course was made necessary by our aim of circling Australia. To reach the middle of the country by car, we had two choices: either drop down to

the center from the north, or rise up from the south. No road worthy of
the name runs across central Australia from east to west.

In Melbourne we found the latest edition of Harold Cogger's *Reptiles
and Amphibians of Australia*. The monumental tome would make our car sag
on its springs; we bought it because we couldn't bear the idea of visiting the
interior deserts and not recognizing the reptiles we met along the way.

We skipped the city zoo, a place where John Muir had looks at lyrebirds, bowerbirds, platypuses, and echidnas. The Californian was nonplussed by the native animals but taken by lions and tigers, which he
found "fine." In Melbourne's municipal cemetery, we passed on a chance
to visit the graves of statesmen and explorers, instead asking a young man
using the cemetery as a shortcut if he would direct us to the Elvis Presley
Memorial. Without needing to scratch his green hair or tug on the gold
ring that pierced his nasal septum, he invited us to follow him. Soon we
stood before a granite monolith, polished to a slippery sheen. On it were
engraved two images of a man who never set foot in the southern hemisphere. Why visit a stone dedicated to the "evergreen memory" of a pop
star who wouldn't know a platypus from a pizza? Perhaps it was our taste
for the bizarre.

We also visited the Botanic Garden. Our chief interest there was a
colony of grey-headed flying foxes, a kind of fruit bat. Great numbers of
flying foxes roost in the garden in a thicket of eucalypts, palms, and tree-
ferns.

Australia is home to many of the world's most beautiful bats, as well as
several of the most ugly. On the good-looking side, if you accept attractive bats as something other than an oxymoron, are the flying foxes. The
black flying fox, for example, is as cute as a chihuahua. The Queensland
tube-nose bat, decorated with snazzy yellow spots on its wings and ears, is
a knockout, too, at least if you can ignore its nose, which suggests a
double-barreled shotgun whose barrels have decided to part company. On
the ugly side lurk bats out of nightmares: the ghost bat, with a face that
might have been torn up in an industrial accident, and several kinds of
horseshoe bats. Among the latter, take your pick of the most hideous: the
greater wart-nosed, the lesser wart-nosed, and the long-eared. Grey-
headed flying foxes hover between the two camps, beautiful and ugly all
at once.

Beris Caine, with whom we were staying again, warned us not to look
up at the bats with mouths open. It proved good advice. When we found

the colony, liquid spattered down on the sidewalks. Was it urine? There was little smell of ammonia in the air. Binoculars suggested a different explanation. Above our heads, several hundred bats were gleefully conducting the wildest orgy imaginable. The shower was partly composed of semen.

The bats demonstrated every sex act we could think of—fellatio, cunnilingus, intercourse ranging from the acrobatic to the sedate, all conducted to the accompaniment of savage biting and weird, unnerving screams. A band of ancient Greeks, no prudes where sex was concerned, would have been impressed.

My observant wife, aided by binoculars more powerful than my own, twirled her lenses. She began to call out the play-by-play like a sports announcer. "Oh my God," she cried. "Have you seen the penises on these things?" I said nothing. Debbie didn't know it, but a crowd of gray-headed women had gathered around us. They wore skirts and blazers marked with the insignia of a garden club. Debbie's intense scrutiny of the treetops had attracted them.

"What is she seeing?" asked one of the women, catching my eyes with her twinkling blue irises.

I stood speechless. There was no way I could give Debbie an elbow without being obvious. "Wow!" gasped Debbie. "The penises on these guys are amazing. They're black and twisted like a corkscrew and half a foot long, with little knobby heads at the end. Look—he's biting her on the neck and shoving it in from behind!" I turned to see the garden club ladies fleeing.

Sexual theatrics aside, the grey-headed flying foxes impressed us. I had never seen a bat much larger than an open hand. But these were immense—the size of big hawks. Funereal black, their wings appeared to be made of tough leather, and their rounded heads and substantial bodies suggested small dogs. The typical insect-eating bat of North America or Europe has dark, beady eyes and oversized ears perfect for collecting radar, but these fruit-fanciers had wide, soulful eyes and small ears. In locating fruit, nectar, and flowers, vision serves grey-headed flying foxes better than radar ever could.

In the 1980s, a brief excitement ran through the scientific world when a biologist suggested that flying foxes might not be bats at all but primates, cousins of humans. The tentative conclusion was based on studies of brain shape. Flying foxes, it was argued, had simply evolved batlike anatomy and behavior. The theory was soon rejected. Mitochondrial DNA work proved that flying foxes were bats after all.

Back in Beaumaris, plans were brewing. Debbie and I had had a casual discussion with Beris and the MacLeods about the possibility of visiting the Grampians, a mountain range west of Melbourne. When we returned from Tasmania, preparations for a trip were in full swing. Breads were being baked, meats purchased, wine set aside, and a cabin rented. The Lotos-Eaters were at it again. Keith's warning about keeping us captive now sounded prophetic.

By the time we returned from the "Gramps," the Easter holiday would be upon us. No point in setting out immediately for the west, we were told. Roads would be crowded, campgrounds full, ferries turning away passengers. The only solution was a second excursion—to the MacLeods' weekend retreat near Mansfield. They had a house at the edge of the Great Dividing Range, and it would make the perfect place to rest before our push inland.

For three weeks we tossed the plot of the *Odyssey* aside and put ourselves in the hands of Philemon and a pair of Baucises. The wine flowed endlessly. The bread broke into a thousand pieces. And because things that Americans have decided are unhealthy to eat are still good for you in Australia, we feasted on roast beef, mutton, and potatoes swimming in gravy, supplemented by Debbie's sumptuous vegetarian lasagnas and my own French toast and pumpkin pies.

By the time the diversion was over, we had added an inch or two to our waistlines. Inertia set in. In the middle of it all, I had an accident. One morning at Mansfield, I was climbing over a barbed wire fence to get close to a Nankeen kestrel when I lost my footing and tumbled. As I fell, I grabbed instinctively at the nearest source of support. As if in slow motion, I saw my hands reach for the fencing wire, experienced a sickening thought of what was to come, and felt my weight drive in the barbs. Bloody and dazed, I limped back to the house. One ankle was sprained, and a piece of my flesh remained impaled on the fence. A hole gaped in each palm. Through the openings I saw muscles and tendons.

Lacking health insurance, I was glad the MacLeods owned a good first-aid kit. I squeezed blood from the wounds to cleanse them, then Debbie applied antiseptic and bandages. There was no doubt I had come to the right place to convalesce. For the next several days I lived like a sultan.

Debbie, Beris, and the MacLeods catered to my needs, feeding me morsels from their fingertips. Not wanting to hire a doctor to sew me up, I avoided using my hands until the wounds closed tightly.

The American writer Paul Theroux, a consummate complainer, came to Australia and found the friendliness of the natives excessive. "Australians," he writes, are "like people who had only recently been domesticated, like youths in their late teens sitting among adults, rather upright and formal and wooden, because as soon as they loosen their grip or have one beer too many they slip into a leering familiarity and all hell breaks loose." Theroux spends too much time in pubs, methinks. Loutishness and cheesy intimacy thrive in such places. I am not surprised the bar-hopping American found Australia "a country where most of the men seemed drunk most of the time." He went to smoky taverns to confirm negative stereotypes, it seems, and succeeded with his usual flair.

Debbie and I stayed clear of the watering holes where Theroux did his socializing. We did so not out of highmindedness, but from lack of interest and cash. Our beans-and-rice budget had no room for pub-crawling. What drinking we did occurred mostly in people's homes. Drunkenness and cloying coziness were not part of the picture. Warmth and generosity were. My only complaint, a minor one, is that three weeks among our friends infected us with the national adverb. It was actually a small price to pay, actually, for while actually picking up the word Australians actually insert in sentences where Americans might say "uh" or "you know," we actually suffered very little trauma.

The excursions to the Grampians and Mansfield provided our first looks at Australia's interior. Driving west from Melbourne, the land grew flatter, the trees more widely spaced, the grasses in the pastures brown and dry. Mark Twain came this way once and exercised his ornithology. "On the way we saw the usual birds," he writes in *Following the Equator.* "The beautiful little green parrots, the magpie, and some others; and also the slender native bird of modest plumage and eternally forgettable name— the bird that is the smartest among birds, and can give a parrot 30 to 1 in the game and then talk him to death." Twain concludes: "I cannot recall the bird's name. I think it begins with M. I wish it began with a G, or something that a person could remember."

We saw birds, too, sixteen new species on the Grampians junket alone. The most beautiful was a purple-crowned lorikeet, the last a brown tree creeper. Most memorable, however, was the quintessential Australian bird that D. H. Lawrence called "a very remote, dirt brown gentleman from the lost plains of time"—the emu.

There were six of them, trotting away from us in single file. The first stood taller than the rest, as high as a man and as giraffe-necked and potbellied as an ostrich. It was almost certainly a male. Father emus do all the work of raising the young once the mother performs the Herculean chore of laying a dozen or more eggs, each weighing over a pound. Hatchlings are striped and short-necked in the early weeks. They trot after the old man until they rival him in size. Emus are native to nearly all of Australia save for its driest deserts and wettest rain forests. There were three subspecies. A Tasmanian emu and a Kangaroo Island emu were hunted to extinction in the nineteenth century. The mainland bird persists in good numbers. Emus have lived in Australia for at least 80 million years. Ranging across the continent through a broad range of habitats, they serve along with the kangaroo, the kookaburra, and the platypus as a national mascot.

In the Grampians we hoped to see eastern grey kangaroos, one of the largest living marsupials. In Mount William National Park on Tasmania, we had glimpsed the bounders at a distance, but close looks never came. Beris, Peg, and Keith predicted success at a picnic area known as Zumstein's.

Driving along a dirt track through the mountains, we were approaching Zumstein's when we spied several eastern greys sprawled on the forest floor. Keith hit the brakes. There were six of them, tall, gangly things with the faces of camels, legs and bodies of oversized rabbits, and long, stout, muscular tails. A kangaroo trademark, the tails serve as counterweights when the animals bound.

"Kangaroo," a D. H. Lawrence poem not to be confused with his novel of the same name, sketches the animal's appearance. The author writes of the "sensitive, long, pure-bred face" of a female kangaroo, and its "full antipodal eyes, so dark, so big and quiet and remote, having watched so many empty dawns in silent Australia." The poem portrays the "great muscular python-stretch" of the kangaroo tail, and how it sits "rabbit-wise, but huge, plumb-weighted." Had we met Lawrence along the track, I would have challenged his notions of emptiness and silence, things he harped on. The Australia we found teemed with life and interest. Emptiness was its antithesis. As for silence, we grew certain that Lawrence had a hearing problem. The laughter of kookaburras, the mad shrieking of parrots, and the chattering honeyeaters, pardalotes, fairy-wrens, and thornbills entertained us wherever we roamed.

I wondered on arriving in Australia if we would find kangaroos abundant or rare. Experience was proving that it all depended on the species. In general, large kangaroos remain numerous, chiefly because they are less vulnerable than their smaller kin to introduced predators such as foxes and housecats. The biggest species, the red and the eastern grey, may today exceed their numbers in Aboriginal times. Irrigation schemes and deep wells bored by farmers for livestock increase the ability of the landscape to support kangaroos. According to recent estimates, eastern greys number about 10 million. Small marsupials, by contrast, are vanishing. Several have become extinct within the twentieth century while others, such as the yellow-footed rock wallaby, persist only within tiny ranges. The latter once spread across the rocky hills of interior South Australia, New South Wales, and Queensland.

With as much calm as we could muster, we slipped out of the car. The kangaroos remained prone, their brown eyes blinking. They had hair on their muzzles, a feature that distinguishes eastern greys from other large kangaroos. In every regard they were substantial, the size if not the shape of deer. We had no way to gauge their weight, but males grow to nearly two hundred pounds and females about half that. From short-legged, squirrellike ancestors that descended from the family tree about 30 million years ago, the eastern grey kangaroo evolved into a terrestrial creature of power and grace. Zoologists place it and all kangaroos in the family Macropodidae, meaning "big-footed."

We raised binoculars. If one of the kangaroos was a female, we might see a joey's head poking out of its pouch. Alas, there were none. Two of the mob were substantially smaller than the others. These were probably youngsters.

Kangaroos breed continuously. Given sufficient food and water, females don't interrupt their estrus cycles during pregnancy as placental mammals do. Kangaroos are always fertile. An eastern grey that kicks a joey out of her pouch generally holds a fertilized embryo *in utero,* waiting its turn. The embryo is called a blastocyst, and it consists of seventy to one hundred translucent cells. When the grazing is good and the pouch is vacated, the blastocyst begins to grow quickly. With birth imminent, the expectant mother cleans her pouch like a human sprucing up a house before the arrival of company. On the big day, the newborn passes up a shortcut that develops between the female's two vaginas. It pops out, and with no time to waste, the tiny joey starts wriggling up its mother's belly, following a moist pathway she has licked through the fur to the pouch. The joey locates the opening and noses inside. A kangaroo at birth is tiny, pink, blind, and hairless.

Within the pouch, the newborn clamps down on a teat. There, development continues. Weeks pass and stretch into months. Nine months after its birth, the joey tumbles out for its first awkward hops. At eleven months it stays out for good. At eighteen months or so, its mother ceases to supply milk. Miffed, the young kangaroo bounds away and adult life begins.

The kangaroos beside the road looked utterly content, sprawled on beds of eucalyptus leaves, legs and big feet splayed, eyes flirting with sleep. I decided to join them. Walking a dozen paces up the hillside, moving in and out of patches of sunshine that broke through the canopy, I halved the distance between us. The ears of the animals pricked up, and their eyes widened. I lay down thirty feet from the nearest and arranged myself on the ground as kangaroolike as anatomy would allow. This was bliss—the Peaceable Kingdom, Australia-style, and I was part of the picture.

The rest of the party were shooting photos when a car roared down the road. Behaving as their ancestors probably did in the presence of *Thylacoleo,* a marsupial lion that stalked Australia during the Pleistocene, the kangaroos leaped to their feet and bounded into the forest. The last we saw of them were their tails, waving in the air like snakes.

Afterward, or a few minutes before—the events of these days of wine and marsupials blur in memory—we spied something that appeared to be a statue of a kangaroo. It stood beside the road, rising from a patch of brush.

The animal was more heavily proportioned than an eastern grey, but less grand overall. The fur was dark brown, the ears short, and a pale stripe ran along each cheek. Was it alive? The answer came a moment later when the swamp wallaby—as we identified it afterward—rose from the ground, executed a 180-degree turn in midair, and vanished into the trees. Later we realized what a lucky sighting this had been. The swamp wallaby ranges across a generous slice of eastern Australia from Cape York to Victoria, yet because it lives in dense, shadowy forests, it is a difficult species to locate. Smelling one is easier. People in interior Queensland and New South Wales call swamp wallabies "stinkers" because they often smell the animal before they see it. We sniffed. Our nostrils filled only with the scents of eucalyptus leaves and sun-baked earth.

After the Grampians, and following our weekend of lotos-eating at Mansfield, I took my bandaged hands and my beloved Penelope and set off for the west. We had covered only a few miles when trouble struck. Outside Melbourne, along a busy highway, our right rear tire exploded. I spat out an unkind word and swung the car to the shoulder.

One of the cheap, resurfaced tires supplied by the dealer had ripped open. There was nothing to do but fish out a jack, lug wrench, and spare. This required a virtual cleaning of the Augean Stables, because nearly everything in the car had to be unloaded to reach them. As our nostrils filled with perfume from a sewage treatment plant, we pried off the old wheel and bolted on the new.

The happy-go-lucky mood in which the day began had turned sober. A flat tire along a busy highway was no catastrophe. Yet we were about to enter the interior. Mechanics and tire dealers would be thin on the ground, and we might drive hours without seeing another car. From now on, the tired old Toyota would serve as our spaceship. In the desert it would provide our only shield against a terrible vastness as uncaring of human fate as the cold, dark vacuum of the cosmos.

After camping near the coastal village of Lorne, we set off the following morning, new radial tires spinning in the rear. The highway was called the Great Ocean Road. Over long stretches we saw almost no one: only dry, rocky grazing country edging up to high cliffs and the deep blue of the Southern Ocean beyond. There were no barns and few houses and towns. The only conspicuous sign of human presence was the narrow smear of asphalt on which we drove.

By the middle of the day, it seemed we had reached the lonely end of the earth. The sky was empty, and so was the road. Yet, pulling into a parking area, we instantly found ourselves immersed in buses, rental cars, and tourists. Engines roared. Multiple languages filled our ears. This was our first real contact with industrial tourism, an important component of the Australian economy.

I found the scene at once awful and wonderful. Japanese, Chinese, Europeans, Africans, Europeanized Australians, and Americans mingled peacefully, united by a common love of landscape. Yet when I stepped behind a bush to address an insistent bladder, I saw the other side of the story. The landscape was strewn with toilet paper, ancient excrement, fresh turds, beer cans, soft-drink bottles, and candy wrappers.

Rock formations known collectively as the Twelve Apostles lay just offshore. These were the magnets that had lured people to the spot. Cut by wave action from narrow headlands, the pillars of stone rose grandly from the sea. Cliffs rose at their backs, and surf foamed at their feet.

We took a short walk, then retreated to the car. I am no misanthrope. I enjoy people. Yet, like wine or whiskey, I enjoy them best in moderate doses. Crowds were easy to find back home. Like many visitors, we had come to Australia seeking elbow room.

The day, born in gloom, matured in sunshine. The Great Ocean Road snaked in and out of deep bays, looped around headlands, and gave so many thrilling views of sea, sky, and cliffs that keeping eyes on the road proved difficult. Darkness finally overtook us from behind. Debbie was at the wheel, driving northwest toward Nelson near the South Australia border, when two kangaroos loomed in the headlights. She punched the brakes. A sickening thud. We stopped, and Debbie turned the car.

At the site of the collision we expected to find a kangaroo dead or bleeding. Instead we discovered a healthy-looking animal, sitting as if nothing had happened. It looked at us, pivoted, and bounded away. Was this the animal we had hit, or was it the other? We couldn't say. On the spot we swore a pact to avoid night driving. We had come to Australia to admire kangaroos, not kill them.

The following morning, in a campground outside of Nelson, we sat in a houseboat mounted on a trailer, enjoying coffee and cake with a retired couple named Keith and Kath. Kath was short and stocky, sounded German to our ears, but proved a Scot. She had emigrated from Scotland to New Zealand, had stayed for two years, then had come to Australia. Keith wore a salt-and-pepper beard and a broad mustache. He had the long, angular face of a Windsor, and had he told me he was George V disguised as a fisherman, I would have believed him.

Keith's voice was low and sonorous. It had a burr, perhaps related to the cigarettes he rolled and smoked in quick succession. He worked most of his life in the fiberglass business, he told us, and had built the boat himself. When I expressed amazement, Keith shrugged. "Oh, I suppose you learn to do something well, and that's what you keep on doing." The couple had spent the Easter holiday camping and fishing with children and grandchildren. Now they were driving to Perth, houseboat trailing behind them.

As we made good-byes, a fly landed near Keith's plate. "You're interested in birds," he said, nodding toward the insect. "Have you made the acquaintance of the dunny budgie?" We had been in Australia long

enough to get the joke. A "budgie" is a budgerigar, a colorful native parakeet. A "dunny" is an outhouse.

That evening, our first in the state of South Australia, was a howler. A
cold wind screamed in from the west, filling the air with dust and leaves
and bending the trees until their branches slapped noisily against the tin
roofs in the campground. Setting up the tent was a wrestling match, cooking dinner a Sisyphean chore. The infernal wind kept picking up the tent
and throwing it. It blew out the stove, blew out the matches I lit to revive
it, and hurled every cup, bowl, and pot on our picnic table toward the
Victoria border.

Before darkness came, we watched three galahs, pink and gray and
white, circle the paddock in which we camped. Galahs are among the
most elegant of parrots, and these provided our best looks to date. They
were gorgeous. Combining the ruddiness of the central deserts, the white
of a salt pan, and the gray of Dividing Range bedrock, the galahs seemed
direct expressions of Australia's national fabric.

The campground's address was Gemini Downs, and it lay along a
stretch of the South Australia coast known as the Coorong. The country
was low, flat, and sandy. It reminded us of coastal Alabama and Mississippi.
An attenuated spit of sand, the Younghusband Peninsula, paralleled the
shore, and between it and the mainland spread a body of water as shallow
and placid as the Mississippi Sound. The sky was alive with gulls, terns,
and pelicans. Coorong, we learned, is a corruption of the Aboriginal
Karangh, meaning "narrow neck of water."

We found the Coorong deserted. The National Park visitor center was
closed, having been extinguished by a budget cut, and the migratory birds
had vanished with the approach of winter. We enjoyed a one-sided conversation with an enormous draft horse we named Duke, and in the
campground one evening we fell in with a foursome of country music
fans heading home from a concert. Cyril, the elder statesman, took a
shine to Debbie and insisted she take a colorful pin from a collection he
wore on his hat. Cyril's mate, Don, eager to give a proper Australian welcome, seemed concerned that I was left out. He presented me with a pin
of my own.

Our cool, windy day on the Coorong began with the winning of
Duke's confidence. Carrots and apples did the trick. The horse was a
Shire, or mostly a Shire, as grand a beast as any I've set eyes on. By the
time we left him, he was nudging our chests with his muzzle.

We explored salt pans, thickets, and mud flats. More than anything we wanted a glimpse of a rare parrot, the orange-bellied, that summers in southwest Tasmania and winters along the Victoria and South Australia coasts. The bird is in serious trouble. Grazing animals, foxes, and housecats have overrun its wintering grounds, pushing it to the brink of oblivion.

We looked for the parrot all day, scrutinizing every unidentified flying object for a blue forehead, green crown, green neck, yellow breast, and luminous orange belly. Meanwhile we discovered other things of interest—banded stilts, red-capped dotterels, and red-necked avocets by the shore, and, in a patch of twisted eucalypts, a black-tailed native hen. One trail led to an enormous earthen mound. It had been made by a malleefowl, one of several Australian birds that build enormous compost heaps of sand, dirt, and decaying vegetation to incubate their eggs.

Of the Aborigines who once feasted on the fish and mollusks of the Coorong, there was no sign. Their absence cast a shadow over the place. Heavily armed foreigners and diseases had decimated their numbers, and the few that survived had drifted away. When we arrived, little remained to commemorate their passing save for a few crumbling piles of oyster shell.

Our interest in the Coorong faced stiff competition from the next place in our sights—Kangaroo Island, one of the premier wildlife-watching locations in Australia. There, with a little luck, we hoped to see western grey kangaroos, wild koalas, and the rare Cape Barren goose. We would visit colonies of Australian sea lions and New Zealand fur seals. The weather would determine our success with reptiles. If it was warm, we might rub noses with the Rosenberg's goanna, a kind of monitor lizard. Goanna, the Australian name for monitor, probably represents a corruption of "iguana."

We set off. A ferry carried us from Cape Jervis, on the Fleurieu Peninsula, to Penneshaw on Kangaroo Island. The boat, named the *Philanderer III,* didn't fool around. I was relieved. The waters between the island and the South Australian coast are notoriously turbulent, leading one to wonder what happened to *Philanderer I* and *Philanderer II.* We sliced into gray, roughneck waves, bound for a smudge on the horizon. Overhead, a great skua crossed the sky, suggesting a bird from Coleridge.

The churning waters and the island that rises beyond them were discovered almost simultaneously in 1802 by English and French explorers. Matthew Flinders, sailing for Britain in the *Investigator,* edged out the French explorer Nicholas Baudin, in *Le Géographe,* but only by a matter of days. Flinders described Kangaroo Island and gave it its name. Stepping ashore on sand untouched by human feet for 2,000 years, he wrote:

> A number of dark-brown kangaroos were seen feeding upon a grass plant by the side of the wood. . . . I had with me a double-barreled gun, fitted with a bayonet, and the gentlemen my companions had muskets. It would be difficult to guess how many kangaroos were seen, but I killed ten, and the rest of the party made up the number to thirty-one, . . . the least of them weighing sixty-nine, and the largest one-hundred and twenty-five pounds. . . . Half a hundredweight of heads, forequarters, and tails were stewed down into soup for dinner on this and succeeding days; and as much steaks given, more-over, to both officers and men, as they could consume by day and by night.

Flinders relished the culinary details, then concluded, "In gratitude for so seasonable a supply, I named this southern land KANGAROO ISLAND." After the voyage, Flinders proposed a name for the great red continent. It appeared on his charts as New Holland, but Flinders decided the place should be called "Australia."

Along the mainland coast, Matthew Flinders met Aborigines. "They seemed to have no idea of any superiority we possessed over them," he wrote in an analysis that sounds naïve today. "On the contrary, they left us, after the first interview, with some appearance of contempt for our pusil-lanimity." He adds, "This opinion, however, seemed to be corrected in their future visits."

On Kangaroo Island, no natives met the English. Archaeological evi-dence documents a human presence from about 12,000 years ago, when rising seas cut off the island from the mainland, until roughly 2,200 years ago. Then humans disappeared, their fate unknown. Perhaps they fled after depleting Kangaroo Island's game. Tim Flannery and others theorize that about five hundred men, women, and children lived on the island, then succumbed to interbreeding, natural disasters, or both. It was the Tasmanian story all over again, only more severe because of Kangaroo Island's smaller size.

From the moment our car rolled off the boat, we found the island a mixed bag. At first the scenery disappointed us. The interior consisted

mostly of dry, dusty paddocks, and there were tattered, gray-green eucalyptus groves whose positive points we were still learning to appreciate.
The coasts lay stark and dreary under gray skies. Least appealing were the
roads—smooth enough on the island's eastern, populated end, but rough,
corrugated, and hell to drive everywhere else.

The wildlife, fortunately, provided never-ending pleasure. The first
day, during a drive from Penneshaw to a campsite at American River, we
saw white-fronted chats congregating on wire fences. In an inlet, musk
ducks and chestnut teal hobnobbed with black swans. Geese ultimately
provoked me to swing the car off the road. The birds were plodding
around a corner of a sheep paddock, plucking up grass. Their bodies were
gray and had a pale, blanched look that contrasted with shiny black bills
and lime-green ceres. Aha! These were Cape Barren geese.

The Cape Barren goose looks like a goose, yet biologists say it is a
duck. It descends, apparently, from the ancestral lineage from which ducks
and geese diverged. At one time, farmers slaughtered Cape Barren geese
in great numbers. The birds preferred pasture to water and ingested great
volumes of forage that would otherwise have nourished livestock. Most
nettlesome of all, Cape Barren geese left behind excrement, and lots of it.
The stuff is foul. Sheep avoid it.

By 1955 the goose-ducks were nearly extinct. Protection followed,
and to the delight of authorities and the dismay of farmers, populations
rebounded. Today about 18,000 live in South Australia alone, with additional flocks in Western Australia, Victoria, Tasmania, and the Bass Strait
islands.

American River, our home for a night, took its name from Yankee
sealers who used the mouth of the stream for a base in the early nineteenth century. We found a campsite in a caravan park, but setting up the
tent had to wait. There were koalas to be found and birds to be seen. Only
an hour of daylight remained.

We strolled down the coast road, followed it past holiday houses
knocked together from odd pieces of lumber, and veered onto a dirt
track. To our left opened a paddock; within it, on the far side of a fence,
old farm machinery stood rusting. Each piece was marked with a crude,
hand-painted sign explaining its function. Within the cleared area rose a
one-story house, white, needing paint, and surrounded by trees, shrubs,
and vines that had once formed a garden. In a vegetable patch beside the
building, an old man in blue overalls stood, aiming a stream of water at a

plant. At his feet, dozens of plump gray pumpkins sprawled in a bed of leaves.

"G'day," we said, waving.

"G'day to you," replied the man, his voice crisp and dry.

Debbie asked about a camel that stood nearby. Saddled and heavily laden with expeditionary gear, it looked ready to carry an explorer from Alice Springs to Perth.

"Yes, the camel. I'll leave the load on overnight. Might help keep it warm. Grandchildren are coming tomorrow. They like to ride it." I felt sorry for the camel. It looked ready to collapse under the load.

The man introduced himself and, when he learned we were camping, offered us a pumpkin. We hopped over the fence and took the one he proffered, as big as a basketball. Harry asked what we did to make a living. Debbie told of her recent work as education coordinator at the Walter Anderson Museum of Art. Harry grunted. I said that I worked mainly as a writer, but sometimes did a turn as a park ranger. He grimaced. "Park rangers. More here all the time. Now we have to pay to see things we used to look at for nothing—sea lions, seals, the parks."

We made ready to move on. A peculiar expression came over Harry's face, elevating his eyebrows. "There was a couple here yesterday," he said. "Canadians." A pause. "When they left I got a kiss." Laughing, we waved good-bye.

In tangled, twisted eucalypts, we searched the branches for koalas. Once Debbie spied a dark and promising shape high on a slope. We thrashed our way up, only to find that a reasonable facsimile of a koala had been created by a swollen bend of trunk. The hunt continued until darkness forced us home.

In the morning we rose early, awakened by the screaming of galahs. A cold Antarctic wind had rattled the eucalypts all night, but with daybreak the gusts ebbed and sunshine fell on the coast. We walked eastward before breakfast. The waters along the island's north shore lay as placid as pudding. Knee-deep in the water, sacred ibises with long, sicklelike bills probed for snails and crabs. We saw Australian pelicans contorting themselves, preening in the morning light, and massive Pacific gulls whose black backs and white bellies matched the elegance of penguins. The gulls stood on rocks and pilings, waiting for the appearance of a fishing boat.

After breakfast we spied three hawklike birds, black and angular. They stroked the air with powerful wingbeats and landed near each other in the crown of a gum tree. Up went binoculars. We saw crests on the birds' heads, and brilliant bands of crimson curving across their tails. Good heavens! This was the glossy black cockatoo, an endangered species of parrot.

The cockatoos flapped off, perhaps seeking a drooping she-oak, the species of casuarina tree that on Kangaroo Island provides their sole source of nourishment. Sadly, drooping she-oaks are scarce. The clearing of land for farming, grazing, and forestry has eliminated all but a few. Ironically, it was a miracle that made the situation so grim. In the 1930s, scientists discovered that Kangaroo Island's soils, notoriously unproductive until that time, lacked copper, cobalt, and selenium. With the addition of these minerals, the farming boomed. Oats and barley grew briskly where they had withered before, and sheep flourished on pastures long unproductive. The good news meant hard times for the drooping she-oak and the glossy black cockatoo.

Efforts to conserve and expand Kangaroo Island's she-oak groves are under way. By a slender lifeline, meanwhile, the cockatoos survive to dazzle bird lovers with handsome plumage and acrobatic flying.

From American Bay we moved west to Kingscote, the island's busiest town. Along the bustling main street we purchased one newspaper, two bananas, a telephone calling card, a tank of petrol, and admission passes to the island's national parks. The newsagent's shop was memorable. It sold virtually every magazine published in the English language, including the grandest assemblage of pornography south of Times Square.

Continuing westward, we put the civilized part of the island behind us. At a blink-and-you-miss-it place called Cygnet River, we turned up a side road. A sign at the intersection said KOALAS.

The dirt track, barely wider than our car, led between tall, gray eucalypts. Ahead we found a half-dozen cars and a van parked along the shoulder. Fifteen or twenty tourists stood beside a tanned, mustachioed guide dressed in khaki. "Koalas," someone whispered to us, pointing to a tree. A pair of amorphous shapes moved in the canopy. With binoculars we transformed them into animals every child in the world could identify. One koala slept. The other advanced from branch to branch, its movements slow and deliberate. It shinnied up a limb, reached out a paw, and hauled in a salad of eucalyptus leaves. I could see why koalas are sometimes mistakenly called "bears." They were as rotund as well-fed grizzlies, although in miniature, and their broad faces, short ears, and forward-aiming eyes were bearlike, too. Biologists groan when people call the koala a bear, but they're not being fair. Their own name for the animal, *Phascolarctos,* sounds very technical but simply means "bear with a pouch."

Eucalyptus leaves provide nearly all that a koala needs for sustenance, even though the foliage contains toxins. An Aboriginal word, *koala* is said to mean "no drink." Koalas get by on food alone, taking in what little moisture they require from the leaves they chew and swallow. On Kangaroo Island, where surface water is scarce, not needing to drink is a blessing.

Koalas arrived on Kangaroo Island in the twentieth century, carried there by humans. In recent years they have outgrown their food supply, a fact that is readily apparent. Bare gum trees were easy to find, and the ones that had koalas in them were losing foliage fast.

Delighted by our first glimpse of the marsupial teddy bear, we cruised on. Where to go? We had no firm idea. Odysseus aimed to arrive home via the most direct route. We hoped for the opposite.

Following a series of whims, we continued south and west to Kangaroo Island's southern shore. The sun was down by the time we arrived at Vivonne Bay, the night moonless and black.

In a primitive campground consisting of a lawn a few feet above sea level, separated from the ocean by dune, we nosed our car among a dozen others and switched off the lights. The other campers had gone to bed. I couldn't see my hands. To complicate things, our only working light was a pocket-sized flashlight with tired batteries. Bravely, Debbie suggested a reversal of our usual roles. She'd erect the tent while I prepared dinner. "How about a cup of tea?" I asked jauntily. Debbie's tone told me her morale was sagging.

I marched to the cooking shelter—a roof propped up on stilts with a few picnic tables beneath, bordered by men's and women's bathrooms. I lit a candle lantern after six tries, and in the "Gents" I found a water tap. Wind blew in icy gusts.

Water in hand, I surprised myself by lighting the stove on the first try. Soon two cups of tea were steaming on the table. When mine had cooled, I raised it and drew a mouthful. Shit! I spat out the stuff. It was vile. Puzzled, I tried again. Revolting! I marched angrily to the men's room and tasted the water. The stuff had come straight from the sea.

Dinner offered a slight improvement in the trend. On our budget, an evening meal usually consisted of a package of flavored noodles. If we were ravenous, tuna or salmon was forked in from a can, producing a

casserole that stuck to one's ribs like concrete. Tonight's special was salmon
and curry-flavored noodles. Debbie attacked her portion with enthusiasm. My mouth, insulted by briny tea, couldn't abide the stuff. Oh, hell. I
pried the top off a warm beer and drank it for dessert.

Morning opened our most eventful day on the island. Before breakfast
we wandered to the shore. Immediately we found an uncommon shore-
bird, the hooded dotterel. It was an elegant creature. A black cap contrasted handsomely with a white nape, and red outlined the eyes and
framed the base of the bill. As calm as a sitting Buddha, the bird stood on
a patch of sand, the sea raging behind it.

From Vivonne Bay we backtracked a few miles to Seal Bay. The lure
here was a colony of Australian sea lions. When Flinders and Baudin had
poked around the island's coast, sea lions thrived in great colonies from
the Bass Strait to the coast of Western Australia. Then came the sealers.
From Europe, the U.S.A., and elsewhere they descended, hacking and
skinning and coloring the ocean red. Sea lions all but vanished. Today
about 10,000 exist, ten percent of them inhabiting Seal Bay.

The Australian sea lion is closely related to the walrus and the fur seals.
The so-called "true seals" are distant kin. It is a massive animal. Males
reach weights of six hundred pounds and more. Like other seals, the sea
lion has a peculiar habit of swallowing stones called gastroliths, some as
large as oranges. Why sea lions eat rocks is unknown. Five theories compete for favor: that the stones serve as ballast, helping the animal adjust its
buoyancy; that they fill the sea lion's belly when it isn't eating; that they
help mash food, serving like the grit turkeys and chickens swallow to pul-
verize seeds in their gizzards; that they destroy parasitic worms that would
otherwise plague the animal's digestive tract; and that they serve as emet-
ics, enabling the sea lion to cough up indigestible crayfish shells, squid
beaks, and fish bones.

On a boardwalk leading to the colony, we met an ill-tempered park
ranger. He greeted us by threatening to ban us from the beach if we
stepped anywhere near a sea lion. The animals were extremely dangerous,
he said. A minute later he led us so close to a mother and pup that the
young animal had no trouble wriggling over the sand to drop its chin on
my foot. I blanched, but to my relief the mother paid no attention.

For an hour we wandered the beach. Our guide, tourist weary and
cynical at the start, warmed to his work. Soon a smile was forming
beneath his salty beard. About three dozen sea lions occupied the sand,

some snoozing belly-up at the base of dunes, others nursing at their mothers' breasts. A few played tag. Two of the animals had jagged scars on their flanks. "These are great white waters," said the ranger. "I wouldn't recommend a swim. Sharks feed on these sea lions. They'll bite you, too, if you give them the chance."

There was little risk of our swimming. Winter was coming. You could feel it in the cold, damp air and in the drops of ocean spray that stung our faces like hornets.

One thing about the colony struck me as odd—the smell. There wasn't any. I asked the ranger if something was wrong with my nose. Fur-seal colonies I had visited in New Zealand reeked like canneries. "These animals are very clean," he said. "They do their excreting in the sea."

From Seal Bay we drove westward to the Kelly Hill Caves. The place sounded like a busy tourist stop we could easily skip, yet the passes we had stretched our budget to pay for included admission, and we aimed to get our money's worth. I emerged from the car desperate to see something, anything, alive. Along the thirty miles of screw-loosening road that lay between Seal Bay and the caves, we had counted seventy-two dead mammals (in varying states of decomposition), one moribund bird (a New Holland honeyeater, flattened in its prime), and two expired, sun-dried Rosenberg's goannas. Each of the lizards was about three feet long.

The carnage saddened us. Each corpse sprawled within view of the next, and hidden by tall grass along the shoulder there must have been dozens more. Nearly all the mammals were kangaroos. It seemed a pity that we had to roll past a hundred dead ones before the first live western grey thumped into view.

Walking into the bush, we promptly came across something to cheer us. It was an echidna, picking its way over a fallen tree. The animal, about the size of a cantaloupe half, waddled awkwardly and soon reached a branch that blocked its progress. *No worries.* The echidna started to detour down the side of the trunk. Gravity got the better of it, however, and it fell to the ground, head over heels. Not missing a step, the echidna righted itself and marched away.

"In an excursion today, Lieutenant Guthrie killed an animal of very odd form. It has no mouth like any other animal but a kind of duck bill which opens at the extremity, where it will not admit the size of a small pistal [*sic*]. Quills or prickles are all over its back." This description represents the debut of the echidna in the English language. The author was William Bligh.

Echidna was a Greek goddess, a scaly Pan, half woman and half snake. The animal's scientific name is *Tachyglossus aculeatus.* The first part, the genus, refers to the echidna's swift and nimble tongue; the species name refers to its formidable coat of spines.

Typical of its species, the echidna shuffled along the ground, rocking and weaving like a drunk. Every few paces it stopped to probe the ground with its snout. The nose-and-mouthpiece of the animal is both rugged and sensitive, able to root in hard soil and slip under heavy logs, but also supremely sensitive to touch, movement, odors, and electrical impulses. According to the biologists Michael Augee and Brett Gooden, a captive echidna once used its beak to nudge a refrigerator across a kitchen floor. This represents a considerable accomplishment for a mammal that weighs fifteen pounds at most.

We enjoyed watching the echidna pursue ants and termites. It showed no interest in our presence but simply went about its business, probing under logs, delving into hollows. How much it ate, or what it caught with its six-inch tongue, we couldn't say. When we finally left it, the monotreme had righted itself after a second tumble and was plodding over the hill.

Our next stop, reached by clattering for miles over corrugated high-way, was Flinders Chase National Park. The land in the island's southwest corner looked parched, defeated, and lifeless. It reflected the "curious sombreness of Australia" that D. H. Lawrence described in *Kangaroo,* a "sense of oldness, with forms all worn down low and blunt, squat." The island was certainly squat. There were no snow-capped peaks and lush green valleys of the sort one takes for granted in New Zealand, but just smooth or rolling country, much of it looking badly in need of compost and watering. Short on leaves, with the bark of many species peeling like sunburn, the eucalyptus trees appeared half dead. Yet proof that the place was anything but lifeless lay strewn along the shoulder—dead kangaroos, possums, and goannas. We saw no live animals because most were noctur-nal, and the weather was too cool for lizards.

A welcoming committee of one emu and a half-dozen tame kangaroos watched from the shoulder as we rattled into the campground. Our win-dows were down, and the emu, spying a cracker I was nibbling, stuck its head in the car and tried to snatch the prize from my fingers. I pushed the bird away, feeling its hot neck and the stiff bristles that passed for feathers. The bird was affronted. It coughed out a low, rumbling sound and with red-brown eyes glared at me as if I'd said something insulting.

When we stepped out, three kangaroos crowded in, eager to succeed where the emu had failed. They sniffed the air, wiggled their noses, and made begging gestures with their forepaws. They were western greys, darker than the eastern greys we had seen in the Grampians. Their short, dense fur was colored a minklike brown.

The biology of the western grey kangaroo is much like that of its eastern cousin, with two major areas of divergence. The western grey's reproduction moves along at a faster pace, resulting in an estrous cycle, gestation, and pouch occupancy all shorter than that of the eastern grey. The other significant difference regards tolerance of fluoroacetate, a poison widely used in predator control. Fluoroacetate kills eastern greys, but western greys are immune. The difference suggests that western greys evolved in Australia's Southwest, where fluoroacetate (known commercially as Compound 1080) occurs naturally in shrubs. Eastern greys, evolving in the east, developed no such resistance.

As the kangaroos studied our movements, Debbie and I pitched the tent. A park ranger had warned us not to leave food inside. The reason became clear. A pup tent stood in the site next to ours. Beside the mesh door, a kangaroo sat on its haunches, nuzzling and pawing the zipper. I looked away. When I glanced back a moment later, a kangaroo tail trailed from the tent door. Then a hairy face appeared, a bag of bread dangling from its teeth.

I ran toward the kangaroo, clapping my hands. It dropped the prize, hopped thirty feet away, and turned toward me, looking crestfallen. The plastic bag had several bites in it, and so did the bread.

The man who owned the tent returned and took the news in good humor. Soon he was sitting on the ground, heating soup on a backpacking stove. Around him five kangaroos gathered, rocking on their haunches, leaning attentively toward the flame. It looked like a cooking class.

Although the scent of food started our stomachs growling, we decided to invest the last hour of sunshine in reconnoitering the area. The days were growing short. Clutching handfuls of nuts and raisins to mollify our appetites, we set off up the track.

Highwaymen descended before we covered twenty feet. An emu as tall as I was poked its beaky face near mine, rasping its hot skin against my arm as it tried to steal the food. I could hear its breathing. There were kangaroos, too, jostling each other for the privilege of first assault. The winner thrust his dark face and harelip under my right arm, caught a look at a peanut, and reached out to grab my hand with its forepaws. On the other side, another kangaroo tugged at my left arm. It felt like a mugging. I pushed and ran. When I glanced back, Debbie was running, too, the emu sprinting in pursuit.

After shedding the pursuers, we slipped into a grove of sugar gums. The branches were very nearly denuded by koalas. We kept going. The path led to a putting green of a meadow on which dozens of western grey kangaroos and Cape Barren geese hopped, waddled, and grazed. The color of the close-cropped grass was wonderfully vivid, yet any chance of beauty was ruined. Bird and mammal droppings littered the ground by the millions.

That evening, and the one immediately following, we used a picnic pavilion for a kitchen and office. The place had a roof overhead but was open on the sides, which meant that we had to bundle up against the night air. There were benefits to the arrangement. We could hear the night sounds of the surrounding meadows and forests, and we could get looks at any animal that passed through the glow of the pavilion's electric lights.

Squeals, grunts, and growls came to us from time to time, but no animal appeared. Then, as we downed the last of our rice and beans, a brush-tailed possum padded up to our table. It leaped on the bench beside me and reached for a loaf of bread. I pushed it away, but the possum came back as soon as it regained its balance. Again I shoved it, gently but firmly enough to deliver a clear message. This time the animal got the idea and moved on to a gas barbecue recently vacated by a German couple. The surface was covered with fresh grease. The possum lapped up every bit, and when it was done it cleaned the turner, too. When that was done, the animal squatted over the grill and produced a large, gleaming shit. Aghast, we vowed to avoid campground barbecues.

The real entertainment of the evening began a half hour later. A koala, looking like a demented old man walking on all fours, ambled into view. It sniffed the base of a eucalyptus tree whose limbs arched over the pavilion. Then, with the arms-first, bottom-second movements of a telephone lineman, it swiftly scaled the bole.

Soon a second, smaller koala walked onto the stage. Like the first, it had a bulging Roman nose and a dark smear across its chest, meaning it was a male. Reaching up with clawed forepaws, koala number two grasped the tree as if intending to climb.

Now the silence of the night gave way to one of the most hideous sounds in nature. High in the branches, the first koala hissed and bellowed. The volume was shocking. Every shriek and roar sounded as if it might be the animal's last.

Stepping out of the shelter, we aimed a light into the tree's crown to assure ourselves that these were koala sounds, not the cries of a *bunyip,* a monster of Aboriginal lore that emerges at night and devours people. Red eyes burned like coals. We watched as the koala, ears back and head up, looking thoroughly pissed off, screamed again and again.

Meanwhile, the second koala ignored the fuss and hauled itself up with its forearms. As it lifted its bottom, the claws lost purchase on the scaly bark. The animal dropped to the ground with a thump. It landed on its derriere, and for a minute it sat there, seeming to gather its thoughts. Gruesome noises showered down from above.

Collecting thoughts does not come easily to a koala. Its brain is small, occupying less than half the volume available inside the skull, forty percent smaller than the brains of other marsupials its size. Kangaroos and kin, as previously noted, are not famed for the abundance of their gray matter, and among marsupials, koalas are relatively brainless. Complicating matters, the hemispheres of the koala's brain are separated from each other. Perhaps that's why koalas always look baffled. About everything they are literally of two minds.

Eventually the thinker tried again. The operatic performance in the balcony, which had ceased, now resumed with greater fervor. Whether the tumble rattled it, or the attempt at intimidation had its desired effect, I cannot say. But the koala's second climb seemed halfhearted. A fall came quickly, and this time the animal turned and ambled away.

Thirty feet from the tree, the koala paused, looked thoughtful, and turned back toward the place of its defeat. The aerial onslaught now reached a crescendo. The koala on the ground moved closer and closer. Then it surprised us. It passed the tree without a second glance and plodded into the shadows. We heard it scratching up another, smaller tree, and silence reigned once more.

What we had witnessed was a territorial interaction between rival males. Koalas of both genders lead solitary lives, keeping within home ranges of two to six acres, feeding inside the perimeter. Interactions occur along borders. Conflicts are frequent, more so between males than between females. Occasionally they turn aggressive. Males biting other males leave serious wounds. To avoid trouble and conserve energy, a koala sniffs the base of every tree it climbs. If the coast is clear, it trickles urine at the bottom of the bole. If the animal is a male, it rubs its chest against the bark, too, depositing pheromones from a sternal gland. The next koala that plods along knows the tree is occupied. Unless food is extremely scarce, as it is on Kangaroo Island, koalas avoid conflict by feeding and resting in unoccupied trees.

The breeding of koalas follows a pattern like that of wolves. Battling among themselves, males establish a dominance hierarchy, at the peak of which sits a top "dog," or alpha male. This animal enjoys the favors of females while rivals watch jealously from the sidelines. Occasionally a nondominant male scales a tree with a female in it. When this happens, he may force her against a branch, bite the back of her neck, and, as she howls in protest, rape her. If the alpha male lies within earshot, he races to the scene and drives off the miscreant. Koala pregnancies, however, rarely occur from rapes.

Typical matings proceed with dignity. An alpha male approaches a female slowly and calmly, makes his intentions known with a few well-placed sniffs, and mounts. For a minute or two he thrusts his pelvis, inserting a penis attached not forward of, but behind, his scrotum. When the pair separates, the male often roars loudly. If fertilization occurs, after about thirty days a baby koala crawls out of one of the female's dual vaginas. It wriggles through belly fur, enters a backward-facing pouch, and clamps on one of two teats in a place that is always warm and cozy. Meanwhile the mother goes about her business of sleeping, climbing, and eating. By six months of age, the young animal is fully furred and feeding on its mother's partially digested feces. It stays with her about a year, spending more and more time outside the pouch. One day the youngster wanders off, perhaps never to see its mother again.

Our final notable encounter with Kangaroo Island wildlife occurred two days later. A brain-jellying ride on corrugated roads brought us to a parking area at the end of a rough track. A walking trail led off into a grove of eucalypts. According to a map, it would bring us through the Ravine des Casoars, named by French explorers for the extinct Kangaroo Island emu. (To the French, the emu looked like a *casoar,* or cassowary.) The ravine emptied onto a beach. There we would enjoy our last look at the Southern Ocean before setting off for the Center.

We were just beginning to descend when a fellow *Homo sapiens* puffed up to us, glistening with sweat. She was a woman of forty, flushed from reclaiming the altitude we were about to surrender. "How did you enjoy the hike?" I asked.

The woman sucked a breath, then spoke. "I didn't have a torch," she said, which was hardly an answer. "But I walked a little way into one of the caves and saw a few fairies." Report delivered, the woman turned and charged up the hill.

Caves? She must have been referring to sea caves. We had read that the trail ended at a place on the coast where waves had battered hollows in the limestone cliffs. Fairies? Being birdwatchers, we guessed her meaning, although I chuckled to think what anyone else would have thought.

On we marched, through a eucalypt forest untouched by axes and saws, into a valley of shadows. Several times we stopped to investigate activity in the trees. In one place tiny, drab birds called striated thornbills skulked among the leaves of gums and wattles. In another we looked up to investigate movement and found purple-gaped honeyeaters snatching insects from the air. A deep, brooding silence reigned. There were no roads nearby, and the sky, as is typical in wild Australia, was deliciously empty of airplanes.

The path led westward and steadily downhill for two or three miles, then disgorged us on a flat. A narrow creek dribbled over the sand, flowing seaward. We followed the water, leaving oversized footprints, until we came around a bulge of rock and heard the crash of waves, and saw the ocean. Stirred by a gusty wind, curls of blue-gray water tumbled onto the beach.

Had it been warmer, and had these waters not been full of great white sharks, we might have leaped in for a swim. As it was, we looked elsewhere for entertainment.

Cave mouths gaped to the left and right. We decided to explore the one on the right. The entrance was high and wide enough to pass through standing up. Footprints in the sand showed that others had gone before us, and the fact that some led out as well as in suggested an absence of Homeric monsters.

Debbie and I had barely stepped over the threshold when a weird voice echoed out of the depths. It began as a cry, segued to a falsetto wail, and culminated as a groan of utter and hopeless misery. Zeus protect us! Debbie switched on a light. We could see only wet, dripping rock and impenetrable blackness. The voice started again and this time was joined by others.

For a moment my blood ran cold. Yet I felt certain of the source of the chorus and waved Debbie onward. "Ladies first," I said. We advanced. One tortured soul wailed more loudly than the others, and we crept in its direction. Soon the light struck a pair of yellow eyes.

Before us, wobbling on pink feet, stood a penguin. It was the species ornithologists call the "little penguin," New Zealanders know as the "little blue," and Australians fondly dub the "fairy."

This particular fairy stood about a foot high, or perhaps a few inches taller. It had no tail worth mentioning, sorry excuses for wings, and a short, dark bill perfect for grabbing fish. Conforming to the penguin dress code, the back was dark, the chest and belly white. The elegant appearance of the bird contrasted sharply with its foul, fishy smell. For a minute or more we lingered, keeping our distance. Eventually, as if embarrassed to have been caught in its Great and Powerful Oz act, the penguin wiggled away.

On the way out of the cave, we saw two more fairies. They stood silently, trembling like frightened Greeks. Suddenly it dawned on us. In this *Odyssey* parallel, we were the monsters.

By the following evening we had caught a ferry to the mainland and driven up the Fleurieu Peninsula to Adelaide. We entered the city, the capital of South Australia, at rush hour. Japanese cars driven by freckle-faced Australians poured onto the highway in torrents. In the middle of the maelstrom, I could have imagined myself on the Bronx River Parkway, fighting my way into New York at daybreak.

Even at five o'clock on a weekday, Adelaide remained the "fine town" John Muir admired in 1903. A few things had changed, of course. The botanic garden in which Muir admired a giant "Aboriginal" eucalyptus tree now included an Elvis memorial. The buildings were as grand as ever, handsome, magisterial, the boulevards running between them shaded by giant trees. Every green space was lovingly tended. We picked our way through the downtown. As darkness fell, we slipped onto a narrow road that plunged into forest. It wound through gorges, climbing higher and higher, until it brought us to Cherryville, a hamlet in the Adelaide Hills.

A woman named Wendy Willow had offered to put us up for a couple of nights. Finding her house proved a challenge. We drove a dark, steep, winding road until our headlights found a sign saying FIRE LANE. The lane was more a goat track than a road. It was navigable with care and led us down a steep hill to a brightly lit house. Inside stood two women, talking beside the cooking range. Neither one was Wendy, they said, but if we continued down the track, we would find her. A second house, surrounded by trees and vines, appeared. A light outside the door shone brightly. "Ed and Debbie?" asked the woman at the door. There are few pleasures to equal being greeted warmly on a dark evening in a strange, faraway place.

A fiftyish woman with short brown hair, our host announced that we must be starving (which was true) and produced bowls of steaming chestnut soup. By bedtime, which came soon afterward, we learned that Wendy was a social worker by profession and a granddaughter of Sir Hans Heysen (1877–1968), a distinguished Australian artist best known for his landscape paintings and pencil drawings. Wendy wanted to know about our wildlife watching. "Yes," she said, on hearing of our plan to drive north from Adelaide, into the Center. "You'll want to go by way of the Flinders Ranges," referring to mountains north of Adelaide. "Grandfather painted there. You can see some of his work tomorrow in the art museum in the city." When I told Wendy we intended to visit Ayers Rock and the Olgas, she frowned. "You really must learn the proper Aboriginal names," she said. "Ayers Rock is *Uluru*." Wendy placed equal emphasis on the three syllables. "And the Olgas [a famous cluster of rocks near Uluru] are known as *Kata Tjuta*."

When morning came, we awoke in paradise. Wendy had given us the run of a rammed-earth studio built across the lane from her house. Two of its four walls were made of glass, so sunshine flooded in, waking us gently. Around the place spread a bucolic scene that could have passed for rural England. Pastures defined by wire fences plunged steeply into a valley, and on the far side, dark pines crowded against each other and rose to the crest of a ridge. Naked, I stepped out a back door, feeling a delicious coolness as bare soles met wet grass. A ewe brayed in the distance, calling to lambs. I felt like Adam in Eden.

After breakfast, Wendy bustled off to work. We intended to venture into the city shortly afterward, but we had not reckoned on the allure of the valley. After a week amid the broken rock and parched forests of Kangaroo Island, Wendy's farm seemed splendidly lush. We lingered.

As the sun climbed, the trees filled with motion. We had gotten pretty sharp at identifying common birds, so it was relatively easy for us to pick out the pardalotes from the thornbills, the brown-headed honeyeaters from the white-naped, and the Adelaide rosellas from other parrots. Yet something new caught our eye. It was tiny enough to fit in the palm of a hand, and the colors stopped us in our tracks— black on the head and back, bright red on the throat and breast, white on the belly with streaks of black and gray, and pink under the tail. Something about the bird was odd. Every time it landed, it twitched and turned as if agitated.

The restlessness gave away the bird's identity. It was a mistletoe bird, a male. The species has a peculiar life history. Mistletoe birds eat bugs and berries. The insects find their way into the stomach, a virtual cul-de-sac, where acids and enzymes digest them. Berries, on the other hand, especially those of the parasitic mistletoe, speed down the gastrointestinal tract unscathed. Of course, what goes in must come out. Sticky, berry-filled droppings emerge from the cloaca, and the bird, by twitching and shifting, glues them onto bark. When the seeds germinate, threadlike roots penetrate the tree's cambium. Before long a mistletoe plant thrives on the spot. In time it produces berries, which attract birds. Studies show that Australian mistletoes rely heavily on the mistletoe bird to disseminate their seed.

In Adelaide we drove wide, tree-lined boulevards, eventually finding a parking place among a throng of cars. The day was sunny and cool. It was lunch hour, and handsome men and women in business clothes crowded the sidewalks. People were talking, smiling, and laughing. *Joie de vivre* filled the air.

Anthony Trollope, a career employee of England's postal service, came to Adelaide and described it as a "pleasant, prosperous town" with a particularly handsome post office. A few years later Mark Twain found Adelaide "a modern city, with wide streets, compactly built; with fine homes everywhere, embowered in foliage and flowers, and with imposing masses of public buildings nobly grouped and architecturally beautiful." Laurence Olivier, touring Australia in 1948 with his wife, the actress Vivien Leigh, came to Adelaide to perform in the play *The Skin of Our Teeth*. The highlight of his stop was a look at kangaroos. "Vivien had seen kangaroos in Perth," Olivier recalled, "but these were my first and I was ravished."

Into one of Adelaide's grand buildings—the South Australian Museum, hard by the Art Gallery of South Australia—we marched. Cut from the same cloth as London's British Museum and New York's American Museum of Natural History, the South Australian Museum combined Victorian order with plummy Edwardian elegance. It served up South Australia's natural history and Aboriginal lore as cleanly as a funeral director lays out an accident victim. Not that we were complaining. The place felt comfortable and familiar. Without the distractions of video monitors, computer screens, digital sound effects, and the toothy robotic dinosaurs one often finds in museums these days, we quietly followed our interests.

Mine led straight to a hall of bones. Here was assembled one of the great collections of Australian megafauna—extinct, oversized cousins of today's kangaroos, wombats, possums, and devils. Unlike dinosaurs, which vanished from the earth tens of millions of years before humans evolved, the monsters that owned these skeletons coexisted in Australia with the ancestors of modern Aborigines.

The first skeleton to seize my attention was a *Diprotodon*. It was enormous! I stand nearly six feet tall, and this animal's shoulders stood even with the crown of my head. From stem to stern it measured almost ten feet, longer than a prize bull. Massive leg bones once supported great weight. Interestingly, the rear legs exceeded the length of those in front. *Diprotodon* must have walked perpetually downhill—perhaps a godsend in the flat monotony of Australia's interior. The skeleton's neck arched to support a massive skull. Out of sockets as wide and deep as coffee mugs, eyes had gazed out on the prairies where *Diprotodon* found its tucker.

The front teeth of the monster were paired like the front choppers of a wombat. This feature led Richard Owen, the nineteenth-century English anatomist best known for coining the term *dinosaur,* to label the rhinoceroslike grazer *Diprotodon,* meaning "two-toothed." Owen had seen only a jawbone.

While Richard Owen had no way of knowing it, the animal he named was a marsupial, a cousin of the wombat. It carried its young in a pouch and gorged on flowers. According to paleontologists, the species *Diprotodon optatum* was the biggest marsupial ever to walk the earth.

Diprotodon skeletons abound. Just as mammoth and mastodon remains turn up in great concentrations in the northern hemisphere, *Diprotodon* boneyards surface from time to time. By way of example, a team from the South Australian Museum excavated a salt pan at Lake Callabonna and sorted out the remains of 360 of the extinct grazers. The site also included giant emus and giant kangaroos, both considerably taller and more robust than surviving species. Analysis revealed that the bones were about 80,000 years old. When the animals lived, the place where they were found was wet and lush.

Another, more recent trove of megafauna was excavated in a place called Lancefield Swamp, in Victoria. The site was discovered and probed superficially in 1843, forgotten for more than a century, then rediscovered and investigated in the 1970s and 1980s. Bones belonging to thousands of animals were identified. The majority belonged to *Macropus titan,* a giant kangaroo. There were *Diprotodons,* too, a giant bird called *Genyornis,* and a monstrous wallaby known as *Protemnodon.*

The museum's bone gallery gave a crash course in Australian paleontology. Snooping from rib cage to rib cage, we learned about *Phascolonus,* a larger-than-life Pleistocene wombat, *Palorchestes,* a dairy-cow sized marsupial that resembled a sloth, *Zygomaturus trilobus,* a beast often called the "marsupial rhinoceros," and *Procoptodon,* an oversized kangaroo that stood eight or nine feet tall, weighed four hundred pounds, and had a face like a bulldog.

With great numbers of plump, plodding plant-eaters roaming the country, opportunities for predators were bountiful. Australia had no lions, tigers, jaguars, pumas, or wolves. Instead it had its own unique flesh-eaters—among them the thylacine and the Tasmanian devil, both of which roamed the length and breadth of the continent before the dingo arrived, and there was the so-called marsupial lion, too, a creature known to scientists as *Thylacoleo.*

During the Miocene and Pleistocene (in other words, until recently and for a very long time), *Thylacoleo* prowled far and wide in Australia, searching for sustenance. The nature of its diet has been debated. The animal had powerful jaws, prodigious fangs, third premolars and first molars shaped like steak knives, and eyes that faced forward. Despite these features, which are typical of predators, some experts considered *Thylacoleo* a herbivore until well-preserved skulls were unearthed. Examination of their teeth revealed wear patterns typical of carnivores. What sort of flesh did the marsupial lion fancy? No one knows. The best guess is that it favored *Diprotodons,* wombats, and kangaroos. *Thylacoleo* had opposable thumbs, like those of arboreal possums and gliders, and may have captured its victims by leaping on them from trees.

Having feasted our eyes but ignored our stomachs, we ventured outside for apples and granola bars. Thus fortified, we walked next door to the Art Gallery of South Australia.

Doing justice to the painting and sculpture gathered within the grand old edifice would have required several days. As it happened, this was a glorious afternoon and our second museum, so we hurried. Bustling through hall after hall, we saw an impressive cross-section of nineteenth-

and twentieth-century Australian art. Most interesting to us were several works by Hans Heysen. His landscapes would have merited attention under any circumstances, but because several portrayed the Flinders Ranges, our next stop, we gave them a careful look.

My favorite Heysen was titled *Red Gold*. It depicted a rural scene, painted boldly on a canvas the size of a billboard. Red-and-white cattle ambled down a country lane, and giant eucalypts cast dappled shade. We recognized the bulging trunks as those of river red gums, *Eucalyptus camaldulensis,* a quintessentially Australian tree that thrives across much of the continent. Keith MacLeod had explained the origin of the river red gum's species name. In 1829 and 1830, Frederic Dehnhardt, a botanist in the employ of the Count of Camalduli, published a list of the plants growing in his boss's garden near Naples. Three eucalypts were included, one of which was the river red gum. The species had been known as *E. rostrata,* but when a subsequent revision of the genus called for a new name, *camaldulensis* was coined.

Robert Hughes, art critic for *Time* magazine and author of a history of Australian art, dismisses Heysen as a tradition-bound technician not worthy of remembrance. Sweeping and harsh, Hughes's judgments flash down like thunderbolts. Yet the critic protests too much, methinks. I think I see the source of the rub. We esteem most in others what we admire in ourselves, and Hughes, a self-styled iconoclast, saves his praise for painters who cast away the old. Heysen respects tradition and uses it as a starting point, and Hughes cannot forgive him for it.

Heysen, like many painters, steeped himself in the classics. After achieving local fame in his teens, he spent four years in Europe under the sponsorship of several Adelaide businessmen. During that period he roamed through England, Scotland, Germany, the Netherlands, Switzerland, France, and Italy, sketching, painting, learning. Upon returning to Australia, he found inspiration in the dry, stark landscapes of the Flinders Ranges. His career flourished. Heysen's paintings and drawings found homes in major public and private collections, and the artist and his family enjoyed a bucolic life on an estate near Adelaide. In 1959, Heysen was knighted by Queen Elizabeth. He died in 1968.

Standing before *Red Gold*, I agreed with Hughes that Heysen offered little that was arresting in subject matter and composition. The subject matter—beasts of burden—was pedestrian. Yet there was quiet power in the painting, a strength rising from its mastery and vitality of detail. Every object in this and the other Heysen canvases we saw appeared robust and noble—farm animals, people, gum trees. In another place, the effect might have seemed cloying. But in Australia, plants, animals, and people overcome staggering odds to endure in harsh environments, and the ordinary wears the mantle of the heroic.

Regarding emotion, which Hughes finds wanting in Heysen, I can see the trouble. Heysen's human figures appear detached. Yet how this man loved trees and sunshine! His passion for river red gums borders on the sexual. Inflamed by the grand specimens he found in the Flinders Ranges, the artist endows the trunks, limbs, and foliage with sensual energy. Such trees! They rise heroically from desiccated, eroded landscapes that defy life to endure. The red gums in particular appear strong, elephantine, and at times anthropomorphic. An Elysian glow illuminates gnarly limbs and ponderous, twisted boles.

Leaving the gallery, we could hardly wait to see the ranges for ourselves. We returned to Wendy's. This time, in bright sunshine, we relished the journey, following a narrow road that turned away from the city and threaded its way among green hills. Mark Twain covered the same ground nearly a century earlier and admired it without irony. "The road wound around through gaps and gorges," he wrote, "and offered all varieties of scenery and prospect—mountains, crags, country houses, gardens, forests—colour, colour, colour everywhere, and the air fine and fresh, the skies blue, and not a shred of cloud to mar the downpour of brilliant sunshine." Glory for glory, the splendor of our drive matched Twain's.

On a warm Wednesday morning we bade good-bye to Wendy, promised to visit again after we had circled the continent, and set out for the Flinders. The drive occupied two leisurely days. From Adelaide we followed Highway 1, the road that nearly circles Australia in a great crescent stretching west, south, east, and north, from Darwin in the Northern Territory to Mossman in Queensland. Our route paralleled the eastern shore of Gulf St. Vincent, then turned due north across the base of the Yorke Peninsula. At Port Pirie, an industrial hub at the head of the Spencer Gulf, we passed a night in a caravan park. There were few trees and even fewer people. The place felt deserted.

The following morning we came to Mount Remarkable National Park, a quick detour off our route. Our chief interest in the place was the rare and nearly extinct yellow-footed rock wallaby, a species considered by

many to be the most beautiful kangaroo in Australia. A remnant population survived in the park.

We took a hike, scanning rock faces for movement. We saw a good
deal, every bit of it human. People were everywhere—laughing, shouting, barbecuing. To get away from the commotion, we descended into
a ravine, followed the bottom between cliffs of red rock, and climbed
back to the car. Still, the landscape echoed with voices. The reason
for the bustle eventually dawned on us. It was April 25, Anzac Day, a
holiday Australians take more seriously than any other. It honors the
Australia–New Zealand Army Corps of World War I (ANZAC), particularly those who on a day in 1915 came ashore at Gallipoli, Turkey, and
were slaughtered by the hundreds. For Australia the event led to an un-
written Declaration of Independence. It burned into the national psyche
the hard truth that blind obedience to England and its imperial aims ran
contrary to Australia's interests.

A few hours of walking yielded no wallabies, yellow-footed or otherwise. Disappointed, we rumbled out of the hills, turned north, and
continued toward the mountains.

After two hours of traversing dry grasslands, we stopped for a rest in
Hawker, a dusty cattle town. At a newsagent's shop we bought a newspaper, tea, and scones, and at a table on the sidewalk we sat, sipped, and
tossed crumbs to English sparrows. We could have been in Texas. Only
the rabbit-felt hats of the men and the Toyota trucks, not Chevrolets and
Fords, betrayed the geographical truth.

North of Hawker, mountains intruded on the horizon. The Flinders
Ranges are ancient, part of a chain pushed up 600 million years ago in
eastern Gondwana. Two fragments persist—the Transantarctic Mountains
of Antarctica and the Flinders. Having endured eons of rain, wind, and
the corrosive effects of plant acids, the ranges are worn to stubs like the
teeth of an old cow. St. Mary's Peak, highest of the Flinders, rises to a
mere 3,900 feet above sea level. Looming above flat country, however, the
mountains are more imposing than their elevations suggest.

We shot in from the east, skirting the base of red, knobby bluffs garnished here and there with clumps of green. In dry washes that cut down
slopes and burrowed under the road, massive red gums of the sort Heysen
painted testified to underground moisture. The trees impressed me
immensely. To see giant redwoods or Tasmanian eucalypts soaring into a
wet sky is one thing, but to find these stalwart monsters rising defiantly

out of a desert was another. The river red gum may well be the world's champion water-finder. Its roots exceed the mass of the rest of the tree, and in country too dry to support most other trees, a big red gum pumps a ton or more of water a day. Passing among the trees, we marveled at their ability to triumph over grim odds.

Our base for two nights was a caravan park. It was located at the mouth of Wilpena Pound, a deep mountain basin once home to a cattle and sheep ranch. As the road curved north, then veered west toward the Pound, it sliced like a game trail through tall grass. The last sunlight of the day gilded the blades, performing an alchemy that transformed everything but the sky into gold. We pulled over to the side of the road, climbed out, and took in the scene.

Suddenly we saw it. A towering, musclebound figure rose above the gold, looking like Arnold Schwarzenegger in a kangaroo suit. The head was square-jawed and the ears long and donkeylike, but black and white streaks on the muzzle made it handsome. The rest of the animal was brick-red, a striking change from the grays and browns of other kangaroos we had seen. Before us stood the largest of living marsupials, *Macropus rufus,* the red kangaroo.

In size, eastern grey and red kangaroos are rivals. Individual eastern greys may be heavier than certain reds, but on average the red kangaroo represents the biggest bounder of them all.

Scientists estimate that reds are the most abundant kangaroo in Australia, perhaps numbering as many as 10 million. Ironically, they are difficult to see alive. Draw a circle enclosing the driest parts of Australia, the places where rainfall never reaches twenty inches, and you have the red kangaroo's range. The big marsupial is to Australia's fauna what the river red gum is to its flora: a hardy survivor in places lethal to most forms of life.

Like other kangaroos, the red is a creature of the night. It sleeps by day under bushes or trees, emerging at dusk to feed on grasses and wild herbs. During the blistering heat of summer, the red kangaroo cools itself by panting and licking its forearms. Patches of skin on the arms are criss-crossed with capillaries, and as the saliva evaporates, the body cools. In extreme heat, red kangaroos lie low and subsist on amounts of food and water unthinkably small for animals that weigh up to 200 pounds. Part of the trick is recycling mechanical energy from each bound, and using some of it to pump air in and out of the lungs. The red kangaroo can even eat saltbush and drink brackish water if it needs to, purging the deadly excess salt by excreting urine of high sodium and low moisture content.

Lush green grass surrounded the big kangaroo. Times were good in the Flinders, which probably explained why the animal, almost certainly a male, appeared at the peak of condition. He would make a formidable opponent in the boxing matches that determine pecking orders among males. If the kangaroo was top dog, he would mate with all the local females. As they came into heat one by one, he would brush aside retinues of lesser males, draw a female toward him, and, rearing up on his powerful haunches, pull her down on his penis. "Copulation usually lasts fifteen to twenty minutes and is accompanied by multiple ejaculations," says Strahan's *Complete Book of Australian Mammals.* No wonder the kangaroo appeared to be smiling.

About the time twilight faded to darkness, the big red pivoted sideways in midair, then hopped away. We watched his thick, velvety tail trail stiffly behind him until he vanished among distant trees.

In the morning we awoke to a cacophony. Doors slammed, motors roared, men and women laughed, and children debated who would sit where in the car. We crawled out of the tent. It was as if we had camped in the middle of a film set, and shooting was about to begin. People, tents, camper vans, tables, chairs, and cookstoves were perched on every knoll and filled every declivity. Laughter, wails, cooking, eating, belching, and argument crowded the air.

Heightening the sense of chaos, red gums lorded over the scene, their bent, sun-bleached limbs and gray-green leaves forming a tattered canopy overhead. In them, Australian ravens perched and called. There were so many of the birds that their vaguely malevolent cries (*Ha, ha, haaaaaa,* they said over and over) formed a background drone as monotonous as that of a diesel generator chugging in the distance.

During breakfast, a ruckus in a tree engaged my attention. Its source was a flock of gray-and-white birds. A close look with binoculars revealed yellow and black facial markings and cottony white rumps. According to the most up-to-date of our bird books, I was seeing yellow-throated miners, an odd name for a bird with a gray throat. The older of our books called the birds white-rumped miners. At first I thought the birds were mobbing a predator, perhaps an owl or a python, but a close look turned up no such threat. Yellow-throated miners often breed in extended family groups, and they are known for performing collective displays called "corroborees." Perhaps that was what I was witnessing.

To complete the picture, there was music. On a rocky slope overlooking the campground, hidden from view by leaves and limbs, a man sat singing. His voice carried far, and there was a wild, reckless quality to it suggesting he was either "crazy as a galah" (Australian for "bonkers") or under the influence of alcohol, drugs, or *joie de vivre*. First came "Sitting On Top of the World," Al Jolson–style, then Simon and Garfunkel's "Feeling Groovy." The man was having the time of his life. Smiling, we set off on a hike.

Fourteen miles of walking lay ahead, and we moved briskly. Our route would follow a zigzag course up a slope of red-brown quartzite, passing boulders the size of railroad cars. We would hike north and west until we crested the rim of Wilpena Pound at Tanderra Saddle. There we planned a picnic. From the ridge, a second trail would bring us into the Pound. An old farm road in the bottom led through the basin's narrow mouth and back to the clamorous campground.

Ten minutes after we started, we fell in with a company of young men from England. They were students spending a term in Australia, and all were jolly. Their jokes made light of their physical fitness, or lack of it. Our legs throbbed, too. Two visits with our lotos-eating friends had left us with expanded waistlines and flabby muscles.

"Where in England are you from?" I asked, making small talk.

"Kent."

"Where in Kent?"

"Canterbury." We were all walking in company now, Debbie in back chatting with the rear guard, me in front posing questions to a tall, raven-haired fellow named Simon.

"Perhaps," I suggested, "you could tell us some Canterbury tales." Guffaws followed. I think they thought me an idiot—either that, or that I was joking. In fact, I was perfectly serious, genuinely interested in Canterbury. This seemed just the crew to tell stories worth hearing. With no birds in view, no flowers in bloom, and no lizards basking on the rocks, a few ribald tales would have been the thing to divert our attention from weary muscles.

There were several hesitant offers to regale us, but none bore fruit. These guys were tongue-tied. We returned to idle patter, and I was left wondering whether a decline in the storytelling arts from Chaucer's day to ours could be attributed to radio, television, and motion pictures.

Today we hire professionals to tell us stories, while our gifts as raconteurs gather moss.

Over the course of the day we saw rocks, rocks, and more rocks. A few agamid lizards, or dragons, basked on sun-warmed boulders, but every time we approached one to examine its markings, it fled before we could get a look. At Tanderra Saddle, a knife-edge, the views were worthy of the effort it took to get there. On one side lay the broad, capacious Pound, a nearly perfect bowl surrounded by hills. On the other, the slope dropped perilously toward dry, rolling country that stretched to the eastern horizon. Somewhere out there, just east of us, lay Ediacara, a fossil bed that forced paleontologists to rewrite the story of life on Earth.

Older, indirect evidence of life exists elsewhere in the world, but the fossil jellyfish first identified near Ediacara in 1946 represented the earliest known remains of actual living organisms. Reports of the discoveries met widespread disbelief. The fossils revealed animals more primitive and ancient than others known at the time, and acknowledging them required an evolution of evolutionary thinking. Once authenticated, the fossils were found to be 600 million years old. The invertebrate animals they preserved, known to zoology students today as the "Ediacaran fauna," have since turned up in digs around the globe.

At the saddle, our Canterbury friends set off on a pilgrimage to St. Mary's Peak while Debbie and I picked our way down into the Pound. It had been a cool morning. Now, descending a west-facing slope in afternoon sun, we peeled off sweaters and shirts and trudged along in T-shirts. We looked for birds, saw few, watched for flowers, saw next to none, scanned the ground for lizards, spied only tails moving in the opposite direction, and scrutinized the shrubby vegetation for signs of kangaroos or other mammals, to no avail. The Pound was still. We plodded on for miles, tired, sweaty, bored. Only when we were nearing the mouth of the valley did movement catch our eye in the bushes.

Kangaroos! At first we couldn't say what species they belonged to, but both of us were immediately certain we had stumbled on something new. The two animals looked a bit like gray kangaroos, yet their bodies were chunkier, shaggier, with noses black and bare. Whatever their identity, they were fetchingly handsome. Round, dark eyes looked at us from soft, curious faces.

We watched. One kangaroo stood a foot taller than the other, about four feet compared to three. I guessed we were seeing a female and a well-developed joey. If this was the case, the larger animal's pouch probably contained the smaller animal's sibling, still only a moist, hairless thing clamped on a nipple. Both kangaroos nibbled halfheartedly on grasses, looking up at us every few seconds and blinking. They looked sleepy.

Clumping along like hoofed animals on blistered feet, we left the marsupials and started for the campground. Our mammal book, too heavy to carry on the hike, would tell us what species of kangaroo we had seen.

We passed through a gap in the Pound's walls where a stream draining the basin poured into the lowlands. The rocky slopes on either side offered our last, best chance for spying a yellow-footed rock wallaby. We lingered and scrutinized every boulder. No luck. We did find a spiny-cheeked honeyeater, an exquisite little acrobat with a salmon-colored throat and breast. The bird, Debbie told me later, represented the 170th species we had identified since arriving.

Sipping tea back at the campsite with my feet up, I flipped through the mammal book. The kangaroos we had seen proved to be common wallaroos, members of a species that ranges over much of arid Australia. In the West, the wallaroo is known as the "euro." Among marsupials it is one of the country's "big four," the other heavyweights being the red kangaroo, the eastern grey, and the western grey.

What next? We might have lingered in the Flinders Ranges for weeks, sleuthing for rock wallabies and wandering in the footsteps of Heysen. Yet our sights were fixed on the Center. Seventy-five days had passed since we stepped off the airplane in Melbourne, seventy-five days of self-restraint during which we had suppressed our urge to race for the heart of the country and plant our palms on its most venerated icon—the great breadloaf of ruddy sandstone known as Uluru, or Ayers Rock. Now the time had come.

In Port Augusta, a frontier town at the head of the Spencer Gulf, we loaded up on groceries. We also stopped at an auto parts store. Following recommendations made by the Royal Automobile Club, we purchased spare radiator hoses, fan belts, a supply of crankcase oil, a special epoxy made for plugging leaking fuel tanks, and a putty suitable for closing rips in oil pans. We lacked the second spare tire and wheel that were also recommended, but it seemed a greater risk to burden our overloaded vehicle with additional weight than to drive and take our chances. The most critical item we loaded aboard was water—gallons and gallons of it. If our car broke down between nowhere and Timbuktu, we could survive several days until help appeared.

Before setting off, we searched for a post office. As we climbed out of the car in Port Augusta's downtown, a thin, dark-skinned man in wrinkled clothes staggered toward us. He had the deep-set eyes of an Aborigine. I smelled alcohol and noticed that the whites of his eyes were the color of Merlot.

"Hey, where are you going?" the man asked. His voice was soft and friendly. "Could you give me a dollar-eighty so I can get something to eat?"

Behind the man, behind a glass storefront, a shopkeeper watched coldly, his lips pulled back in a snarl. There was tension here, and I wondered what to do. My first instinct was to give the man nothing, reckoning that he'd run straight across the street to the pub. Its door gaped open, and in its black maw two men stood, smoking, watching. My second instinct was to give the man some cash. The Aboriginal man saw my hesitation and resumed speaking. "Please," he said. "I would like to know where you come from. Tasmania, eh?"

"America," I said. "I was born in New York, but we lived in Mississippi before the trip."

"Mississippi, eh? The blues come from there. Cotton, too. Mississippi is cotton country."

Before I could reply, a second Aboriginal man appeared. I recognized him as one of the two figures standing at the pub's door. This fellow was the antithesis of the other, robust, tall, radiating power. A mane of black hair surrounded his head, and he wore a long beard streaked with white. "Be careful of him," said the second man. "He's got HIV." As swiftly as he'd appeared, the bearded man vanished. Now there were four players on the stage: Debbie, me, the thin man, and the remaining figure outside the pub. The town was virtually deserted.

What to do? We were flummoxed. I sensed, or imagined, a touch of menace in the air. Should I produce a wallet and offer money? Hop back in the car and drive away? Excuse ourselves and hunt for a post office? We chose the third option, which gave us time to think. As we began to walk away, the thin man called after us. "Okay, okay, have a great time in Ozzie, eh?" he said. The post office was closed, and a glance at a calendar inside the window told us why. It was Sunday. After more than two months of spontaneous living, we had lost our sense of time and date.

Rattled by our brief stop in Port Augusta, we were glad to leave town and turn north on the Stuart Highway, a road that bisects Australia north to south. It is the only avenue of consequence to the Center, and one must either follow it south from Darwin or drive it north from Adelaide.

Miles raced by, the red sun of afternoon turning the car into an oven. The country grew rapidly drier and the vegetation thinner. There were a few tattered eucalypts at first, then no trees at all, but only shrubs, and then a moonscape of broken rock known as "gibber." The gibber was garnished with pale, low-growing desert herbs and spiky clumps of spinifex grass. Our latitude was about thirty degrees South. At this parallel, and at thirty degrees North, dry air descends toward the Earth's surface, bringing no rain, soaking up moisture, creating the great deserts of the world. We were entering the vast, dry region that occupies more than half of the Australian continent. Rolling along in our Toyota on a paved road, we counted ourselves lucky not to be on foot or horseback.

A glance at a map showed enormous lakes: Lake Eyre, Lake Frome, Lake Torrens, and Lake Gairdner, to name several. They are not lakes in any traditional sense. Wordsworth would find no "waters on a starry night" to inspire him here, unless he happened to arrive in one of those rare years when rain tears up the desert like machine-gun fire. A few times a century, the basins fill and the country around them turns lush, but with poignant brevity. In wet years plants sprout, flowers blossom, amphibians claw to the surface and sing in raucous choruses, and birds appear from afar to nest by the hundreds of thousands.

I pulled the car onto the shoulder and stepped out. The ground lay red and rocky underfoot, as crunchy as corn flakes. All was silence, save for a light wind that whistled against the hats we wore to keep off the glare. The sun punched a round, red hole in a sky that screamed blueness. There were no clouds, no birds, no airplanes, only a cobalt dome that seemed a million miles away. I felt a dizzying sense of space, a vertigo of flatness. The vastness was incomprehensible. There was nothing to hold on to, no distant landmark or hint of change. Two lanes of asphalt led north, and in the opposite direction, an identical set pointed south. Fall asleep and lose orientation here, and only the sun sweeping across the northern sky would provide a sense of direction.

Debbie commented on the wisdom of coming to central Australia in autumn rather than summer. The air felt hot, but tolerably so, and a breeze promised cooler hours to come. On a summer day the temperature in this place might reach 120 Fahrenheit or more. The sun would be so strong one would need a welder's mask to gaze on the salt pans. Alan

Moorehead reports that the explorer Charles Sturt, struggling across this region in 1844 and 1845, found the heat so brutal that it drove the mercury to 157 Fahrenheit, ignited matches that fell, drove screws from wooden boxes, forced lead out of pencils, dried ink before it could write, and caused the fingernails of the explorers to shatter like crystal.

In Sturt's day the northern reaches of South Australia were inhabited by seminomadic Aborigines. They eked out hard lives, moving in bands from water hole to water hole, digging up edible roots and using spears and clubs to kill animals and supply themselves with protein. In the second half of the nineteenth century, Europeans crept in and drove the Aborigines out. A lucrative pastoral economy sprang up, and fortunes were made. Then the boom went bust. Unable to endure the grazing pressure of sheep and cattle, the desert's slow-growing plants perished. Without vegetation, winds and violent rains blasted away the topsoil—a thin layer that took eons to form, a fortune saved a penny at a time. The ranchers fled, and the central Australian desert spread farther over the map.

As barren as the country appeared, there was abundant evidence of wildlife. We saw dozens, perhaps hundreds, of red kangaroos over the course of the day. All lay dead and decomposing. After it was paved in the 1980s, the Stuart Highway became a godsend for truckers, Odysseans, and eagles that gorged on kangaroo corpses, but for terrestrial wildlife it developed into an abattoir. Most of the killing occurs at night. Kangaroos emerge to feed when road trains (powerful trucks hauling three or four trailers) roar down the roads at more than sixty miles per hour. Kangaroos stare blindly into headlights, and the big rigs, drunk on momentum, smash them mile after bloody mile.

As the hours passed, we began to note eagles lying beside kangaroo carcasses. The birds were coming down to salvage the remains, then being struck by vehicles themselves. Debbie proposed a plan. Every time we saw a carcass, we would stop, get out, and drag it onto the shoulder. If we took turns, the chore could be endured, and a few extra eagles would sail the skies thanks to our passing.

The job became routine. At the sight of a red-brown lump, whoever was driving would brake the car. One of us bolted out, took a deep breath, and ceased inhaling long enough to wrap hands around the soft tail and pull the corpse into the desert. The tails were sturdy and massive, some of them as thick around as a salami. Wedge-tailed eagles, perched vulture-like in trees, followed our work with interest. As we drove away, we often looked in the rearview mirror and saw dark shapes floating in, eager to make bad luck good.

In deserts, details reveal themselves slowly. We began to notice that the land we were driving through was less bereft of vegetation than it had first appeared. The plant called mulga, *Acacia aneura,* added regular touches of green. Some of the mulgas were barely tall enough to be called bushes, while others were proper trees, reaching thirty feet from blue-green crown to base of trunk. Aborigines made boomerangs from mulga wood. The stuff is red in the middle, yellow toward the outside, and in many areas is the only wood available.

In several mulgas we spied bright, slender parrots with golden foreheads. They had green backs and bellies, red and yellow underparts, and wings marked with blue and yellow. The length of the tails astonished us, nearly as long as the birds themselves. We flipped frantically through the books, hunting for the answer before the question disappeared. Of course—they were mulga parrots!

Approaching Woomera, a remote oasis where we would camp for the night, I began to think about lizards. We were crossing herpetological hallowed ground. The Australian interior is so harsh, so poorly endowed with water, nutrients, and energy, that warm-blooded creatures such as mammals, with their high food and moisture requirements, play second fiddle to energy-efficient, water-conserving reptiles. Lizards reign. In fact, the deserts of central and western Australia hold a greater diversity of lizards than any other place on Earth. One could say that the country is infested with them, and it is common for dozens of species to inhabit a single patch of rock and sand.

Strangely, we hadn't seen a lizard all day. Perhaps the weather was too cool, or too hot. Reptiles are like that. When the temperature is right, they're everywhere. When it isn't, they're not. Of course, it was possible the road had wiped out every lizard for miles, just as it had succeeded in slaughtering red kangaroos. On cool days, lizards bask on warm rocks. A strip of asphalt offers a sunbather's paradise. Pave a road through a desert, and lizards and snakes are flattened by the thousands.

Woomera. We turned off the highway as the day culminated in golden stillness. Buildings loomed ahead. We had left behind the ageless Australian desert and arrived in suburban America, circa 1964. Fossil water accumulated over millennia in aquifers was being pumped to the surface here and used to nurture lawns, shade trees, and trellises bursting with roses. Several white-fronted honeyeaters, classic birds of the arid country, perched on a utility wire. A ranch house loomed in the background. Ironically, the birds looked out of place while the house, tucked among others like it, appeared perfectly at home.

The woomera is an Aboriginal spear-throwing device. Its namesake village has long served as a Cape Canaveral and White Sands rolled into one, a place where British, American, and Australian military personnel have made mischief since the 1940s. Satellites are fired into space from a launching pad nearby, missiles are tested, America's space shuttle is tracked, and nuclear waste lies festering in subterranean repositories.

Visits by civilians and vagabonds have been allowed since 1982, but only to the peaceful bedroom community where scientists, technicians, and their families sleep and play. The serious stuff takes place in the immense Woomera Prohibited Area. This zone of mystery stretches two hundred miles and more to the north and west, blotting out broad swaths of our road atlas. At Maralinga, in the western reaches of the zone, seven mushroom clouds darkened the sky in the 1950s. Unfortunately, nobody did a thorough job of warning soldiers and local Aborigines regarding the dangers of fallout. A few deaths were immediate. Many others, of radiation-related cancers, came later.

Something about this neat, trim, surreal outpost in the desert reminded me of the Mississippi coast. For four years we had lived near Biloxi, home of Keesler Air Force Base, and the houses there looked like those of Woomera. I said to Debbie, half joking, "There are Mississippians here. I can feel it."

The first person we saw was a black man. His features weren't Aboriginal, and he wore slacks, a tennis shirt, and running shoes. "Hi," he said, sticking out a hand when we hailed him. "I'm Michael." Michael came from Mobile, Alabama, and had lived several years in Biloxi. As we talked, I noticed tubes poking from the ground beside every tree and bush in sight. They trickled water sucked from the aquifer.

The following morning, cruising northward on a right-of-way through the Prohibited Area, we made sure no one was looking each time we dragged a kangaroo corpse across the threshold of national security. Desert oaks, or casuarinas, trailed weeping masses of gray-green branches, aiming to filter solar energy out of the dry air at little cost of moisture. Casuarinas are primitive plants. They are classified as flowering angiosperms but look more like gymnosperms, the group to which pine trees and cycads belong. We looked closely at one of the trees and saw that its spiky twigs acted the part of leaves. Rich in chlorophyll, the twigs harnessed the sun's energy and used it to build carbohydrates. The actual leaves consisted merely of scales, ringing the branches like decorative afterthoughts.

There were birds in the casuarinas—variegated fairy-wrens, drab and brown at this season but still carrying their exclamation-point tails, and black-faced woodswallows, gray with white-tipped tails and dark faces that lent them an air of mystery. Woodswallows resemble ordinary swallows in size and appetites, but ornithologists consider them relations of currawongs and butcher-birds. Often we would spy a woodswallow sitting like a king in the crown of a tree, surveying its parched domain.

We drove for hours, seeming to get nowhere in a landscape flat in most places, rolling in others, and utterly devoid of landmarks. There were no signs of human activity, save for the occasional car that passed us on its way south. The exception was a watering hole and fuel depot called Glendambo. Here the Toyota, Debbie, and I slaked our mighty thirsts. Then we set off again. We drove with fingers crossed, hoping that the engine would keep running. Our car had reached an age when problems crop up, and this was no place for a breakdown.

At midafternoon, having covered more than two hundred miles, we pulled into Coober Pedy. This speck on the map would be unknown, had not opals been discovered there in 1915. By the end of the twentieth century, the place had become a mecca for people hoping to make a fast buck, either by finding gems or stealing them. For miles around, the land looked as if giant moles had churned it. Dirt heaps lay everywhere, and abandoned excavating machines and automobiles rusted beneath the sun. Film directors wanting to depict a postnuclear wasteland come to Coober Pedy to work. Parts of *Mad Max III* were filmed there. A substantial part of the town's population lived underground, like rabbits in warrens, avoiding the mercurial desert and hanging paintings where windows might have been. For recreation, people in Coober Pedy drank, shopped for opals, and eyed each other's treasures. Since we had neither the money nor the interest to join in, we exchanged suspicious glances with a few roadside characters, refueled the car, and sped on.

Soon the heaps of dirt vanished behind us and we were back to old tricks, scanning trees for birds and clearing the road of corpses. The light faded, and the desert, bleached of color at noon, regained the ruddy glow of morning. Just at dark we arrived at a place called Cadney Homestead.

With the tent pitched and dinner consumed, I ambled over to the petrol station. A road train rumbled out of the darkness like a fire-breathing dragon, its headlights blinding me, its roar terrifying. I found a telephone. My brother-in-law, Andy, was celebrating a birthday in North Carolina, and I surprised him with a call.

"Ed?"

"Yes."

"We're relieved to hear you're all right."

"Why wouldn't we be?"

"I guess you haven't heard." Andy told me that a man carrying a bag had walked into the café at Port Arthur, the old prison we'd visited in Tasmania, where he took out an automatic weapon and shot a large number of people. He was still on the loose, and Andy, my sister Maggie, and their kids were watching the live action on CNN.

Debbie and I slept poorly that night. Had we plotted our meanderings differently, we might have been strolling around Port Arthur, not gathering dust in the desert. In the morning we awoke groggy, but feeling grateful for our well-being. The gods, it seemed, were with us.

If the expedition's chief ornithologist had named the bird she most wanted to see during our travels in the Center, it would have been the pink cockatoo, widely known as the Major Mitchell. The parrot has a Napoleonic look about it, square of head, round of belly, full of its own importance. White wings, a white crown, a pink breast, and cheeks that glow strawberry red round out the Major's portrait.

The flashiest part of a Major Mitchell lies concealed, except when prospective mates appear. Then the crown unfurls to form a Japanese fan of red, yellow, and white. The thing looks as gaudy and glamorous as the ceremonial headdress of a Plains Indian. The bird's namesake was Major Thomas Mitchell, a self-important man who served Britain's New South Wales colony as Surveyor-General in the early nineteenth century.

We were driving along quietly when Debbie screamed, "Major Mitchells!" I punched the brakes and swerved to the shoulder.

In a tree hard by the road, two fat parrots bounced on flimsy branches. They were pink with white wings. Debbie was right. Unfortunately, the stopping of the car provoked the birds into tactical retreat. We saw a pink flash, like firecrackers going off, and then both Mitchells were gone with the wind.

For the rest of the day my inconsolable Penelope and I pushed north-ward. Our eagle-rescue program continued, and by the time we had driven 206 miles to the Ayers Rock turnoff, our hands (and, by extension, the inside of the car) reeked of moribund kangaroo. The bull's-eye of Australia still lay 160 miles to the west, yet it was within striking distance now. We grew restless with excitement.

The afternoon wore on, slowly. We crossed into the Northern Territory, and the road led through hot, bleak country. The car became a sauna. Heat causes friction, and friction heat; soon the cycle was rolling forward under its own steam. Debbie and I, cooped up for days in the same cramped space, each on the nerves of the other, struck sparks like flint on steel.

An actual, typical exchange:

> *That's Ayers Rock, there in the distance.* (Debbie).
> *No, it's not.* (Me).
> *What is it, then?*
> *I don't know. You tell me. You've got the map.*
> *I think it's Ayers Rock.*
> *How do you know? It doesn't look like Ayers Rock. Ayers Rock is*
>   *rounded. This thing is square.*
> *It doesn't look square to me. It looks like Ayers Rock.*
> *How can it be? That hill is only a few miles from here. The rock is still*
>   *sixty miles away.*

This time, but far from always, I won the argument. The thousand-foot-high block of red conglomerate and sandstone we quibbled over was Mount Connor. Like its famous sibling to the west, Connor is a child of the Petermann Event, a geological upheaval caused 600 million years ago when the world's southern continents collided, forming Gondwana. A thousand-mile range of snow-covered mountains buckled up. Over eons, the mountains degraded to piles of rubble, and three of the heaps fused to form Mount Connor, Ayers Rock, and the Olgas.

Three-quarters of an hour later, the Rock (generally spelled with a capital *R*) appeared at last. We spied it on the horizon at a considerable distance. There was no mistake this time. In shape the monolith suggested a loaf of rye bread, rounded on the ends, long and slightly humped in the middle. The color was brick red, as we expected it to be, but the texture surprised us—not smooth, as it often appears in photographs, but rough. In the slanting light of afternoon we could see that the Rock was built of flat plates lying hard against each other, in parallel. It was plain that they had been upended by geologic forces, and wind and water had gnawed at their interfaces. Low ridges and shallow grooves were the result, and the ribbed surface reminded me of an old cast-iron radiator.

Ayers Rock—there was no escaping the fact—was gorgeous. We understood instantly why William Christie Gosse, the first European to examine it closely after Ernest Giles spotted the monolith from a distance a year earlier, called it "the most wonderful natural feature I have ever seen." Gosse climbed to the summit, the first in a long line of European tourists to do so. Ignorant of Aboriginal names for the landmark, he proclaimed it "Ayers Rock," after Sir Henry Ayers, the Premier of South Australia.

The Aboriginal name of Ayers Rock is often said to be Uluru, and the monolith is designated as such on official documents. The truth of the matter may be another story. Aborigines of many groups tramped to the rock and its freshwater springs for 20,000 years or more. Given that several hundred languages were spoken in pre-European Australia, Uluru is undoubtedly only one of dozens or even hundreds of Aboriginal names.

Charles Mountford, an anthropologist sympathetic to the Aborigines, visited central Australia in 1940 and reported that in the lexicon of his native guides, the name *Uluru* referred not to the formation as a whole, but to a water hole near the summit. Mountford attempted a visit to "Uluru Water," but his guides lost their way, or at least feigned disorientation. Later, Aboriginal elders told Mountford of the monolith's creation. In their tale, Uluru Water plays a central role.

Mountford recounts the story in his classic *Brown Men and Red Sand* (1948). In ancient times, according to the tale, before humans came into being, ancient ancestral creatures inhabited central Australia. Among them were the Mulga Seed Men, who lived in mountains west of the Rock, Carpet Snakes (sentient creatures, not the modern-day reptile), who inhabited a region to the east, and Marsupial Rats, who lived around the Rock itself. In this magical time, Ayers Rock, or Uluru, was far lower and less massive than today.

Trouble arose. The Mulga Seed Men organized an important ceremony and invited the Carpet Snakes and Marsupial Rats to attend. With the best of intentions, the Snakes started on their way, but at Uluru Water, they ran into Sleepy Lizard Women, with whom they fell immediately in love. The Snakes married the Lizard Women, forgetting the ceremony they had promised to attend, and settled down to life on the Rock. Meanwhile, the Marsupial Rats decided they had better things to do than participate in a ritual that meant little to them. Instead, they sat back and relaxed.

Word reached the Mulga Seed Men that the Carpet Snakes and Marsupial Rats had decided to snub the ceremony. Furious, they sent Poisonous Serpents to destroy the Snakes. A hideous monster called Kulpunya was then cobbled together from a mulga branch, forked sticks, women's hair, the teeth of a small marsupial, and a bandicoot tail. Kulpunya's job was to rub out the Rats.

From two directions simultaneously, the Poisonous Serpents descended on the Carpet Snakes. The attack came as a surprise, and many Carpet Snakes died. In the middle of the melee, one of the Poisonous Serpents found the Lizard Women and burned them to ashes. This was too much for the Carpet Snakes to bear. They fled the scene, and soon thereafter, their leader succumbed to wounds suffered in the battle. Heavy with despair, the survivors circled around the corpse and committed collective suicide. According to Mountford's informants, the violent fighting had created the ridges, caves, and gullies of the southern face of the Rock and the grooves on its windswept summit.

Kulpunya, meanwhile, moved against the Marsupial Rats. He attacked with fury, but the Rats fared better than the Snakes. Many survived and escaped to surrounding country. As legend has it, the struggle between the Marsupial Rats and Kulpunya gave rise to the tortured contours of the Rock's northern flank.

As for the pockmarked western side of the monolith, the Aborigines told Mountford that the holes were created by the digging of Marsupial Moles and the scratching of a lizard called Tatiya. As one story went, Tatiya lost a boomerang and, in attempting to find it, cut declivities in the Rock's smooth face.

After the fighting ended, Ayers Rock, Uluru, or whatever one calls it, rose above the surrounding desert. To this day it remains a reminder of the importance of social commitments, and of the perils of breaking them. Several writers, including Tim Flannery and Mountford himself, point out that the powerful social bonds maintained between Aborigines may have provided a key advantage in surviving the harsh conditions of the outback. Getting along with one's neighbors and fellows was of supreme importance because the man, woman, or group you befriended or insulted today might be in a position to rescue you from catastrophe tomorrow.

As we neared the Rock, it slipped from sight behind a swell of the landscape. Simultaneously, civilization burst into view. Buildings—square, tidy, alien—rose like a mirage above the spinifex grass and desert oaks. This was Yulara, the Ayers Rock resort.

I am tempted to pronounce Yulara an abomination, a glittering eyesore in the wilderness. Having never set eyes on the shabby and scabrous desert flotsam of structures it replaced, however, I sheath my pen. Yulara seems better than the tourist ghetto it replaced, if only because the old camp cluttered the base of the Rock, while the new resort lies ten miles up the road.

We passed the turnoff to Connellan Airport, where jumbo jets disgorge bellies full of well-heeled, time-poor travelers from the far corners of the world. Where a sign said "Turn," we veered onto Yulara Drive. It led us past the Desert Gardens Hotel, administrative offices, the Emu Walk Apartments, the entrance to a supermarket and shopping complex, the Amphitheatre, the Sails in the Desert Hotel, tennis courts, the Town Council Meeting House, a police station, and the headquarters of a fire brigade. At last the campground appeared on the left. We checked in, paid eighteen Australian dollars, and pitched our tent on a thick green lawn. A covert irrigation system watered the grass, which was home to several coin-operated gas barbecues.

Covered in red dust after our traverse of the desert, we felt more akin to Aborigines and early European explorers than to the well-groomed, shopping-bag-toting tourists we saw bustling around the resort. Self-righteous impulses were tempered, however, by honest acknowledgment. Driving the smooth, paved road that brought us to Yulara from Adelaide was a far cry from a camel ride. We hadn't dropped in by jet, but neither had we slogged to the Center the hard way.

We set up camp. Crested pigeons bobbed over the lawn, pecking at crumbs and watching us. We paid the birds little attention. One thought commandeered our brains—the prospect of witnessing one of the great wonders of the world, sunset on Ayers Rock.

It was six. Creeping toward the horizon, the great orb's color intensified from pink to red as its power ebbed. We sped down the road and quickly reached the park boundary. At the gate, a blond woman of about forty with a tanned, creased face relieved us of twenty dollars. Our passes provided entry to Uluru National Park for five days. Then on we raced, knowing the sun was fading. The Rock was hidden by a low hill.

A few miles ahead, we were surprised to see a sign pointing down a dirt road. It said SUNSET VIEWING AREA. Oh, really? With no time to waste, I punched the accelerator.

Rounding a bend, our eyes confronted a sight I'll always remember. There was an asphalt parking area, long and narrow and stretching nearly as far as we could see, and filling it, like eggs in a carton, were hundreds of Range Rovers, Land Cruisers, sedans, and station wagons, old and new. In front of the fleet stood a thousand or more people of every conceivable shape, size, and color. Beyond the mob and the chrome rose the Rock.

The only parking space we could find was a slot so narrow other cars had avoided it. I liberated Debbie and squeezed inside.

Emerging in the soft evening air, we inhaled a double-barrel jolt of diesel fumes. Buses growled, poised to whisk passengers to four-course meals and plush beds as soon as the reddening sun faded into desert night.

The crowd was thick, a palisade of bodies. It took several requests to find someone, an elderly woman, willing to let me poke through the wall with a camera. By the time I succeeded, the Rock had lost its brilliance. Cars coughed to life, and buses revved. We lingered, enjoying a conversation with a couple from Sacramento, California. They wore German binoculars worth far more than our car, and were in the middle of a round-the-world birdwatching safari.

Gasps came from those who remained. The Rock was lighting up again. The sun's afterglow colored it mauve, pale at first, then richer and deeper. In describing the scene, I grasp for words. *Magical* and *otherworldly* come to mind, but the truth is that the spectacle was perfectly ordinary. Before us a routine drama played out, staged on a landscape very much *of* the world, rather than apart from it. The Rock had witnessed millions of sunsets, and this was merely one.

In the morning, Debbie and I drove back into the park in the profound darkness that anticipates first light. Mobs might gather to watch sunsets, but only a few, we reckoned, would rise at an ungodly hour to cheer in the dawn. Ours was the only car on the road.

Near the turn for the sunset viewing area, our headlights illuminated another sign. It pointed to a SUNRISE VIEWING AREA. Why not? Dawn was imminent, and we wouldn't want to miss it.

Imagine our chagrin when we rounded a bend and found an ocean of people and cars. More than a dozen buses were lined up end to end, roaring. Inside we could see people sitting in illuminated seats, basking in warmth until the sun commenced its passion play. The eastern sky brightened. Buses emptied. The black hump before us turned pink, and five hundred cameras clicked like a field full of grasshoppers.

We stood between the sun and the Rock, filling the foreground with tall shadows. Words of approval filled the air, and faces smiled. Then something remarkable happened. One moment the place was aswarm, and the next we stood alone. Everyone had bustled off to breakfast. We were left behind like toy boats when the plug is pulled from a bathtub.

Leaning against the hood of the car, I ate fruit and granola, feeling confused. Part of me was ready to flee this place. Here we were, in the middle of an odyssey, making plans and choices, heeding Emerson's advice in "Self-Reliance" to be our own "taskmaster, . . . doctrine, society, [and] law." Yet everywhere we turned, tourists mobbed around us, doing the same things we were doing. Only the presence of neatly dressed guides and paunchy bus drivers, shepherding their charges like sheep, differentiated their adventures from ours.

I was frank enough with myself to concede a nettlesome truth. It was easy to look down our noses at the mortals who were escorted from place to place like children on school trips. Yet I had to admit that their per capita impact on the Australian environment might be lighter than ours. We traveled in that glass-house-on-wheels known as the automobile, the most convenient but least efficient means of moving people around a continent ever devised. Not everyone was as fortunate as we in being able to uproot ourselves for the better part of a year, free of cares. Would the universe be better served if the Rock existed by itself, alone in the desert, and no one came to see it? I would not argue the case. So I vowed to suspend judgment and enjoy the place for what it was, rather than what it might have been.

Ayers Rock stands 1,100 feet high, stretches two miles end to end along its greatest axis, and measures six miles in circumference around the base. The walls are steep and end abruptly at the desert floor, as if the monolith were a giant house of stone. The first thing a great many visitors do on reaching the Rock is climb it. We had yet to decide this would be a good idea. In several places we had read that the Aborigines who lived nearby asked people to stay off because the formation, to them, was a sacred site. To climb it would be like going to France and scaling Notre Dame. If this was so, I would stay at the bottom. Yet I would wait to hear the objection firsthand before making up my mind.

Meanwhile, we walked around the Rock. Under a sun that burned its way across a sky of desolate blue, we began the journey in the company of a park ranger, a dozen fellow pilgrims, and 100,000 flies. This was our first introduction to the six-legged scourge of the Australian outback.

Looking like tiny house flies and showing no tendency to bite, the insects sought moisture wherever they could find it—in the corners of eyes and mouths, between lips, up nostrils, and deep inside ears. The tickling of little feet in sensitive places provided annoyance enough, but the worst offense came from thoughts of where those feet had been—skating across fresh dung, perhaps, or probing a rotting corpse. Bush flies transmit serious eye diseases. Not relishing the idea of contracting one, we quickly mastered the art of sweeping flies from our faces with incessant, windshield-wiper-like sweeps of the hand. This form of self-defense is known as the "Australian wave."

Eric Pianka, a University of Texas herpetologist who studies monitor lizards in Australia, offers a cure for flies. Dig a hole in the ground, he says. Defecate in it. Instantly the bugs will forsake your face for the new-found bonanza. When they do, bury them. You walk away calmly, Pianka promises, harassed only by a few survivors.

Our guide, whom I'll call Karen, had a suntanned face with delicate crow's feet spreading from the corners of her eyes. Her nose was thin and aquiline, and straight brown hair hung to her waist. She wore a green shirt decorated with an emblem or two, matching shorts, and hiking boots. On sturdy legs streaked with dark hair, Karen stood six feet from sole to crown.

She led us to a cave. It was all mouth and no depth. The inner wall curved up and away like an ocean wave. Squinting at us in the glare, Karen told a story we had heard often in Australia, especially in national parks. Its protagonists were a kind, gentle people who lived in perfect harmony with their environment, embodying all that is good and admirable, and a greedy, cruel race, monumentally arrogant, irreverent, and wicked. The cruel people drove the gentle ones from their lands, killed the majority of them, and forced the survivors into poverty and degradation.

Karen's grim tale contained much truth, but common sense and background reading also informed us that a saga of saints and sinners presented a narrow and highly colored reading of facts more complicated than is sometimes supposed. Perhaps she had studied the *Lonely Planet* guide to Australia. The Aborigines, it said, "never hunted an animal to extinction or harvested a plant species to the point where it was threatened with extinction. Like other hunter-gatherer peoples of the world, the Aborigines were true ecologists."

Karen ended the soapbox portion of her presentation with a joke. There is a cave at Uluru, she said, that the Aborigines call "Bus Fella's Dreaming." It is so named because bus drivers who brought gullible tourists there made up bogus Aboriginal legends about it. Karen's audience, entirely European in composition, chuckled uncomfortably.

Our guide probably wanted to right ancient wrongs, but was she succeeding? To my ears, her tales of godlike natives, and of invaders who were half monster and half buffoon, sounded like a glib recycling of the old noble-savage myth. The interpretation smacked of racism—a droll, sanctimonious, prettified racism that beatified black Australians and degraded whites. In so doing it simply replaced one form of mean-spirited prejudice with another.

Let it be said plainly: Australia's Aborigines received, and continue to receive, much abominable treatment at the hands of the continent's European conquerors. In many places they were shot or poisoned like rabid dogs, often with the government's acquiescence or even its active participation. Torture and mutilation were commonplace. As in North America, however, intentional harm paled beside the accidental carnage wrought by pathogens. Smallpox and other diseases decimated Aboriginal populations in much the same way that they wiped out tribe after tribe of American Indians.

The treatment of the Aborigines seems especially ghastly because it happened so recently in history, at a time when its perpetrators had reason to know better. Yet even nineteenth century intellectuals witnessed the tragedy blithely. "Of the Australian black man," wrote Anthony Trollope after visiting Australia, "we may say certainly that he has to go. That he should perish without unnecessary suffering should be the aim of all who are concerned in the matter." The Norwegian zoologist Carl Lumholtz felt similarly. Speaking uncritically of a Queensland rancher who killed every Aborigine that appeared on "his" land, Lumholtz recounts that the rancher "shot all the men because they were cattle killers; the women, because they gave birth to cattle killers; and the children, because they would in time become cattle killers." Elsewhere, Lumholtz sums up the matter baldly. "On the borders of civilisation," he writes, "men would think as little of shooting a black man as a dog." Both Trollope and Lumholtz considered the Aborigines, in the Norwegian's words, a "doomed race."

While Europeans often met Aborigines with violence, black Australians were not always the meek, gentle people they are sometimes claimed to have been. Aborigines fought back and sometimes attacked first. Lumholtz reports the stalking of whites by blacks in Northern Queensland, attributing it to a "war of extermination between the two races." European settlers succumbed to surprise attacks with spears, and in brushy portions of the outback, natives were known to creep up on Europeans and set the bush around them afire. To portray the Aborigines as pushovers is to demean them. They stood their ground, successfully at times, just as did the Indians of North America. Tragically, however, smallpox, gunpowder, and grazing animals proved invincible adversaries over the long haul.

The notion, in vogue at the moment, that Aborigines lived in perfect harmony with Australia's plants and animals crumbles under scrutiny. "Many people," writes the biologist Jared Diamond, "still cling to the Rousseauvian fantasy that [human destruction of the environment] did not appear in us until the Industrial Revolution, before which we lived in harmony with nature. If that were true, we could have nothing to learn from the past except how virtuous we once were and how evil we have become."

Tim Flannery marshals interesting evidence in *The Future Eaters*. (The title refers to the author's thesis that humans, no matter their race, disrupt any ecosystem they enter, undermining the capacity of the environment to sustain life.) Flannery notes that the traditional explanation for the extinction of large animals, or megafauna, over the last 50,000 years attributes the losses to climatic change, ignoring telltale correlations between the arrival dates of *Homo sapiens* in ecosystems and the sudden disappearance of animals that were big, meaty, and easy to kill.

Australia lost ninety-four percent of its megafauna, says Flannery, a proportion significantly higher than the seventy-three percent lost in North America. Tellingly, the extinctions took place around 35,000 years ago, well before climatic changes associated with ice-age cooling reached their most severe. The timing matches the period when humans dispersed across the continent. In North America, megafaunal extinctions peaked

11,000 years ago. Large mammals that survived several ice ages and endured the warming periods that followed them vanished at a time when harsh climatic conditions were actually abating. Why did they die? The case is not yet closed, but it is hard to sidestep the fact that the extinctions coincided with the arrival and dispersal in North America of the first human beings.

In New Zealand, a diverse megafauna of giant birds called moas survived ice ages in great diversity and numbers, only to perish in the last thousand years. What happened? This extinction is documented by archaeological evidence. The first Polynesian settlers arrived in New Zealand a millennium ago. As Flannery's thesis predicts, they quickly set about devouring their future. The last moa died shortly before the appearance of Europeans.

Terence Dawson, a biologist at the University of New South Wales, concurs with Flannery. Dawson explains why some animals survived the onslaught of two-legged hunters while others did not. Most of the large kangaroos that perished, notes Dawson, browsed on woody vegetation. These animals moved slowly because their diet required them to have capacious stomachs in which slow-to-digest leaves and twigs could be carried. They offered easy pickings for the first human hunters. If Dawson is correct, then the kangaroos that survived humanity's appearance should be fast-moving grazers with small stomachs. This in fact is the case.

Admittedly the argument for a profound, human-caused disruption of Australia's ecosystems rests almost entirely on circumstantial evidence. There is no smoking gun, no set of archaeological sites that prove the matter conclusively. Yet the indirect evidence is so extensive that it is hard to refute. Fleet-footed animals that climb trees, and animals that burrow underground, survived to see European sails break the horizon. Big, fleshy, plodding animals that lived in the open, beasts that had endured the vagaries of climate through a succession of ice ages and warming periods, vanished once humans appeared. The plant community changed dramatically, too. Ash and charcoal become prominent in soil cores around the time that humans appeared on the stage, and at once the diversity of plant life plummets. Eucalypts, which thrive in the presence of fire, burst into dominance. Eucalyptus leaves contain toxins, and few animals can eat them. Flannery and others suspect that Australia's megafauna disappeared not only from overhunting and harassment, but from revolutionary changes in plant communities brought on by human-caused fires.

Australia's first humans made a mess, it seems, then saw the light. When the giant browsers disappeared, dead leaves and stems they would have eaten piled up, promoting catastrophic fires of the sort that scorched Yellowstone National Park in 1988. The Aborigines, Flannery suggests, learned to burn the landscape routinely to prevent fuel from building to dangerous levels. In so doing, they encouraged the growth of grasses. Green grass made life easier for kangaroos and other surviving herbivores. Thus the "future eaters" metamorphosed into conservationists.

Eager to interpret Uluru for ourselves, we said good-bye to Karen and set off around the base. Dry air pinched our nostrils, as it does in the deserts of Texas, and red rock underfoot reflected the heat of the sun.

The scenery offered stark contrasts. On one side the landscape was all flatness and monotony. On the other it swept into the sky, presented a frieze of curves and crevices, and gave off a fiery glow that was nearly blinding. The Rock's rusty color made a perfect counterpoint to the overwhelming blueness of the sky.

Black-faced woodswallows monitored our progress from perches on dead, sun-bleached limbs. A brown goshawk, harried by magpies, zoomed in over the desert sand and vanished in a rocky cleft. Slowly, swatting flies with mounting frenzy, we picked our way in and out of bulges and invaginations, our feet crunching on bits of the monolith's shed skin.

We saw five or six people; that was all. Silence prevailed. Time stopped in its tracks. For a couple of hours we felt like the first humans staggering out of the desert. We pressed palms against the Rock's warm flank as if touching a live dinosaur, and were awed.

An animal stood near our car when we returned. It was a dog, but not a dog, long of leg, powerful of body, and yellow. We had glimpsed the animal, or one like it, slinking through the campground the night before, flashing into view, then dissolving into shadow. It was a dingo.

The dingo blinked an eye already half closed against the sun. Planted on four paws that looked surprisingly delicate for a beast the size of a police dog, it looked up at us with the practiced, woebegone look of a creature that prefers handouts to hunting. We would have liked to feed the dingo, but knew that doing so would be hurtful in the long run. This was a wild creature, partly tame, but potentially dangerous.

"A beautiful creature—shapely, graceful, a little wolfish in some of his aspects, but with a most friendly eye and social disposition," wrote Mark Twain of Australia's wild dog. Twain saw a dingo in a zoo and was taken with it. For a century and more, scientists have tried to puzzle out exactly what sort of beast the dingo is, and Twain wondered, too. He asked a naturalist, and this, according to Twain, was the response. "The dingo [is] not a dingo at all, but just a wild dog; and . . . the only difference between a dingo and a dog [is] that neither of them barked; otherwise they [are] just the same."

Twain was close to the mark. The dingo was, and perhaps will always remain, a cipher. Look the animal up in a book, and depending on the year it was published, you will find the animal listed as a dog (*Canis familiaris dingo*), a variety of wolf, (*Canis lupus dingo*), or as a species all its own, (*Canis dingo*). What is it, really? No one can say for sure. Wolves, dogs, and dingoes share so much in common, including an ability to interbreed if given the chance, that some experts suggest lumping them into a single, variable species.

The question of where exactly the dingo came from, and how it arrived in Australia, has never been answered. Almost certainly the dingo arrived from Asia via islands to the north of Australia, but the exact point of origin and route of entry are unknown. Since dingoes could not have dog-paddled across Wallace's Line on their own, someone must have brought them. Who? We can't say. When? The fact that dingoes never populated Tasmania suggests that they entered Australia sometime after 14,000 years ago, when rising seas at the end of the last ice age severed the island from the mainland. Flannery estimates the introduction took place around 1500 B.C., or 3,500 years ago.

Whatever the timing, the dingo's impact on Australia appears to have been profound. The fleet-footed carnivore probably made short work of small and medium-sized marsupials that survived the megafaunal extinctions. Some species vanished. Among them were mainland populations of the Tasmanian tiger and the Tasmanian devil. The dingo either ate its competitors or drove them out of business by taking away their livelihood.

After leaving the dingo, we visited the park's Aboriginal Cultural Center. It was a splendid place, low and designed to blend in with the desert. The inside teemed with brightly painted murals and collections of artifacts. A ramp wound through the building like a snake, and during our stroll along it we enjoyed the congenial company of a guide.

He was stocky and white-haired, with eyes that twinkled and skin the color and sheen of polished mahogany. On his head he wore a cowboy hat. The man told stories of his family's ancient connection to the Rock, of magical forces that brought about the monolith's creation, and of "bush tucker" his people found in the desert. There were a few touches of the "black man good, white man bad" thesis, but for the most part the old man told thoughtful stories and left the axe-grinding to others. We listened eagerly.

Near the end of the tour, an Englishwoman asked how the Anangu, the local Aborigines, felt about tourists climbing the Rock. I expected a speech about sacredness and sacrilege. Instead the old man smiled broadly, adjusted his hat, and said that the problem his people had with climbing was that the doing of it was dangerous. "We are your hosts at Uluru," he said, "and we take our job very seriously. When people fall from the top, or die from a heart attack, we feel very sad." The woman pressed him. Was it not an act of very bad manners to climb? Our guide laughed. "No, no," he said. "We simply want you to be safe, to go home happy." The woman looked disappointed. I felt a smile coming on. Deep down, I wanted to reach the top.

An hour of daylight remained. The blue of the sky was deepening in the east, and the westering sun had transformed the monolith into something extraterrestrial—a fallen chunk of star, perhaps, or a glob of the universal protoplasm from which all life erupts. Low in the sky, a nearly full moon was glowing. On impulse, we set off for the place where a chain leads up the Rock's western bulge.

We arrived, contemplated, and hesitated. People streamed down from above, their faces radiant with exertion and accomplishment. A few scrambled upward. The sun sank ever lower, and the hike to the summit might take more than an hour.

As the heat of midday gave way to the cool of evening, we started to climb. Debbie advanced a hundred feet, then stopped. Doubts about loose-fitting shoes and fear of bringing on an asthma attack during a hasty ascent changed her mind. She would linger at the bottom, she said, look for the dingo, and enjoy the sunset.

I moved on and up, anxious to gain altitude quickly lest I be stranded on the Rock after dark. I reached the chain quickly. It provided more reassurance than help, so I kept my hands free and ascended beside it. The stone underfoot was rough, the footing secure. I paused once to gasp for air when my speed exceeded my wind, and in a few minutes had reached the upper limit of the chain.

I sat down to rest. The vast, almost featureless desert spread out before me, the tops of bloodwoods, desert oaks, and clumps of spinifex catching the last pink wash of sunlight. The scene was all softness and peace, the stone beneath me warm and comforting. Nevertheless, I felt a pang of worry. The horizon smothered the sun and the desert turned dark. Enough glow remained in the sky that visibility remained adequate, yet the blackness pooling in the declivity around me foretold a night that was soon to come.

I stood up and walked on, following markings painted on the Rock's weathered epidermis. A half-dozen people descending passed me during the first leg, but now I was the only animate object in the scene. The first planets and stars pierced the sky, now a rich indigo in the east. Every pit and dimple of the Rock filled with darkness. Should I go on? I held a conference with myself. The high point lay a quarter-mile off, and there was a rosy glow in the west to get me there. But in a quarter of an hour, with the light a fraction of its present intensity, would I be able to discern the markings that led back to the chain and a safe descent? I could barely make out the paint now. Millions of feet had worn it to nothing. The adventurer in me said to keep going, while the survivor ordered retreat.

I turned back. Along the way, I lost the markers once and suffered a passing fright. The weather was mild enough for me to survive the night, but Debbie would have worried, and an unnecessary rescue might have followed. I steadied my nerves and crept in the direction I had just come. *A touch of paint. Good.* Carefully I inched forward until the next mark, and the next.

I was still high on the Rock when I witnessed something astounding. A large kangaroo, a euro, bounded up the steep flank of the next bulge. It had no better reason to be there than Edmund Hillary had in trekking up Everest. There were patches of green in the lower clefts, but none up high. Yet there the animal was. Up and up it hopped, tail thrust out for balance, until it crested a ridge and disappeared down the far side. What was the kangaroo seeking? I might as well have asked the same question of myself.

The following day we drove thirty miles west to Kata Tjuta, or the Olgas, a sort of larger Ayers Rock made of coarser stone. Time had eroded it into thirty or forty rounded megaliths, the highest of which rose hundreds of feet above the desert floor. The explorer Ernest Giles likened

Kata Tjuta's distinctive shapes to "the backs of monstrous elephants." The formation reminded me of witches in red cloaks, hunched over a cauldron.

Over the course of several hot, brain-broiling hours, we scuffed our way up and into the labyrinth among the monoliths. In some places the silence was profound; the only sounds we could hear, if we strained, were the beating of our hearts and the buzzing of ubiquitous flies. In others we heard the stuttering voices of Torresian crows, big black birds with white underfeathers that were revealed every time a gust of wind, like the exhalation of a hot oven, shot through a cleft and ruffled their glossy feathers.

We had just staggered back to the parking area, delirious from the heat, when a lizard caught our attention. About six inches long, it was large of head and tapering of body, like a carrot that had sprouted legs. We opened the car and hauled out a book. The reptile was a central netted dragon, a species that ranged from the continental interior across more than a thousand miles of arid country to the Western Australia coast.

To be active during the heat of a desert day is unusual, except for mad dogs, Englishmen, and wandering Americans. The dragon seemed to manage the feat by moving frequently, perhaps cooling itself with airflow and preventing the hot sand from scorching its delicate feet. We also noticed that it had a habit of raising its head and body well off the ground—another way to stay cool in a world of relentless heat.

Bounding kangaroos and brightly colored parrots attracted the attention of other hikers, but we found that few gave reptiles more than a passing glance. As a lover of lizards and snakes since childhood, I cannot fathom the reason, unless it can be blamed on ancient myths of fire-breathing dragons and the bad rap handed serpents in the Bible. The harmless, insect-eating creature before us was exquisitely marked. The belly was white, the throat softly spotted. Pale gray-white rings circled the eyes, the back of the head was fringed with delicate spikes, and orange-brown spots dotted the green-gray skin of the torso. Its behavior caught our interest. The lizard had a hole in the ground, a dark circle from which it popped like a jack-in-the-box. Once out, it ran a few laps around the sand flat, cast us a sidelong glance or two, and darted back into its lair.

As the afternoon cooled, the sun prepared to set and the moon to rise, and we found a picnic table that afforded a sweeping view across the scrub to Kata Tjuta. There we sat, sipped cool water, and picked idly at nuts and fruit. Seeing the prospect for a dramatic photograph in the reddening light, I set up a camera on a tripod.

While we were waiting for the moment when the deepening blue of the sky would contrast handsomely with the increasingly vibrant red-ochre of Kata Tjuta, an astounding thing happened. I was looking through the camera, focusing, when a woman carrying a crystal wineglass sauntered into the foreground. She was soon followed by a second woman and a man, both with glasses of wine, and then about two dozen more. It turned out that a bus had pulled into the parking lot, and someone was organizing a catered picnic in my foreground. Wine flowed freely, people milled back and forth, and a burly driver in a blue shirt began forking steaks onto a charcoal grill. We were remote from most of the world's population, yet not alone.

A visit to Alice Springs, 276 miles away and the only town of consequence in the middle of Australia, seemed obligatory. So we folded up the tent one morning, said good-bye to the flock of crested doves that had been bobbing around our feet for days, and moved on. "The Alice," as it is sometimes called, was a place we had heard a good deal about. According to contradictory accounts from a variety of sources, it was hot, cold (in the sense of unfriendliness), safe, dangerous, beautiful, and ugly. As old hands at travel, we took what we heard as a summons to judge the town for ourselves.

On an afternoon when the sun felt like a blowtorch and the mercury climbed to 100 degrees Fahrenheit, we were nearing Alice Springs when the Toyota's temperature gauge shot into the red zone. At the wheel, Debbie sounded the alarm and killed the engine, and we coasted onto the shoulder. What to do? We'd die if we tried to walk anywhere. Calmed by thoughts of our five-gallon water reserve, we let the car cool, started it again, and drove a minute or two until another meltdown threatened. From that point on, it became rote: wait ten minutes to cool, start, drive, stop, wait to cool, over and over. After about an hour we spied a sign for a campground at the edge of town. One more run and we were there.

At the office, a slender, silver-haired man was talking with a burly, bearded man with a deep tan. The first was the campground's owner, David; the second, Harry, a traveler from Tasmania. Together the two dove under our hood, and before we could get a look ourselves, they pronounced the problem a broken water pump. "It's packed up," said David. "Pick yourself a place to sleep, and I'll show you a shady spot where you can sort out your problems tomorrow." By this time it was early evening and too late to shop for parts. Harry cheerfully assured us he would pick us up after breakfast and chauffeur us around Alice Springs until we found a new pump at the best price.

And so he did, but only after his wife, Marie, started our day on a cheery note by serving us coffee and muffins straight from the oven. After we returned from town, new water pump in hand, Harry saw me struggling to install the part with adequate but less than ideal tools. Reappearing with his own kit, he coaxed me aside ("Let's have a look," he said) and dove into the job with massive arms and nimble fingers. Twenty minutes later the Toyota idled contentedly, its engine cool.

Odysseus benefited from the intervention of Athena at a few crucial points in the *Odyssey,* and perhaps we, too, had a god on our side. Had the Toyota's water pump ceased its natural life along one of the remote desert roads we had been driving since Adelaide, we might have faced serious trouble. At the very least we would have incurred a long, expensive tow to the nearest mechanic—in central Australia, that might have meant a journey of hundreds of miles and a wait of many days for a new pump to arrive. At worst, heat, thirst, and the wrong passerby might have turned the minor incident into a major hell.

Deciding to give the car a well-earned rest, we walked into the Alice. Our route brought us along a dry creekbed beside which dusty, sad-looking Aboriginal men gathered in twos and threes in the shade of river red gums. They were dressed in T-shirts and trousers, barefoot for the most part, and the ground around them was littered haphazardly with empty bottles and cans. Several of the men clutched bottles of whiskey or beer, and none smiled or looked as though they had reason to. We found the scene dismal—the ugly and all-too-universal result of western mercantile culture mixing with a tribal society. I have gazed on similar scenes in the American West, and experienced an identical sense of loss.

The walk, covering two and a half miles, took us about an hour. From the path near the creek we found our way into a residential area, in the middle of which appeared a tennis club. Dozens of neatly dressed, well-groomed, fair-skinned people exchanged forehands and backhands on courts of manicured grass.

The contrast between the Aboriginal world we had just glimpsed and this privileged western enclave was profound and unsettling. To see descendants of an ancient race of Odyssean wanderers, warriors, artists, and desert survival experts reduced to urban poverty and alcoholism was painful to witness. Fortunately the grim situation in and around Alice

Springs was not typical everywhere. Aborigines in some parts of the country ran thriving businesses on immense reservations, and a few communities had banned alcohol entirely and begun the difficult work of restoring meaning to lives long bereft of them. We'd learned that Aborigines managed ranches and national parks and distinguished themselves in art, fiction, nonfiction, poetry, and cinema. Poverty and alcoholism remained widespread, yet it would demean the successes of many Aborigines to say that the picture was uniformly bleak.

The heart of town was abustle with fair-skinned tourists and Aborigines, two worlds spinning side by side. The tourists were well-scrubbed, and most were busy chatting gaily and poking in and out of shops. The Aborigines, as dark as the darkest Africans but prominent of brow, kept mostly to themselves. Women and children laughed and played in groups on benches and bits of lawn. The men, by contrast, presented a more troubling sight. Most shuffled alone from street to street or, gathering in clusters, stared at passersby with what might have been contempt. In modern industrial society, what is there for these consummate trackers and hunters to do? Each community in Alice Springs, white and black, seemed to keep a close but veiled watch on the other. We saw no interaction, as much as we craved it ourselves.

Yet our chance came. Along one of the main streets we found a shop selling Aboriginal paintings and musical instruments called didgeridoos, which are made from termite-hollowed tree trunks. The place had been recommended as a business that paid Aborigines fairly for their work.

Before we left Mississippi, one of our neighbors, a man named Noah Johnson, had sat on his porch whittling one evening, basset hound curled at his feet, and said that if we found a didjeridoo at a fair price, we should buy it for him and he'd reimburse us for all expenses.

A professional didgeridoo player named Gary, blond and fair, happened to be visiting the store. He loved the idea of helping us find the right instrument for Noah, and soon was producing weird wails and groans from one didgeridoo after another. Finally, in a back room, he found an instrument that was waiting for an Aboriginal artist to paint it, thereby trebling its price. Noah was a man of modest resources with an enormous love of music. We told Gary that if the choice came between a gorgeous instrument with mediocre sound and a raw cylinder of wood with exquisite tonal quality, Noah would want the latter. And this is what Gary found: a tree trunk that, put to his lips, produced throbbing bass notes and otherworldly buzzes. They sounded like the voices of creatures of myth.

As we roamed the shop, which occupied several rooms, we saw Aborigines come and go. There was an old man, his hair touched lightly with gray, dressed like an American cowboy in a plaid shirt, blue jeans, and leather boots with pointed toes. After him came a barefoot couple: a thin man in T-shirt and tattered denim trousers and a chunky woman in a cotton frock. The couple slipped into a back room, sat on the floor, pulled out several pencils, and began poking the erasers into pots of acrylic paint. The colors were daubed on the canvas of a work in progress. Dot-painting of this sort is a twentieth-century innovation. It combines ancient symbols and traditional colors with western-style paint and canvas. In places such as Alice Springs, dot-painting has given artistically inclined Aborigines a valuable product they can market to tourists and art dealers.

I asked the couple if I might sit and join them. "Yes, yes," said the man. "I'm Sammy, and she's Zita. I speak English pretty good, but Zita knows only our native language. Of course, I can translate." Debbie joined us and, after completing the introductions, we settled down to watch and chat.

Sammy applied most of the paint, but Zita directed his hand. She smiled at us and pointed to shapes on the canvas. Through Zita's words, euphonious like the soft tones of a dove but unintelligible to us, and Sammy's translations, we learned that the painting was about "bush tucker" that Aborigines gathered in the desert.

"It's a Woman's Dreaming," said Sammy as he dabbed red inside white circles under Zita's watchful eye. "The circles that run down the middle are wild onions. Good bush tucker, eh?" Some of the dots, Sammy and Zita said, represented the seeds of onions, lines meant digging sticks, and semicircles marked places where women sat on the sand.

Over the course of an hour the conversation branched in several directions. Zita told us through Sammy that their son had drunk too much the night before, had been involved in a fight, and was locked up in jail. The money for the painting would help pay his bail. Zita looked worried, as any mother would under the circumstances. While we talked, I found myself gazing at the Aboriginal woman's feet. The thing that fascinated me about them is that, in size and shape if not in color, they were identical to mine, right down to thick nails on the big toes and the swirls and circles that decorated her soles. I would have liked to press my soles against hers in a gesture of human solidarity, but feared the act might require too much explaining.

Sammy's dark, mahogany-colored eyes looked exotic to me, but his straight hair, cut Beatles-style, looked uncannily like my own. The difference was color: my German-Irish-English ancestry supplied a red-brown mop while Sammy's locks were ebony. He had much to say and soon was telling us about a friend of his in Louisiana and the great deal he knew about America. He asked questions, too: about relations between blacks and whites in the United States, about American Indians, and about movie stars. "Have you met Clint Eastwood?" he asked hopefully.

"No," I said. But seeing his eagerness, I mentioned that on a street in New Orleans, we had once seen Kathleen Turner.

"Ah, Kathleen Turner!" Zita chimed in, nodding enthusiastically, her face stretched by an enormous smile.

I added that I had a friend who once met John Wayne. Sammy cheered. "John Wayne! Fantastic. I like movies, and westerns are my favorites. Cowboys, Indians, and the cavalry, eh?" Sammy's love of westerns seemed ironic. He knew of problems faced by Indians, African-Americans, and other minority groups in the United States, yet he found nothing offensive in Hollywood's depiction of uniformed soldiers battling painted savages—popular culture's version of a history not unlike Australia's.

Wanting to get off the subject of movies and back to earthier ground, I searched my head for something I'd done that would interest Sammy and Zita. Then I hit on it: I used to tap sugar maple trees, collect the watery sap, and boil it down to syrup. I launched into a short discourse on maples, sap flow, and the making of syrup on wood-fired evaporators. The couple grew especially interested when I explained that maple syrup was "bush tucker" for American Indians, made originally by gathering the raw material in bark vessels, pouring it into wooden troughs, and dropping in heated rocks to do the boiling.

About an hour after the conversation began, Sammy put the last touches on Zita's "Dreaming" and the pair made ready to go. We parted warmly. I realized that my feeling of being unwelcome among the Aborigines was gone.

Darkness had settled on the desert by the time we were ready to walk back to the caravan park, and we were nervous about the dark streets and the lonely stretch along the creek with drunken, angry-looking men lurking in shadows. About this time, two young white policeman strolled by. We asked them if the walk would be safe. "No, we wouldn't advise it," said the taller and more square-jawed of the two. "Certain members of the community"—there was a sneering quality to his voice that repelled us—"have a bit too much to drink, and they approach strangers looking for money. If you don't have what they want, or won't give it to them, they can get ugly. Do yourselves a favor and take a cab." There was a haughtiness about the cops that we didn't like, and an ugly tone of racism. Nevertheless, we heeded the advice.

Our taxi driver was a Turk named Serge. He had emigrated to Australia in the 1970s, had lived and driven cabs in Melbourne for years, and then had moved to the Alice. We asked what he thought of the place. "It's magic," he said. "This town is surrounded by beautiful hills and full of people from everywhere." Will he one day return to Melbourne, or Turkey? "Never," came the emphatic reply. "Melbourne was all right, but Alice Springs is my home." At the caravan park, Serge wished us well and drove off into the night.

Outside of Alice Springs, a few brief adventures remained for us in the desert. We would make a side trip to the West MacDonnell Ranges, west of Alice Springs, and there scuff over ancient Precambrian rock. Flock pigeons, abundant, elusive birds of the interior, would wing overhead, and we would watch black-footed rock wallabies materialize from dark shadows at dusk and creep to a water hole. A colony of boisterous birds called white-crowned babblers would hold our attention for an hour, and we would add a new Australian expression to our growing mastery of the indigenous tongue, one meaning "very early." While delivering a public lecture, a park ranger told the audience that he rose at "sparrow-fart" every morning to pursue his interest in birds.

Yet the winds of Aeolus had begun to blow. Before long they pushed us back to Melbourne, where, still smeared red by desert dust, we relished another round of lotos-eating with Beris Caine and the MacLeods. Pulling away was hard, but a new leg of the odyssey beckoned.

5

Land of Laestrygons

ODYSSEUS'S REQUEST FOR a second bag of wind was greeted with anger. "You've got to be kidding," said the Lord of the Winds, or something like that. This time the Greeks set off the hard way, under oar. Rowing six days and nights, unaided by breeze or wind, they made landfall on the seventh day at Lamos, in the land of Laestrygons. All the Greek boats save one tied up in the harbor. Ever wary, Odysseus roped his vessel to a rock lying off the end of a peninsula. The Laestrygons were giants, after all.

At first all went swimmingly. Three men rowed ashore on Odysseus's orders and met a girl fetching water from a spring. The daughter of the Laestrygonian chief, the girl brought the Greeks home to her father. The moment he saw the sailors, he picked one up and ate him. The survivors ran for their lives. By the time they arrived at the harbor, an alarm had been raised and the sky rained boulders. One ship after another broke into splinters. As the Greeks swam for their lives, the giants speared them like fish. Odysseus, meanwhile, fled with his crew to the end of the peninsula, escaped to his tethered boat, and rowed out to sea.

In setting out from Melbourne a third time, bound for Sydney by way of the Victoria coast, Debbie and I would heed Homer's lessons. Girls gathering water would be avoided, and their fathers, too. Above all we would tread carefully in Sydney. The city's giants were buildings, and among them ogres might roam—ogres of the type that covet flesh, blood, and money.

Pulling away from the MacLeods' in late morning, we started across the part of Victoria known as Gippsland. The region is named for Sir George Gipps, governor of New South Wales from 1838 to 1846. The terrain rose and fell like an unmade bed. There were fields of green and others plowed to brown, and, here and there, quiet towns consisting of a few shops and petrol pumps. In patches of eucalyptus forest, the trunks stood pale and gaunt, and limbs and leaves drooped as if overcome by melancholy. This was bucolic Australia, a striking contrast from the parched red-brown country of the Center.

The creature I most desired to see in this corner of the continent was neither mammal, bird, reptile, nor frog, but a worm. *Megascolides australis,* the Gippsland earthworm, is the largest terrestrial invertebrate in the world. It grows up to ten feet in length and is found, says the zoologist Alan Keast, by the "weird gurgling sounds" it makes as it squeezes through tunnels underfoot. Unfortunately this titan of nightcrawlers is difficult to locate under the best of circumstances, partly because it has grown rare. The only real hope we had of seeing it was to visit a museum whose mission was to make the annelid famous.

Driving south through Koo-wee-rup, Lang Lang, Grantville, and Bass, we at last spied the place. There was no mistaking it. One story high, brown, long, pointed on one end, blunt on the other, the building unquestionably took its shape from *M. australis.* Windows were carefully camouflaged, and walls curved to meet the roof. The museum, recently expanded to include a wombat exhibit, was called Wildlife Wonderland.

Inside, Japanese tourists filled a sprawling souvenir shop hawking giant earthworm keepsakes. We shook hands with the business manager, a young woman with whom I had spoken by telephone. Keith and Peg MacLeod had come this far with us, and it was Keith who noted a prominent love bite on the business manager's neck. "She has a hickey," whispered Keith, fighting a grin. "Do you suppose it was caused by her boyfriend, or by a giant worm?"

A likely answer presented itself in one of the galleries. On a bulletin board, the staff had tacked up magazine and newspaper articles. Everything one might want to know about giant earthworms appeared there, including some lighthearted items. One story reported that the employees had organized a betting pool. To win, a staff member and another person (not specified) had to engage in sexual relations inside the portion of the building that simulates the worm's intestines.

Of all the museum's parts, the worm-intestine hall impressed us the most. Hidden loudspeakers broadcast slurping and grinding noises as we strolled beneath a low, glutinous ceiling painted to suggest an alimentary canal. Exhibits told of the worm's diet and digestion. At the end, we came to a doorway and squeezed out the building's rear end. The effect, it was clear, was to make departing visitors feel like shit.

Humor aside, the worm ranks among Australia's wonders. Before entering the intestine, we had walked through a gallery whose walls and ceiling formed a giant worm farm. The panels to our right and over our heads gave no sign of *Megascolides,* but things looked promising on the left. The soil was dark and damp, and in a half-dozen places I could make out an inch or two of worm, red-brown, and circled by fine grooves like the nightcrawlers used for fishing bait. Unfortunately, the overall effect proved disappointing. We had no way of telling whether we were looking at six small worms or one the length of a python.

Late in the afternoon, a few hours after exchanging hugs with the MacLeods, we left behind the farms of Gippsland and turned south toward Wilson's Promontory. The peninsula, surrounded on three sides by the Bass Strait, forms the continent's southernmost reach.

The air was cool and gusty. We rolled up windows, drove through dense, low-growing forest, and snaked up and over granite ridges covered in heaths and banksias. In the end the road descended to a flat beside an estuary. Once a training base for Australian Army commandos, the place now served as a campground.

Hardly had we stepped from the car than parrots spilled over us in a rush of wings and beaks. They were crimson rosellas. People had been feeding them, and with shrieks and gentle nibbles the birds made it clear they expected us to do the same.

After pitching the tent, we made our way to a cooking shelter where three walls offered respite from the wind. Darkness fell as we sipped tea and prepared a meal of fish and noodles. We were not alone. Four haggard schoolteachers joined us. From campsites nearby came a clamor of teenagers.

We were washing dishes when a pair of girls burst out of the gloom. "A possum!" they cried. "Come and see!" Debbie and I joined the throng. Perched ten feet up a gum tree, a brown, mouselike face peered down at sixty excited humans. "It's a ringtail," announced one of the girls. Indeed it was, the common ringtail possum that inhabited wet, forested areas in Tasmania and on the mainland.

With binoculars and the help of the students' flashlights, we found the white tip of the possum's tail. It looked less like a ring than a rope that had been dipped in white paint. The tail was doing what evolution had designed it to do: wrapping itself around a branch, like a fifth foot. In all likelihood the possum had a nest in a hollow nearby or a dense clump of mistletoe. It was out for a night of leaf, flower, and fruit-eating.

Wondering if the animal might be carrying offspring, we strained to see its underside, to determine its gender, and its back, where young often go riding. The job was difficult. The possum was the size of a large squirrel, and a branch blocked our view of all but its face, feet, and tail. Eventually we gave up. The possum had no intention of budging while a mob loomed beneath it.

Hardly had we turned away than a dark shape plodded past us. At a glance it looked in silhouette like someone's dog—a bulldog, perhaps. Yet this was Australia, land of the weird. The apparition, of course, was a wombat.

Only a few of the campground's five hundred sites were occupied. The rest were quiet and dark, offering a perfect pasture on which wombats could graze and shuffle. We followed the first one until it led us to a virtual wombat horde: a convention of a dozen or more animals ranging from marmot-sized youngsters padding after mothers to brawny adults that stood as high and wide as medium-sized dogs. Wombats once ranged all over Gippsland, but dogs, automobiles, and farmers unhappy with their effect on rabbitproof fences have killed most of them. Survivors persist in a few wild corners.

Campground animals often tolerate humans. This was certainly true of the Tidal River wombats. As long as we kept a dozen feet away, they went about their business. It consisted of plodding back and forth, heads down, noses wiggling, cropping grass on the lawn.

Above all things the wombat is good at eating, as one guesses immediately from its blockhouse shape. The animal is also good eating for humans, although few take the trouble. Most wombats killed by farmers are left to rot. Today the common wombat is protected by Victorian law, a status it gained in 1984 following seventy-eight years of being classed as "vermin." Many are still destroyed, despite the law, a few for so-called sport but most out of exasperation.

We saw one wombat squat and then walk away, leaving a cube of blanched grass on a rock. The droppings are remarkably dry and soon fall apart. Pick one up, and it smells like a fine cigar.

At times, wombat droppings represent more than mere excrement. A female entering estrus coats her scats with perfume. Soon males in the neighborhood solicit her attentions. Mating takes place throughout the year, but mostly in spring and summer. Intercourse is remarkably tender for such brutish-looking creatures. The couple lie side by side, and afterward the male vanishes, his involvement in child-rearing over until his next dalliance.

The female wombat gives birth to a single larva about four weeks later. Within five minutes of seeing daylight, the hairless, blind thing, small enough to fit in the palm of a hand, crawls its way along a moist path licked by its mother. The wetness leads through soft hair to the mother's backward-facing pouch. Inside, the baby settles down to eight months of almost continuous suckling, and eight to ten months later it leaves the snuggery for good. If the mother is tolerant, the juvenile noses in the pouch for an occasional drink until about fifteen months of age.

Before conceding the night to wombats, Debbie and I followed a service road away from the campground. We were hoping to find night life—owls, bats, more wombats, maybe even one of the Tasmanian tigers that a Melbourne tabloid newspaper claimed were sometimes seen in Gippsland. Five minutes of walking led to a parking area. A street lamp blotted out the stars, and moths fluttered in great numbers around the bulb. Among them we glimpsed a shadow gliding from left to right. What was it? We would wait and see.

Patience was rewarded. A brown owl hardly larger than a city pigeon darted into view, snatched a moth from the air, and landed on a branch in plain view. It was an old friend of mine, the bird New Zealanders call the "morepork" because its plaintive hoots sound like a hungry sailor crying for a second helping of pig. In Australia the species is most often called the boobook.

The owl was gorgeous—chocolate brown on the back and wings, the pale breast handsomely dappled with brown. Its face looked as if someone had drawn a bold white X in the middle. The eyes, jade encircling ebony, radiated intensity of purpose.

We watched the bird finesse a few more flying objects into its bill, then shuffled back to the campground. *Boo-book,* cried a plaintive voice on the hillside above us. *Boo-book,* answered a sad neighbor somewhere deep in the valley.

The next day we puttered around the "Prom," as Australians call Wilson's Promontory, enjoying the company of king and crimson rosella parrots, watching honeyeaters of several species spirit nectar from flowers, and stepping carefully around wombat droppings. In one place we came upon a new bird, a dove called the brush bronzewing. It had the typical small-headed, plump-bodied look of all doves and pigeons, but with touches of metallic green on the wings. Glossy chestnut spread over the chin, nape, and shoulders, and tangerine glowed like afternoon sunshine on the forehead.

We explored several trails. One led into a leafy gorge crowded with trees called lilly pillies. Botanists place lilly pillies in the family Myrtaceae along with more familiar Australian plants such as eucalypts and melaleucas. The dark green leaves formed a dense canopy. In the somber light beneath them we found our way to a grotto thatched overhead by the fronds of tree ferns. A brook trickled softly. There was a bench, and we sat on it. Debbie pulled out a bag of scroggin (the mix of nuts and raisins known to American hikers as "gorp"), and instantly a bolt of arterial red streaked out of the forest. It was a crimson rosella.

The bird landed on Debbie's shoulder. It flicked its wings, and blue highlights flashed a semaphore in a ray of sunlight. With an open palm, Debbie offered the parrot a snack. It leaned forward, plucked up a raisin in its gray bill, and flung the thing aside. Then the rosella sampled a peanut. *Ah, just the thing.* One after another, peanuts vanished, crumbs falling to the ground. Had tourists newly arrived in Australia ambled by, they would have thought us a couple of eccentrics, sharing lunch with a pet.

Feeding wild parrots is a common practice in Australia. In national parks it is not unusual—in fact it is commonplace—to have a parrot appear out of nowhere and land on one's hand. Taming birds has a downside, especially if the recipients of handouts become pests or expose themselves to danger that completely wild birds would avoid. Nevertheless, the practice has merit. A brilliantly colored animal that trusts humans enough to land on thumbs and forefingers makes a forceful advocate for wildlife conservation. You can't look at a rosella up close without being completely charmed. Binoculars are fine, but as most conservationists have learned, there is no substitute for hands-on contact in forging bonds of affection between people and animals. Watching birds through polished lenses is mere voyeurism beside the feeling of a peck on the ear or hot, scaly toes wrapping around a finger. I applaud Australian park rangers for tolerating a bit of bird feeding. On the whole I'm convinced it's a good thing.

On a bright, windy Saturday morning we pulled away from the Prom and set out for Malacoota, three hundred miles to the east. We felt groggy after a night of wombat watching, and on such a fine day it seemed criminal to lock ourselves in the car. Yet we had a promise to keep. Peter Kurz, a friend of Beris Caine and the MacLeods, awaited our arrival.

Hour by hour we drove to the east. In a place called Sale we picked up the Princes Highway, a scenic road that runs between Melbourne and Sydney. We sped in and out of towns, some of them populous like Bairnsdale, which boasted six hotels, eight motels, and three caravan parks, but most quiet, blink-or-you-miss-them places. In the latter category were Swan Reach, Nowa Nowa, Tostaree, and Cabbage Tree Creek. Unlike routes between major cities in North America and Europe, the Princes Highway was a two-lane affair. It drilled straight through towns and villages like a string through beads.

When we turned off the trunk road at Genoa, beginning the home stretch toward Malacoota, the light failed us. Down fourteen miles of winding pavement, alert for kangaroos, we crept in darkness. Dense forest surrounded us, blotting out the stars, and I had a feeling of being inside a submarine probing some abyssal trench. At last Peter's wooden sign appeared, and wheel ruts led into the bush.

The track brought us to a house with lights burning in upstairs windows. High and turreted like a castle, the place glowed like a Christmas tree, its earthen walls dotted with luminous circles of red, green, and blue. We later learned that the circles were the bottoms of wine bottles, separated from their necks by a glass-cutting saw, taped together to form cylinders, and imbedded in adobe.

"We're so glad you have arrived," said Peter Kurz, shaking our hands and beckoning us inside. He had black hair, thinning on top, the kind of gaze that makes you feel the subject of intense scrutiny, and a German accent. "Come in, come in. You can get your things later. Margaret has prepared a wonderful Indonesian meal." Shivering and hungry, we obeyed.

Walking stiffly because of a back injury, Peter led us into a turret and up two flights of spiral stairs. He pushed opened a door, and we burst into warmth and light. A smiling woman with long brown hair gathered in a braid stepped from the kitchen to greet us. Her mouth was pinched in an impish smile. "I hope you like Indonesian food," she said. Her accent was soft, Polish. "Excuse me. I am Margaret," she said, extending a palm and slender fingers.

As Margaret set out the meal, Peter introduced us to the house. The walls, as we had noted, were adobe. Peter had excavated earth nearby, mixed it with water and straw, and fashioned the mud bricks in wooden molds. The wine bottles in the walls, he said, were designed to fill the rooms with color by day, and decorate the exterior of the place by night.

The walls, Peter said, were ten inches thick. They kept the place cool in summer, warm in winter. The beams holding up the roof and floors were salvaged from a highway bridge demolished to make way for a ferro-concrete replacement. Peter and a friend had salvaged the timbers, hewn from old-growth eucalyptus. The room's door came from an old elevator.

We could hardly see the walls for the bookshelves. One wall seemed devoted to science fiction, another to natural history, a third to miscellaneous novels and copies of *National Geographic*. Four ring-necked turtle doves blinked down at us from shelves, and a fifth sprawled on its side on a chair whose seat was strewn with seed. The birds, it was clear, enjoyed the run of the place. Droppings dotted the floor and rugs like chalk dust.

Margaret introduced us to the recumbent bird, which she called Francesca. Eight years earlier, a cat had crippled the dove. Paralyzed, Francesca was kept alive on a diet of seeds, fruit, and tenderness. But Margaret worried. Francesca had eaten little or nothing all day. With delicate hands that had once helped Margaret earn a living as a pig farmer, she picked up the cripple and kissed it. Looking on, Peter said that the bird was old for a dove and might be nearing the end. Margaret's eyes grew moist. "I am not eager to lose her," she said.

During dinner we learned how Peter and Margaret had come to Mala-coota. From his boyhood home in Stuttgart, Peter had set off in the 1960s on a journey around the world. He'd ventured widely, found that a vagabond's life suited him, and eventually turned up in Australia. Five years of wandering among the kangaroos ended in Malacoota. Peter had found his vision of paradise, and he vowed to never leave.

In the early days, Peter's income came chiefly from abalone diving. A near-fatal attack of the bends persuaded him to find a less risky way to make a living. He bought a block of land and started experimenting with adobe. The tests led to the building of a shed. Convinced he could build a mud-brick structure capable of enduring Malacoota's wet climate, he constructed the first of the half dozen houses that dot his property. The grandest of them was a wildly imaginative "VIP bungalow." It featured a rooftop viewing platform, reached by a series of bloodwood steps notched into a tree trunk. The trunk lay diagonally from ground to roof. To descend, the lucky VIP could either use the steps or drop to the lower level via a fireman's pole.

Margaret had arrived in Australia more recently, following a brother who emigrated from Poland to Melbourne. Back home she had raised pigs. An invitation from her brother led, ultimately, to Malacoota and Peter. Now she spent the majority of waking hours caring not for swine but for the couple's collection of poultry. They had several hundred birds, ranging from ordinary chickens and turkeys to birds as flamboyant as belly dancers.

Peter managed six adobe flats, as well as the VIP bungalow, a honeymoon cabin, and a three-bedroom farmhouse. Most of his clients were "holidaymakers," as he put it, busy people from Sydney and Melbourne who came to rest and play along the shores of Malacoota Inlet. The village was surrounded by Croajinolong National Park, in which leafy forests and rocky beaches were traversed by hiking tracks.

Peter spoke of Malacoota's wildlife the way an artist might gush over Picasso—with a passion bordering on infatuation. The way he reckoned it, he had disrupted animal habitat by building his mud-brick village, and in return for what he had taken, he owed the animals restitution. He paid it by maintaining an open compost heap on which possums, gliders, and satin bowerbirds dined alfresco, by dishing out fruit and seed on a second-story balcony for parrots and possums, and by serving handfuls of mince-meat every morning to magpies. "It's the least I can do," Peter said, the words escaping between his straight white teeth. "We feed all sorts of creatures here—possums, parrots, finches, magpies, currawongs, bower-birds, kookaburras, antechinuses, and bush rats." The antechinus is a small, predatory marsupial that looks like a cross between a crocodile and a mouse. The bush rat, *Rattus fuscipes,* is a close relation of the Norway and black rats that conquered the world with the help of European sailing ships. When and how the bush rat's Eurasian ancestors reached Australia is unknown.

"Let's see if we have visitors now," whispered Peter. He switched on a light over the balcony. Through a window we could see a plump brush-tailed possum, larger than a squirrel, hunching over what remained of a banana. The animal's fur was gray, edged in black. "Lovely, isn't it?"

"Once," said Peter, "we had a wonderful encounter here between our guests and a possum. The husband, Werner, was from Switzerland, and the wife, Alex, from Italy, although they had lived some years in Australia. One night a possum they had been feeding walked into their flat and climbed on Alex's lap. When I arrived to help, it was giving birth! The family stayed up until midnight, the parents and the kids, taking photos and making videos. The mother possum leaned against the back of the sofa, keeping the path moist between her birth canal and her pouch by licking. Eventually the baby wriggled out, a tiny thing, and found its way to the pouch." Peter grinned in triumph. "That family complained about the possums when they arrived here. By the time they went home, they were in love with them. You are naturalists. Do you think my feeding of the animals here a bad idea?"

I opined that while handing food to large predatory animals would be dangerous, a little doling out of treats to small animals in a country without rabies probably accomplished significant good, promoting feelings of kinship between man and beast. Peter laughed. "Well, then," he said. "Please join us—all of us—for breakfast. Say, eight o'clock?"

We awoke in multicolored light cast by the wine bottles embedded in the bedroom walls. When Margaret beckoned us into the kitchen, Peter was out on the veranda. We walked across the room, past Francesca (who, to Margaret's delight, had just pecked at some food), and joined Peter. He put ground meat in our hands. It felt sticky and cool. Australian magpies, crowlike birds daubed white on the back, scurried over to greet us. "Ouch!" said Debbie. A magpie had missed the meat and pecked her palm. A moment later I echoed the sentiment. Other magpies flapped in, and Peter resupplied us. Meanwhile, parrots, squawking at each other, made short work of nuts and raisins spread along the railing. Beyond, blue sky met blue water and the rising sun suffused both with light.

After breakfast, Debbie and I rode with Peter in an old utility vehicle. A trailer rattled behind us as we drove to a quarry a mile or two up a gravel road. Surrounded by bush, the operation was modest, only a few hundred feet square and perhaps twenty feet deep. The town council, Peter said, mined it for rock and earth that it used for road repair. Peter needed to fill holes in his entrance drive. We helped him fill the trailer. The morning was cool, the air as refreshing as chilled wine.

Driving back to the house, we came around a bend in the road and saw a bird with a long tail skipping along ahead of us. Peter jerked us to a halt. "A lyrebird," he said, switching off the engine.

Indeed it was—a superb lyrebird, a representative of one of the world's two lyrebird species. Both are Australian endemics. The superb is by far the more abundant, ranging from the mountains of southern Queensland down through the Great Dividing Range of New South Wales, and into the forests of Gippsland. It also thrives in western Tasmania. The other species, Albert's lyrebird, occupies a few hundred square miles of montane forest along the Queensland–New South Wales border. In a few weeks, we would enter its range and try to find it.

A second lyrebird appeared. For several minutes we watched as the two ran in and out of the road, half flying, half running, vanishing into the ferny growth along the shoulder and rematerializing in the open just when we thought they had fled. We could see at once that the bird deserved its name. From the rump forward it was utterly undistinguished, a dull brown of back and ashen gray on the belly. The beak was small and dark, the eyes round and black, and the head and torso offered nothing in the way of crests, colors, or embellishment. Yet the tail was everything the rest of the bird was not—preposterous, extravagant, utterly superb. It was just shy of two feet long and it trailed like the train of a wedding dress. The lyrebird struggled to keep it airborne while running along in the dust.

Sixteen feathers make up the superb lyrebird's tail. We could see that the outermost pair, banded light and dark like a raccoon's tail, curved out, in, and out again to form a lyre. The inner feathers were wispy and filamentous like the foliage of certain aquatic plants, except for the middle two, which looked like gray ribbons.

Peter rolled down his window. "They're young males. Listen."

We had no choice. Sound poured through the window. Amid the torrent, we noted a few familiar calls—the sharp cracking of an eastern whipbird, the whistles of a shrike-thrush, the nasal *currawong* of a pied currawong. The mimicry was audacious, showing an exquisite mastery of tone. The species being imitated would have been flattered. We also heard unfamiliar notes that represented original compositions.

Lyrebirds look like cousins of pheasants and peacocks, yet they are primitive passerines, or perching birds. Fairy-wrens and honeyeaters, crows and finches are closer kin than the gallinaceous species the lyrebird resembles.

In wooing females, no bird in the world goes to greater lengths than a lyrebird male. For seven or eight years he trots around as a journeyman, slowly developing the filigree tailfeathers he will eventually shake over his head in nuptial dances. Month by month, year by year, the unsophisticated vocal apparatus in his throat learns to duplicate every sound in the forest.

Once the apprentice lyrebird has developed a proper tail, an extensive repertoire, and the strength and skill to defend a territory, his labors of love begin. He has trysting places to build. Kicking dirt and leaf litter with scaly reptilian feet, the lyrebird piles up mounds that average about six inches high. He constructs as few as a dozen and as many as ninety, but typically forty or fifty. Each day during the breeding season, he awakes in a treetop, sings his way in increments to the forest floor, spruces up his mounds, and displays. The show is dazzling. On the top of one of his home-made prominences, the lyrebird fans his tail, folds it over his back and crown, and vibrates it as he sings and struts. He keeps this up for four months. Females drop by, take in a performance. If the song-and-dance man offers the *je ne sais quoi* a lady fancies, she mates with him. Whether lyrebirds keep faith with a particular harem, or mate with any vamp that struts along, is uncertain. Whatever the case, fathering duties end with copulation. Females build nests, lay eggs, and nurture offspring without help from anyone.

Engrossed in lyrebird song, we failed to notice a pair of cars speeding toward us in the opposing lane. Peter's "ute" (short for utility vehicle) and trailer partly blocked the road. As the vehicles squeezed by, the second one paused long enough for the driver, a Crocodile Dundee lookalike, to roll down a window and curl his upper lip. "We were watching two beautiful lyrebirds," Peter started to say.

"Right!" snarled the man, making two syllables of the word. He punched his accelerator and sprayed us with gravel.

"That's a pity," said Peter. "Did you notice the first car? Parents and children. They couldn't be bothered to stop for the birds. We are surrounded by a national park, but not everyone cares about the forest and the animals." In a voice tinged with sadness and frustration, Peter told of trouble he had had with neighbors. Several years earlier a family in Malacoota began felling old eucalyptus trees in violation of local conservation laws. Peter called the police. That night, at midnight, a car rolled up Peter's driveway. Two men stepped out, wielding sledgehammers. They walked up to Peter's boat, which sat on a trailer, and smashed its Evinrude motor to pieces. In the morning Peter visited the police station. The constable in charge told him that if he had kept his mouth shut, the trouble would never have happened. From now on, mind your own business. The vandals were never apprehended, and shortly after the incident, someone ring-barked the surviving eucalypts. (Ringbarking means hacking through bark and sapwood, thereby killing the tree.) When the trees were dead, the man who wanted them out of his way gained legal permission to fell them.

Peter gripped the wheel tightly and drove us back to the house. In the late-morning light, the adobe looked several shades lighter than it had at dawn, like coffee to which milk has been added. The wine bottles sparkled. "Go!" said Peter, waving his arms. "I'll finish the job. Take a walk and enjoy Malacoota."

It wasn't difficult. For the rest of the day, and the two that followed, we walked in forests, visited Margaret in the poultry pen, watched six-inch gray-green slugs scour algae from the brick patio, and made the acquaintance of several new birds. Among them were the royal spoonbill, the wonga pigeon, the Lewin's honeyeater, and the eastern whipbird. The whipbird's calls were already familiar to us, a sharp *crack!* uttered by the male and an antiphonal *chip, chip* uttered by the nearest female. We had not seen their makers until Debbie and I converged on a thicket a short walk from the house. Somewhere in the middle, a male snapped his whip. As we neared the spot from opposite directions, a long-tailed, plump-bodied bird about the size of a North American blue jay leaped into the open. A crest on its head imparted a look of astonishment. So did red eyes and a pair of white slashes that ran back from the corners of the mouth. The bird's belly was gray. Everywhere else it was greenish black, like leaves covered in soot.

The whipbird cast a nervous look at us, then dove into a tangle of ferns.

While our conquest of the whipbird led to triumph, our hunt for reptiles around Malacoota proved a dismal failure. We looked for snakes, venomous and otherwise, and found none. We searched for lizards—by day for skinks, by night for geckos—and came up empty-handed. There were no turtles, at least none that we saw, and we were far from the range of crocodiles.

Confessing disappointment to Peter, we received directions to a waterfall. He said that if we visited the place, we would be sure to find eastern water dragons, members of the agamid tribe, sunning on rocks beside the water. An hour later we were there. Rocks abounded. Unfortunately the sun that warmed them had vanished. So had the lizards.

The reptile I most wanted to find at Malacoota was the lace monitor. One of the longest, heaviest lizards in the world, it can measure six feet from nose to tail, climb the tallest trees, and swallow possums. Lace monitors range from Melbourne to northern Queensland. We were squarely in their territory. What were our chances? Peter grimaced when I asked. "I'm afraid you've come at the wrong time of year."

Perhaps we had. It was the twenty-first of May. For more than three months we had dashed around Australia's coasts and outback. Now the days were growing short and cool, the nights long. The sun swept low across the sky. If we had any intention of immersing ourselves in the country's herpetofauna, there was only one solution. Head north. Get Sydney and Canberra behind us, and strike out for the tropics. In the torrid zone between the Tropic of Capricorn and the Equator, we were sure to find our quarry. Or vice versa.

On a goosebump-inducing Wednesday morning, we made our reluctant farewells. Hugs and handshakes were exchanged, and we started for the car. "Is there anything you need?" asked Peter. "Any item that you could use but don't have?" He gestured beneath the house. Heaps of boxes and tools were stored there. "I might be able to help you."

"No, thank you," I said automatically. Then I remembered there was one thing we needed very much—a stove to cook on. Our little mountaineering rig was on the blink; the last time we'd used it, at Wilson's Promontory, it had set fire to a picnic table. Getting the parts we needed to fix the thing might be difficult. "There is something," I said.

Like a magician reaching into a hat, Peter plunged into the shadows. Boards shifted, boxes slid to other piles, and metal clanged against metal. Then he emerged wearing a look of satisfaction, carrying a propane tank topped with a chrome burner. "Could this be helpful to you?"

Peter's brother had visited from Germany, purchased a car and camping gear, and traveled around Australia. Before leaving, he'd sold the automobile and given the gear to Peter. It came with instructions to give the stuff away to the first person who came along and needed it. "It's yours," said Peter. "I don't want it back. Give it to someone else when you're finished." And so we came to own the camping stove that would heat our coffee and food the rest of the way around Australia.

Northward we charged, leapfrogging from the Nadgee Forest Reserve, where we tramped through wet coastal forest ringing with lyrebird song, to Wonboyn Lake, just over the New South Wales border. Beris Caine's neighbors Max and Eva Redlich had a holiday house at Wonboyn, and in it they hosted us for two nights of grand conversation and fine eating. From Wonboyn we moved on to a place called Murramarang Resort. There, in a campground within earshot of South Pacific surf, I experienced an epiphany, a dream become flesh.

While Debbie strolled off to find the campground's "ablution block," as toilet-and-shower complexes in Australia's caravan parks are called, I pitched the tent. Our site was merely a corner of the lawn that lay between the resort's buildings and a line of dunes. I could hear waves crashing and taste salt in the air.

Day was nearly done. A pale blue light lingered in the sky. The air had turned cool. I slipped on a sweater.

As I knelt to slip tent poles into sleeves, dark shapes on the lawn's periphery, shapes I had taken for bushes, started to move. They approached awkwardly, neither walking nor hopping, but rocking back and forth on short arms and long legs. The motion reminded me of contraptions I'd seen pumping oil from the ground in Texas. As the forms grew closer, I could see that they had faces with big dark eyes, donkey ears, and snouts that culminated in black noses.

Kangaroos.

I have no belief in ESP or reincarnation. Yet the déjà-vu that came over me as the animals approached, and the realization that my old recurring dream of kangaroos at twilight had come to life exactly as I had envisioned it, was unnerving. By some weird alchemy, fantasy had become reality. What to make of it? I drifted off that night to a fitful sleep, making no sense of it at all.

In the morning kangaroos—and their raisinlike droppings—lay everywhere. The nearest animal appeared a scant ten feet from our mesh door. An eastern grey, it sprawled on its side, brown eyes blinking in the sunshine, looking like someone who had dropped in his tracks after swilling too much booze. More than twenty of his mates lounged nearby. Outnumbering the tents, they peered from behind heavy eyelids at the campers stirring around them.

Of all the kangaroos we had seen in Australia, these struck me as the most handsome. Their gray represented the epitome of grayness, a rich silvery color that gleamed in the morning light. The fur was clean and velvety, as if freshly shampooed and blow-dried. Black fur covered the animals' forepaws like dress gloves, and matching hind feet suggested shoes.

A kick from an adult kangaroo can disembowel the unwary. When I decided to join the mob for a sprawl, I made sure to approach cautiously, uttering soothing words. The ploy worked. I found a trio reclining in the vicinity of each other, defining a marsupial triangle, and plopped down in the middle. Debbie saw me and laughed, recalling the time I'd fallen in with a herd of peccaries in the Chisos Mountains of Texas. For an hour I'd roamed with them. So great was my fondness for the pig-like animals, and so deep their tolerance of me, that they led me to a secret wallow. The honor was not lost on me. I might well have leaped into the hole and rolled in the mud like the hairiest of them, had I not watched the peccary in line ahead of me spray the mud with urine.

In the afternoon we drove north to a quieter, cheaper campground, at Ulladulla. There we stayed two nights, resting, relaxing, scribbling articles for the newspapers I write for, and catching up in journals. We found so much that interested us in Australia that at times we needed to retreat for a couple of days, hole up in a congenial place, and digest the movable feast. "A blessed day of rest and recovery," I wrote that day. "I lounged, read the newspaper, drank several cups of coffee, and not much else."

The month of May nearly over, the antipodean winter was nearly upon us. Nights had grown cold, and sitting around campgrounds after dark was becoming a test of fortitude. Darkness came early, right about suppertime. It was getting to the point where a greater fraction of each day was spent inside sleeping bags than out of them. Too much sleep is tiring, and it led to a resolution. We would cross the mountains to Canberra, enjoy a couple of indoor nights with a friend there, and then hurry on to Sydney.

Our car nearly overheated a half-dozen times as we labored up and over the Budawang Range. The road led to Braidwood, an old-fashioned country town that retained much of its Victorian flavor. We splurged on tea and scones at the Café Albion, sitting at a table on a veranda, basking like lizards in the afternoon sun. The engine now cool, we cruised the rest of the way to Canberra. A modern planned city, the federal capital lay on a limestone plain ringed by wooded hills.

We coasted into town an hour before dark. Immediately the place provoked thoughts of Washington, D.C. The buildings were bone-white and grand in the manner of American public edifices, and ornamental trees and shrubs bordered streets that spread out geometrically. Soon we found ourselves at Parliament House.

Debbie waited in the car while I scaled a grass-covered glacis. On top, beneath chrome-plated arches supporting a flag and flagpole, I discovered a promenade. It looked down on the building, which didn't impress me much, and out over the landscape. The sun was setting, amber ripening to pink, and the temperature suddenly took a nosedive. Shivering in a T-shirt, I looked out to hills blackened by shadows on their eastern flanks. A manicured swath of green led in one direction to a bridge, beyond which I could see the city's downtown. Canberra looked clean and new. Most of the public and commercial buildings had risen since World War II, and the population, a mere 39,000 in 1958, had jumped to 300,000 by the mid-1990s.

Walter Burley Griffin, namesake of the reservoir in which Canberra's most important buildings admire their own reflections, would have been pleased by the city as we found it. A Chicago architect, Griffin worked with Frank Lloyd Wright. The launching of his career coincided with the 1901 elevation of Australia from colony to Commonwealth, and in 1912 Griffin was declared the winner of a competition to design the new Australian capital. The luster of victory was tarnished somewhat because English and Australian architects boycotted the competition, indignant at a $3,500 prize they deemed beneath their dignity. An up-and-comer, Griffin accepted the honor gladly. Immediately he was hired by the Australians to put his scheme in action.

We lingered two days in Canberra. Our friend Ruth Lathlean, a school librarian and teacher of photography, sheltered us on two freezing nights in her cozy house in a suburb. During a day spent poking around the city, I developed mixed feelings for it. I liked the trees and shrubs that stood along the avenues in orderly ranks, and I appreciated the fact that wild hills were always in view. Strips of green followed the roads, softening their stark lines, and the public buildings, while monumental, hunkered low enough to avoid intimidating pedestrians. Commerce except of the most delicate sort was absent. There were restaurants and shops, but no factories or car dealerships. Only when we ventured to Fyshedale, an industrial excrescence on the city's pretty skin, did we find automobile sales yards, mechanic's garages, discount stores, and warehouses.

But few things about Canberra made me recoil. I loathed the preternatural tidiness and found certain public works absurd. The Captain Cook Memorial Jet, for example, ejaculated at regular intervals all day, spewing rockets of water into Lake Burley Griffin and accomplishing little more than disturbing the serenity of platypuses. An eighteen-projector slide show in the mausoleumlike visitor center made the evolution of Canberra seem bland and bloodless—the old story of European conquest over nature and savages, jazzed up with slick photography and ponderous narration. Times being what they were, several politically expedient nods were made to the Aborigines, who had lived in the basin for millennia until guns and smallpox arrived to "disperse" them.

The program, like the city it celebrated and the plush theater it was shown in, radiated cash. A flood of it pours into Canberra every day, as many Australians ruefully told us. While some view their national capital with pride, others see it as a parasite's nest, a gravid tick on the national hide. Perhaps the truth lies somewhere between. Meeting in Canberra since 1927, Australia's parliament has run the country smoothly through a turbulent century, at least in general. The country's worst crisis of government came in 1975. Gough Whitlam, a progressive Labor Party prime minister, plunged into political hot water with provocative acts: ending the draft, pulling Australian forces out of Vietnam, recognizing the People's Republic of China, strengthening Australia's social welfare net, and granting land rights to Aborigines, to name a few. Whitlam might have kept on in this fashion, earning the hatred of reactionaries at home and abroad, had he not moved to limit CIA activities in Australia. In the middle of a hullabaloo over closing down a secret American spy base in the Northern Territory, a financial scandal hit the news. Right-wing politicians of the Liberal and National parties, enemies of Whitlam from the start, reacted with a parliamentary maneuver to cut off the government's money supply. Whitlam could do nothing. From the right, cries rose for his resignation.

In a shocking and unprecedented move that some Australians believe was engineered by Richard Nixon and the CIA, the Governor-General of Australia, appointed not by the country's parliament but by Queen Elizabeth, exercised a power few knew he possessed. He dismissed Whitlam and his government on the November 11, 1975.

No such drama took place during our stay in Canberra. The closest thing we found to revolt was a student protest outside Parliament House. The country's new prime minister, John Howard, had taken office when Debbie and I were on Tasmania, and he had set to work selling off government assets on sweet terms to investors and cutting funds for education and the environment. As demonstrations go, this one could not have been milder. Dressed in cap and gown, a lone student stood at a lectern, reading softly from a treatise of dissent.

Having seen no mammals in Canberra other than *Homo sapiens,* no reptiles, and few birds, we aimed the car toward Sydney. Ruth fortified us the night before our departure with roast lamb, baked pumpkin, Australian wine, and gin and tonics.

Arriving in Australia's largest metropolis was a nightmare. Slicing in from the southwest, we struck suburbs at nightfall, just as rush hour began. I was fully acclimated to driving on the left by this time, but after thousands of miles of open-country motoring, I was unprepared for the blitzkrieg. We tried avoiding Sydney's 3.5 million inhabitants by circling the city, rather than skewering its core, but the idea proved a mistake. The core was exploding, flinging hundreds of thousands of trucks and cars toward the fringes. Our destination was Manly, a seaside town on the city's northeastern shore. Unfortunately, Manly lay on the far rim of a storm.

Lanes came and went, and trucks did their best to flatten us. We thundered along with the stampede, fighting to make the appropriate turns, struggling to reorient ourselves when we failed. At about eight o'clock, two hours later than expected, we arrived. I stopped at a pay telephone and rang Tom Quigley, son of the Reverend Thomas Quigley, once rector of St. George's Church in Hobart. Tom lived about a mile away and was expecting us.

A slender man whose bold features and kindly face reminded me of the explorer David Livingstone, stood on the sidewalk as we pulled up. Tall and fit, a youthful seventy-six, he spoke when I rolled down a window. "Come into the drive," he said. "There's a car park in the rear." The words uttered, Tom bustled into the darkness. We followed, stowed the car where he directed, and stepped into the open air. The night was cool, but far warmer than the wintry temperatures of Canberra. We shook hands and introduced ourselves, a bit awkwardly. When distant relations meet for the first time, no one knows what to expect, nor what is expected.

In a shadowy room overlooking Steyne Street and the beach, we met Margaret, Tom's girlfriend. Shapely and dressed in a miniskirt, I guessed her age at twenty-five until she stepped into the light. Delicate wrinkles fanned from her eyes and mouth, covering her cheeks like spiderwebs. She wore rouge. "Has anyone ever told you you look like D. H. Lawrence?" she asked. No one had. "Have you read *Kangaroo?*" Margaret was referring to the novel Lawrence penned at Thirroul, a seaside village south of Sydney. I hadn't, not yet. Margaret told us she was just back from Europe. She had a lively interest in writers, past and present, and an impressive knowledge of the places where they lived and traveled.

The following morning, Debbie and I woke to find the flat flooded with light. A picture window opened to the east, allowing the blue-tinted glow of morning to stream in from the sea. Tom's was a second-story place. It looked out to a row of Norfolk Island pines that stood along the seaward side of the boulevard. Each looked like the potted Norfolk Island pine we had left in the care of friends, except that ours reached my waist, while these stood a hundred feet or more from base to crown. Branches fanned out in whorls, rising until they disappeared above the window frames. In existence since the Jurassic, Norfolk Island "pines" are ancient plants, not really pines at all but members of the Auracaria family. The group includes the monkey puzzle tree of South America and the kauri of New Zealand. *Auracaria heterophylla* takes the name of its natural home, Norfolk Island, an Australian possession that rises from the sea between New Zealand and New Caledonia.

From Manly, a place John Muir called "a sort of Coney Island for Sydney," we caught the morning ferry to Circular Quay. Tom served as guide. He pointed out Manly Cove, discussed our passing of Dobroyd Head, and smiled the triumphant smile of a man in love with history and geography as we turned south and west into Port Jackson. We were following a course pioneered in 1770 by James Cook, the first European to cruise these waters. Eighteen years later, Arthur Philip sailed in his wake, delivering Australia's first load of convicts.

Port Jackson reached its many fingers miles inland. We followed Tom's gaze to George's Head and the Taronga Park Zoo on the north shore, and to Point Piper and Darling Point on the south. Any doubt that we had arrived in the Land of Laestrygons vanished when we saw two giant landmarks rising ahead—the Sydney Harbour Bridge, muscling its way into the northern suburbs, and the Opera House. The English travel writer Jan Morris sees the bridge as "a very British, very 1930-ish, very George V–like, very male, very strong, graceless and orthodox thing," and so we found it—gray, stolid, proud. Far more attractive, the celebrated Opera House suggested a mass of billowing sails.

I had never seen a more picturesque harbor. The water glittered, green hills rumbled down to the shore, handsome homes lined the heights, and ferries and speedboats churned to and fro, streaking the water white. It was easy to see what Joseph Conrad saw in the place. In an autobiographical memoir, the author of *Lord Jim* hailed Sydney Cove as "one of the finest, most beautiful, vast, and safe bays in the world." Coming from a man who had seen all the great ports, this was high praise. As we edged up to the pier, a replica of Captain Bligh's *Bounty* passed us under sail. It offered a poignant contrast between days of yore and the steel-and-glass skyscrapers that towered over the gangway. Before us lay "huge, restless, modern Sydney," as D. H. Lawrence described it, "whose million inhabitants seem to slip like fishes from one side of the harbour to the other."

After months in the backcountry, we found Sydney's noise and bustle hard to bear. It didn't help that we had drawn parallels in our minds between the thunderous metropolis that engulfed us and a place where Odysseus came close to grief.

Used to picking faint birdsongs out of the tops of eucalypts, our ears winced at the clamor of cars, buses, and trucks. Our noses, accustomed to fresh air, smarted at a miasma of auto exhaust and diesel fumes that colored the air like a sepia photograph. People swarmed over the quay. Wading among them, I felt almost claustrophobic enough to jump back on the boat.

"When a stranger from America steps ashore," Mark Twain wrote of Sydney, "the first thing that strikes him is that the place is eight times as large as he was expecting it to be." Twain came to the capital of New South Wales in 1895. A century later, Sydney was eighty times larger than we expected it to be. To Odysseans fresh from the outback, it loomed like a cruel and ravenous giant.

Tom led the tour. First we made a short foray up Bennelong Point to pay our respects to the Opera House. It was an exuberant, unfettered piece of architecture, and well it should have been, for by the time the last doorknob was screwed on in 1973, the cost of the place had mushroomed to ten times the original estimate. The building was handsome as buildings go, but I would have preferred to find wombats grazing on the site, or a family of Aborigines roasting fish. Instead we found an enormous carapace of concrete and steel, the back of a giant turtle. Inside were theaters, a concert hall, a library, and shops eager to handle our Visa card.

According to Alan Moorehead, Bennelong Point was named for an Aborigine. In 1789 or thereabouts, a young native named Bennelong was captured by soldiers on the Governor's orders, taught a smattering of

English, fitted with European clothing, and "kept as a sort of pet at Government House," as Moorehead puts it. Once he was deemed able to comport himself like a gentleman, Bennelong traveled to England. There he remained for more than a year, making the rounds of polite society, sipping sherry, smoking cigars. After he returned to Australia, things went awry. The story is sketchy, but it seems that Bennelong had a wife, and in his absence she had taken a lover and become pregnant. Learning this, Bennelong shed his waistcoat and skewered his rival with a spear. The unfaithful wife died in childbirth soon thereafter, and, in the tale's tragic denouement, Bennelong snatched up the bastard, burned him on a pyre where the Opera House now stands, and fled for the bush. He died in a tribal war some years later.

Bennelong's kin were nowhere in sight the morning we joined dozens of other tourists milling around the point. We saw only white skin, leisure attire, and running shoes. Where were Sydney's Aborigines? In Redfern, said an article in the morning newspaper. Redfern was an Aboriginal enclave south of the city center. Deeded to the Aborigines in 1973, it was the first piece of land owned by black Australians under modern law after 40,000 or so years of occupation.

Tom whisked us to a train platform. There we met Margaret, who again insisted that I looked like Lawrence. People rushed to and fro, red-faced and exhibiting the universal do-or-die manner of travelers hurrying for trains and appointments. Few were the "shabby-looking, loafing sort of men" that disconcerted Lawrence in Sydney in 1922. In fact, we would have welcomed a little shabbiness and loafing. Most of the people here, male or female, wore tailored business clothes and moved at breakneck speed. Many had cell phones glued to their ears and were as well groomed as poodles.

Our first stop was the Art Gallery of New South Wales. We reached the grand old Neoclassical hall by walking up Macquarie Street, passing Parliament House and Sydney Hospital, turning left at Queens Square, and following Prince Albert Road. The last part of the walk brought us through the Sydney Domain, a green space in which Australian eucalypts and wattles met ornamental plantings from all over the world. Enormous white parrots croaked in the trees, occasionally erecting yellow head-dresses. They were sulphur-crested cockatoos.

Although the morning passed pleasantly, we were glad when lunch in the museum's upmarket café was over and we were back in the sunshine.

From the gallery, we walked over a motorway on which traffic shrieked southward. On the far side lay the Royal Botanic Garden. It proved a balm for the soul, a quiet place of lawns, giant ferns, and grand old trees.

The gardens were tidy and the plants well kept, yet I was saddened to think that for many visitors to Australia, especially those on short city-to-city tours, this manicured place might represent the closest they would come to wildness. Such was the case for John Muir. He arrived in Australia on the sixteenth of December, 1903, stayed until January 11, and returned again for a little over three weeks in March. A champion of North American wilderness, Muir saw little more of the Australian bush than the botanic gardens of Perth, Melbourne, and Sydney. Nevertheless, he came away enchanted. "The most interesting garden I have yet seen," wrote Muir of Sydney's Royal Botanic Garden. He visited again and again during his stay in the New South Wales capital, partly because he lacked the time and means to venture farther afield. "Curious how this strange country is taking possession of me," he observed before leaving.

For us the day's highlight was watching a flock of cockatoos sort out relationships on a lawn. As we sprawled nearby, resting before the walk back to the ferry, the birds squawked at each other, basked like reptiles, furled and unfurled their extravagant headgear, flapped into trees, fluttered to the ground, and chased each other. In the occasional quiet interval, they ripped apart fruits on the ground. We had seen sulphur-crested cockatoos before, but never at close range. They were marvelous—as robust as owls and nearly the size of chickens.

Coming from a continent where the lone native parrot, the Carolina parakeet, succumbed to extinction in September 1914, we still felt a touch of the surreal every time one of Australia's fifty-six parrot species materialized before our eyes. When the birds were as big as cockatoos, appeared in the middle of a city, and wore crests like Indian chieftains, we could do little more than mumble platitudes and gape. Australia's parrots captured our interest and never let go. Large, small, black, white, and multicolored, they dished out a smorgasbord for the eye that we never tired of.

At Tom's apartment, parrot sightings came daily. Every evening, great flocks of rainbow lorikeets appeared in squadrons from all but the seaward direction, and shrieking like demons, they converged among the Norfolk Island pines. For an hour the mad cacophony would continue. Standing in the living room, I felt a victim of role reversal. Here I was the caged bird, confined in a small space with a few objects to amuse me and tidbits to eat.

Outside, the lorikeets whooped it up, laughing, screaming, reveling in freedom.

Manly's lorikeets enjoyed the good life. By day they dispersed among Sydney's treetops to lap up nectar and pollen from the prettiest flowers. At night they commuted home to the shore. Afternoons, as the sky turned pale and pink, the lorikeet flocks would swoop in, bank the most improbable of turns, and sort themselves among the limbs.

One day Tom had things to do, and Debbie and I rode the ferry on our own. It was a cool, luminous morning, the kind that adds bounce to one's step and fills the brain's dark corners with optimism. Perhaps Paul Theroux, the most acerbic of travel writers, saw Sydney on such a day. In his ironically titled *Happy Isles of Oceania,* Theroux writes of Port Jackson: "It was the most beautiful harbor I had ever seen in my life, long and wide, spangled with sunshine and filled with coves and bays." Theroux recoiled from interior Australia, but loved Sydney. We could see why. Nowhere could a finer array of peninsulas and passages, headlands and shoals, channels and embayments congregate more handsomely. The water sparkled like sapphires, and skyscrapers, wharves, bridges, lighthouses, stately homes, bungalows, and ferry boats cast flattering reflections on the surface.

Through noisy streets we strolled, stopping to collect mail at the ponderous old post office and walking toward Hyde Park. Along Elizabeth Street, a young man with long hair crouched apelike, drawing on the sidewalk. With a thick piece of yellow chalk, he was adding golden locks to a portrait of a woman with green eyes. Beyond him, and on the far side of a hedge, dark-haired, bronze-skinned men from the Middle East gathered around paving stones converted into a chess board.

Across Hyde Park we found the Australian Museum. The grand old institution had remade itself in recent years into a world-class center for the study of the natural sciences, and we were eager to see the inside. First we would need to find a bank machine.

Pausing on the museum steps for a lunch of apples, we were approached by a man in white and black. His pink face was crisscrossed by arteries, and a band of snow-white hair curved around his dome like a wreath. He twitched nervously. "Where are you from?" he asked in a voice resonant with breeding and culture.

Our response triggered introductions. I'll call the man Ted. He was, he said, a museum docent out for a bit of air. Would we like a tour? Debbie explained our budget and present lack of cash. "Oh, there'd be no cost for the tour," he said with a courtly bow, "especially for such a lovely woman as you." Ted refused to let us walk to a bank. "Come inside with me," he said. "Your bank card will be accepted at the ticket office, and if it's not, I'll see what I can do."

At the gate, the card produced a blank stare. "So be it," cried Ted. "They'll be my guests, then. This way!" We scurried away, beginning a peculiar hour.

Ted knew the museum well, and spoke about the exhibits with child-like enthusiasm. His commentary, however, was adults-only. He pawed Debbie, giggled to Debbie, put a hand on Debbie's back, encouraged Debbie to look at this and that, cooed to Debbie, and wept for Debbie. Standing irrelevant on the sidelines, I didn't know whether to be bored, angry, or amused.

Beside a case containing an enormous cockroach, Ted said (I'm not making this up), "Do you know that cockroaches are all males?" We answered with baffled looks. The punchline followed a pregnant pause. "You haven't heard of vagina roaches, have you?"

At an exhibit on primates, Ted called our attention to the fact that the *Homo sapiens* male has a bigger penis than any other primate. "It's to please the females," he said, touching Debbie's arm. I felt that at any moment I might spray Ted with my lunch.

"The human female," he continued, warming to the subject, "is the only ape female that has enlarged breasts even when not lactating." A sigh. "All that unnecessary protein and flesh, but, oh, they're so lovely to touch, to hold, to stroke!" Ted was gushing. As far as I was concerned, he had gone over the top. One part of me was ready to make for the administrative office and report Ted to the boss. Yet the absurdity of the situation made me curious to see where things would lead.

We continued. At several points, Ted turned to face us, demanded to know if he was doing a great job, and feigned a tantrum when we were slow to respond. Meanwhile the lurid innuendo continued. Ted had told us he needed to leave at one-thirty, and as the time approached, his effusions reached a climax. "You are beautiful!" he blurted to Debbie, as if the words craved expression and had torn loose from his soul. At 1:30 P.M. sharp, Ted flushed red, faced Debbie, and put his hands on her shoulders. "I love you," he cried, and was gone.

We were left to see the place for ourselves. My favorite exhibits featured bones—rhinoceros-sized *Diprotodons*, racehorse-sized extinct birds, dinosaur bones, a wooden antipodean dinosaur skeleton that kids could dismantle and rebuild, and human bones. A vein of wry Aussie humor ran through it all. There was a "Bone Ranger," for example, a man mounted on a rearing horse. Both rider and mount were devoid of flesh. Nearby, through a plate of glass, we looked into a domestic scene. There were easy chairs and bookcases, a bird in a cage, a man in a rocking chair, a dog by his side, and a cat chasing a mouse. All were skeletons. Across the room, a sign beside an exercise bike invited visitors to pedal. I climbed on and started pumping. Six feet away, inside a glass case, an identical bike moved in synchrony. On it sat a skeleton, its femora, tibiae, and fibulae pushing the pedals just as mine did, bony fingers clutching the handlebars. The effect was a bit unsettling—like seeing one's skeleton in motion.

The most poignant exhibit in the place had to do with frogs. Many of Australia's frog species are vanishing. The loss may or may not be related to amphibian declines elsewhere, the causes of which are uncertain. The facts were alarming. Seven Australian frog species had vanished in my lifetime. The southern gastric brooding frog, a bizarre species in which the females swallow their eggs and brood tadpoles in their stomachs, had not been seen alive since 1981. The northern gastric brooding frog, not since 1985. The southern day frog, 1979. The Eungella torrent frog, 1987. The Nyakala tree frog and the tinking frog, 1990. The sharp-snouted frog, 1995. Three more species, the torrent tree frog, the Day's tree frog, and the creek frog, had perished in all places but a few.

The villain or villains behind Australia's frog declines were unknown. If pollution was at work, it must have been widely dispersed and toxic to frogs in minute quantities. Most of the sites occupied by the lost frogs still consisted of virgin wilderness. No smoking factories lurked up the road, nor were the frogs mashed in the treads of bulldozers. The prime suspect, said the exhibit, was an unknown pathogen. It could have been a bacterium or virus carried into Australia via the pet trade, or a home-grown microbe suddenly turned virulent. Stress from pollution might have been part of the problem. DDT, for example, found its way into the bloodstreams and fatty tissues of animals all over the world. DDT, or some other poison, could have been compromising amphibian immune responses, much as HIV disables the human immune system. If this happened, formerly innocuous microbes could have become lethal.

Saddened by the notion of a world without frogs, we headed for the door. A guard halted us midway. He was standing at the entrance to a hall in which people were clearing tables. "Help yourselves," he said, gesturing to cakes and custards left over from a luncheon meeting. We wolfed down several, feeling like a couple of tramps but not minding the sensation in the slightest. In the museum bookstore, another guard appeared. He was carrying a tray like a waiter. "Would you like one?" he asked. We declined, but only because Tom had promised a dinner of blue-eyed cod.

On another day, we left Tom's apartment in Manly to visit Australia's oldest and second-oldest national parks. Royal, a few miles south of Botany Bay, which in turn lies a few miles south of Sydney, came into being in 1879, seven years after the creation of Yellowstone. A brochure handed to us at the entrance asserted that while Yellowstone was set aside by Congress in 1872, it was not declared a "national park" until 1883. Ergo, the world's first national park was Royal.

Which came first mattered little to us. We were, however, intrigued by Royal's beginnings. Its hills and dales not only provided sanctuary for plants, animals, and frazzled residents of Sydney, but also, in the early days, served as a "rifle butt or artillery range" and a place for the "exercise or encampment of military or naval sources." How a wildlife refuge could operate simultaneously as an artillery range was beyond us. A promontory in the park was still known as Artillery Hill. I shudder to think what a hike up it would have been like, watching birds and dodging shells, hoping not to miss the sign marking the rifle range.

Today, Royal can still be a dangerous place. In 1994, between the sixth and eighth of January, bush fires roared through the park, charring, to varying degrees, ninety percent of the acreage.

Behind the visitor center we found a snack bar. Indulging in a pair of "veggie burgers," we ate at a picnic table set in a sunny glade. Eucalyptus trees surrounded us. Hardly had we settled onto a bench than sulphur-crested cockatoos and silver gulls descended. At the same time, we noticed an old man with a mustache like a hairbrush. He was dressed in a white shirt and black pants and sat beside a middle-aged man with similar features. The two conversed in Italian.

The snack bar sold birdseed by the cup, and the old man had purchased some. He held the vessel in his right hand. On his shoulder a cockatoo perched, towering over the man's head and dipping every few seconds into the seed. Occasionally the man looked up to admire the bird and utter a word of praise.

Suddenly, with the cup still half full, the parrot snatched the container in its bill and flapped across the lawn. I was certain the seed would spill. It didn't. The top remained uppermost, and still clutching it, the bird landed gingerly in a eucalypt. Transferring the prize to its left foot, the cockatoo resumed its meal.

The central event of the day was a hike along a trail named the Forest Path. The route struck deep into a leafy forest, traced the bank of a river, and curved nearly full-circle around the base of a hill. A sign informed us that the trail was there to "afford convenient access to the finest forest trees." Twice in the early nineteenth century, unfortunately, the convenience was enjoyed by loggers. Not until 1922, after much public outcry, were the timber raids halted for good.

Saws and axes had made their marks in the bush, but the wounds were no longer conspicuous. The forest was full of stout trunks reaching high into the sky, and ferns and palms turned the underwood into a salad. The palm's scientific name, *Archontophoenix cunninghamiana,* seemed to incorporate the entire alphabet. The common name was bangalow.

Each bangalow palm sent up a fountain of jade-green fronds. The foliage seemed to spout from the earth and rain back on itself in a viridian shower. Even though not a drop of rain had fallen all day, the plants appeared to be dripping.

The farther we walked, the darker and more mysterious the forest became. The soft trickling of the stream inspired thoughts of water sprites and platypuses.

At one point a superb lyrebird half-flew, half-ran across the track ahead of us. It looked like a cross between a peacock and a mockingbird, the head small and round, the tail comically long. We stopped to listen. The quiet glade rang out with the full repertoire—whistles, rattles, buzzes, chips, chirps, whip-cracks, gargles, honks, laughs, shrieks, squawks, crackles, and hisses. Music synthesizers have nothing on the lyrebird. In addition to duplicating the calls of whipbirds, wattlebirds, kookaburras, cockatoos, and grey shrike-thrushes, this one gave us the clamor of an entire flock of lorikeets.

On another fine day we joined Tom, an ordained Church of England minister like his father, on a field trip with the Scripture Union Bushwalking Club. Tom left the ministry in 1958, worked in factories in England, then returned to Australia and took a job with the New South

Wales National Parks and Wildlife Service. He remained active in religious groups, and this one planned an all-day hike in Australia's second oldest national park.

Ku-Ring-Gai Chase lies about as far north of Sydney as Royal does to the south, which is to say, a jaunt away by car, train, or bus. We left the Toyota in Manly, caught a bus, then a train, and completed the last minutes of the journey on foot.

The Scripture Union contingent gathered near a park that backed up to the railway station. On the green lawn, a dozen men and women in jogging suits practiced t'ai chi. West met East, while the spiritual practices of the Aborigines had long vanished from the place.

As we waited for latecomers, I spied a squirrel-sized animal lying inert at the foot of a utility pole. Venturing near, Debbie and I saw that it was a ring-tailed possum, freshly dead. "What is it?" someone asked as the group gathered around us. We were stunned. Only the Americans recognized the identity of a common Australian mammal.

Tom conducted a short prayer while the t'ai chi people exhaled like whales behind us. Then we set off. Tom was nearly impossible to keep up with, his fitness extraordinary for a man soon to turn seventy-seven. We marched through streets flanked by houses, each surrounded by lawn and ringed by a hedge or fence. At a streetcorner, we paused beside a monument consisting of four bronze lions crouching at the bottom of a fluted column. A globe and a cylindrical rod crowned the top.

Inside an adjacent cottage, on September 22, 1918, we learned, the voice of the Marchese Marconi, speaking from Wales, had come over the radio receiver of a T. T. Fisk. Australian troops, he said, had pushed back the Germans at Amiens. It was an epochal moment. Australia's long isolation was over.

The national park boundary appeared at the end of a dead-end street. Tramping beyond, into a valley thick with the forest Australians call dry sclerophyll ("sclerophyll" means hard-leaved), we recognized eucalypts, wattles, banksias, and melaleucas. The terrain grew steep and wet. In the shade, ferns and mosses covered the ground, and the air turned cool. We donned sweaters. There were fallen trunks and roots to climb over, and progress was slow.

Every time we spotted a bird, Debbie and I fell farther behind the group. One species, the rock warbler, was new to us. It looked vaguely like the white-browed scrubwrens we had been seen in recent weeks, but it lacked the alabaster brow. The rock warbler lived only in this corner of New South Wales, and we had not expected to see it.

Shallow pool led to shallow pool, separated by foot-high waterfalls. Eventually the ravine spilled out at Bobbin Head. The air was warm and scented with brine. At the base of a boulder, I spied a lizard basking in the autumn sun. It was unusually scaly, as fat around as a bratwurst, and had black skin liberally sprinkled with brown and white. Later, field notes helped me identify it as a Cunningham's skink, a species that subsists on fruit and seeds.

When we caught up with the bushwalkers, they were zipping packs and starting up the escarpment. We wolfed down a few bites of lunch, cast a wistful glance at river mangroves that might have yielded birds and reptiles, and ran to catch up. Tom was taking the group home by a different route.

Everyone seemed more interested in catching an early train than in enjoying the surroundings. The pace quickened, the terrain grew steep, faces reddened, and mouths gulped air. Debbie and I walked beside a man named Patrick.

During the home stretch, Patrick went mad over banksias. Every time he saw flowers on one of the shrubs, he crashed off to sample the nectar. Banksia reproductive structures are woody and look vaguely like corncobs, although corn is a grass and banksias belong to the family Proteaceae. Bankias are ancient. They arrived in the world around the same time dinosaurs were leaving it, about 65 million years ago, and, from the start, have been pollinated not by featherweight insects but by vertebrates. This may explain the sturdiness of their stems and flowers.

Honeyeaters probably do most of the pollinating of banksias. In return the birds receive copious nectar, rich in proteins and amino acids. Mammals pollinate banksias, too, among them flying foxes and pigmy possums. If we succeeded in reaching Western Australia, we would hunt for the most intriguing banksia pollinator of all—the honey-possum, not properly a possum at all but the last survivor of an ancient line. The honey-possum is the only terrestrial mammal in the world that feeds exclusively on nectar and pollen.

Perhaps Patrick was a honey-possum at heart. With childlike glee he would surround a banksia flower cluster with his hands and squeegee his way up it until clear, sweet nectar glistened on his thumbs and forefingers. "Ah," he would cry, and lap the stuff up. Curious, I gave it a try. Avoiding the spiny leaves, I squeezed and pulled as if coaxing milk from a cow. The banksia supplied a reward. I tasted it. The stuff was sweet, although a sour aftertaste lingered on my tongue.

The railway station eventually appeared. As we stood waiting for a train, I marveled at the hiking opportunities available by bus and train from Sydney. I know of no American city where national parks as wild and inviting as Royal and Ku-Ring-Gai Chase loom so close to a downtown area. Sydney had other parks within easy reach, too. In one of them, Wollemi, a world-class botanical discovery was made in 1994.

David Noble, a Wollemi ranger, was tramping through a remote corner of the reserve when he found branches and leaves lying thick on the ground. Investigating, he found that the material had fallen from a tree that looked like none in the books. Experts were summoned, and great excitement ensued. The tree represented a primitive, hitherto undiscovered genus and species of the Auracaria family, an ancient group that dates back more than 200 million years. Botanists named the tree *Wollemia nobilis,* honoring Noble and the site of his discovery.

Aside from its novelty, *Wollemia nobilis* is notable for its inability to shed leaves individually. The tree is evergreen and sometimes called a pine, but even pines and pine lookalikes such as Auracarians must jettison old, worn-out leaves from time to time in order to make way for the new. The Wollemi "pine" accomplishes the job by dropping entire branches, leaves and all. A veritable junk heap accumulates at the base, and it was just such a compost pile that led Noble to his find.

Our final bit of fun in Sydney involved a social call. From Tom's apartment, I spoke by telephone with Mike Vance, a Melbourne neighbor of Beris Caine. Mike was a television producer with the Australian Broadcast Corporation (ABC), and had worked on wildlife documentaries with David Attenborough. He knew the general shape of our odyssey, and it occurred to him that we might enjoy meeting his friends Densey Clyne and Jim Frazier. Densey is a distinguished natural history writer, newspaper columnist, and nature photographer. Jim Frazier, her friend and business partner, is a world-class photographer and inventor. Together they run Mantis Wildlife Films. Mike explained that they were busy with a project, but told us that if we gave them a call, they would invite us over for tea.

The visit provided two of the most memorable hours of our trip. On a Sunday morning at ten, we knocked on Densey's door in one of Sydney's leafy outer suburbs. The house was a one-story brick structure that looked like a thousand others. But inside we found a unique world. There were cameras and lenses, floodlights on telescoping stands, canisters of motion picture film on racks, and books by the thousand. Silver-haired and wearing glasses, Densey looked much like any other handsome woman her age, but the keenness of her eyes told us she was a person of great gifts. Jim was a tall, slender man with a shy, boyish smile. Both he and Densey welcomed us warmly.

Densey led us out a side door to a patio. At a table where scones and jam awaited, we sat while Jim poured coffee. We talked of mammals and birds, reptiles and amphibians, of exciting things we had seen and of those we would search for. Densey and I discovered that we had published similar books—she a collection of newspaper columns about Australian animals, I a set of columns about American fauna. As we talked, a white pigeon with a blue-green back stirred the air with wings that whistled. It landed on a limb overhead and looked down on the table. "Is that a white-headed pigeon?" Debbie asked. It was, the first we had seen in Australia.

Eventually the conversation came around to *Atrax robustus,* the Sydney funnel-web spider. Some people in Sydney boast about the spider the way New Yorkers brag about rats the size of St. Bernards. The spiders, however, are real.

I had boned up on the spider. Males roam widely and are "extremely hostile," according to a book I found in our local library. When *Atrax robustus* bites you, hope it's a male. Males inject venom three to five times more potent than that of females, which means your ordeal will be over more quickly. The fangs jab and pierce. You have stabbing pains at the site of the wound. Then the spot goes numb. Don't start planning for the future. You sweat buckets, develop mild nausea, then feel like puking out your guts. Your lungs fill with fluid. You can't breathe. You turn blue. If people are watching, they start to cry. Cramps, terribly severe, stab into your legs and guts. You're almost finished. Mercifully, you grow delirious right about the time convulsions begin. Muscles twitch violently, then cease activity permanently. Coma descends, and soon the undertaker is ringing the doorbell.

If you prefer a more scientific explanation, consider this from Keith McKeown's *Australian Spiders.* "The venom stimulates smooth muscle," McKeown writes coolly, "interferes with the conduction of nerve impulses and disturbs the electrical activity of the cerebral cortex. In animals and man the effects of the venom resemble those produced by stimulation of the parasympathetic system. . . . Death is caused by failure of respiration. The venom consists of at least six different toxic fractions." Etc., etc. In other words, the Sydney funnel-web spider is hell on eight legs.

"Have you ever seen one in the yard?" I asked Densey, herself the author of a book on spiders. Before she could answer, Jim spoke. "We have one in the kitchen," he said, chuckling. "Would you like to see it?"

Of course we did. Inside, Jim produced a jar and set it by the sink. "There," he said. Debbie and I stood with mouths agape. The spider, Jim explained, preferred a private life despite its reputation for aggression. It was unhappy with life in the bottle, and Jim planned to release it as soon as he shot some photographs.

Looking closely, we could see that the spider was black and hairy. It was larger than the big wolf spiders that roam the forests of my native New York, and smaller than big tarantulas I had seen in Texas. Unusually prominent, the fangs rose from tufts of red hair. "Most spiders have fangs that face each other," Densey explained. "Fangs of that sort are useful for poisoning small prey such as insects, but it's almost impossible for them to puncture human skin, except between toes and fingers." Densey was warming to her subject. "The funnel-web spider has downward-pointing fangs. Long and sharp." She raised the middle finger and forefinger of her right hand and slashed downward through the air. "A funnel-web spider can bite you anywhere."

I had read about several fatalities—a two-year-old boy who died in ninety minutes, a five-year-old girl who expired in an hour and a quarter. A woman of twenty-six lasted thirteen hours, a forty-six-year-old woman succumbed in eleven. Jim's offer came as a surprise. "Would you like a better look at the fangs?"

Unscrewing the top of the jar, he took a pencil and prodded the arachnid with the eraser. One poke, two pokes; no reaction. On the third the spider, which until this time might have been dead, leaped up on pointed legs and struck down with its instruments of doom. This was old-hat for Densey and Jim. Debbie and I shuddered. We had glimpsed a bit of the darkness that lurks beneath Australia's sunny surface.

While making good-byes, Densey presented us with one of her books, *The Best of Wildlife in the Suburbs.* Jim appeared from an adjacent room and gave us a print he had made. The subject might have been Wollemi pines captured in prismatic light, but in fact Jim had created the scene on glass out of salt crystals and illuminated it with colored lamps. Grateful, we promised to send a book from America, waved good-bye, and headed for the Blue Mountains.

Odysseys involve twists and turns, some dictated by fickle gods, others willed by heroes. Our westward jog into the Blue Mountains was of the latter sort. Acting on little more than a whim, we drove into Sydney's western suburbs, turned onto the Great Western Highway, and aimed for a high plateau.

West of Penrith we crossed the Nepean River, named for Sir Evan Nepean, Under-Secretary to Britain's Home Office when Sydney's penal colony was founded. "Early in the morning we crossed the Nepean in a ferry boat," wrote Charles Darwin, traveling west from Sydney on the January 17, 1836. The future author of *Origin of Species* was twenty-six, homesick, and weary of his voyage on the *Beagle*. His destination was the same as ours, a dissected sandstone plateau, rising to just over 3,000 feet. The massif formed the same kind of physical and psychological barrier to westward movement in colonial Australia that the Appalachian Mountains presented to Europeans in North America.

"With the exception of two or three small inns, there are no houses or cultivated land," wrote Darwin of his climb up the escarpment. "The road, moreover, is solitary, the most frequent object being a bullock waggon, piled up with bales of wool." A hundred and sixty years later, the bullocks and waggons were gone. Otherwise little had changed. "Scrubby trees of the never-failing *Eucalyptus* genus" still ruled the slopes, and in late afternoon, the two-lane road was all but empty of vehicles.

Night had fallen by the time we reached Leura. Here we would meet Tom and Margaret the following morning. The village was deserted. Ours was the only car on the streets, and judging by the icy feel of our windshield, the temperature had dropped below freezing. Where to stay? A week in and around Sydney had killed our budget. The only way to resurrect it was to sleep in a campground. We found one near the railway station. Our site consisted of a patch of lawn, hard against the back of a cabin. Inside, people were cozy and warm. The ground shook when trains thundered by.

By the time our numb fingers had wrestled the tent into shape, we had given up all thoughts of dinner. To warm ourselves, we crossed over the rails and walked down Main Street. People were eating meals, drinking wine, and laughing in the three restaurants that were open. It was tempting to trample our budget once and for all, yet we recognized the predicament as a test. To carry on, to complete our goal of circling Australia, we would have to steel ourselves to cold and hunger.

I remember little of our first day in the Blue Mountains, perhaps because I was constantly shivering. We slept in clothes and sweaters, but still the chill found us. Tom and Margaret appeared at the appointed hour. After a round of coffee and pastries at a quiet café, we set off on a walk.

The geography of the Blue Mountains suits the city-based explorer. You can ride a train from Sydney to Leura or any of several other towns on the plateau, hike all day or for several days, emerge from the wilderness at a railway stop, and catch the first train home.

Down a narrow path shaded by tree ferns and eucalypts, we followed Tom until the land fell away before us. Far, far below we could see the green pinwheels of treetops. Forest spread for miles and miles until it folded over the horizon. As we took in the view, a cacophony of squawks filled the air, followed by a whirring of wings. Birds landed in a leafless tree above us. They were as big as hawks and black save for yellow markings on their cheeks and tails. The bills were massive and hooked. Suddenly it clicked—these were yellow-tailed black cockatoos, a species of parrot we had seen on Tasmania. The cockatoos promptly began ripping off strips of bark, hunting for the larvae of moths and beetles.

We picked our way along the brink, seeing other walkers occasionally, but mostly having the bush and the view to ourselves. Birds flitted, flapped, croaked, and sang—New Holland honeyeaters, eastern whipbirds, golden whistlers, and exquisite little finches called red-browed firetails. Vertigo set in on a few occasions. When the track broke free of bush, we found ourselves standing on rocky knobs. There were no railings. One misstep, and the result would be a long and hopeless fall.

There were waterfalls, the grandest of them called Bridal Veil. A run of clear weather had dried out the stream, and the veil had contracted to a rope, white and twisted. After the flatness of the interior and the urban mayhem of Sydney, we found the Blue Mountains a feast for the eye.

John Muir, however, was unimpressed. Visiting in January 1904, he wrote that the Blue Mountains were "sadly in need of lofty white summits." "The falls," he said, would "be thought nothing of" in California.

The crystal light of midday yellowed, then reddened as the afternoon wore on. We burst out of the trees and found ourselves among several dozen tourists milling around an overlook. Ahead, across a chasm, lay the Three Sisters, the best-known natural landmark in New South Wales.

Presented to good advantage in rosy light, the Sisters rose from a peninsula of rock that extended from the cliff edge. Each consisted of a pinnacle fifty or sixty feet high, separated from the next by a narrow gap. The Sisters were all but naked. Erosion and gravity had scrubbed them clean, revealing horizontal layers of sandstone. Beyond them lay a deep valley, miles across and filled with blue haze. A mist of eucalyptus oil exhaled by the forest give the mountains their eponymous hue.

We gawked, heard conversations conducted in a half-dozen languages, and took the obligatory photos. A Japanese family recruited me to shoot their picture, and so did a group of Indonesians.

The Three Sisters, according to legend, were once a trio of Aboriginal girls whose father turned them to stone. The father's intent was to protect his daughters while he was away on a journey (he would delithify them upon his return), but warriors killed the man, and the girls stayed stoned. Late-twentieth-century Americans fancy themselves inventors of the dysfunctional family, but tribal legends such as this challenge the patent. All over the world, fathers, daughters, mothers, and sons have galloped roughshod over each other since the beginning of time.

After a restaurant meal in Leura, Tom and Margaret went off to a backpacker's hostel while Debbie and I retired to the tent. I wondered who was more frustrated with her husband: the elegantly dressed, stone-faced woman we saw in the restaurant consuming a dinner by candlelight while her mate sat opposite, transacting business on a cell phone, or Debbie, whose mate had hauled her into the cold mountains on a shoestring.

Our second night proved more bitter than the first. It was 20 degrees Fahrenheit when we wriggled into our sleeping bags, and not much warmer when we crawled out in the morning. No wonder the Aborigines avoided the Blue Mountains until recent times. The oldest archaeological site, at Lyrebird Dell near Leura, dates to 12,000 years ago, but most signs of human occupation date to only the last three millennia. The mountains, it seems, were too damned cold.

In the morning we caught a train to the village of Wentworth Falls. Tom and Margaret met us and directed us to a Bavarian bakery. The cold air, German accents, and bundled-up look of the customers could have convinced me someone had drugged us during the night and transported us to the Alps. Tom had a plan. We could hike the Charles Darwin Trail, enjoy fine views of cliffs, valleys, and bush, and wind up at a place called the Conservation Hut. There we would stop for tea.

Treading in the footsteps of Darwin provided a near duplicate of the previous day's adventure. We trudged through bush thick with tree ferns and banksia, walked in the shade of wattles and eucalypts, and gazed down like Greek gods into a forested valley that seemed to go on forever. I thought about heaving a stone into the void, as Darwin did, but resisted the temptation. Tourists were scarce here in 1836, but this is no longer the case.

We followed the cliff edge as it snaked in and out of the massif. Erosion had carved great crescents from the escarpment, and Darwin called the cutouts "bays." The label was apt. With a little imagination I could see the clifftop as a shoreline, the blue-green canopy below as a sea stirred by wind, and the indentations coves in which ships might anchor. Darwin pronounced the view "extremely magnificent," displaying an enthusiasm that was rare for him in a country he found, at least for the most part, desolate and ugly.

After tea at the Conservation Hut, we enjoyed a second round in the dining room of the grand but careworn Hydro-Majestic Hotel. Then we made good-byes. Tom and Margaret were heading back to Sydney.

I had developed a great affection for this long-lost cousin of mine, and perhaps he for us. Farewells came hesitantly. Knowing our travels were unlikely to bring us back to Sydney, we expected that the good-byes we were making were final.

We checked into Gardiner's Hotel in Blackheath that night, unwilling to face another night in the freezer. The hotel was a stodgy old place, pub downstairs, spartan rooms upstairs, hard by the Great Western Highway that ran through the middle of town. Darwin had slept here, the proprietor told us, and what was good enough for the Father of Modern Biology, we reckoned, was good enough for us.

In the Charles Darwin Lounge, the air was tropical. A woodburning stove hissed and crackled in the corner, and by a stroke of luck, the off-track betting parlor with nine television monitors in the next room stood empty and silent. I threw the budget over the brink and ordered a tumbler of Scotch, a cup of boiling water, and a schooner of Guinness Stout. Cutting the whiskey with the scalding water as my old New Zealand friend

Peter Miller used to do, I gave my insides the warming they needed. Debbie ordered a Bailey's, then another.

While sipping, I leafed through a history of the hotel. Andrew Gardiner, the original proprietor, had won a free ticket to Australia by being convicted in Oxford of a felony. The year was 1818. Gardiner's sentence was "transportation," which meant seven years of labor in Britain's Australian penal colony. After his liberation, Gardiner procured a land grant from the New South Wales governor and built the hotel. It opened in July 1831, five months and sixteen days before a twenty-two-year-old naturalist named Charles Darwin set sail from Devonport, England, on the *Beagle*.

Reading on, I learned that the edifice we would sleep in was not the building Darwin had visited. The original hotel was sold by Gardiner in 1847, converted to a pigsty, refurbished, reopened, run into the ground, and, in 1938, demolished. Later a new inn rose from the ruin of the old. We groaned, having just laid out seventy dollars to sleep on a sagging bed in a cold room without bath in an edifice that Darwin had never set foot in.

The day that was supposed to be our last in the Blue Mountains brought trouble. All was going well. We had visited Govett's Leap, a waterfall named for a Devonshire man named William Romain Govett. Govett never leaped from the Leap, but rather surveyed the area around it in the early nineteenth century. Enjoying a warm, cheery day hiking the sunny cliff edge, we looked at birds, admired the crimson blossoms of a shrub called mountain devil, and steamed the chill from our marrow. By the time we drove away, the sun was setting and the valleys had filled with blackness. The temperature plummeted. We decided to pass without stopping through the last of the mountain villages, descend to an interior plain, and camp where the air would be warmer.

We had passed the village of Mount Victoria and were approaching the place where the highway plunged off the edge of the plateau when we heard a loud *snap!* The car's life functions ceased. Powered only by momentum, I swerved onto the shoulder.

Debbie said something unladylike, I words inappropriate for a gentleman. It was cold and dark. We were stranded on a lonely stretch of road, the car loaded, its engine as dead as a *Diprotodon*.

For lack of a better idea, I turned the key. The starter motor spun and whined. Something was amiss. The engine wasn't turning. I tried again and again. "Timing chain," I said finally, too depressed for verbs. "Big money." Odysseus would have blamed Poseidon.

We walked. A quarter mile back toward the village, we came to a garden center. It was past closing time, but a friendly woman named Margaret welcomed us inside. She asked if we were members of the Automobile Club. We were, thank Zeus. On Tasmania we had signed up for a "Plus" membership. It entitled us to free towing and, if a mechanical problem was big enough to maroon us for forty-eight hours, three nights of lodging and a rental car. Margaret made the call. A mechanic, she reported, was on his way to meet us.

Ten minutes later, a white pickup truck displaying the Automobile Club insignia parked behind the corpse. Two young men jumped out, one tall and blond, the other shorter, with dark hair that stood up as if charged with static electricity. The tall one was Paul, the other Oliver. "Let's have a look," said Paul politely. "Please unlatch the bonnet." Within seconds we had the diagnosis. "It's your timing gear," Paul said. "This car has a gear rather than a chain. It's made of something like fiberglass. Yours has probably shattered. You won't be going anywhere for a while. I'm sorry."

We were sorrier. Our bruised and bloodied budget, in guarded condition after our stay in the mountains, had gone the way of the gear. Yet we knew we were lucky. Had the problem occurred on the Stuart Highway between Adelaide and Alice Springs, we would have been up a creek, a perilously dry one. As it was, Paul and Oliver offered to drive us around town until we found lodgings. Our car would be towed later. "Take what you need for the night," Paul said.

The drama continued. Every hotel and guest house in town was full. Same story for the next town. It was the Queen's Birthday weekend, a three-day holiday. Every Blue Mountain bed had someone sleeping in it. Paul and Oliver had the patience of chess masters, driving us places and helping make telephone calls. In the end, despite all their efforts, no place would take us in.

Debbie remembered a sign she had seen for a guest house somewhere up a side road. Oliver knew the place. "Worth asking," said Paul. His tone of voice said otherwise. The most elegant place in town, this would be the last place to have a vacancy, and its prices would exceed the hundred dollars per night the auto club was willing to pay.

We knocked. A rosy-cheeked woman beckoned us inside, smiling. "I'm so sorry," she said after hearing our story. "With the holiday, we're all full up." A pause. I could see thinking going on beneath curly locks. "Are there four of you?"

"Oh no," said Debbie, as Oliver and Paul chuckled behind her. "Just two."

Delight broke over the woman's face. "This is what I can do. We have a small room with single bed that we normally don't let to guests. However, seeing your predicament, do you think you could manage?" We could. But there was the matter of cost. I explained our ailing budget, the likely cost of repairs, and the hundred dollars the club would pay. Under the circumstances, we could pay no more. "That'll be fine," said our benefactress. She introduced herself as Annette Lenton, and shook our cold hands.

The Royal Automobile Club of Tasmania would pay for three nights at the Manor House. The night we arrived, Annette led us past a library in which guests sipped sherry beside a roaring fire, past a billiard room, past a lounge in which children sat around a television, past a door that led to a hot tub we were encouraged to use, and down a dimly lit corridor. Our room was number twenty-five. "I bet you could use a little dinner," said Annette. "Freshen up, and join us in the dining room."

Grilled calamari, prepared with exquisite delicacy, segued to chicken served with spicy tomato sauce. Dessert consisted of cream-filled pastries made with wattle seed, doused with chocolate sauce and fresh cream. Annette had suggested I run across to the Imperial Hotel and fetch ourselves some wine. What was another ten or fifteen dollars on top of a five-hundred-dollar repair bill? The wine, the meal, the congenial company, the plush surroundings, and the hot tub soothed our tattered nerves.

Declining the Automobile Club's offer of a rental car, we spent our forced holiday reading, writing, and resting. Nearly everyone in town, the postmistress, the antique dealer, the pianist up the street, the old woman in the secondhand bookshop, soon knew our story. People saw us on the street and inquired about progress.

Immersing myself in Rupert Murdoch's *Sydney Morning Herald,* I caught up on the news. Some of my gleanings:

Over the holiday weekend, five people died in highway accidents in New South Wales, four hundred drivers were arrested for drunkenness at the wheel, and 7,290 received speeding tickets.

Exotic weeds now made up fifteen percent of Australia's flora.

Makers of didgeridoos were wiping out mallee trees.

Four hundred sixty-three exotic pasture plants had invaded Australia since 1947, ninety-five percent of which were of no interest to cattle and sheep.

A story titled "Killer Weeds: The Most Dangerous Half-Dozen" told of the rubber vine, which choked Queensland's rivers; the blue thumbergia, which "smothers" native plants; the hymenachne, which threatened tropical wetlands in a manner not explained; the para grass, which among its many crimes "destroys bird breeding grounds"; the bitou bush, which crowded out native coastal vegetation; and the cithel pine, which "displaces native trees, salinises soil, and reduces animal resources," whatever that means.

My favorite item: "Meat Study Sparks Health Fears over Sausage-Shaped Pet Food."

The morning our car was to be ready, it wasn't. David Hopkins, the friendly mechanic in charge of the job, explained that a part that belonged in a box with another part was missing. He had ordered the absent item. Its arrival was imminent.

At two in the afternoon, we hiked up the road to the garage. Another night in the Manor House was out of the question. If a fourth night in Mount Victoria became necessary, we would camp on someone's lawn.

At three the car was ready. Paul, finishing the job for David, turned the key. The engine cranked but no cylinders fired. David was summoned. It turned out that the distributor was mounted incorrectly. Soon the motor roared to life.

David and I took the patient for a test drive. A superb lyrebird hopscotched across the road as we started out, and David delivered an impressive account of the bird's life history. He had learned it all at a lecture by Jim Frazier.

When we returned to the garage's driveway, I expected to see triumph on Debbie's face. Instead I saw a wrinkled brow. "What's that stuff leaking from underneath the engine?" she asked.

It turned out that one of the transmission's cooling lines had cracked, probably during the course of repairs. Up went the car, and off came the line. David tried welding it, without success. A frown spread over his face. "Might have to order a new one," he said. "Wouldn't be here until tomorrow."

At this point a truck driver sauntered over. We had spoken with him earlier in the day. He told us that he and his wife would spend their next holiday visiting the Mack Truck factory in New Jersey. "Let's have a look," he said.

The man was a wizard with a welding torch. In a twinkling the hole was neatly closed. "No charge," he said, laughing.

The telephone rang while we waited for Paul to install the line. David answered it. "For you," he said, handing me the receiver.

It was Colin Lenton, Annette's husband and the co-owner of the Manor House. "Ed, Annette and I have decided that you and Debbie should have a rest and make a fresh start in the morning. No worries about the cost. This one's on us."

And so we spent one more night in palatial comfort. Annette and her children were making Christmas decorations, and we lent a hand. The fact that this was June, not December, bothered us only a little. Days were short, nights long, and the air after sundown turned crisp and cold. A chorus of carolers would have seemed fitting. Several years earlier, a clever person in the Blue Mountains had conceived a scheme in which hotels, guest houses, and restaurants would stage "Christmas in July." Australians who were tired of celebrating the holiday in the scorching summer could come to the mountains and enjoy an old-fashioned, northern hemisphere Christmas. The idea caught on, and the Manor House was getting prepared.

In the morning we set off at last. We drove all day, threading through small towns and traversing miles of grazing country. The place names along the way were as distinctly Australian as the gum trees beside the road—Cullen Bullen, Mudgee, Gulgong, Dunedoo, and Mendooran.

The drive's highlight came along a quiet stretch of road. On the pavement ahead of us we spied a group of birds, dark and vaguely crowlike, running along like a high-school track team. We stopped and climbed out. The birds flew into a gum tree and perched side by side on a limb. Binoculars revealed them to be apostlebirds, named for their habit of associating in groups of twelve.

Consummate cooperators, apostlebirds stick together through thick and thin. They build nests, incubate eggs, brood and feed nestlings, eat, drink, preen, and sleep communally. In summer they feed mostly on insects and spiders, and in winter on seeds. Studies show that groups vary from six to eighteen but always consist of a breeding pair and a mob of offspring.

Max and Pat Mapleson had dinner waiting for us in Coonabarabran. Pat was a poet, artist, mother, and housewife. Max ran a biological supply house in Sydney for years, sold it, and retired. He and Pat searched for a country town where they could accomplish two things: enjoy a quiet life amid congenial surroundings, and contribute in some way to the economy and cultural life.

Coonabarabran won out because it was a friendly place, near Warrumbungles National Park, and in need of an astronomical observatory. The
area already possessed a world-class observatory known as Siding Springs,
which attracted astronomers from around the world, but the public could
only visit it during the day. People could look *at* the telescope, one of the
largest in the world, but not *through* it. "This town," Max said, "needed a
public observatory, and we built one."

In a workshop attached to the Maplesons' house, Max constructed the
observatory's dome, one piece of lumber at a time. Contractors built the
edifice it sat on. Inside, Pat painted murals depicting the constellations and
the legends associated with them. Together they bought telescopes, hired
the staff, and paid the bills. The place was called Skywatch.

During dinner, Max checked his watch several times. Halfway through
dessert, he stood up, saying, "We'd better get going." We looked to Pat.

"You go," she said. "I'll look after the dishes."

Clad in an old sweater and blue jeans, Max sprang out the door. A few
minutes behind him, we followed his directions as best we could, picking
our way through a patch of bush, stepping between strands of barbed
wire, and emerging on the observatory lawn. Inside, beneath Pat's painting of Orion, a half dozen people gathered.

Soon a young, square-jawed man bustled in, introduced himself as
Rob, told us a few things about Skywatch, and led us out a door and into
the cool night. Everything was dark save for a tinge of rose in the west. We
walked up a ramp that curved to a second-story viewing platform. Several
telescopes were mounted there on pedestals.

"Let's orient ourselves," Rob said. "First of all, who can show me the
Southern Cross?" Hands shot up. A boy of eight aimed an index finger
straight at the mark. "And the pointer stars?" Half the hands came down.
A lesson followed about navigating south of the equator. Find the cross,
and extend an imaginary line through its long axis. Then strike a perpendicular bisector through an imaginary line connecting two so-called
"pointer" stars. The perpendicular bisector and the cross's extended axis
intersect at the south celestial pole. The southern hemisphere has no pole
star, no antipodean Polaris.

All this was old-hat. We had camped in the bush dozens of nights and
used stars to find our celestial bearings. Only when Rob spoke of a great
emu in the Milky Way did our interest quicken. The emu was a dark,
long-necked shape than ran through the constellation's north-south axis.

It looked as advertised: long of leg, round of body, serpentine of neck. I wanted to ask what sort of phenomenon the dark bird in the glittering galaxy represented, but before I could speak, we were whisked into Max's homemade dome.

I know little of telescopes and so will be vague rather than inaccurate. The monster we looked through was powerful. "Fantastic," said Rob, who had been struggling to find something. "It will be faint and you won't see much of a tail, but have a look. I've found a comet that the experts say will give us some fine viewing next year." And so we had our first look at Hale-Bopp.

In due time people would be calling Hale-Bopp the comet of the century, automobile collisions would be caused by drivers craning their necks to admire it, and a houseful of crazy Californians would commit collective suicide on the orders of a guru who maintained that a spaceship parked behind Hale-Bopp would carry them to a better world. This night the comet looked like a fuzzy star.

The following day we hiked among the Warrumbungles, a group of old volcanic dikes and necks that rose like the ruins of castles. Max and Pat had encouraged us to spend the day climbing to a cluster of rocky outcrops known as Grand High Tops.

The morning was cool enough for sweaters, yet warm enough for shorts. From the park's visitor center in a grassy basin, we drove into the forest and parked at a trailhead. A footpath led steadily upward, passing clumps of introduced prickly pear cactus and crossing and recrossing a brook. The valley was littered with boulders and shaded by tall trees. Among the leaves, birds abounded. We had just set off when Debbie identified two species new to us—the yellow-tufted honeyeater, a greenish bird with a black mask and yellow tufts that looked like ears, and the crested shrike-tit. The shrike-tit had a striped black and white coiffure that Elvis Presley might have envied, and its belly glowed electric yellow. Paying us no heed, it ripped off strips of bark in an energetic search for insects.

Eventually the track broke free of eucalypt forest. We stepped quickly past the Bread Knife, a towering dike isolated by erosion so that it formed a freestanding wall of rock. Slashed by faults and only a few feet thick, the Knife looked ready to topple at any moment.

On the first of the several summits known as Grand High Tops, we paused to rest and soak up the view. Below lay gray-green forest, above aquamarine sky. To the west spread the tawny, arid plains of the New

South Wales interior. It pleased me to think that Ayers Rock or Uluru lay beyond the western horizon.

We were beginning our descent when Debbie's sharp eyes picked a koala out of a dark tangle of eucalyptus leaves. We investigated. Indeed, a koala was cuddled there in a fork, shaded by foliage, sound asleep.

Looking closely, we could see that the animal's forepaws grasped the limbs with two digits opposing three, a koala trademark. The nose was small, and the dark stain that males have on their chests was missing. This koala was a female.

The koala is an animal that benefited from European settlement, at least initially. Aborigines had a taste for the fleshy marsupials, which they captured with long poles fitted with loops of rope. Once on the ground, a koala was killed with a club. Roasted, it offered a feast of protein, something Aborigines enjoyed infrequently. Archaeological evidence shows that koalas declined sharply in range and number during Aboriginal times. After English settlement, murder, mayhem, and disease made Aborigines scarce, koala populations began to rebound.

The biologists Anthony Lee and Roger Martin tell of a place near Sydney where koalas vanished before the English settled the area in the early nineteenth century. By 1870, koalas were numerous there again. Yet the charmed relationship between the slow-moving marsupial and Europeans came to a predictable end. Furriers in London discovered the beauty of the pelage, and soon koala coats and embellishments became the rage. Fashion led swiftly to slaughter. By the time the species was granted protection in New South Wales in 1909, millions had been shot or trapped.

Luckily for the koala above us, the exportation of its skin was no longer legal, and our stomachs were full of Pat's roast lamb sandwiches. The only thing we asked of it was a photograph. I climbed a nearby tree to get a pleasing angle. The koala slept. I shouted and waved an arm. The koala slept. "G'day," I cried. "Wake up!" The koala slept. Masters of slumber, koalas may snooze nineteen hours a day.

A few minutes later, after some patient waiting, the animal roused. It reached out a gray, velvety arm, pulled in some leaves, and chewed. Five minutes later it was dozing again. Meanwhile I came away with a photo.

The rest of the walk seemed an anticlimax. We wound our way back to the car through a gum forest blackened by wildfire. Birds ran afternoon errands in the trees, among them yellow robins, speckled warblers, striated pardalotes, brown-headed honeyeaters, and a laughing kookaburra that sat immobile like a porcelain reproduction of itself. On and under rocks we looked for lizards. We had still not seen a goanna, and our longing for a sighting had grown into infatuation. Perhaps the air was too cool. No lizards of any kind appeared, not even one of the brown, striped, you've-seen-one, you've-seen-them-all skinks that scurry everywhere in Australia. We hoped our luck would change in Queensland.

Out of the woods and back in the meadow, we found the sun still shining brightly. It cast a warm glow on kangaroos bounding and grazing on the green. The animals were eastern greys, taller and lankier than the brush-tailed rock wallaby we had seen near the end of the hike. Their tails were long and sleek, like snakes. Kangaroos no longer surprised us. Eastern greys seemed as familiar now as white-tailed deer back home. The blush of novelty had faded.

In a luminous sky brushed lightly with cirrus clouds, a wedge-tailed eagle traced figure-eights in an updraft.

We were turning onto the road leading out of the park when a flash of color arrested us. "Out of this world!" cried Debbie, and so they were—turquoise parrots, the most exquisitely marked bird we had seen in Australia. There were about two dozen, all trailing long, slender, lime-green tails trimmed in gold. The bellies of the birds were a vivid yellow, while turquoise ringed their eyes and beaks.

Like falling leaves, the parrots fluttered to the ground amid a patch of weeds. Creeping closer, we saw them plucking seeds from withered flowers. We noted now that the yellow of the male turquoise parrots crept far up their breasts, and that both genders had wings trimmed with indigo. Males also sported a finishing touch—scarlet epaulets. We might have lingered, gawking, until the light failed entirely, but the birds sent us home by levitating in unison and rocketing away to the far side of the valley.

Our final adventure in the land of Laestrygons brought us close to an apparition that bore a striking resemblance to *Archaeopteryx,* the earliest fossil bird. We had said good-bye to Max and Pat more than twenty-four hours earlier. Bound for the Queensland border, we were rumbling down a dirt road when the navigator sounded the alarm. "Something ran across the road and dove into tall grass," said Debbie. "It was a bird, I think."

We bustled out. Debbie led the way to the spot where the thing had vanished. We could see a parting of the blades where an animal had slipped beneath a strand of fencing wire and plunged into the grass.

"How big was it?" I asked. When in doubt about a wildlife sighting, always interrogate the witness.

Debbie held out her hands wider than her shoulders. About thirty inches.

"That's big," I said. "Color?"

"Sort of a rusty brown all over."

"General impressions?"

"Well, it must have been a bird, because it had a beak. It looked unkempt, like it could use some grooming. And the tail—it was long like a pheasant's, but thicker."

"This is perfect pheasant habitat," I said, nodding toward the fields that bordered the road. "Ring-necked pheasants were introduced to Australia, just as they were to the United States. Do you suppose the bird was a—"

"No way. I've seen plenty of pheasants. This thing was bizarre."

Just then, off to our left, we spied a rusty shape. It burst through tall grass into the open, then darted back where it came from. We hurried over for a look. Following the field edge, we glimpsed the bird three more times. Unfortunately, on each occasion it vanished the exact moment we spied it.

In hopes of finding the bird in a book, Debbie walked back to the car. I advanced along the road, thinking it might flush one more time.

For a hundred strides I saw only grass, blue sky, and a pied currawong flapping overhead. Then, at the point where the lane plunged into forest, a thing that looked like a miniature hang-glider shot across the road at chest height. It had red eyes and feathers streaked with white. The apparition—it was a bird—sailed into a lower field, making a few uncertain beats of stubby wings along the way. I lost sight of the UFO when it plunged into the forest.

When I reached Debbie, she had Graham Pizzey's *Field Guide to the Birds of Australia* open to the mound-builders, pheasants, and lyrebirds. A forefinger touched our suspect—the pheasant coucal.

The evolutionary biologist Alan Feduccia points out that *Archaeopteryx,* were it alive today, would closely resemble the pheasant coucal, which, in fact, is not a pheasant at all, but a cuckoo. Like the coucal, *Archaeopteryx* probably flew with little grace and spent a good deal of time running and climbing. Even the diets of the birds were similar. The pheasant coucal eats lizards, birds, birds' eggs, and a variety of other small, helpless creatures. All these would have appealed to *Archaeopteryx*, which lived in Bavaria before the invention of schnitzel.

Francis Ratcliffe, author of the Australian natural history classic *Flying Fox and Drifting Sand,* said the coucal suggested to him "an urchin dressed up in a big brother's cast-off suit." This is an apt description of a bird so bumbling on the ground and clumsy in flight that one wonders how it manages to survive.

Debbie's discovery of the koala and the coucal underscored a truth that had grown increasingly clear: Odysseus made a mistake in leaving Penelope at home.

6

Circe

SHORTLY AFTER ODYSSEUS escaped the Laestrygons, he landed on Aeaea. Circe, the resident witch, daughter of the sun, and an incorrigible seductress, promptly turned two and twenty of the Greeks into swine. She tried making a pig out of Odysseus, too. It happened thus: she gave him a potion, tapped him with a wand, and cried, "Get you to your sty, wallow there with your friends!" Yet the Trojan Horse's inventor outmaneuvered her. Hermes had given him a magic herb. Odysseus swallowed it, gained immunity to Circe's magic, and avoided swinedom.

Seeing that the tables had been turned, Circe implored the Greek to ravish her. "I pray you sheath that sword," she begged, "and let us two lie together that we may mingle our bodies and learn to trust one another by proofs of love and intercourse." It was a dirty job, but somebody had to do it. For a year Odysseus mingled shamelessly with Circe and cultivated her trust. Meanwhile the pigs became humans again, and all fell into a life of ease and contentment.

Debbie and I were transformed into swine, too, then fell into a state of bliss. It happened like this. I had written ahead to a place called O'Reilly's Rainforest Guest House, known to many Australians simply as "O'Reilly's." The guest house occupies an Aeaea of private land high amid Lamington National Park, a 50,000-acre tract of temperate and sub-tropical rain forest just over the New South Wales border. O'Reilly's seemed the perfect place to introduce ourselves to the seductions of Queensland. There was only one hitch. The plush beds, fine food, and first-rate naturalist programs would bankrupt us. So I wrote to Peter O'Reilly, the hotel's grand old man. I told him the truth: that a poor, wandering writer and his wife could use a bit of relief from one-pot cooking and a couple of nights in a soft bed. In return I promised to write about the visit in my weekly newspaper column, and to mention O'Reilly's in a book I would write if we managed to survive the snakes, spiders, and crocodiles. Frankly, I had doubts about the ethics of accepting handouts from a place I would later describe for readers. In order to guarantee that I could face myself in a mirror the next time I came across one, I made a vow: I would tell the plain truth even if it meant biting the hand that fed me.

The reply reached us in Sydney. It was signed by Trevor Burslem, the marketing manager. "We would be happy to host you and your wife for two nights," he said.

And so it came to pass that we threaded our way up a narrow mountain road that ended at the guest-house door. Night was coming on, and in our hurry to reach the dining room before the evening meal, we nearly drove over several brown and king quail out for their evening constitutionals. Shan, a young, raven-haired woman with a fetching smile, led us through a labyrinth of corridors and covered walkways to a second-story room. From the picture window, we looked out to find the entire western sky aflame.

In the dining room, in the fifth month of our beans-and-rice expedition, we feasted merrily on salads, breads, meats, vegetables, puddings, cakes, and coffee. At first I had no idea why the well-dressed people with whom we shared a table cast us disapproving glances. Then it struck me. Faced with delicacies we hadn't seen in ages, we were transformed into swine.

From padded chairs, we looked out a picture window to a wooden shelf. Pieces of fruit lay scattered there, and among them crouched a mammal a little larger than a chipmunk. It had round, bulging eyes, Mickey Mouse ears, and skin that hung from its flanks in folds. "Zeus!" I cried, choking on a medallion of pork. Before us loomed a creature we had searched for in vain since the day of our arrival—a sugar glider.

While we wallowed in main courses and desserts, the glider nibbled on fruit salad. The marsupial was a dead ringer for the flying squirrels we had left behind in North America. The only giveaway was the head. It was striped, not plain.

The sugar glider is a cousin of Australian possums. For about seventy days each spring, the female sails from tree to tree with a pair of offspring in her pouch. Flights can reach a staggering 150 feet. At times, sugar gliders eat sugar. They find it in the form of honeydew, the sweet excretions of certain sap-sucking insects. Sugar gliders also lap up eucalyptus resins that other arboreal marsupials cannot digest. The trick is having an oversized cecum (a cul-de-sac of the intestine) loaded with helpful bacteria. The bacteria break down the resins and, in payment for rent, share the spoils.

Debbie and I kept glancing at the glider, hoping to see it sail. Unfortunately, it was there one moment, gone the next. After a few courses of dessert, we shuffled off to an evening program optimistic that gliders would float across our paths often in days to come. We didn't know it then, but this would prove our only sighting of a sugar glider in Australia.

Before landing on a mattress that night, we borrowed a spotlight from Tim O'Reilly and set off to see what animals, if any, were hopping, gliding, and prowling out in the darkness. The night was cold. Inside thick sweaters, we shivered as we traced the forest edge, sweeping the terrain ahead with the beam. All was quiet. We heard only the distant hum of a generator and an occasional drift of laughter from the cocktail lounge.

Then came a new sound—a soft thump. I aimed the light in the noise's direction. Three kangaroos appeared, hunched over the lawn, grazing. One stood in profile, one faced us, and the third offered us its tail.

The animals cast us stoical glances, squinted, and went back to their chewing. We looked them over. With more than forty species of kangaroo to sort out in Australia, one must examine each animal carefully. These were chunky, small as kangaroos go, and in general almost exact duplicates of the Tasmanian pademelons we found at Mount Field. Their fur was gray-brown above, dirty white below. The faces looked timid and sheep-like. Yet something was different, and soon we realized what it was—rusty fur spread like a mantle over the kangaroos' shoulders and napes. Before us stood red-necked pademelons.

Kangaroos masticate like people who count how many times they chew before swallowing, which is to say slowly. Although their digestive processes are similar to those of sheep, macropods do not mash cud, as sheep do, but grind it right the first time.

On our way back to the lodge, we detoured a hundred feet down a track plunging into the rain forest. At one point the light struck eyeshine. The source proved to be a possum, dark and furry, its body shaped like a pear. It looked like a giant mouse with a weight problem. Tim O'Reilly had told us to watch for mountain brushtail possums, which tend to be almost black in color. Mountain brushtails have smaller ears than common brushies, and this animal fit the bill.

In the morning we clawed our way out of bed before first light. Michael O'Reilly, a soft-spoken man who had greeted us during our first swinish performance in the dining room, was leading a bird walk at 6:45. Coffee and muffins awaited downstairs. We fortified ourselves, then stepped outside. The air stung our faces, yet a hint of sunshine in the tree-tops promised warmth. Michael appeared, his neck wrapped in a plaid scarf. About twenty early risers appeared, and Michael, a man of prodigious memory, greeted every one by name.

Our leader held five plastic bags in his sinewy hands. Each held something different: seed, scraps of bread, ground meat, sultanas, shredded cheese. Without a word, Michael pulled out a few sultanas and tossed the fruit at our feet.

Before the first morsel hit the pavement, birds shot in like bullets. There were two, identical in size and shape. One was jet black, the other olive brown with scalloping on its upper back and belly. Brilliant orange-yellow spread over the nape and wings of the black one, and a dab of tangerine appeared like egg yolk on its forehead. The arrivals were regent bowerbirds, an attention-getting male and a camouflaged female.

Celebrities of the bird world, bowerbirds live in Australia, New Guinea, and nearby islands. All but a few species make complex display arenas called bowers, which are built by the males. There are "avenue bowers" that consist of two parallel walls of upright sticks rising above a twiggy platform, and "maypole bowers" consisting of one or two towers of sticks built around small trees. The trysting place of the regent bowerbird consists of a patch of forest floor, cleared and decorated with bric-a-brac such as bits of shell, leaves, and fruit. Within this area rise two palisades, about eight inches long, built of foot-high sticks erected ten inches apart. This structure is the bower.

Most of the year, the male regent bowerbird tends his masterpiece. Any time a prospective mate appears, he plucks up an item from his collection, dances, sings, and, if the female is willing, snuggles his cloaca against hers. At the height of the dalliance, the male excretes a smear of semen. He has no penis. Freud might postulate that the bowerbird builds his bower out of feelings of inadequacy. Who knows? The encounter over, the female ambles off to build a nest. She is a single parent. The male, trapped by his own possessions, cannot leave his bower. If he does, neighboring males come, trash the place, and raid his precious collections.

"Would you like a closer look?" asked Michael. He dropped a pinch of sultanas in my hand. Before I could ask Athena for luck, a male bowerbird was clutching my forefinger with hot, clawed feet. I nearly swooned.

Moving beyond the guest house's two-story buildings, we approached the rain forest. Trees formed a colonnade around the lawn, and from them came a cacophony of shrieks. "Parrots," someone whispered.

Indeed they were. Within seconds, Australian king parrots and crimson rosellas were bobbing at our feet. Others landed on our heads, raking sharp nails across our scalps, and fluttered on our shoulders. A mob of magpies dashed in, too. Michael moved like a windmill, dispensing seed here, sultanas there, cheese one moment, ground meat the next.

"One morning," he told us, "when the weather was warmer than it is today, we stood where we're standing now and looked up to the gutter over there. We saw a python. This wasn't unusual. The snakes crawl out on the roofs and gutters here to bask in the morning sunshine. A few of us were troubled because the python was in the process of swallowing a female bowerbird. Just having his breakfast, I suppose."

Farther along the forest edge, a turkeylike bird stepped from the shadows. It had an Elizabethan frill of yellow around its neck, and a head as red as an apple. We had seen the bird before—on Kangaroo Island, where it was introduced. Before us, strutting and pecking on its native soil, was an Australian brush-turkey, a common bird of Queensland rain forests and scrub.

A woman with a razor-edged nose asked if brush-turkeys were edible. "Rather than answer the question directly," Michael said, "let me give you a recipe developed by the O'Reillys when they settled here. Put a brush-turkey in a cooking pot along with a rock and some water. Then turn up the heat. When the rock is soft, the bird is ready for eating." We all laughed. It was an old joke, recycled deftly.

Our interests were turning to breakfast when Michael led us into a grove of trees. Beside the trail, he pointed to a structure that looked like a fairy house. Twigs were interwoven to form a carpet, and two parallel walls of foot-high sticks arched toward each other, nearly touching at the top. The attention to detail amazed me. The builder had even wallpapered the inside of the edifice with mashed-up leaves.

The carpet of twigs extended well beyond the walls. Littering it were odds and ends colored either blue or yellow-green—drinking straws, parrot feathers, bottle caps, flowers from a nearby bush, a plastic knife, a matching fork, and clothespins.

"G'day, Jacques," said Michael cheerfully. "Where are you this morning?" A bird hopped into view. It looked like an overfed blackbird, except that the longer you looked at it, the better you could see it wasn't black at all, but a very deep shade of bluish-purple. "Meet Jacques Aloysius McSatin," said Michael. He gave us the bird's résumé—star of two David Attenborough films, featured performer in numerous other documentaries, expert architect, ten years as resident Romeo of the bower before us, and seven years' work as an apprentice, learning the arts of love, bowerbird-style. The bird's feathers gleamed like satin, and its bill might have been carved of ivory.

Jacques was a satin bowerbird, and he proved himself to be fearless. Ignoring the mob of primates looming over his bower, he hopped down to snatch up sultanas. "I only give him a few," said Michael. "If food accumulated here, the brush-turkeys would come looking for it, and they might knock apart the bower."

The bowerbird vanished for a moment, and while he was gone, Michael picked up a greenish-yellow flower and dropped it inside the bower. "To the rest of us, the collection of odds and ends looks like rubbish, carelessly assembled," explained Michael. "But to this satin bowerbird, the individual items are as carefully arranged as flowers in a bouquet."

A moment later, Jacques was back. He cocked his head quizzically to one side, hopped into the avenue between the upright sticks, and snatched up the flower. He carried it out and dropped it exactly where Michael had found it.

Male bowerbirds take years learning how to build and tend a bower. In the beginning, the prospective architect's constructions are feeble. But slowly, by shadowing older males and helping them maintain existing bowers, and by playacting the role of the female in display-and-mating rehearsals, the apprentice learns the trade. The fact that bowerbirds live considerably longer than the average songbird probably has much to do with the long period required to attain breeding success. Females spurn the inept, bestowing their favors only on males that build, decorate, sing, and dance with panache. Evolutionary biologists speculate that females thus pick the males with the best genes, and in so doing they invest their energy in raising young with the greatest chance of flourishing.

With no female or juvenile on hand, Jacques had little to do but stare. We gawked, too, but stomachs rumbled. Soon we were marching back to the dining room. Thus began a day of walking, talking, learning, and feasting that ended after morning tea, lunch, afternoon tea, dinner, and a ten o'clock supper of bread, butter, and cold cuts.

The following morning we grunted to wakefulness an hour before dawn. Out the entrance road we walked, trudging a quarter-hour before our flashlight beam picked out a trail branching off to the left. Our urgent errand was to reach the base of a particular tree described to us by O'Reilly's resident wildlife photographer, Glen Threlfo. We had walked with Glen the preceding afternoon and found him a treasure-house of knowledge. He told us how to find the sleeping place of a particular Albert's lyrebird, one of the most elusive birds in Australia. If we arrived before first light, we would hear its morning chorale.

The bird, said Glen, would sing from the tree's uppermost branches at the first touch of sunshine. A mimic, it would belt out every song of the forest and probably toss in imitations of forest fires and an old-fashioned radio being tuned. Glen said the bird would work its way in increments to the forest floor, caroling at great volume as it descended.

Huddled with Debbie at the base of the tree, the forest around us a sea of blackness, I felt a pang of fear. There were no tigers prowling here, no lions, leopards, jaguars, or grizzly bears. Aside from deadly snakes, lethal spiders, and the dreaded, venomous gympie-gympie tree, there was really nothing to worry about. Our chances of surviving to enjoy another O'Reilly's breakfast were excellent. Why the anxiety? I couldn't explain it. The feeling was primordial, perhaps an utterance of ancient genes.

A shrill whistle, then another. From above? Again, two whistles. Yes. Either someone with a tin whistle was entertaining himself in the canopy, or an Albert's lyrebird was announcing the arrival of dawn.

As green light began to sift down to us, the lyrebird continued its performance, descending steadily toward the earth. We heard strange whistles and chatter, yet for the most part the air shook with imitations of other birds—southern logrunner, eastern whipbird, laughing kookaburra, Lewin's honeyeater, green catbird, grey shrike-thrush, satin bowerbird, paradise riflebird, and crimson rosella. Every voice of the mountains, it seemed, rang from the lyrebird's versatile throat.

In the middle of the show, the impressionist mimicked a woman coughing.

After breakfast, and after we checked out of our room, Glen Threlfo led us to a secret place where the Albert's lyrebird we visited at dawn staged courtship displays. The theater consisted of an opening in the woods where a tree had fallen. Vines lay over the ground, weaving in and out of each other to form a rope. They attached on one side to a sapling tree, on the other to a leafy bush. "Sit quietly," whispered Glen. "George will be with us shortly."

On cue, an Albert's lyrebird strutted into the clearing. One moment the bird seemed to sing far away, and the next it was creeping onto the vines. Glen whispered. We were sitting on a log about thirty feet from the display area, partly concealed from it by foliage. "Listen for three clicks that come before the whistle," Glen said. "They let you know George is doing his territorial call." The bird obliged. "Now watch him. He knows we're here, but he's relaxed. George and I are mates. I know what he fears—dingoes. When he hears the cracking of a stick, he thinks it's a dingo coming to eat him. So watch where you put your feet and hands."

Arms in our laps, boots planted on the ground, we waited. George raised his tail and folded it over his head. As he did, the filamentous inner feathers fanned out to form a silvery veil. Suddenly the veil began to shake, and the bird stood beneath it, hissing, crackling, and plucking the vines with his feet. "Watch," said Glen. "He'll play those vines like the strings of a guitar, and they'll make the tree and the bush on either side shake. That will get him really excited." We watched, awestruck. The bird sang, the veil shivered, powerful scaly feet plucked the vines, and the bush and the tree shook as if tossed by gusting wind. The show lasted about a minute.

"He has no steady girlfriend," said Glen, "so he shakes the trees, makes himself handsome, and produces all this noise. Partly it's for the benefit of Ernie, the lyrebird you hear in the distance. They shout abuse at each other all day. But George is really hoping a female will come along. If one does, and she's thoroughly impressed, she'll mate with him. Then she goes off and lays an egg. He does nothing because he's busy finding another girlfriend.

"The incubation is unusually long. The female doesn't go near the egg for several days, and then she sits on it only when she's inclined to, sometimes leaving for hours and letting the egg grow cold. After about six weeks, it hatches. With continuous incubation, scientists can hatch the egg in three. After the little one is out, it stays with the mother for a long time. About ten months."

The display completed, George trotted away. A minute or two later we heard him sing again, deep in the forest.

Life after O'Reilly's proved nearly as agreeable as the salad days when we were house guests. We ate now not in a wood-paneled dining room but in a meadow with a sunset view and rain forest all around us. Our bed was harder and lumpier than the one we had surrendered, but it had the advantage of birdsong in the morning and proximity to a satin bowerbird's playground. The campground lay only a short walk from the guest-house door.

At the bower near our tent, a dress rehearsal was staged. An immature male satin bowerbird, identical to the female save for a greenish throat streaked faintly with white, played the part of the ingenue. He strolled in and around the bower with the calculated diffidence of someone shopping for diamonds. The older male meanwhile squeaked, rattled, hissed, and produced a sound that Michael O'Reilly had likened to "two pieces of corrugated iron dragged over each other."

Both birds took the drama seriously, or so it seemed. We laughed when the older male picked up a flower in his bill and carried it to the faux-female. He was completely in earnest, yet looked silly, like a teenage boy who arrives at a girl's house with a corsage, holding it like a dead fish. The charade went on and on. We left before finding out whether the males stopped shy of consummating the liaison or went all the way, like Greek sailors of old.

Despite our shift to primitive accommodations, Debbie and I still enjoyed the run of the O'Reillys' library, thanks to visiting rights extended by Michael O'Reilly. This was a good thing. The winter solstice was only a couple days away, and evenings were dark and cold. The library offered warmth and comfort not available in a tent. Its drawback was that it was located beside the dining area, up a short flight of stairs. To get to the library we had to march past a salad bar, a buffet of main courses and side dishes, and a table covered with pies and pastries. Appealing fragrances drifted up to us, and houseguests filled the air with laughter, the clink of wineglasses, and the sound of knives skating over china plates.

Our third day in Lamington brought an eleven-mile hike. Lush subtropical rain forest flourished on the lower reaches of the plateau, nourished by volcanic soils, and a sparer, temperate rain forest covered the high

ground. We chose a route that traversed both habitats—along the Main
Border Track to Mount Bithongabel and a forest of Antarctic beech,
along the rim of an ancient volcano, and back to the campground by way
of Emerald, Toolona, Chalahn, Guongurai, Triple, and Elebana Falls.
Nothing inspires a hike more than crawling out of a sleeping bag on a
goosebump-provoking morning. We rose, dressed hurriedly, downed a
perfunctory breakfast, and set off.

The forest teemed with marvels. There were titanic trees alive with
birds, the trunks and limbs draped with vines, mosses, ferns, liverworts,
club mosses, and leafy epiphytes. We could hardly see the trees for the
vegetation plastered over them. Two hanging ferns were especially eye-
catching, the staghorn and the elkhorn. Each had a grotesque fleshy base
and fronds shaped like antlers.

More than a thousand species of plant inhabit the Lamington forests.
Our growing but rudimentary knowledge of Australian flora allowed us to
identify a fraction of them—booyong, satinwood, Australian red cedar,
foambark, hoop pine, and gympie-gympie. Eucalypts were generally conspicuous by their absence. Interestingly, while the genus *Eucalyptus* nearly
monopolizes the continent's desert and semiarid landscapes, its strangle-
hold loosens in the rain forest. No longer is every tree some kind of gum.
In the three-tenths of one percent of Australia covered by rain forest,
diversity rules.

The person who did more than any other to establish Lamington
National Park and preserve its forests was Romeo Lahey, a lumber tycoon.
Like a thoughtful hunter, Lahey killed what he loved, yet found space in
his soul for the paradox. He came to scout timber on the plateau in 1908,
stood humbled by the splendor of the rain forest, and underwent a roadside conversion. The Queensland government at this time was doing its
best to lure settlers into the area. The idea was to bring down trees and
replace them with dairy cows. Among the takers were the O'Reillys.

A born-again conservationist, Romeo Lahey lobbied to defend the
forest against the industry that had made him wealthy. Lamington was
declared a national park in 1915. For the O'Reillys, the news was catastrophic. Roads the government promised to create would not be built,
and without roads the transport of butter and cheese to market would be
impossible. What to do? The O'Reillys had an idea. They hacked a horse
path up the ridge to the farm, and, with a few modifications, converted

their ramshackle buildings into a guest house. The place opened for business in 1926. Today, O'Reilly Rainforest Guest House and Binna Burra Lodge, a facility founded by Lahey, serve as Lamington National Park's de facto visitor centers.

Along the trail we saw leaves, stems, and trunks, but little else. The vegetation was so thick that seeing through it to find a singing bird was usually impossible. We did manage a look at a logrunner, a striped, portly bird that ran along logs. Eastern whipbirds cracked often, and at several points we heard Albert's lyrebirds breezing through their repertoires. The bird we most wanted to see, the rare, elusive rufous scrub-bird, never poked its face from the scrub.

Several times we stopped to lift the hatch of a trapdoor spider. They abounded in the rain forest, and Glen Threlfo had shown us how to find their lairs, which had silken lids that looked like silver dollars. Most of the lids had spiders lurking behind them, poised to subdue passing insects. According to Glen, the spiders enjoyed long lives and averaged between twenty and thirty years of age. Were they deadly? "No," he said in deadpan. "If one bit you, you'd welcome death, but you wouldn't die."

Spiders disgust many people. I am drawn to them, and my trust in their good nature has never been violated. Only one organism in the forest made my skin crawl—*Ficus macrophylla,* the Moreton Bay fig tree.

Moreton Bay is a natural harbor near Brisbane, the capital of Queensland. The fig that bears its name is a strangler. It begins life as a tasty fruit, hitchhikes a ride in the digestive tract of a bird, and launches its diabolical career when the bird defecates. If a seed lands in a moist crotch between tree limbs, it germinates, puts out leaves, stems, and roots, and begins the long, ugly process of engulfing its host. Along the trail we saw dozens of trees that had aerial fig roots swarming over them like the arms of an octopus. Years are required for the roots to reach the ground. When they do, the soil provides a sudden influx of nutrients. A growth spurt follows, and swiftly the host is boxed in by fig roots. Over time the host dies and rots. The result is a fig tree whose trunk consists not of ordinary wood, but of a mass of scabby roots.

Midday brought a rendezvous with Jeanette Conway, Colleen Morgan, and a few other people we'd gotten to know at the lodge. Picnics are an art form in Australia. This one involved breads, cheeses, and meats carried by our friends from the hotel kitchen.

The meal's setting was glorious—mossy shade beneath a ceiling of Antarctic beech, enormous trees with leaves the size of thumbnails. Through a gap in the forest we enjoyed one of the grandest views in Australia. Jungle spread across a deep abyss, green mountains rumpled away to the horizon, and cottony clouds hung like dirigibles in a sky of electric blue.

At midafternoon we made good-byes and trekked on. We would have to move quickly to make it out of the woods by nightfall.

The light grew soft and dim as we picked our way past the boles of giant trees and through gorges crowded with the foliage of the stream lily, *Helmholtzia glabberima*. The lilies produced masses of narrow leaves that often stood taller than we did. Crowding up to streams, the plants manage to survive the torrents that thunder down the ravines after heavy rains.

There were two animals we wanted to search for, but the imminence of darkness demanded that we keep advancing. One object of interest was the platypus. With its shallow pools and mossy banks, Toolona Creek looked like platypus heaven. We also wanted to see the marsupial frog. This bizarre amphibian has a brown back and black sides, measures a smidgen more than an inch, wears a thin coat of slime, and resides only in and around the McPherson Ranges. The reproductive system of the frog startled scientists when it was discovered. The female lays eggs, and the male, clinging to her back, anoints them with sperm. Business as usual, at least for a frog. But here the amphibian's life history takes a weird turn. The male pushes into the fertilized egg mass, and tadpoles, bursting from gelatinous capsules, nose into pockets along the sides of their father's back.

From this point on, the male carries a hidden cargo. The tadpoles grow, sprout legs, reabsorb their tails, and eventually occupy so much space that they push against the stomach of the suffering father, making it hard for him to eat. In the end, about ten juvenile frogs pop out of the folds. The fact that the marsupial frog lives only in the land of mammalian marsupials is an extraordinary coincidence.

One birdcall held my attention more than any other that day, perhaps because I had just learned to recognize it—a mew like that of a wounded cat. We managed to focus binoculars on the vocalist and found it to be plump and radiantly green. It was a green catbird, unrelated to the gray catbird of North America. The plumage seemed like a mirror reflecting all the highlights and shadows of the rain forest. The green catbird is an oxymoron, a bowerbird that makes no bower.

Aware that we, too, would lack a bower that night if we failed to cover ground, we turned away from the bird and trudged on. Mile gave way to mile, waterfall to waterfall. The stream ran quietly after a stretch of clear weather, although we could see places where floods had recently scoured the banks.

The pools below the falls offered good spots to look for platypuses. Alas, none appeared. Nor did we find a marsupial frog. To all appearances, the forest was empty of wildlife and people. Only the occasional whistles and rattles of birds relieved our sense of aloneness.

Anticipating dinner, the guests at O'Reilly's were adjusting slips and neckties in brightly lit rooms. Meanwhile we slogged through dark woods. When the light failed, we felt for the track with our boots.

At the base of a massive brush-box tree, we sat, put heads in our hands, and discussed the idea of giving up and spending a cold, damp night in the forest. Courage revived with rest, however, and we crept on, probing for the path, stumbling, cajoling. Just as the blackness grew complete, the glow of lights seeped through the trees. It was the guest house porch, and we homed on the light like moths.

The following evening, our last in the McPherson Ranges, we piled into a bus driven by Rob South, O'Reilly's well-spoken and friendly maintenance chief. He was hauling a load of houseguests to a eucalyptus grove down the road. His aim was to find a greater glider, the largest of Australia's parasailing marsupials. Greater gliders are difficult to locate and rarely give away their presence by sound. Rob knew that a particular grove of trees hosted a population of them, and he invited us to join the hunt.

Twenty people in dinner dress climbed out of the bus and shuffled up a rough track. A few of us carried lights, and we did our best to help the crowd avoid falls and fumbles. The forest, only a few miles from the hotel, was open, dry, and characterized not by an extravagance of foliage but by tall, stately eucalyptus trees, thin of leaf, widely spaced. Through gaps in the canopy we saw stars glitter brightly.

On a sandy flat, Rob gathered the group in a circle and talked for a few minutes about the glider. It was absent in the rain forest, he said, and occurred only in eucalyptus groves that grew on the drier parts of the ridge. Like the koala, the greater glider fed almost entirely on eucalyptus leaves. It employed the same means to digest them, an oversized cecum loaded with cooperative bacteria.

The greater glider was an impressive animal, Rob said. It could measure nearly a meter (about three feet) from nose to tip of tail and occurred in two color phases, charcoal black and dirty white. It slept by day in a hollow tree, emerged after dark, and often made several glides to reach a feeding area. Rob said that scientists have measured flights and found that some exceed one hundred meters (more than three hundred feet).

As we walked, Rob scanned the trees with a spotlight. At last he spied something: two eyes shining high on a limb. "There." Those with binoculars focused on the spot. I saw a ragged looking mammal that looked like a plump possum, except that its tail was unusually long—twice the length of the body. One moment the glider was there, the next it was gone. Half the crowd never had a look.

In the morning, Debbie and I celebrated the sunrise by playing cat-and-mouse with George. I had staked out the most frequently used of the lyrebird's display arenas with photographic gear. The subject failed to appear. Rejoining me short of breath, Debbie said that George was staging performances on his other soundstage. Moving my gear, I set up at this other place. A half hour later, the bird appeared and danced.

That afternoon we were driving down the ridge toward Brisbane when a snake appeared in the road. It was a gorgeous thing, about four feet long, cream-colored with olive blotches. Immobile and twisted in a way that looked unnatural, the reptile appeared to be dead.

The snake was so handsome of color and pattern that I hated the thought of a car mangling its body. I pulled the Toyota onto the shoulder. Walking over to move the carcass, I saw the long, smooth torso grow taut. The snake was alive!

Roads provide perfect surfaces on which to warm cool blood, and they destroy snakes with merciless efficiency. If I failed to move quickly, this strip of asphalt would claim another victim. I found a stick. As I prepared to nudge the animal aside, I heard a car approaching at high speed. The snake's only hope was for me to snatch it up in my hands.

One matter had to be settled first: the snake's identity. This was Australia, venomous snake capital of the world. I believed the reptile to be a python. Pythons are nonvenomous. They kill by squeezing, and this one was too small to do me serious harm. To test the theory, I cast a hasty look at the lower jaw. If this was a python, I would find a row of heat-sensitive pits, organs that help the snake find its tucker. *Yes.* With two quick motions I pressed the snake's neck to the asphalt, grabbed it behind the head with my free hand, and pulled it from the ground. A second later, a dark sedan flew around the bend.

Meanwhile the ungrateful python squeezed foul-smelling musk onto me from glands beside its cloaca. Simultaneously it looped coils around my right arm and tightened like a blood-pressure cuff. The strength of the grip amazed me. I had handled captive pythons, some of them a dozen feet long and as thick around as a human thigh. This snake was a third that length, and far less imposing of girth, yet its strength was much greater. No wonder. Captive snakes laze around cages all day, while this reptile scaled tall trees and survived by the strength of its coils.

Freeing the python proved difficult. It refused to let me go. Eventually I coaxed it off my arm onto the limb of a tree. The tree had fallen well away from the road, and its demise had cut a hole in the canopy. Sunshine streamed in, giving the snake a perfect place for basking.

On the shortest day of the austral year, we drove into Brisbane, fetched a packet of letters from the Central Post Office, and turned the car north toward the Tropic of Capricorn. Ahead lay warm days in central and northern Queensland.

Reaching Buderim by day's end, we skipped the zoo, the koala farm, and the Dino Fun Park, and holed up for three nights with Ian Thelander, brother of our friend Beris Caine. The Thelanders, Ian and his wife, Gwen, were retired medical doctors. We were suffering from postpartum depression after leaving Lamington, and diagnosing our affliction, the Thelanders medicated us with home brew, deviled macadamia nuts, hot food, wine, and song. Gwen had launched a second career as an accompanist. Ian, active in local musical comedy productions, crooned for us in his booming baritone. As Gwen played accompaniment on a grand piano, we sang from early evening to midnight, working our way through "Lullaby of Broadway," "Swanee," "Old Kentucky Home," "Night and Day," "Two Sleepy People," and "Coming In on a Wing and a Prayer."

North of Brisbane, Australia's warm, tropical side began to reveal itself. The first morning we awoke in Buderim, we drifted into consciousness to find the air scented by flowers. Strange birdsongs filtered through the windows. It seemed as if we had climbed into bed in one country and stepped out in another.

Perhaps we had. Many people in Victoria and New South Wales spoke of Queensland as a savage place, a part of Australia in which we were likely to encounter misanthropic beasts and rednecks. The condescension and fear with which many Australians view the country's second-largest state reminded me of feelings in the northern United States toward the South. Indeed, we heard Queensland called the "Deep North." During World War II, when Singapore fell and it seemed that the entire western Pacific might be ruled by Tokyo, Australian leaders met in secrecy and agreed to a division that became known as the "Brisbane Line." North of the line, which passed close to Brisbane, Australian territory would be conceded to the Japanese without a fight. South of the line, the country would be defended. Mention the Brisbane Line to a dyed-in-the-wool Queenslander, we were told, and you can always provoke a lively discussion.

Queensland had occupied more than its usual share of the national spotlight lately. The election to Parliament of Pauline Hanson, the owner of a Queensland fish-and-chips shop, stirred the pot. Hanson was speaking out against Aboriginal land rights and Asian immigration, winning her a few friends but also making a rising tide of enemies.

To us, Queensland seemed a paradise. Broad swaths of the state had been converted to grazing land and sugar cane plantations, but the place still seemed largely an unfallen Eden, a wildlife lover's nirvana. Strolling around the Thelanders' neighborhood and tiptoeing through the acre of rain forest they tended behind their house, we spied six new birds. One species, the figbird, appeared while I was writing newspaper columns. Color flashed outside the window, and I looked up to find a half-dozen birds, each a duplicate of the next, swaying on branches barely strong enough to hold them. They had green backs, yellow bellies, black caps, and patches of bare skin around the eyes so luridly red that they appeared to be bleeding.

Stunning as I found the figbirds, their Technicolor feathers paled beside the blazing plumes of the scarlet honeyeaters we saw in the afternoon. Hovering, fluttering, darting their curved bills into flowers, the honeyeaters looked like well-fed butterflies.

Of all the birds we saw in Buderim, the one that engaged my interest most was number 235 on our list: the spangled drongo. We would later see this black bird with its fishlike tail all over eastern Queensland, yet the first sighting gave us the biggest thrill. We found a single individual, perched on a utility wire. Its body was sleek, its plumage glossy black and irregularly speckled with green. The tail was flared and notched like a fish's, and red eyes imparted a hint of the demonic. We guessed the drongo to be a member of the crow family until we saw it hunting insects. The thing flew like a flycatcher. It was deadly, chasing down every bug and butterfly we saw it pursue. Back at the house, we consulted our traveling library and learned that the spangled drongo is the lone Australian representative of a family that spreads across Africa, India, and Asia.

North of Buderim, we followed the Bruce Highway. It began as four lanes, narrowed to two, and soon plunged us into a sea of sugar cane that stretched all the way to Cairns and beyond. The cane grew where coastal rain forest once had stood, and although the present state of the landscape was far from natural, we found it green, leafy, and pleasing to the eye.

A harvest was under way. Signs warning of "cane trains" often delivered what they promised, pint-sized locomotives pulling carts loaded to the sky with cut cane, rattling down narrow-gauge tracks. In one place we saw smoke billowing into the air, and drawing near, we found a fire that had swept across a cane field to the highway. Hawks called whistling kites circled over the inferno. Stopping to watch, we saw one of the kites dart to earth, then flap off with a rodent in its talons. The birds know that fires send rodents running for their lives, and they hunt them mercilessly.

Our destination for the day was Rockhampton, a place Anthony Trollope proclaimed "so hot that people going from it to an evil place are said to send back to earth for their blankets." Trollope came in summer, we in winter. At noon the day was warm enough for T-shirts.

Near Mount Morgan, an old gold-rush town west of Rockhampton, we had arranged to stay with our friends Ian and Cathy Herbert. Telephoning to confirm the time of our arrival, Debbie asked if we could save the Herberts a trip to town by picking up groceries. The pantry was well stocked, Cathy reported, but fresh bananas would be appreciated.

In a country town made up of a newsagent's shop, a hotel (in rural Australia, "hotel" means a legal excuse for a bar), a grocery, and a farm supply store, Debbie went off to find bananas while I hunted for motor oil. We met later in front of the grocery. Debbie was grinning.

"You've got to see this," she said. The inside of the grocery was a shrine to Elvis. Glossy, larger-than-life photos of the Mississippi-born Presley hung on the walls, while an Elvis clock behind the cash register marked time by gyrating its pelvis. Debbie introduced me to the proprietor. He was a gaunt man, about Elvis's age, with hair pouffed and oiled. Black sideburns framed his bony face. Standing behind the counter, he pointed to a complete set of Elvis movies on videotape. He told us about his pen pal, a New York State park ranger who worked in the Adirondacks and exchanged information with him about Elvis.

Ian and Cathy put us up in an old farmhouse. By the time we arrived at the 1,300-acre property they call Belgamba, night had fallen, and the only wildlife we saw were translucent geckos that stuck by the dozens to the outside of the house. Like tree frogs, the lizards had adhesive toe-pads to help them hold on, and they eyed us warily. The Herberts ordinarily run the house as a bed-and-breakfast, but generously gave us the run of it. Up the hill, they inhabit a newer, more spacious home. Its deck afforded long views over a property that consisted of abandoned pastures and rocky, forested hills.

Ian, an electrical engineer, worked for the phone company until he and Cathy came to Belgamba. Now he taught part-time at the local state university, spending the rest of his time improving Belgamba, repairing equipment, and enjoying the fresh air. Cathy, born in London, spoke in crisp English that contrasted with Ian's relaxed Brisbane argot. She worked on the property full-time. Together the Herberts were making the former ranch into a wildlife reserve. The work consisted of stopping and reversing erosion on overgrazed slopes, digging out exotic plants, and reintroducing native vegetation destroyed when the land was cleared for pasture. Tracks maintained by the Herberts wound through Belgamba, each marked with wooden signs.

In the morning the Herberts served us breakfast and led us on a hike. We wore shorts, the winter air warm and agreeable after the dawn chill. Cathy gave us a four-page list of plants she had identified on the property so that we could keep track of things we saw. On the list were intriguing names such as "love flower" and "dysentery plant, or dog's balls."

As we climbed out of the valley, a creek ran beside us. Like so many watercourses in Australia, it was dry. Cathy and Ian called the stream the Dee.

We gained altitude slowly. Our hosts shot out hands like gunslingers: There a river casuarina, there a cycad, *Cycas megacarpa*. The cycad suggested a thirsty tree fern. Botanists consider it and its kind the most primitive seed-bearing plants in the world. They are relics of the Mesozoic. About 185 species survive today, most of them tropical.

The cycads at Belgamba ranged in size from young, ground-hugging specimens to eight- or nine-foot-tall Methusalehs. The big ones were several hundred years old, Cathy said. Gray and knobby, the trunks reminded me of the surface of a pineapple. The fronds of the cycads formed pinwheels on the tops.

Cycads are gymnosperms, which means "naked seeds." (A gymnasium, literally, is a room in which people run around naked.) Pines, spruces, and Auracarians such as the Norfolk Island pine are kin. Botanists believed until recently that wind pollinated cycads, as it does gymnosperms in general. Recent studies, however, have proved otherwise. A primitive beetle, rather than Aeolus, serves as Cupid; it reproduces inside male cones, ferries pollen to female plants, and leaves the pollen to germinate on its own, burrow into female reproductive structures, and release swimming sperm. The sperms of cycads are the biggest in nature—magnificent, tadpole-like things that botanists observe with the naked eye. The seeds they sire are toxic. In 1770, Captain Cook's crew ate cycad seeds at the mouth of Queensland's Endeavour River and became miserably sick. Aborigines knew better. They leached the toxins out of cycad seeds by soaking them in ponds or streams, then consumed them without discomfort.

Perspiring as the terrain steepened, we moved toward the spine of a ridge that would afford views of the surrounding country. On the way up, the Herberts pointed out trees. Lemon-scented gums had leaves that smelled as advertised. On the trunks Ian showed us wounds oozing sap. Yellow-bellied gliders, a kind of phalanger, were tapping the gums for sap. Cathy found a bat-wing coral tree. Its leaves were shaped like bats in flight. We also saw pink and brown bloodwoods; swamp mahogany, flourishing on dry soil; peppermint, a eucalypt whose leaves smelled minty; stringy-barks; gum-topped boxes; narrow-leaved ironbark, which had trunks covered by rough, corky skin; blue gum, a massive eucalypt with a hint of blue in otherwise pale bark; and a grass tree called *Xanthorrhea latifolia*. We had seen grass trees in other places but these were the finest specimens. Vaguely human in size and shape, they had short limbs sticking out from the main trunks like arms, and on their crowns they wore hairlike masses of wiry leaves. European settlers called grass trees "black boys" because at a distance they could be mistaken for Aborigines.

As we crested the ridge, a view opened. Before we could comment, Ian raised a finger to his lips. Two brush-tailed rock wallabies stood frozen on a boulder before us. They turned a moment later and bounded out of sight.

Cathy opened a thermos. As we sat and sipped tea, a vaguely deerlike face appeared from behind a boulder. One of the rock-wallabies had crept back to inspect us.

Like the other rock-wallabies we had seen, these had attenuated tails. The extra length probably helped the animals maintain balance as they traversed cliff faces and steep talus. All kangaroos are vaguely pear-shaped, light in front, heavy at the rear; the pattern is exaggerated in rock-wallabies.

John Muir saw brush-tailed rock-wallabies in New South Wales in 1904 and found them peculiar. "Many are about the size of a large wood-chuck," he wrote, "perhaps a little larger. They climb or rather jump well. Look in the face like a chipmunk and are the queerest, most ridiculous-looking [creatures] conceivable." At Belgamba, we were close to the northern limit of the brush-tailed rock-wallaby's range.

Circling back to the house, we shifted attention from plants to birds. Cathy showed us a sandy bank where spotted pardalotes nested. Overhead, pardalotes were calling in the trees. She taught us to distinguish the spotted pardalote, which sang three syllables, par-da-lote, the first note lower than the second and third, from the striated, which delivered three notes on the same pitch. By the time we and our hosts diverged for afternoon naps, we had learned several new calls and seen scaly-breasted lorikeets, white-throated honeyeaters, scarlet honeyeaters, Lewin's honeyeaters, noisy min-ers, figbirds, Australian magpies, pied currawongs, a pheasant coucal, and a scrofulous-looking honeyeater called the noisy friarbird. The friarbird had few feathers on its head and had all the charm of a vulture.

Nearing the end of the walk, Debbie spotted little lorikeets, brilliant green parrots with crimson faces. By the time I raised my binoculars they were gone.

The most exciting bird I saw came last. Approaching a wattle bush covered with yellow flowers, we froze in our tracks. A creature with a green back and black and white underside, its cheeks gleaming a magnifi-cent electric blue, was probing the blossoms for nectar. It was a blue-faced honeyeater.

Debbie set off the next morning with Cathy to fetch mail and gro-ceries from Rockhampton. I felt a twinge of jealousy. The short journey would carry Debbie across the Tropic of Capricorn, a line we had crossed only by air. Ian meanwhile had recruited me to help with trail work, and I was eager to lend a hand.

We set off in convoy. Ian drove a tractor, and I followed in an ancient Land Rover. The drive brought us gently up a valley until, bucking up a rocky slope in low gear, we climbed to the summit of a ridge. Descending the far side, we came to a place where a downpour had cut a jagged gully across the track. Ian explained that he wanted me to help him out of a jam if he got in one. The hill was steep, and rolling the tractor was a risk. He told me to do as I pleased, but listen for the tractor. If something sounded amiss, I should hurry back.

I poked around the bush, staying within earshot. All was deathly still—no birds in the trees, no rock-wallabies hopping among the boulders, few insects buzzing in the parched air. After wandering for an hour, I rejoined Ian. We brewed tea in a billy, heating it on a Swedish alcohol stove that looked as if it had been dug up by an archaeologist. The risky part of the job was over, said Ian. He advised that I spend the next couple of hours exploring a gully that would lead, if I followed it far enough, into a cool thicket of palms.

Ducking under limbs and dodging spiderwebs, I pushed farther and farther into the dry hills. The gully made a good track, impossible to lose if not always easy to walk. Vegetation crowded in at times, and I scuttled like a crab. In time the tractor's roar fell away, replaced by a silence so profound that a shout might not have broken it.

Where the gully broadened into a floodplain shaded by palms, I found a rock and sat. The stillness was getting on my nerves. No bird sang. Only the buzzing of an occasional fly and the fluttering of a butterfly broke my sense of the surreal.

I found myself thinking of Ludwig Leichhardt, the nineteenth century explorer who crossed this country three times in the course of expeditions into the interior. At times Leichhardt flew into a kind of ecstasy, and at others he found the country empty and oppressive. "Wandering about in the bush becomes very tiresome in the long run," he wrote to a friend. "Eucalyptus trees with their whitish bark, casuarinas with their articulated leaves that are so like pine-needles, and unchanging undergrowth, are with you for hundreds of miles."

Leichhardt's love-hate relationship with the interior eventually proved his undoing. He and his party vanished in the course of an 1848 expedition. Despite much searching, no remains were ever found. The question of whether heat, hunger, hostile natives, or mutiny ended the German's career has never been settled. Leichhardt was notoriously incompetent at managing men and supplies. There is a good chance that he simply succumbed to thirst and hunger in some lonely corner of the outback.

I came up behind Ian's tractor just as the grading bar dislodged a bread-loaf of rock. In the hole I spied a snake. It was about a foot long, no thicker around than a pencil, and marked with black and white bands. My first instinct was to grab the reptile, which looked like a rubber novelty, but I reminded myself where I was. Snakes with eye-catching colors are often venomous.

I tried to coax the thing into the open with a stick. To my surprise, it did something I had never seen a snake do: it mashed its head into the ground as if bent on self-destruction, meanwhile arching its torso in the air.

Back at the house, I pulled out Cogger's *Reptiles and Amphibians of Australia*. The snake was a bandy-bandy, a species that produces venom but has little ability to inject it into humans. Handling the snake might have been safe, but I had no regrets. I wanted close looks at Australia's serpents, but was determined to avoid foolish risks.

One night at Belgamba, we hiked into the bush with Ian to look for yellow-bellied gliders. We visited dozens of lemon-scented gums, examining the bark for toothmarks and sap. Evidence of glider feeding turned up on several trees. For a half hour we waited quietly, hearing faint rustlings in the leaves and the occasional buzz of an insect. No gliders appeared.

During the walk back to the house, Ian stopped abruptly and pointed to his right ear. We listened. Somewhere in the distance, dingoes yipped and wailed. They sounded like people turned into dogs, mourning the lives they had lost.

After three nights with the Herberts, we made good-byes and thank-yous and slipped across the Tropic of Capricorn. Just north of 23½ degrees latitude, in the coastal city of Rockhampton, we took a short walk in a botanical garden. Birds rather than plants were our quarry, but as it happened the thing that monopolized our attention was Krefft's river turtle, a reptile. There were dozens of them, many the size of dinner plates. All had carapaces rendered dark and shaggy by algae. Parents and children off on school holidays were tossing bread to the turtles, which elbowed each other aside to get at the stuff in a water-churning frenzy of rudeness.

Krefft's river turtle is named for Gerard Krefft, curator of the Australian Museum from 1861 to 1874. Krefft was a herpetological pioneer and curmudgeon. Dismissed on charges of "occasional intoxication," "willful smashing of a fossil jawbone," and "condoning the sale of pornographic photographs in the museum," Krefft defied an order to vacate the building. According to the herpetologist Richard Shine, he was ultimately carried from his office by a pair of hired toughs, his backside still firmly pressed to the curator's chair.

By the time we turned north on the Bruce Highway, we had seen six new birds. Our favorites: a comb-crested jacana, or lotus-bird, that walked across lily pads on long, spindly toes, and a forest kingfisher hunting seafood along the shore.

Raising cane for a world obsessed with sugar appeared to be the sole industry of Queensland's coastal plain. A narrow strip of asphalt ran between green walls, and we shot up the middle, feeling like Moses parting the sea. Rockhampton, the city of 63,000 we had just departed, called itself the "Beef Capital of Australia." Mackay, the town of 53,000 we reached after a drive of two hundred miles, dubbed itself Australia's sugar capital. It was easy to see why.

As we passed through Sarina, a refinery town south of Mackay, olfactory cues reinforced the visual. A reek of molasses filled the air, thick and cloying.

Outside Mackay (pronounced *Mah-KIE*), we stopped to examine a kingfisher perched on a utility wire. It was nearly chicken-sized like the laughing kookaburra, but something was odd. The crown was streaked and fluffed, as if the bird had just visited a hair stylist. Kookaburras in the South had washes of blue on the wings, but this specimen wore epaulets of dazzling turquoise. The rump was turquoise, too, and the tail was brown. Out came binoculars and a book. The bird was a blue-winged kookaburra, or howling jackass, a bird whose call Graham Pizzey likened to the sound of a "machine-driven hacksaw."

I wanted to hear the bird sing, but it refused to cooperate. In fact, a brown tail told us the kookaburra was actually a queen. She sat, looked down her prodigious beak at us, and squirted out a prodigious shit.

In Mackay we found a campground. Situated on a grassy flat shaded by enormous eucalypts, the place was overrun with teenagers. Laughing, shouting, flirting, fighting, and teasing each other, they presented a sharp contrast to the weary schoolteachers who watched from the sidelines.

The thing I remember best about our night in Mackay, aside from its clamor, is that when dusk came on, dark clumps in the trees began to move. Soon broad, leathery wings were flogging the air, creating *whoosh-whoosh-whoosh* sounds and blotting out large portions of the sky. They were flying foxes, our first since Debbie shocked the garden-club ladies in Melbourne. Back and forth they flapped, playing a game of tag uncannily similar to the horseplay of the students below them. We sat, sipped tea, and took in the show until the troupe vanished over the treetops.

In the morning we drove west. Rain-forest-clad mountains rose abruptly inland from Mackay, and we aimed to coax our overloaded car up and into the heart of them. Our destination was Eungella National Park. A river running through the park offered excellent prospects for observing platypuses.

Driving between cane fields west of town, we passed a farmhouse separated from the road by a tall hedge. Mandarin orange trees heavy with fruit grew around the place, and above them, perched on a wire, a brightly colored bird caught my eye.

It proved to be one of the most stunning creatures either of us had ever set eyes on, its plumage a crazy quilt of blue, green, gold, orange, and black. As we stood watching, a woman in a cotton frock, with a young girl clinging to each hand, marched out a door. She wasn't smiling, and she was bound in our direction. She probably thought we had designs on her oranges.

"We've stopped to admire one of your birds—a rainbow bee-eater," I said, putting on the widest smile I could muster.

"A rainbow what?" The woman sounded skeptical.

I explained that bee-eaters were best known from Africa, but they also ranged across southern Europe, Asia, and Indonesia. Australia had one species, and it was catching insects among her orange trees.

"I see." A look of pleasant surprise came over the woman's face. Soon a meeting that had nearly begun in hostile confrontation developed into a friendly chat. An offer of tea and all the oranges we could carry followed. Courtney and Shenise let go of their mother's hand and started collecting. Reluctantly, we declined the tea. It was important to reach Eungella before nightfall. With thanks, we set off with an armload each of fruit.

The road to Eungella was winding and steep. Three times during the ascent we pulled onto the shoulder and let the Toyota sigh and ping and cool. Far below, fields of green cane spread across the valley. In the east we could see Mackay, and beyond it the aquamarine Pacific.

Chugging along in low gear while running our heater to help cool the motor, we crested the ridge. Rain forest engulfed us, a welcome change from the monotony of the cane country. The road led into the park, and we followed it to a bridge over the Broken River. On the far side, we turned onto a dirt track. It led to campsites at a place called Fern Flats.

Finding far more ferns than flats, we set up our tent on an earthen terrace worn into a hillside by previous campers. Job done, we set off to find a designated "platypus viewing area." A wooden platform had been built along the edge of the Broken River, and from it, a ranger told us, platypuses could be seen feeding at dawn and dusk.

Before we reached the place, we detoured onto the bridge that had earlier carried us over the river. I was surprised to look into the water and find a platypus directly below, stirring the water with rapid motions of its bill. We stood and watched. The animal dove and surfaced, again and again, hauling crayfish and insects from the bottom in cheek pouches and mashing them in its bill. This was our first look at a platypus from above, and I was astounded by the shape of its forefeet. They looked like the fins worn by scuba divers—wide, flat, marvelous tools for propulsion.

At dusk we stood with a dozen fellow campers at the observation platform. The viewing was disappointing compared to our luck from the bridge.

Back in the campground, we found mayhem. The site next to ours had been empty when we left, but now a man and a woman stood in the middle of it, screaming profanities at each other. After a while, he stormed up to the access road on the hill above, revved his old hulk of an automobile (a "Yank tank" in the lingua franca), and crashed it through the rain forest understory until it came to rest in the campsite. The shouting resumed.

For more than an hour the couple hacked away with machetes, inflicting great damage on the surrounding vegetation. The cuttings fed an enormous bonfire that belched flames high into the night. Meanwhile threats and accusations flew back and forth, the verbal repartee so violent that we feared a physical assault might follow.

Debbie and I meanwhile did our best to enjoy the brush-tailed possums, northern brown bandicoots, and long-nosed bandicoots that plodded and snuffled past our picnic table. We were especially drawn to the bandicoots. Looking something like small kangaroos and somewhat like oversized, short-eared rabbits, they moved by gentle hops. Debbie pointed out that there were two kinds.

The northern brown bandicoot seemed the handsomer of the two. It had a sleek brown body that started narrow at the pointed snout and grew ever wider until it culminated in a round, shapely rump. A ratlike tail hung on the end like an afterthought. The long-nosed bandicoot, by contrast, was slightly smaller and had an attenuated nose and long, rabbitlike ears. It appeared to be wearing white socks, and generally had a more clumsy look than the brown bandicoot. Both species shared a world record. Bandicoots give birth to newborns twelve and a half days after conception, the shortest gestation known among mammals.

Like American skunks, bandicoots earn widespread disdain by digging up suburban lawns. In both cases, the animals serve as exterminators, ferreting out grubs that harm the roots of grasses. Unfortunately, the services are rarely appreciated.

Bandicoots, unlike skunks, have toothsome flesh. The explorer Carl Lumholtz considered them "good eating even for Europeans, and in my opinion the only Australian animals fit to eat. They resemble pigs, and the flesh tastes somewhat like pork."

We watched the bandicoots dig holes, then poke their noses inside. The excavations they left behind were exact duplicates of holes we had seen in the lawn at O'Reilly's.

By midnight we were asleep, despite the drama next door. At nearly three, I awoke to the sounds of violent retching. "You ruined my life," screamed the man between upchucks. "Getting involved with you was the worst thing that ever happened to me."

The accusation started the woman howling. "What a joke! You ruined my life ten times worse than I ruined yours." So it went for another hour. We had come to take our personal safety for granted in the bush, but the warring pair reminded us of our vulnerability. There was no ranger here to turn to for intervention, no police, no telephone. If the man had attacked the woman, or us, we would have had to face the situation alone. I lay awake for a long time, dreading the prospect of violence.

At sunrise we left on a bird walk. Next door, all was silent. When we returned several hours later, our neighbors were gone. We guessed that someone had met the park ranger when he reported for work and the couple had been evicted.

The chief excitement of our first full day at Eungella came unexpectedly. Late in the morning we were sipping tea at the table beside our tent when Debbie went to fetch her journal from the car. Then I heard a scream. Running to investigate, I found Debbie talking with Olaf and Rosalie Perfler, Californians from Sacramento whom we knew from chance meetings in Melbourne and on Kangaroo Island. The odds of meeting them again in a country as vast as Australia were small, yet here they were, sauntering down a remote Queensland byway at the exact moment Debbie had gone to the car.

We also made new friends that day. In another campsite at Fern Flats, an Australian family, the Wardlaws, were finishing "tea," the evening meal, when Debbie and I came trudging past. Friendly waves led to conversation, and before we knew it, the six of us were exchanging news of platypuses, lizards, bandicoots, and birds. Peter and Ros Wardlaw had two children, Amy, about fifteen, and Matthew, around eleven. They were as surprised by our knowledge of the local flora and fauna as we were by their enthusiasm. When we finally set off to make supper, Ros sent us away with peach crumble, still warm from her camp oven.

The following morning the Perflers came with us on a hike. In long pants worn to defend our flesh from stinging trees, we followed the most straightforward route the map offered, a trail along the Broken River. Progress was slow and sweaty.

We threaded our way through leafy forest, running along the riverbank at times, then diverting away. Birds abounded, although in the extravagant foliage we heard far more than we saw.

Lewin's honeyeaters outnumbered the other birds, and on several occasions we tried to turn one into the rare, endemic Eungella honeyeater. In every case, however, the bird turned its cheek, revealing a yellow patch behind the eye, dashing our hopes. The Eungella has silver where the Lewin's has gold.

Far more colorful than the honeyeaters were the Ulysses butterflies we saw flitting through the forest. With wings as wide as dessert plates and metallic blue scales that shimmered in the sunshine, the insects looked like pieces of the sky.

We were discussing the idea of turning back when Debbie raised an arm and pointed. Rosalie, Olaf, and I traced her line of sight. On a branch about twenty feet before us sat a sparrow-sized kingfisher. It was stunning—brilliant blue, like a clear winter sky.

The azure kingfisher comported itself in typical kingfisher fashion, sitting still, gazing down its daggerlike bill into the water. It lingered just long enough for us to get a fix, then shot out wings and flapped downstream, saying "Pete!" twice. As it flew, we glimpsed its rusty brown underside and cherry-red feet.

Evening brought a second visit with the Wardlaws. In the middle of things, Matthew led me down an unmarked path to a place where he had found an eastern brown snake coiled beside the trail. The reptile was still there, and we admired it from a distance. The eastern brown is one of the world's most dangerous snakes. Ranging through most of Queensland, New South Wales, and Victoria, with a few isolated populations elsewhere, its venom is far more potent than that produced by America's most feared reptile, the diamondback rattlesnake. This snake did what most snakes do: lay there quietly and minded its own business.

The Wardlaws told us they would leave in the morning, a day ahead of us. Eager to see more of each other, we made plans to meet again at Cape Hillsborough, their next destination and now ours, too. We made goodbyes. They would be leaving early, and I had plans to spend the morning hiding behind a bush, photographing duck-billed platypuses. Debbie announced her intention to sleep late and catch up on rest.

We crawled into our sleeping bags at midnight, having been visited again by a series of bandicoots and possums. I slept fitfully, knowing an alarm would call me to action well before dawn.

It was cold and black when I wriggled into damp clothes, shouldered a load of photographic gear, and set off for the river. My Penelope slept soundly. The time was a quarter past six.

Down the dirt road I moved in long strides, illuminating my footing lest any eastern brown snake be out for a crawl. I soon reached the river. In the dim light of imminent dawn, I could see that the surface lay as smooth as a tabletop. I crossed a bridge, walked along the river's ten-foot-high bank, and descended through ferns toward the shore.

Chilled and groggy, I thought of hot coffee and midday sun and set up a camera, tripod, and flash. I wanted to be ready if a platypus appeared. Over the last few days I had observed that this stretch of river was a hotbed of activity. Perhaps the river bottom supported a high concentration of insects or crayfish, or the platypuses had a burrow in the bank. I was excited to think that a female might curl in a chamber beneath my feet, warming eggs with her hot body or suckling newborn offspring.

In the top of a gum tree on the far shore, a black and white bird caroled in the dawn. It was a pied butcherbird, also known as the "organ bird" or "break-o'-day-boy." Butcherbirds in nearby trees joined the first. The resulting music was sacred and stirring. I closed my eyes, listened, and felt happier than I had in years.

Suddenly, bubbles appeared in the green water before me. I cocked my camera, switched on the flash, and held my breath. *There—there—there—*I was struck dumb by good fortune. A black, rubbery bill wider than a duck's pushed through the surface immediately before me. It was followed by webbed feet, a hairy face with beady black eyes, and a furry brown body about the size of a muskrat's. I fiddled with the camera. The platypus was so close that my lens could not focus.

The platypus vanished, leaving a raft of bubbles. I counted the seconds. Ten. Twenty. On the count of twenty-two, the animal bobbed up like a whale, farther from me than before. I focused as best I could in the dim light and squeezed the shutter. The flash popped. An image of uncertain quality was mine.

Down went the duckbill for another helping of breakfast. As I awaited its reappearance, I heard the scratching of a large animal. Turning, I met the source eye-to-eye: an Australian brush-turkey, red, black, decked out in yellow wattles, more svelte than the wild turkey of the Americas. The brush-turkey was kicking sticks, leaves, and dirt onto an enormous mound. I had taken the earthwork for a bulge of riverbank, but now I saw that it was a nursery. The mound was about five feet high and a dozen feet across. Thousands of pounds of material composed it, heaped there by the bird one kick at a time.

I couldn't see them, but inside the mound lay the eggs of one or more females, kept at optimum temperature by the insulating earth and by heat generated during the bacterial decomposition of leaves. A brush-turkey tests the temperatures of its mound with a sensitive mouth lining. When adjustments are called for, the bird effects them by adding or subtracting leaves and earth. This bird was enlarging its mound, and it went about the work with no regard for my presence.

Morning light began to settle. The pea-soup color of the water gave way to the colors and inverted shapes of trees. Watching the transformation was like observing the development of a Polaroid photograph. All was idyllic, save for the clamor. From gum trees across the river came voices that suggested demons from Dante or some ghastly, blood-sucking beast out of Homer. I looked up to see a dozen or more sulphur-crested cockatoos, quarreling with each other at terrible volume. With each delivery of bombast, their alabaster bellies puffed out like rising bread dough.

Again the platypus surfaced. Sunlight drenched the forest now, and turned water droplets on the fur into gemstones. I shot several photographs, but my heart was not in the work. The most singular of mammals was simply too marvelous, too novel, to peer at through a lens. I craved an intimacy that photography ruined. So for an hour I sat and did nothing but watch. The platypus dove and swam, and there were times when its eyes, tucked in pink recesses that closed when it submerged, looked at me. I'm not sure which was more exciting: seeing a platypus or being seen by one.

In late morning, Debbie and I struck camp and loaded the car. On our way out of Eungella we joined the Perflers on two short adventures. The first was a search for the Eungella honeyeater. Walking up a dirt road just beyond the park boundary, we heard and glimpsed a bird that seemed to match the rare bird's description. Each time we neared it, however, it darted into the jungle and was lost.

The saving grace of watching birds is that when you fail in pursuit of one species, you stumble upon another. We were discussing our bad luck when I spotted a large bird in a tree. It combined the size and shape of a falcon with the crest of a blue jay. The feathers were gray above, striped on the belly, and eyes as yellow as lemons watched us suspiciously. The erect crest reminded me of whipped cream teased to a peak by a beater. Our books identified the apparition as a Pacific baza, or crested hawk, a raptor that snatches lizards and insects out of the treetops.

Our second round of excitement that morning came as we were leaving Finch-Hatton Gorge, a corner of Eungella National Park we reached via a road in the valley. We had taken lunch to a picnic area at the gorge because people told us it was a sure bet for goannas. Experienced wildlife watchers know, of course, that sure bets rarely turn out that way. The place proved barren of lizards. As we rumbled back to the main highway, I spied a farmer walking across a cane field. He was attired in the *de facto* uniform of Queensland men—wide-brimmed felt hat, gray button-front shirt, green shorts, and elastic-sided work boots. His face looked thoughtful, so I guessed he might be able to settle a question that was nettling me.

After some pleasantries, I asked the man if in his travels about the farm he had ever seen a taipan. I meant the coastal taipan, *Oxyuranus scutellatus,* perhaps the second-deadliest snake in the world. Its venom is eight times stronger than that of a king cobra. Tests show that a single load of the coastal taipan's venom packs enough punch to kill 50,000 mice. But there is one snake even more dangerous. Perhaps the deadliest of all the world's poisonous reptiles is the inland taipan, *O. microlepidotus.,* whose bite contains enough toxin to kill 109,000 mice, at least in theory. The coastal taipan inhabits Queensland's cane fields, while its fearsome cousin rules the state's arid interior.

"Yes," said the man. "From time to time I do. Heaps of snakes around here." He picked up the limp carcass of a serpent lying dead in a furrow. "Tractor got this poor bugger," he said.

"What kind is it?"

"Dunno," he said. Eager to identify the snake, I was about to crash through the brush that separated me from the man when I stopped short. Anything could have lurked in the tangle, including a taipan.

"Almost all snake bites take place because a snake has been interfered with or inadvertently trodden on," asserted a Park Service pamphlet that we had picked up at Eungella. This made sense. In the taipan's range, we would grant every serpent the right-of-way. I had no wish to imitate the naturalist David Fleay, who made a strong impression on Elspeth Huxley by picking two taipans out of a cage and letting them crawl up and down his arms.

Arriving at Cape Hillsborough after dark, we stomped noisily around a campsite for several minutes, sweeping the ground with flashlights to make sure the coast was clear. Then we pitched the tent. The night was cool, the air scented with salt and mud. Exhausted, we ate a perfunctory dinner and fell asleep to the sound of waves spanking a nearby shore.

Several times that night we awoke to weird, gurgling cries in the bush. What made them—a monster from Homer, a soul pleading for release from the Underworld? In time we identified the source as the orange-footed scrubfowl, a mound-building bird closely related to the brush-turkey.

Hardly had we burst from our chrysalides in the morning than Debbie managed to get herself bitten. The culprit was a large, green ant. A glorious thing to behold, the insect shone like polished jade. Grasping the thorax gently between a thumb and forefinger, I coaxed the little warrior off her arm and onto the top of our picnic table.

For Debbie it was a rude introduction. Welcome or not, here was one of the most interesting animals in Australia, the green ant, *Oecophylla smaragdina*. It ranges from Queensland to India. "Their stings were by some esteemed not much less painful than those of a bee," wrote Joseph Banks, running afoul of the insect more than two centuries before Debbie did.

While enjoying our usual breakfast of muesli, sliced banana, powdered milk, and tea, we noticed that several gum trees in the neighborhood had green-ant nests built around their boughs. The smallest of them were the size of cantaloupes, the largest as plump as rugby balls. Constructed of leaves pulled together by ants working cooperatively in teams, the nests were held together by strands of silk squeezed from conscripted larvae.

According to Bert Holldobler and Edward O. Wilson, green-ant nests are virtual cities, and may contain a half-million or more ants. Scale insects may live in the colony, tended and milked by the ants for sweet excrement. The caterpillars of a butterfly may also take shelter there. The adult lays its eggs on or near a green-ant nest, and larvae find their way inside.

A green-ant colony often consists of several nests. Those on the edge of the group's territory serve, say Holldobler and Wilson, as "barracks" for over-the-hill workers. Beyond their prime, these ants serve the colony as guard dogs, charging out to fight attackers from rival colonies and nipping at the skin of humans. One nest in each colony contains a queen. She is fat, lazy, and important, and she rules the waves of workers that teem around her. The secret of the queen's success is a potion. Excreted from a gland on her head, the stuff contains chemicals that induce workers to collect infertile eggs and feed them to her. She gulps them down like popcorn. All fertile eggs in the colony come from Her Highness.

Eating breakfast in shorts, T-shirts, and sandals, we did our best to ignore the fact that every square foot of the forest floor included at least one green ant, marching somewhere with a purpose. Some had insects clutched in their jaws, and others wrestled jaw-to-jaw with members of their own species. A few minded their own business. Green ants would be with us throughout our wanderings in the North, and we would have to grow accustomed to having them around.

We spent the next couple of days squishing along the fringes of mangrove swamps, plodding across mud flats at low tide, and thrashing through coastal rain forest. At every turn, new birds popped up. We spied Brahminy kites, hawks that looked like miniature bald eagles, and watched them sail across cobalt skies. Along the shore there were mangrove herons, reef herons, beach stone-curlews, and sacred kingfishers. Two birds we saw had reached Australia on their own wings and were old friends from North America: the gull-billed tern and the Caspian tern. We also identified a whimbrel. An oversized sandpiper, the whimbrel is streaked and spotted, with a great sickle of a bill used to probe mud flats for invertebrates. There is an American whimbrel that flees Northern Hemisphere winters for New Zealand, but this was the Eurasian species. It flies to Australia from Siberia.

Of all the birds we found, the most colorful were yellow-bellied sunbirds. The Old World's answer to the hummingbirds of the Americas, sunbirds reach their greatest diversity in Africa. There are more than a hundred species. I was ignorant of the fact that one inhabited Australia until we spied three of them darting in and out of a flowering shrub.

One of the sunbirds, a male, had a throat that shimmered a deep metallic blue. The others had lemon-yellow throats, and we identified them as females and juveniles. Watching the birds probe blossoms, lapping up nectar and insects, we marveled at their similarity to hummingbirds. Experts say the resemblance is only skin deep. Hummingbirds are related to swifts, even though they look nothing alike, and sunbirds, more recently evolved, are lumped with the Passerines, or perching birds. The "sun" in "sunbird" fits perfectly. Whenever the birds caught the light, they flashed reflections of the tropical sun, sullen and heavy above us.

Clumping across a mud flat one afternoon at low tide, watching fish and crabs scuttle across shrinking pools, we picked our way into dense bush on the far side. Mangroves gave way to a more diverse array of trees, dwarfed and knotted by wind and spray. Not far in, we came to an enormous mound. Debbie caught a glimpse of a vaguely chickenlike bird bustling off into the shadows. A crest stuck up on the back of its head, she said, and the legs and feet were orange. It could be nothing else but the orange-footed scrubfowl.

Eager to see the thing myself, I circled quietly among the trees. Soon I found it, moving furtively, running in bursts and keeping trees and tangles between us. The pointed head suggested someone who had gone to bed with wet hair. When I returned, Debbie was sizing up the mound. It measured about thirty feet across and rose to a height of four feet in the center. Like the brush-turkey, the scrubfowl creates mounds to incubate eggs. Ornithologists pronounce its handiwork—or footwork—the largest structure in the world built by a bird.

It pleased us to have the Wardlaws along on excursions. Matthew was impressed when we took him back to see the scrubfowl mound, even though the bird failed to appear. Amy leaped with joy over sunbirds. Like most children, the Wardlaw kids proved keen observers. One afternoon we led them and their parents to a mangrove swamp behind our campsite. On earlier visits we had spied—but never gotten a fix on—a small brown animal that dove into holes in the mud before we could get a look. Within a minute of arriving, Amy cried, "Fish!" Matthew ran over, squinted, and echoed her pronouncement.

Where? The four adults in the party had to crouch. Were the creatures really fish, or frogs? Colored gray-brown like the mud, the things measured about as long as index fingers. They appeared to be satyrs of a sort, half-amphibian, half-fish. One remained when the others fled, sprawling on a mangrove root. Its eyes bulged like a frog's, its head was square and wide, and crooked pectoral fins stuck out like props. The body, covered by spotted skin, tapered like a carrot to a tail.

One of us moved. Alarmed, the frog-fish flicked itself onto the mud, skipped toward a hole with rapid snaps of its tail, and vanished like a rabbit. Behavior clinched the identification. We had just made the acquaintance of a mudskipper.

A fish struggling to be a frog, the mudskipper is a cousin of the goby. There are five species in Australia, each adapted for survival out of water as well as in. Why the surf-'n'-turf lifestyle? It probably evolved at least in part as a defense against predators. Big fish prowl the shallows of mangrove swamps at high tide, snapping up smaller ones. The mudskipper keeps its options open. It can dart into a burrow if it has one, or climb out on a limb or root.

Surviving out of water is no mean feat for a fish. The mudskipper manages the job in two ways: by swishing oxygenated water like mouthwash around its jowly cheeks, and by soaking up oxygen through its skin, as a frog does. When the tide runs out, the mudskipper goes to work. It drops to the mud, crutches itself along on jointed pectoral fins, and feasts. Typical items on its menu are worms, insects, isopods, crabs, other mud-dwelling crustaceans, and algae.

As we ogled the mudskipper, a bird sang in the apex of a mangrove. It was modest of size, crimson of back, black everywhere else, and cocked a long tail up toward the sun. It was a bird we had stalked without success since leaving Sydney—the red-backed fairy-wren, a garrulous minstrel of mangrove swamps and woodlands.

The next morning we parted company sadly with the Cape and the Wardlaws. Traveling north, we followed a road that ran along the narrow coastal plain. To our right lay the blue Pacific, to the left mountains green and shaggy with jungle. Cane fields stretched for miles, broken occasionally by small towns peddling fuel and groceries. Rainbow bee-eaters and blue-winged kookaburras surveyed our progress from power lines.

The second night out, we camped at Bowling Green National Park, just inland from a cape of the same name. Flat and grassy, the peninsula reminded Captain Cook of the bowling greens of England. The campground was small and cozy, a sunny clearing in the bush.

When we arrived, brush-turkeys roamed the picnic area. One had found an unattended table and was standing on top of it, using its feet to send a family's lunch flying in several directions. As the afternoon light faded, agile wallabies and unadorned rock-wallabies filtered in from the forest. The rock-wallabies dragged exaggerated tails behind them, as all rock-wallabies do, and the agile wallabies presented the handsomest faces of any kangaroo we had seen. Light and dark stripes ran down the cheeks, and the snouts tapered to delicate muzzles.

In the next site, beyond a tree lately climbed by a brush-tailed possum with a baby on its back, camped a Canadian couple in their late fifties. Jack and Joanie, three years earlier and with modest sailing experience, had piloted their yacht out of Vancouver. Jack's brother, an expert seaman, came with them as far as San Diego, making sure the couple knew what they were doing. After a shakedown cruise to Mexico, the brother flew home. Jack and Joanie were on their own. They crossed the Pacific to the Marquesas, sailed on to Fiji, Tonga, Tahiti, the Cook Islands, and New Zealand, and eventually landed in Queensland. In Brisbane, Jack and Joanie bought a camper van and set off to see Australia.

Driving into Townsville the following afternoon, we found Queensland's third largest city deserted. It was a scorching winter day, the air parched and dusty. The general atmosphere was one of neglect, except down by the harbor. There a grand, newly built aquarium offered a vicarious introduction to the Great Barrier Reef.

After weighing pros and cons, we decided to skip the aquarium. Why tantalize ourselves with glimpses of a paradise we could not afford to visit? The world's largest coral reef had been with us since Rockhampton, lying well offshore at first but edging closer the farther we moved toward Cairns. Someday, finances replenished, we would return and give the great wall of coral its due. In present circumstances, however, we had no choice but to turn our backs. Reef cruises and diving trips were costly, and even the cheapest of them would sink our budget. Our resolve was unshakable: circle Australia or bust.

A reconnaissance of the Townsville Common proved that we had left Victoria far behind, entering a world as different from Australia's Southeast as Florida is from Maine. The Common was not a green in the center of town, as we expected it to be, but a wild place at the city's edge. Dry and sunbaked above the high-tide line, rank and salty below, it teemed with animal activity even in the middle of a steamy day.

Just after entering the Common, we spied two strange, leggy birds strutting across the road. They looked vaguely like shrunken ostriches, plump of body, long of neck, colored a silvery gray except for black crests and mud-brown backs and wings. "Bustards!" I cried. It was a wild guess. I had no firm idea what a bustard looked like, but as luck had it, I was right. They were Australian bustards (not to be confused with Australian bastards). During his travels along the Queensland coast with Cook, Joseph Banks pronounced the bustard the tastiest bird he had encountered since leaving England.

Bustards are the heaviest birds that fly. Male Australian bustards can weigh thirty pounds or more. Somehow they manage to get off the ground, especially when flight offers access to a feeding or resting place not accessible on foot. The species is famed for round-the-clock breeding displays. A lusty male puffs up his chest like a balloon, creating a feathery bag that dangles nearly to the ground. Swinging it like a pendulum, he folds his tail over his back, points his extended neck toward the sky, and roars, according to Graham Pizzey, "like a distant lion."

I stopped the car, hoping the bustards would give us a show. Instead they raised their heads like snobs at a country club and dashed into the scrub.

Debbie and I were picking at each other again, a situation aggravated by hot sun, glare, and the knowledge that while we were scuffing through dust on the Common, most tourists in the area were cruising over the Barrier Reef, sipping piña coladas in glass-bottomed boats. Still, we mustered enough interest and teamwork to add six new birds to our list. After the bustard came the olive-backed oriole, the fairy martin, an exquisite little singer called the golden-headed cisticola, and two species of mannikin, the chestnut-breasted and the nutmeg.

Unlike manikins, which stand behind department store windows, mannikins are finches. They are not members of the "true finch" or Fringillid family of the Northern Hemisphere, but cousins of the sparrows, weaverbirds, and grass-finches. There are four kinds in Australia. In one bush at the Common, we found two.

The native chestnut-breasted mannikin was the handsomer of the pair, an elegant little bird with argyle plumage (black, white, and brown) and a short, sturdy bill perfect for seed-cracking. Several dozen flitted in and out of view, and among them we spied nutmeg mannikins—plainer, darker, with scalloped breasts and bellies. The natural range of the nutmeg mannikin stretches from India to Indonesia. Bird merchants imported them to Australian pet stores, and more than a few gained liberty. Nutmeg mannikins spread today along the Queensland and New South Wales coasts from Cooktown to Sydney.

The next day we continued north, driving from Jourama Falls to Mission Beach by way of Ingham, Cardwell, and Tully. Ingham, claiming the biggest sugar mill south of the equator, was populated largely by Italians and Basques. We stopped there to buy a distributor cap and rotor for the car. Noticing a garage nearby, we decided to have our front end aligned. The mechanic was grumpy but honest. After tinkering with the Toyota's steering, he raised the car high on a lift and called us over. "Look," he said, pointing to crimps in the undercarriage. "This car has been in a wreck. The front end can't be aligned properly. I've done my best. Drive sensibly and you'll probably be all right." We cursed the Tasmanian car salesman one more time.

Through the long day I pondered Queensland's homey, undistinguished coastal towns and wondered why I felt so pleased with them. Part of the charm was size. The settlements were neither too small nor too big. Ingham had a population of 6,000, Cardwell 1,500 or so, and Tully something in between. People on the streets looked happy, not harried, puffed up, or predatory, as did so many in Sydney and Melbourne. Perhaps the main thing was proportion. I only feel genuine affection for a town when it is dwarfed by its surroundings, put in place by mountains or water. Ones that spread like cancers, obliterating everything of beauty in a selfish rush for growth, sadden me. When a place garnishes its natural surroundings like a sprig of parsley on a filet of broiled salmon, I find it good.

Approaching Mission Beach, named for a missionary base obliterated by a 1918 cyclone, we crossed and paralleled the route taken by the explorer Edmund Kennedy in 1848. In the grand tradition of Victorian exploration, Kennedy landed near Cardwell with a party of men, three horse-drawn carts, and a mob of one hundred sheep. He proposed to slog hundreds of miles thus equipped through merciless country, across dozens of rivers aswirl with crocodiles, into territory inhabited by hostile Aborigines. It sounds like madness, and it was. Yet to Kennedy the journey was logical. His goal was Cape York, the northern tip of the Cape York Peninsula.

He almost made it. Sixty miles short of his goal, perilously short of supplies and demoralized by disasters, he sent all but one of the party, an Aboriginal guide named Jackey-Jackey, to seek better luck on the coast. Meanwhile Kennedy and Jackey-Jackey plodded on. Crossing the last river that lay between them and the Cape, Aborigines attacked. A spear struck Kennedy and he bled to death, his last sight the channel dividing Australia and New Guinea. Jackey-Jackey ran for his life. The locals pursued. He was wounded but somehow managed to reach the coast. There a ship waiting to take the triumphant party home learned the terrible news. The ship's captain traced the coast southward, hunting for survivors. Only two were found.

Our night in Mission Beach was a far cry from Kennedy's. We camped at the Tropical Hibiscus Caravan Park. When a storm blew in, we sat it out in comfort under the tin roof of a cooking shelter. Rain rattled down, drumming on the roofs of caravans. Soon over, the tempest gave way to a sprinkle and a warm breeze spiced by flowers. Crickets trilled. Old people with white hair and pink faces bustled between toilets and caravans. In the shelter, a dozen barefoot men and women, in their early twenties and all tanned and happy, swapped yarns. They were fruit pickers, here from the U.K. and Germany to work in orchards at winter harvest.

Coconut palms loomed near the tent. During the night, vegetable cannonballs struck the earth, stirring us half awake. In the morning we rose with mild anxiety. The reason was obvious. We had come to Mission Beach to hunt for the fearsome cassowary, the bird that inspired the immortal rhyme:

> *If I were a cassowary*
> *On the plains of Timbuctoo,*
> *I would eat a missionary,*
> *Cassock, band, and hymn-book too.*

Sometimes attributed to William Thackeray, this bit of doggerel is credited in the *Oxford Dictionary of Quotations* to the Bishop Samuel Wilberforce.

Two words sum up the cassowary: majestic and dangerous. It is a primitive bird, close kin to the emu, the African ostrich, the South American rhea, and New Zealand's kiwis. When it wants to, a cassowary stands six feet in height. It looks smaller than an emu but is much heavier.

There are three species. The one that occurs in Australia, from Mission Beach northward, is a monster. It may weigh as much as Muhammad Ali in his prime, run thirty miles per hour, and disembowel a man or woman with the slash of a toenail. Attacks are airborne. Able to jump five feet in the air, a cassowary can slice through clothing and flesh with its middle toes, each armed with a five-inch long, rapier-sharp claw.

A Queensland National Parks and Wildlife Service pamphlet on rain-forest safety provided the following warning:

> This large, flightless bird has powerful legs that it will use to defend itself or its young. They have caused human fatalities. If encountered, stand still—their eyesight is poor. If the bird acts aggressively, attempt to look as large as possible by raising your arms overhead holding a camera, hat, or bag. DO NOT RUN. . . .

When Debbie and I ventured into the rain forest near Mission Beach to hunt for the feathered terror, I believed that the warnings about its behavior were exaggerated. After we returned home, I learned the truth. In 1995, the year before our visit, eighty cassowary attacks were reported in Queensland. I nearly fainted when I read that statistic in 1997. By then it was too late.

It was also too late when I visited the American Museum of Natural History in New York and met with Mary LeCroy, an ornithologist renowned for her work in Australasia. I asked about cassowaries. Is the danger overblown? "I don't think so," she said. "I keep my distance from them." LeCroy told me a story related to her by a colleague. In New Guinea, a woman was walking past an enclosure in which a cassowary was housed. Without warning or apparent provocation, the bird leaped into the air, cleared the fence, and struck. One of the woman's arms was opened to the bone from shoulder to wrist. LeCroy's friend stitched up the wound.

What were our chances of seeing a cassowary? We had little idea. We knew what to look for—an emu with a stoop, dark, stocky, with a gaudy red necklace of exposed flesh, a pale blue head darkening to an indigo neck, and a horny fin, or casque, on top of the head. The casque's exact function is uncertain. It may help the bird penetrate dense forests, intimidate rivals, attract mates, or some combination of these. The body is massive and covered by black, strawlike hair. In photographs, the bird looks like it's wearing a grass skirt. Holding it all up are stout legs, far heavier than an emu's, and shorter. The legs are covered with black scales and look as though they belong to a dinosaur. Each culminates in a trident of toes and claws.

Our search began after breakfast. In the cool, green light of morning, at a place called Licuala Forest, we left the car and walked into the forest. Overhead, the fronds of the fan palm, *Licuala ramsayi,* unfolded like parasols. There were vines, too, and dozens of plants regarding whose identity we were clueless. Among the branches we spotted Macleay's honeyeaters, birds that always look as if they're molting. Graham Pizzey writes that the Macleay's sings "a free TV, a free TV." These were silent.

The orange, fleshy fruits of the fan palm are prized by the cassowary, and so are the fruits of other rain forest plants. A nursery near Mission Beach sells the plants whose seeds the cassowary feeds on, encouraging people to plant them. They get their stock from a ready source: cassowary feces. The birds litter the rain forest floor with droppings that look like pizzas. Instead of peppers and olives, the pies are garnished with seeds that pass through the birds' digestive tracts unharmed.

The forest was eerily mute, save for the clatter of fan-palm fronds rattling against each other in a breeze. Everywhere we looked, there were things of interest. We admired the red, cigarette-shaped flowers of the climbing pandanus, a kind of vine that festooned many of the trees. Darting tongues into the blossoms were Macleay's honeyeaters. Other birds winged into view as well—yellow-breasted boatbills with luminous lemon undersides, and spectacled monarchs that worked the foliage for insects.

In sunny patches, skinks congregated. The lizards had bronze heads, gray backs speckled with black, and an iridescent sheen over them from snout to tail. A few in each group had dazzling pink necks and throats, reminiscent of hummingbirds. The colorful individuals faced off against each other, twitching their tails. I guessed them to be males, engaged in ritual combat. Later we identified them. They were rainbow skinks, *Carlia rhomboidalis.*

An hour of walking returned us to the car. Of giant birds we had seen nothing—not a feather, not a pizza, not an egg. As we started down the road, however, a brown shape appeared in front of us. One moment it was there, the next it was gone. (I was reminded of snippets of film purporting to show the bigfoot, or yeti.) Licuala held Australia's greatest concentration of cassowaries. There was nothing else the apparition could have been.

Why was the cassowary brown? We found the answer in a field guide. Adults were black, juveniles brown.

We left without having had a clear look. Disappointed, we drove up the road to a place called Lacey Creek. A short hike into the forest, a clearing opened. A pavilion there displayed information on cassowaries, and nearby, sapling trees marked with interpretive signs told about their diet. We were interested to learn that females grew taller and bulkier than males. If we met a cassowary along the trail, the exhibit advised us to cower behind a tree until the bird left the area.

Thus informed, we padded into the bush, listening, watching, hoping, unsettled by the prospect of consummating our desires. Fan palms were absent at Lacey Creek. In their place grew a diverse mix of tall trees, vines, and epiphytes. Along the track we met a pair of young women, one from Detroit, Michigan, the other from Innsbruck, Austria. Both physicists, they were in Australia attending professional meetings. A day trip from Cairns had brought them to Mission Beach.

During the hour that followed, we saw the women on and off. Mostly they stayed ahead of us, but each time they stopped to examine something of interest, we caught up and led the way until their faster pace overtook us. At one point, after ten minutes without seeing them, we came around a bend and found them crashing off the trail. They reached a stout tree, circled behind it, and froze. Only then did we spy the birds—two cassowaries, an enormous red, black, and blue adult and a sandy brown youngster. The adult stepped toward us, its lethal feet striking the ground tenderly.

The juvenile was smaller than the subadult we had seen at Licuala, but far larger than a chicken and quite imposing. Fear struck us like a sudden chill. We knew that large, dangerous animals were more likely to act aggressively in the presence of young.

Seeing a prize-winning photograph in the making—terrified physicists on one side of a tree, cassowary on the other—I dropped my pack to the ground, ripped open its zipper, and rummaged for a camera. The act nearly proved my undoing. The young cassowary ran over and poked its bill in the pack. Its stiff feathers bristled against my hand and wrist, and I shuddered at the hotness of its neck.

What to do? I looked up. To my relief, the parent bird seemed unconcerned, pecking idly at the ground. Yet I was not out of the woods. A cassowary may attack without warning, running toward a chosen enemy and striking simultaneously with its feet. I was painfully aware that by crouching, I had placed my head in a perfect position for it to be kicked like a ball into the treetops.

Nudging the bird gently aside, I backed away slowly. The parent preened, pulling at its flanks with its bill. I noted the legs and feet. They might have been borrowed from a velociraptor.

At a more comfortable distance, I fitted a flash to a camera and loaded a roll of film. I crept forward, uttering soothing words. The cassowaries ignored me. There were no threats, no charges, none of the deep rumbles that are said to precede an attack. I circled the larger bird, shooting several frames. Eventually the cassowaries drifted into the forest. Laughing and looking relieved, the physicists resumed their walk.

Debbie and I saw no more giant birds that day. Back at the car, a hard truth dawned on me. I did not remain as calm in the shadow of death as I thought I did. In the heat of the encounter, I'd failed to synchronize the camera with the flash. My photos were ruined.

So appealing were the forests around Mission Beach, and so seductive were their flowery perfumes and emerald light, that we might have lingered for weeks. But the calendar spurred us on. It was the ninth of July, and we still had the north of Queensland and the Northern Territory to explore. By September we wanted to reach Western Australia. There we aimed to enjoy one of the greatest shows on earth—the state's spring eruption of wildflowers.

We set off, eager to reach Palmerston National Park by nightfall. Palmerston perches halfway up the great bulwark of slopes bordering the Atherton Tableland, a high plateau covered by rain forest, dairy farms, tea plantations, coffee groves, and villages. In Innisfail, a coastal town, we stopped to buy fish. If we couldn't see the Great Barrier Reef, at least we could enjoy a bit of seafood. Leaving Innisfail, we turned away from the coast and climbed west into jungle.

Our radiator was about to whistle like a teakettle when the pull-off for the park's Henrietta Creek campground appeared. The facilities consisted of an outhouse, a shelter with picnic tables, and several acres of lawn hacked out of impenetrable forest. It was hardly the Tropical Hibiscus Caravan Park. The tent went up, the sleeping bags down. A half hour after arriving, we were swapping stories with Igor and Alison, a couple from Sydney. They had a cask of wine and shared two rounds of Riesling.

Although the campground lacked charm, the rain forest possessed it in plenty. Birds were everywhere. In one direction we heard the cry of some kind of dove, mournful, calling high in the canopy. In another we heard a loud, rollicking call that was completely novel.

When the wine had been drained and our neighbors turned to preparing a meal, we set off to find the birds. The dove proved to be an immense thing, as fat as a pigeon, and strikingly colorful. A luminous jade green painted the feathers from nape to tail, and the wings were marked with yellow. Juicy purple oozed down the breast, the underparts were golden, and the head placed eyes and bill of cherry-red on a sober gray background. It was a wompoo pigeon, or wompoo fruit-dove, one of the most glamorous birds in the world. *My name is Wompoo,* the bird seemed to say, at least to a man who had just downed two glasses of wine. *My name is wompoo. How do you do?*

While moving toward the second call we were waylaid by a marsupial. It was a musky rat-kangaroo, the most primitive of living kangaroos.

Dark and hairy, the rat-kangaroo was smaller than a cat. It hopped along quietly just inside the forest edge, pausing from time to time to rummage in the leaf litter. Aside from an upward glance, it ignored us completely.

The rummaging was done with delicate forepaws. When the rat-kangaroo found a bug or a fruit, it picked the thing up in its mouth and chewed. The animal gathers nest material in much the same way. Forepaws do the searching, the mouth picks things up, and the tail, which is naked like a Norway rat's, does the carrying. To get the stuff onto the tail, the rat-kangaroo drops what it has picked up, pivots, and kicks the material into a position where the prehensile tail can grasp it.

The musky rat-kangaroo is the only kangaroo to raise two young at a time, rather than the usual one. And there are other distinctions. It has big toes on its hind feet; other kangaroos don't. In fact, the small feet of the musky rat-kangaroo more resemble possum feet than the Michael-Jordan-sized thumpers of its cousins. The rat-kangaroo hops on four feet, rather than two. Whereas other kangaroos digest high-cellulose diets in complex stomachs and oversized cecums, the rat-kangaroo has an ordinary stomach and a compact cecum. It will swallow just about anything—worms, bugs of all sorts, and wild fruits.

Watching the mammal hobble away, we turned toward the bird singing over and over, at staggering volume, beyond it. I was in the process of inventing a mnemonic device to remember the call when Debbie spotted the maker. It was a drab, dusky thing with gray rings around the eyes and a white belly. According to the bird book, it was a chowchilla, also known as the northern logrunner and auctioneer-bird. Appropriately, the bird chanted *chowchilla* like a loudmouthed huckster.

Darkness came on swiftly. As I scrubbed dishes in the washbasin we'd purchased in Tasmania, the sky flooded with stars. Igor and Alison appeared soon thereafter. They were setting off for a platypus-viewing area ten minutes down the trail. Would we like to join them?

Moonglow helped us navigate through the forest. Silent plodding brought us to the summit of a high bank, and twenty feet below, catching the moonlight, flowed a stream. We lingered for forty minutes, hearing and seeing nothing. Our nostrils filled with earthy scents, and the damp night air slowly drenched our clothes.

Stopping for a single night at Palmerston but lingering three, we caught up on rest, mended holes in clothing and sneakers, and filled pages in our journals. Igor and Alison said good-bye the first morning, to be replaced a few hours later by Vincent and Solange. Vincent looked like the actor Gerard Depardieu, Solange like Yvette Mimieux. They were French-speaking Swiss, and spoke little English. With smiles, gestures, and our fossilized high-school French, we managed to get to know each other.

Vincent and Solange had landed in Melbourne. Like us, they'd bought a disreputable-looking station wagon and set off to see the country. Then our stories diverged. Three weeks after arriving, they'd parked their car on a busy street in Adelaide. It was a weekday afternoon. They were away two hours. When they returned, the car was empty. Everything had been stolen—their clothes, alpine-grade sleeping bags, mountaineering tent, tripod, several cameras, lenses, a hundred rolls of film. The only thing remaining was a windsurfer, still tied to the roof. Fortunately, Vincent and Solange had met a friendly, French-speaking restaurant owner. They ran to him in tears. For a week he housed and fed them, helped them file a police report, and drove them around Adelaide, searching for things the thieves might have jettisoned. Nothing was found. Travel insurance covered part of the loss, and the pair carried on.

Debbie and I listened to the story with dread. We drove a better-looking car than Vincent and Solange's, traveled with equipment of greater value, and owned no insurance policy. If thieves emptied our car, we would catch the next plane home.

Our two full days at Palmerston passed like a dream. We read, wrote, ate, and slept. One afternoon, eager to see more of the rain forest, we hiked to a waterfall that poured a thin stream of molten silver into a deep, shadowy basin. We were nearly scared out of our wits along the way by a loud grunting at close range. It was a feral pig. The animal never material-ized, but we could see where it had ripped apart an entire hillside with its tusks and hooves. Pigs existed in plague-like proportions in Queensland's forests, and we knew of assaults on people.

The forest swirled with feathers and wings. We saw pale yellow robins and Macleay's honeyeaters, wompoo fruit-doves and lemon-bellied fly-catchers, chowchillas and Victoria's riflebirds. The riflebird belongs to a group known as the birds of paradise. Like many hummingbirds, the males have brilliant, iridescent patches on their throats and crowns, and stage extravagant song-and-dance routines. A male sometimes surrounds a female with his wings and sings and sways as he wraps her in a feathery cape. Debbie managed a look at a male riflebird and pronounced it breathtaking. Until my luck improved several weeks later, I saw only females, shapely but drab.

On our final night at Palmerston, we walked to a shallow pool across the highway. It was dusk, and we found the water stirred by a platypus. Fetching Vincent and Solange from the campground, the four of us watched the world's most peculiar mammal surface and masticate, dive and retrieve, until daylight failed.

We were off the next morning. The highway climbed higher and higher up the flank of the Tableland, passed a tea plantation, and crested the top. We pulled over to gawk. The scene could have passed for Vermont or Bavaria. The air was cool, the sun warm, the sky blue, the pastures almost shockingly green, the cows black and white. It seemed as if we had left the rest of Australia behind.

Jane and Paul Rodwell of Umala Brook Farm on the Tableland had invited us to stay a few days. Driving country roads that grew narrower by the mile, we reached their gate near Ravenshoe (pronounced *raven's-hoe*). A sprawling, homemade adobe house stood against a backdrop of dark forest. Jane, sixty-four, a retired hospital administrator, and Paul, ten years younger, a farmer, builder, and part-time prison guard, started with a worn-out piece of agricultural land, put in a biodynamic garden to feed themselves, and erected a mud-and-straw paradise. The place was gor-geous. With the Rodwells lived a russet-haired mongrel named Ruthie.

On a shady veranda, we enjoyed a vegetarian lunch fresh from the Rodwells' garden and chatted about our travels. Jane asked what we wanted to see and do on the Tableland. Aside from an interest in simply poking around, we arrived with two specific goals: to see elusive, indigenous marsupials such as the Lumholtz's tree-kangaroo and the striped possum, and to get a look at the amethystine, or scrub, python. The python is Australia's biggest snake and one of the largest in the world. It reaches twenty-five feet in length. Exquisitely beautiful, its polished scales radiate a purple-blue sheen of amethyst. The python spends most of its year in the jungle, gorging on flying foxes, bandicoots, gliders, rodents, and the occasional tree-kangaroo. In winter it forsakes the cool woods to congregate on sun-heated rock outcrops and along the warm fringes of lakes.

The Rodwells listened carefully. Jane was soon on the phone with John Winter, a distinguished mammalogist who lived down the road. The result was an invitation to Sunday-morning tea and an offer to join Winter on a nocturnal spotlighting expedition. A tree-kangaroo expert from Massachusetts was in town, a woman who had done Ph.D. work on the Tableland in the 1980s. John was taking her and her family into the jungle to see if they could find old friends, and we were encouraged to participate.

Regarding pythons, Jane and Paul gave precise directions. Lake Barrine, an hour's drive from the farm, hosted an annual winter gathering of the snakes. By taking the day's first boat cruise, at 10:15 A.M., we could be certain of seeing pythons basking on a bed of lakeside plants.

The following morning, a Saturday, we were cruising over deep, cold waters filling a 95,000-year-old crater, scanning the shoreline for reptiles. Ian, the boat captain, laughed at our request to get as close to the snakes as possible. He would do what he could.

Nosing the bow into a cove, Ian killed the motor. The boat drifted. A hissing filled the air, the sound created by the passing of the hull's aluminum skin over water plants. "Look there," said Ian. Half of the boat's twenty passengers retreated. The rest of us pushed toward the bow.

A pair of pythons lay peacefully over a tangle of reeds, soaking up sunshine. The morning was cool, but the light was warm and the snakes were heating their blood. Although often labeled "cold-blooded," reptiles in fact must stay warm like the rest of us. If chilled, they cannot move freely or fully digest their food. We produce heat by metabolizing what we eat. They keep comfortable by moving in and out of sunshine and on and off warm surfaces.

At first we could see only portions of the snakes: the head of one, coils of another. Scales caught the light and threw it back at us in such a way that a hologram of purple hovered an inch above their skin. Ian estimated the snakes to be around four and a half meters in length, or about fourteen feet. They were thicker than my forearms.

Seeing giant snakes in a zoo is one thing, in the wild quite another. Before us loomed paragons of their species, not the lazy, overfed specimens covered by rotting scales and abrasions such as we have often seen in cages. Lean from climbing and curling, fresh from morning dips in the lake, the Lake Barrine snakes radiated glamour and good health. When they at last began to move, at one point I could see ten feet of cylindrical torso, culminating in a fleshy head. The tail of the snake was lost in the reeds, or tangled in the coils of the other. A forked tongue darted in and out, and eyes fixed us in a glassy stare.

On shore, we treated ourselves to a Devonshire tea in the café, then set off on a hike around the lake's four-and-a-half-mile perimeter. Rich, basaltic soils watered by heavy showers had given rise to extravagant rain forest, a universe of leaves. We stepped past stinging trees, heard the mewing of green catbirds, and spied an unfamiliar brown-backed bird with streaks on its breast. It proved to be a tooth-billed bowerbird, a species sometimes called the "stagemaker" because the male clears a stage about seven feet in diameter, and over it spreads dozens of fresh-cut leaves, bottoms-up. On a branch above the arena, the male whistles, chortles, and imitates other birds. If the stagemaker is lucky, a female comes along, takes a fancy to his concert, and by some subtle gesture invites him to approach. He drops down, snatches up a leaf like a bouquet of roses, and dances. If the female is impressed, she surrenders herself like a groupie to a rock star.

Tooth-billed bowerbirds are rare and seldom seen in July. We were fortunate to find one, but our luck nearly led to grief. My attention shifted to the branches overhead, and I was not watching my step when I came around a hairpin bend and nearly stepped on a snake. It was five or six feet long, black of back, lurid red below, and thicker around than a broom handle.

When I startled it, the snake was lounging full-length across the trail, soaking up sunlight. In a flash it shot up and over the buttress-roots of a tree and vanished into a hollow. I stood frozen. No book was needed to make the identification. This was a red-bellied black snake, venomous and dangerous.

Like most snakes, red-bellied blacks are docile around humans unless backed into a corner. Only during the spring breeding season are they aggressive, and then only when a male meets another male. Males engage in ritual combat similar to thumb-wrestling. Each tries to force the head of the other to the ground. A no-biting rule seems to be in effect—a good thing, for venomous snakes are generally susceptible to their own toxin. When the contest concludes, the victor gets the girl.

Saturday was memorable for reptiles, Sunday for mammals. Early in the morning we tramped down the road to the next driveway, walked up a lane into the woods, and enjoyed tea and pumpkin scones with John Winter, the mammalogist, his partner Helen, and a research assistant named Alex Thomas. Plans were discussed for the evening. After supper, John would pick us up and whisk us away for a hunt with spotlights.

We had just returned from an after-dinner ramble when John's Land Rover raced down the drive. We had seen a platypus and mentioned our sighting to John. He listened patiently, but I could tell his interest lay elsewhere. Seeing a duck-billed platypus here was an everyday occurrence, no more newsworthy a happening than spying a gray squirrel in Manhattan's Central Park.

Into the night we flew, the car speeding over rough roads and rattling our teeth. Around every bend, and there were hundreds, we cringed at the thought of meeting a kangaroo or car.

We asked John about a small mammal, a bit larger than a mouse, that we had seen in a live-trap at Lake Barrine. The man who showed us the creature insisted it was a rat. We were skeptical. The snout was too pointed, the teeth too numerous and sharp, the look of the thing too alien. What could it have been?

John ruled out the long-tailed planigale, the most diminutive of marsupials and the tiniest mammal in the world, save for the dwarf shrew of Africa. Planigales, which eat insects, were simply too small to be mistaken for a rat. We had probably seen an antechinus.

There were three candidates: the Atherton antechinus, a rare species found only around Ravenshoe; the brown antechinus, a marsupial that has no pouch and drags its young around like a fish hauling lamprey eels; and the yellow-footed antechinus. The yellow-footed sometimes builds its nests inside televisions and easy chairs. It eats insects, mice, flowers, and nectar, and copulates for up to twelve hours. During lovemaking, the male sinks its teeth into the female's neck, a gesture she may fail to appreciate. After a binge of fornication, the male soon dies. Heir only to his genes, the female gestates, delivers, and nurses up to a dozen young. Which gender gets the better deal in the scheme is hard to say.

We reached a parking area at Mount Hypipamee Crater as pitch blackness settled on the rainforest. The Americans were waiting. It was a long time since we had heard Massachusetts accents, or North American diction of any kind. The speech struck us as strange. "Hi" sounded wrong. Why didn't these people say "g'day"?

We strapped on headlamps, tucked heavy batteries into backpacks, and dispersed into the night. Almost immediately I struck gold—yellow eyes, too small and close-set to belong to a tree-kangaroo, yet exciting to me nevertheless. John bustled over. Together we found a trembling rodent wedged into the fork of a shrub. It was a fawn-footed melomys, one of the few terrestrial mammals we had seen that was not a marsupial.

Rodents are placental mammals, a minority group in the land of kangaroos, but the majority everywhere else. At the time of European settlement, about a quarter of Australia's land mammals were rodents, among them such little-known beasts as the water rat, the spinifex hopping-mouse, and the prehensile-tailed rat, known from New Guinea but not discovered in Australia until 1974, at Lake Barrine. Introduced predators, rabbits, and grazing animals had been hard on Australian rodents. Eight species were presumed extinct.

Where did the rodents of Australia originate? Scientific tradition holds that they and placental mammals in general represent a recent invasion from New Guinea. Tim Flannery, however, suggests otherwise. He writes of a 55-million-year-old tooth found in Queensland in 1992, one that he says belonged to a condylarth, a primitive placental mammal. The find supports Flannery's theory that Australia is marsupial-rich not simply because the continent was isolated during an early stage of mammalian evolution, but also because marsupials outcompeted placentals in the country's low-energy ecosystems.

We left the melomys to its life of leaf-, bud-, and fruit-eating and resumed the hunt. A few minutes later I heard a cry in the dark. This time one of the Massachusetts contingent had found a brush-tailed possum. John advised us to note the eyeshine. The more scarce lemuroid ringtail possum inhabited the forest, too, he said, and its oversized eyes would produce bolder reflections than the small eyes of the brushtail.

"Over here!" This time it *was* a lemuroid ringtail, a portly, gray-brown possum with rusty shoulders and a belly tinged with yellow. Perched high in a tangle of leaves, it gazed down with eyes so big they inspired comparison to the goggle-eyed lemurs of Madagascar. Aside from its optical gear, the lemuroid ringtail looked plump but ordinary, like a common ringtail that had eaten too much.

In two hours of searching, we found no green ringtails, which John had been eager to show us, or any gliders. The Lumholtz's tree-kangaroo also refused to appear. We returned home to the Rodwells both disappointed and hopeful. The tree-kangaroo expert from Massachusetts said she had visited her former study site the preceding evening, and in a fig tree had admired a tree-kangaroo at close range. She was glad to give directions.

We visited that tree several weeks later. We were feeling cocky. In preceding days we had enjoyed excellent looks at a striped possum, arguably the most handsome of marsupials, in a tree near Julatten, and we had slogged through a jungle on Mount Lewis and found a bird of exquisite beauty, the golden bowerbird, tending twin towers of sticks. Our success in finding the animals we wanted to find had pumped us up with optimism.

And so we stood beneath the giant fig one dark night, waiting and listening. The suspense was cruel. For an hour or more, we heard little more than our own restless breathing. Then it came: a sound, a whisper of a movement in branches high above. Following the tree-kangaroo expert's advice, we kept our lights switched off and waited for the animal to descend.

Lumholtz's tree-kangaroo eats, sleeps, lives, and dies in trees. It is a genuine kangaroo, a true macropod, although it differs from its earthbound cousins in being able to move its rear legs independently. Tree-kangaroos are more typical of New Guinea, but two species inhabit Australia, Lumholtz's and Bennett's.

Bennett's tree-kangaroo occupies a small range north of the Daintree River, well north of the Tableland. Lumholtz's ranges from the south bank of the Daintree, down through the Tableland, all the way to forests west of Cardwell. Both species feed on rainforest leaves and fruit. Lacking opposable digits and tails that can grasp, Australian tree-kangaroos use sharp claws and a superb sense of balance to move through their jungle-gym world with speed and grace.

The first specimen of an Australian tree-kangaroo was collected by Carl Lumholtz, a zoologist from Norway. Lumholtz was an incorrigible racist who suggested that Aborigines were apelike. In his book *Among Cannibals* (1889), he wrote: "I live among a race of people whose culture—if indeed they can be said to have any culture whatsoever—must be characterised as the lowest to be found among the whole genus *Homo sapiens*." Ironically, Lumholtz depended on Aborigines to provide him specimens. One day they carried into camp an animal they called "boongarry." It was a tree-kangaroo. Lumholtz found it "a better proportioned animal than the common kangaroo" and "the most beautiful marsupial I have seen in Australia."

Lumholtz fancied himself superior, yet it was he, not his Aboriginal helpers, who left the boongarry skin where it could be carried off by a dingo. The dingo ate much of the trophy, then fell sick because Lumholtz had lathered the inside with an arsenic-based preservative. Now the Norwegian had a second problem. The dingo was not a wild animal, but the property of Lumholtz's Aboriginal colleagues. If it died, they might leave him to hunt specimens on his own.

According to his account of events, Lumholtz mixed tobacco with water and poured it down the dingo's throat, inducing the animal to cough up the pelt. The dog lived, the natives stayed on the job, and Lumholtz went on to shoot and skin a second specimen of the tree-kangaroo that would eventually bear his name.

The noise came again, directly overhead. *And again.* Something—we dearly hoped it was a Lumholtz's tree-kangaroo—was descending toward us out of the canopy. Silent and watchful, we waited among the fig tree's roots.

For a minute there was no sound at all. Then we heard a large animal moving across the forest floor, somewhere to our left. Damn! The thing, whatever it was, had slipped to the ground and was making a getaway. We switched on a light. Nothing—no animal, no eyeshine, just leaves and stems against a black velvet background.

Yet we had heard something—something large and about the size of a tree-kangaroo. It had taken several hops. Tree-kangaroos come down from trees at night, looking for things to eat. In all likelihood the animal lurked just beyond the reach of our light. But where? In a state of mounting agitation, we charged back and forth in the bush, hoping no red-bellied black snake was out for a prowl.

Nothing. *Nothing.* In the morning we left the Tableland defeated.

From the Rodwells' we drove to Cairns, the northernmost city in Queensland. The place seemed surreal—more like a theme park than a real metropolis. Most of the buildings looked as though they had been thrown together the day before, and the streets were crowded with foreigners, half of them under twenty-five and skinny, the other half gray of top and round of bottom. Souvenir shops, booking agents hawking reef tours, restaurants, hotels, and nightclubs crowded up against each other in a feverish attempt to gather dollars, deutsche marks, pounds, francs, kroner, and guilders.

We darted in and out of Cairns a dozen times over the course of several weeks. A friend, a woman named Jo Trezise, let us come and go from her apartment in Edge Hill, just outside the city. Thanks to Jo, we enjoyed the benefits of Cairns without being caught in its tentacles. A camera repairman revived an ailing Olympus, a shoe repairman named Theo reunited a set of uppers with soles, and a mechanic replaced bearings in the Toyota's wobbling distributor. Best of all, we rediscovered ice cream.

Ignoring high-gloss advertisements for guided reef cruises and diving trips, we asked the locals if there was any way a couple of paupers smeared with outback dust could finagle a peek at the world's greatest wall of coral. The answer was yes, sort of. Fitzroy Island, named by Captain Cook after Augustus Henry Fitzroy, England's prime minister the day *Endeavour* set sail, lay only a few miles from the Cairns wharf. For thirty bucks we could buy a ticket there and back, and for a few dollars more we could rent a site in the island's municipal campground. A little milk of human kindness sweetened the deal. The only commercial enterprise on Fitzroy, a Japanese-owned resort, gave campers free, unrestricted access to their hot showers, bar, and swimming pool.

Between the hour when a boat deposited us on the island's pier until the moment it hauled us away two days later, we had the time of our lives. We pitched the tent within a hundred feet of the sea, donned masks, bit down on snorkels, and for forty-eight hours lived like fish. A few naysayers had told us that crown-of-thorns starfish, which were killing vast areas of the Great Barrier Reef, had exterminated all of Fitzroy's coral, but they were wrong. A few patches were dead, yet the shallow waters off the beach presented the finest collection of hard and soft coral either of us had ever seen.

The Great Barrier Reef proper lies well beyond Fitzroy Island. It runs along the northeast coast of Australia for more than 1,400 miles, rising

180 feet above the seafloor in places and covering more than 80,000 square miles. The reef is the size of England and Scotland combined. Astronauts on the moon, looking back at the Earth, saw only one sign of life—the reef, a fertile crescent in a vast blue ocean.

To say that the Great Barrier Reef teems with life is like saying the universe holds many stars. There are more than 1,500 species of fish, over four hundred kinds of coral, giant clams that can weigh six hundred pounds, sea turtles galore, thousands of squishy marine invertebrates most people have never heard of, and great white sharks. *Conus geographus* lives there, too. It is a handsome-looking mollusk that most of us would pick up without a second thought. According to an article in *National Geographic,* a shell collector found one a few years ago, dropped it in a pocket, and fell immediately dead. The gastropod packs venom. It had jabbed the man through the fabric of his pocket.

I nearly stepped on a venomous stonefish, sulking on the bottom, and together Debbie and I almost swam into a butterfly-cod, or lionfish. The butterfly-cod looks like a papier-mâché sculpture from a Chinese parade, poisonous spines covering it like porcupine quills. Despite these near misses, we were really quite safe. The cold, deep waters where great white sharks prowl lay miles to the east. For hours we floated in a state of bliss. As long as we looked rather than touched, we knew that the only harm likely to come to us was a bad sunburn. The water was cool and sparkling. Swimming in it was like playing in a tub of champagne.

Everywhere we looked, a new fish swam by, each more colorful than the last. Through masks we admired angelfish and wrasses, butterfly-fish and clownfish, sergeant-majors and firefish, parrotfish, boxfish, unicorn-fish, coral cod, and several kinds of triggerfish. Red, yellow, green, blue, and orange shapes swirled around us. The colors were so electric that the fish looked like hallucinations.

Directly beneath us, giant clams, the kind that in old movies grab divers by the ankle and try to drown them, looked powerful yet benign. Measuring three feet across their prismatic maws, the mollusks never worried us. Clams, giant ones included, are filter feeders. They may weigh four hundred pounds or more, but none preys on movie actors and tourists. Giant clams, paragons of patience, spend their lives glued to the seafloor, waiting for plankton.

Although it would be possible, theoretically, to put a foot in the mouth of a giant clam and have it clamp down in response, the chances of such a blunder happening are slim. There is no missing the colorful mantle that fringes the mollusk's parted valves. Blues, greens, and red-browns seem to be daubed on like lipstick, but in fact are created by algae resident in the mantle. Giant clams cultivate single-celled algae in protective folds, digesting great numbers of them but leaving the majority unharmed. The surviving algae give off color. The clams must live in shallow water because their algal partners need sunshine to survive. Without them the oversized bivalves would quickly starve.

Our greatest excitement in the coral came unexpectedly. We were nosing down into twenty feet of water, following a butterfly-cod at a safe distance. Suddenly a dark shape intruded between us and the sun. What could it be? I looked over my shoulder to see an enormous turtle stroking its flippers. At a distance it resembled a giant water bug, and like that diving insect, the turtle wore a coat of air bubbles that glinted like diamonds.

Debbie and I drifted closer. We watched the turtle bob to the surface for a noseful of air, then row downward with its flippers. Its movements had the quality of fine ballet, each surge of its body powerful and controlled, a study in grace. We could have touched the green, arching carapace, but resisted the temptation.

I was so entranced by the sea turtle that I failed to note the features that would have told us its identity. Later, perusing Cogger's bible of Australian herpetology, we settled on the green turtle, *Chelonia mydas*, a species that outnumbered the other two on the reef. Green turtles occur from Shark Bay in Western Australia, up and over the continent's northern coastline, and south along the east coast to Fraser Island in Queensland. Outside of Australia, the range of the green turtle forms a wide belt around the midriff of the globe.

Green turtles once abounded. Coastal peoples from Florida to Southeast Asia to northern Australia relied on their flesh as a staple. Seafarers relished them, too, turtle meat breaking the culinary monotony of long voyages. Then came the twentieth century. An international trade in turtle soup and turtle eggs sprang up, and in a few short decades the green turtle was driven toward extinction. Today, Australian Aborigines and Torres Strait islanders hunt the reptile for food, but otherwise it enjoys strict protection. Slowly numbers are rising, and encounters such as ours grow more common every year.

Our aquatic interlude over too soon, we rode the ferry back to Cairns. There we shook sand from our shoes, consulted with the locals, and made a decision. We would venture north up the Cape York Peninsula in two separate pushes. The first would bring us up the Captain Cook Highway to Mossman, on to the Daintree River, across the channel by ferry, and north by rough road to Cape Tribulation. The second push would test our mettle. If the car could handle it, we would drive the so-called Peninsula Developmental Road into the interior, then branch off on a four-wheel-drive-only road to the remote wilderness of Lakefield National Park. It was the dry season, and people told us that our car could handle the terrain and river crossings if we were careful.

To travel any farther up the peninsula, we would need not one but *two* four-wheel-drive vehicles; such was the consensus among experts. Two rugged vehicles are advised so that if one gets stuck, the other can pull it out. Hundreds of deep gullies and fords lay between civilization and the Cape, and the road that connected them was unpaved and badly eroded. On a limited budget, in an overloaded two-wheel-drive station wagon, we had to settle for exploring the southern half of the Florida-sized peninsula. If all went well, we would still penetrate far beyond the reach of most tourists, and see some of the wildest country in Australia.

Our first venture into the savage North proved a rude awakening. The country above Cairns was picturesque, and we marveled at jungle-clad mountains that swept down to the highway. On the seaward side of the road, we found sandy beaches with crocodile warning signs and mangrove trees standing bowlegged over mud flats. Cycads dotted the slopes, looking like stodgy palm trees, and the sun blazed cheerfully in an azure sky. Yet something was wrong. The road to nowhere echoed with the hiss of rubber. Cars, trucks, buses, and ungainly four-wheel-drive people-movers sped by us every time we stopped to take in a view. Where were they headed? Surely not to Mossman, a sleepy town that owed its existence to a cane-processing plant. The answer came from a ranger at the National Parks office in Mossman. The crowds were bound for the area called "the Daintree," a much-publicized corner of the 2,223,000-acre Wet Tropics World Heritage Area that stretches from Townsville to Cooktown.

After two days of driving, we arrived at Daintree village and found ourselves among hundreds of visitors seeking excitement in the wilderness. The village was a sort of Ye Olde Frontier Town, erected for the purpose of lightening the wallets of travelers. Instead of a dusty country store with a sleepy dog and a petrol pump out front, we found restaurants, souvenir shops, and booking offices. We pitched our tent in a crowded campground. Overhead, pink, saucer-sized blossoms served nectar to yellow-bellied sunbirds.

For the first time in our odyssey, we cast Emersonian self-reliance aside and hired a guide. His name was Rick, and for fifty dollars, nearly two days' budget for us, he agreed to take us out in a fiberglass boat powered by a Japanese outboard and show us the local wildlife.

A man who pays cash to satisfy a sexual urge must feel something like the queasiness we experienced during our three hours on the Daintree River. In the back of the boat sat Rick, bored, chain-smoking cigarettes, doing his best to sound like a redneck. He knew his birds, however, as no self-respecting redneck ever would, and showed us a fair selection—the jabiru, or black-necked stork; the mangrove gerygone; the long-billed gerygone; a stunning blue-black bird called the shining flycatcher; the little kingfisher, which was indigo of back, alabaster of belly, and barely larger than a sparrow; and a virtual PTA meeting of Nankeen night-herons. The night-herons crowded into a tree up a side channel. They looked at us as if engaged in important discussion and miffed about being disturbed.

Chief among the river's attractions were reptiles. We were not disappointed. Between puffs on his coffin-nails, Rick pointed out a common tree snake here, a northern tree snake there, and an eastern water dragon thrown in now and again for variety. The man had a good eye. Gazing into the green and yellow coils of a common tree snake basking on a limb overhead, I asked if the reptile was poisonous. "Mildly," said Rick, ending the matter as far as he was concerned. If our bow had veered a few inches to the right, it would have bumped the tree, and the snake, baking in the morning sun like a pretzel, would have landed in one of our laps. It didn't worry Rick.

The eastern water dragon hardly lived up to its name. It was a scrawny thing, barely a foot long, and looked no more a challenge for a knight in armor than a malnourished pet iguana. The skin hung loose and brown. Although spikes ran along the nape and ridge of the back, they had lost all interest in standing up. A black swath ran back from each eye, giving the water dragon a mildly sinister look. Otherwise it was about as imposing as the rubber lizards sold in the village as souvenirs.

The day's biggest thrill came from a trio of crocodiles. They were about a dozen feet long, and to eyes accustomed to alligators, their heads looked too big for the bodies. But the size made sense when we thought about it. Alligators eat small things, mostly, such as turtles, frogs, and the odd schnauzer. Queensland crocodiles, by contrast, think nothing of consuming a dairy cow. Judging by the bulge in one croc's midriff, it had eaten a small boat recently. Fortunately, it and its sidekicks wanted only to snooze on the grassy bank.

The Daintree crocodiles left us disappointed. Their discovery had come too quickly, too easily, with none of the struggle or suspense that came from finding things ourselves. Rick had given us our money's worth, it was true. Yet like a couple of johns leaving a brothel, we came away deflated, feeling we had done something not quite ethical. Perhaps paying for something sacred leaves one feeling dirty.

In the afternoon we crossed the Daintree on an automobile ferry. It was an ancient thing, an iron hulk that pulled its way along a cable. The middle of the cable sagged into the pea-green water. Tourists and rental cars crowded the boat. I was reminded of a story that someone had told us in Cairns. It seems there was an evening when the ferry's winch broke down in midriver. A call went out to a mechanic, who appeared a while later. Ignoring the risk of crocodiles, perhaps because he had downed a few pints at a pub on the way and wanted to show off for the pretty women watching from the rail, the mechanic strapped tools to his back and swam out to do the job. Before he reached the boat, the water swirled, a curl of crocodile tail was seen, and the man vanished. According to the teller of the story, the dead man's brother was interviewed on television. When asked if the mechanic had done something foolhardy, the brother protested. "Oh, no," he said. "He'd swum out to the ferry several times before." The incident was blamed on the reptile rather than on poor judgment, and the story ended as such tales usually do. The crocodile was hunted down and destroyed.

From the northern bank of the river, a winding road led through lush subtropical forest, up and down a series of hills, and on to "Cape Trib," as people called it. "I named . . . the north point Cape Tribulation," wrote James Cook, "because here began all our troubles." The day after passing the peninsula, Cook's ship, *Endeavour,* impaled itself on a dagger of coral. Four planks were pierced and three more damaged. As the hold took on water, the ship entered a river a few miles to the north. Today that river is known as the Endeavour, and the spot where carpenters repaired the breach goes by the name of Cooktown.

We spent two nights at Cape Tribulation. In a clearing hacked out of dense bush by Frank and Mark Trezise, the husband and son of Jo Trezise, we pitched our tent and cooked over a wood fire. Gaunt and soft-spoken, Frank greeted us when we arrived an hour after dark, appearing out of the darkness like a specter. He insisted that we camp within a few steps of his door, and, feeling in no position to argue, we did. In the morning Frank asked us to join him for breakfast.

Sitting in chairs beside the open-air fireplace in which Frank cooked his meals, we emptied bowls of steaming porridge and fell into conversation. We learned that Frank lived on a block of private land bordering one of Australia's last great wilderness areas. By design, his house had only three walls, the fourth left open to morning sunshine, birdsong, and the rustle of nocturnal wildlife. Frank grew most of his own food and spent his days as he pleased—reading, penning letters, thinking, and cooking and eating under a tree. His was the life Emerson advocated, one combining action and contemplation. Frank lived much as Thoreau had at Walden.

Frank nodded in sympathy when we told him of our impatience with desk jobs, and of our desire to get out and see the world. He shared our hunger for freedom, beauty, and adventure. "Of course," he said. "You had to go. The only wonder is that you didn't start sooner." Frank's voice was soft and deep, like an owl's.

After Frank Trezise, Cape Tribulation itself proved disappointing. We avoided a beach where a dozen people swam in defiance of a sign warning about crocodiles. Resort hotels beckoned with haute cuisine and cocktails, but we avoided them. Of more interest were a leathery old Boyd's forest dragon we found in the bush, and a bird called the noisy pitta.

For months we had been hearing noisy pittas in Australia's eastern forests, but the bird itself had eluded us. The three-syllable call is whistled at shocking volume. Bird books render it as *Walk to work! Walk to work!*

When a noisy pitta began to call in the rain forest at Cape Trib, I suggested to Debbie that we try to find it. Putting aside thoughts of venomous snakes and funnel-web spiders, we stepped off the trail, pushed through the shrubs and vines, and moved toward the source of the fuss.

A plump, sawed-off little bird burst almost immediately into view. It scurried along the ground, as a pitta should, and had a golden belly, racy orange underpants, a black mask, and a rusty crown. The pitta's back was emerald green, providing perfect camouflage from above. We froze. Ignoring us, the bird snatched up a land snail, placed it on a stone, and pecked. The shell yielded, and the pitta wolfed down the flesh inside.

Then the calling resumed. *Walk to work, walk to work!* At close range the volume stung our ears.

The pitta's beauty demanded contemplation, so I suggested we linger. Finding a nearby log, we sat for about ten minutes. The bird continued to strut and demolish snails. In the middle of the performance, Debbie gasped as if a Tasmanian tiger had walked up behind me. I turned. An old, leathery war veteran of a lizard perched on a limb just above the ground. It had formidable spikes on its head, a cream-colored patch on each cheek, and a scaly dewlap that hung from its jaw like a jowl. From the angular snout to the end of its long, spiky tail, the lizard stretched as long as my forearm. It was a Boyd's forest dragon, an elusive rain-forest creature we had entertained little hope of finding.

Still, the reptile we most hoped to see at Cape Trib was the one that had confounded our efforts to find it everywhere else: the goanna, or monitor lizard. Twenty-five species of goanna occur in Australia, six in northern Queensland alone. We would have settled for any one of them, gladly. By virtue of its abundance and wide distribution, the lace monitor offered our best chance.

Strong and nimble, lace monitors spend most of their time in trees, preying on insects, lizards, snakes, and arboreal mammals. They also drop to the ground from time to time and consume carrion, baby birds, and unattended meals on picnic tables. According to local advice, they patrolled the Cape Tribulation campground. We stopped there on our way out of town for the sole purpose of seeing one.

Turning from the graveled main road into a pair of wheel ruts, we came quickly to a caravan, or travel-trailer. A man and woman, both gray-haired and puckered by too much sun, sat outside eating fried eggs. Their car had New South Wales license plates. "Right," said the man, when I asked if they had seen a goanna. He raised a farmer's meaty hand toward the scrub, pointing. "That's where he went after he strolled past the caravan. Go have a look." The woman smiled uncomfortably, as one might in the presence of lunatics.

For an hour we had a look. We crept through every bushy corner of the camping area, watching for lizards (and snakes), and listening. Every man, woman, and child in our path was interrogated. A few had seen a goanna the previous morning, an unusually large one, but none today. Exasperation set in. We had tried everything—driven thousands of miles, looked in all the right places, seen flattened goannas on the road, and in desperation we bought some sausages, or "snags," and grilled them outdoors. Debbie had read that goannas are drawn to picnic areas by the smell of sausages cooking. For five months we had hunted the lizards, and everywhere they eluded us.

A half-day's drive brought us to Mount Molloy. There we veered north and west on the road to Cape York. We stopped briefly at a public campground to use the toilets, and had the pleasure of gazing up to see a tawny frogmouth sitting owl-like on a branch. The frogmouth is one of the weirdest birds in Australia. It sits around all day, utterly immobile, looking like a cross between an owl and a broken-off limb. At night it flies around, opens its broad and almost beakless mouth, vacuums up flying insects, and plucks frogs, lizards, and mice from the ground. The bird is a Caprimulgid, or goatsucker. Eurasia's nightjar and North America's whippoorwill are close relations. From Tasmania to northern Queensland we had been entertained at night by frogmouths, which utter strings of deep, airy bass notes. It was satisfying to finally meet the bird behind the song.

On we drove. There were no other passenger cars. Occasionally a truck or Land Cruiser thundered past, spraying dust and gravel, but otherwise the road was deserted. The country was flat and increasingly dry, and when a truck approached from the opposite direction, we could see its dust plume far in the distance.

At one point we skirted a shallow lake. A pair of wild horses, or "brumbies," were galloping exuberantly through the shallows, sending showers of glittering diamonds flying into the air with each footfall. Further on, we stopped at a roadhouse, intrigued by the daily special, "Croc and Chips."

The chips consisted of ordinary French fries. The crocodile, breaded and fried, was as delicate and chewy as American alligator. It was unlikely we were eating the croc that swallowed the Daintree ferry repairman. Meat for the restaurant trade, the proprietor assured us, came from crocodile farms.

On we thundered, into country that grew flatter and drier, on and on at the vortex of a spreading fan of dust. This was the real, fair-dinkum outback, although no one seemed to call it that. It was simply "the Bush." There were no towns, no barns, no houses, just the occasional roadhouse selling petrol, radiator hoses, and cold drinks to wash down the dust. Bony cattle grazed the land, and judging by the paucity of plants, they were busy turning the shrubland into desert.

Having left civilization well behind us, we felt a heady mix of exhilaration and terror. Whatever happened here, for good or for ill, would be ours to confront alone. We might discover wondrous things, and we might encounter troubles or outlaws. Like Odysseus, we would have to face the challenges armed with little more than guts and cunning.

In Laura, a one-horse town that looked like the set of a Hollywood western, we topped off our petrol and bought groceries. The fidgety man behind the counter in the shop appeared to be the only white man in town. Three Aboriginal children kicked a ball in the street, casting smiles and glances at us. Dressed in shorts and T-shirts, every square inch of their clothes stained by dust, the kids looked happier than most of their sharply dressed counterparts in Sydney.

Watching everything from the shade of a crooked tree, three Aboriginal men sat with blank faces. They were old and wrinkled, and only an occasional flash of eye-white told us they were awake and paying attention. I was sure they were scrutinizing us and, feeling self-conscious, gave them a friendly wave. There was no reaction. In the periphery of my vision, I could see the grocer peering out the window. He looked clammy and afraid.

Laura was one of many remote settlements in which we sensed a dangerous tension between blacks and whites. We had been reading Australian newspapers long enough to know the usual story. The anger and frustration of each race toward the other results eventually in violence. Violence leads to further violence, and the destruction of property, and in the end, policemen come in with guns and clubs and subdue the hostile mob. Aborigines end up in jail, and some of them die. A few whites are imprisoned, too, but often not for long. Although progress is being made at reform, the criminal justice system seems steeply slanted in favor of the white man. This, in turn, promotes further Aboriginal anger and frustration, which in turn provokes hostile responses from whites, and the sad story goes on and on. In both groups, alcohol compounds the ugliness.

Not wanting to get caught in the middle of something, we bustled out of Laura. A few minutes later we ran into a roadblock. It was a fruit-and-vegetable inspection station manned by three jolly white men.

A few minutes after surrendering our bananas, we passed a sign marking the boundary of Lakefield National Park. Almost immediately, the landscape transformed. Dusty, overgrazed, and scrubby terrain gave way to a forest of eucalypts and wattles. In the afternoon light, the trees cast long black stripes across the road's red dirt.

As the landscape grew lovelier by the minute, the road turned ugly. Deep corrugations scored the surface, and at every speed, the car shook like a hardware store's paint mixer. The only thing to do was proceed at a crawl, hoping the Toyota's nuts remained married to its bolts and our teeth stayed tight in their sockets.

Slow movement brought advantages. Now we were able to take in the sights—all two of them. Poking up in all directions were termite mounds, one kind red, crumbling, and suggestive of a sand castle after a heavy rain, the other shaped like a tombstone, gray, flat, two-dimensional, and gothic, topped with a row of spires. The average height of the crumbling mounds was three or four feet, the tombstones double that. We expected to be impressed by the architectural attainments of Australian termites, but nothing had prepared us for the scale and abundance of their work.

The termites that constructed the mounds were pale, squishy things, each about the length of a human fingernail. One would hardly guess these amorphous globs of protoplasm were capable of getting out of bed in the morning, let alone of designing and building skyscrapers. Yet they managed. Like more than a few famous overachievers, the termites lead sordid private lives. Workers enslave bacteria and use them to digest the cellulose in decaying plants. Other members of the colony feed on the workers' excrement and vomit. Hundreds of thousands of termites inhabit each bustling colony.

To house themselves, the termites build high-rise buildings out of clay, spit, and feces. The edifice raised by the magnetic termite, the builder of the tombstones, stands with its broad front parallel to the planet's magnetic axis. One end points toward magnetic north, the other toward magnetic south. The insects thus avoid the worst heat of midday. Morning light strikes the tombstone's eastern flank, and afternoon sunshine bathes the western side. In the blistering hours, the sun strikes only a thin edge, and the termites avoid overheating.

Just before dark we checked in at the New Laura ranger station. A woman watched through a screen door as we padded up the steps. Her arms were red where they poked out of a khaki uniform, and her thin face was dotted prettily with freckles. "G'day," the ranger greeted us in singsong tones, and introduced herself as Virginia Mini. "You'll be wanting a campsite. Right, then. I have just the place—Catfish Waterhole. If you hurry, you'll make it before dark."

We did not. Advancing slowly, scrutinizing trees for birds and the ground for lizards and dingoes, we saw darkness arrive with a suddenness that shocks visitors to the tropics. We strained to find the dirt track that led from the main road to the campsite. Eventually twin ruts appeared in the grass. The road? We edged forward into pitch blackness, making sure the car kept on course. To one side lay a water hole patrolled by estuarine crocodiles. Virginia had said that crocs abounded in the area and we should keep away from the water's edge at all times.

There were three primitive campsites along the track. Virginia had assigned us to the middle one. Somehow we missed the first and second, for suddenly a lantern appeared, telling us we had gone too far. Beneath the light, three men sat playing cards. They were the only other humans in this corner of 1.3 million acres of wilderness.

Reversing the car into the velvety blackness proved impossible. The backup lights were too dim. Debbie and I climbed out, first checking the ground for snakes. The night air was warm and moist. Insects trilled. What to do? We couldn't go forward. Going backward blindly might put us in the water hole. A flashlight revealed water only a few feet from one of our wheels. Scanning the area near the car, we found a patch of grass. I maneuvered into it and switched off the engine and lights.

As we pitched the tent, mournful voices filled the air. Dingoes! The cries were longer and more full-bodied than the yips and wails of coyotes, yet more piercing than the deep howls of wolves. In the Center, someone had told us that dingoes, once semidomesticated by Aborigines, have not entirely lost their affinity for humans. Wild and wary in general, they are nevertheless drawn by the light of human encampments. Perhaps they retain some dim ancestral memory of a partnership long dissolved.

A few minutes later we heard a stick snap. Were the dingoes near, watching us? A flashlight revealed nothing. On the ground, thousands of green spider eyes glinted in sets of eight. The dingoes called again, farther off. The place seemed less lonely for their wails.

Debbie crawled into bed. Restless, I stayed awake for another hour, sitting in the car and making notes by the glow of a candle. I listened to an Australia Broadcast Corporation news report. Little had changed in the world—the same promise, the same contrapuntal mayhem. It all seemed very far away. At last, still very much awake, I set off on a walk.

I backtracked a quarter-mile up the road, staying well away from the water hole. Rocket frogs hopped to and fro in the grass, long, leggy things with pointed snouts. I tried catching them, but each lunge came up empty. Tiring, I shuffled back to camp. The insects were quieter now, and I could hear Debbie breathing softly inside the tent. Above, stars sparkled in unfamiliar patterns. A sense of deep happiness crept over me. I could feel it in my scalp. "This is living," I said to myself. Curled up beside my Penelope, I felt consciousness slip away as dingoes cried in the distance.

Lest the reader form a notion of me as one of those eager naturalists who bolt up before dawn each morning, ready to seize the day, I will confess the truth. I am a dead weight until nearly midday. Waking in a daily funk, I would, if given the choice between sleeping a few more hours and meeting the last living dodo, burrow under the covers. During the course of our journey, Debbie often had to tease, coax, threaten, and lure me into action with promises of coffee and breakfast.

Yet, on our first morning at Lakefield, I burst into consciousness with glee, proving, I think, that there is no better tonic for the soul than happiness. I had only begun to know this wild place, yet I loved it with a reckless, impulsive passion. The first hints of daylight were seeping into the bush when I stirred, and the trees shook with the voices of birds.

If our odyssey had a single morning that I savor above all others, it would be this one. We wriggled into damp clothes, staggered onto our feet, fetched binoculars, and were off. Birds were everywhere—on the ground, in the water, in bushes, in trees, darting through the air, soaring against the sky. Never, anywhere, had we seen and heard so many kinds in so small an area in such a short interval of time.

In the water there were Radjah shelducks, oversized things with white heads and pink bills. In the air we saw a flock of red-tailed black cockatoos, looking more like an RAAF squadron than parrots. A white-bellied sea eagle flew past at treetop level and looked as big as a Cessna. The eagle passed silently while the cockatoos filled the air with war cries.

From trees came the voices of yellow orioles, bubbling and joyful, and a soliloquy of squawks and hisses that we traced to a great bowerbird. The latter was a plump, gray-suited politician of a thing that sat on a limb and droned like a parliamentarian. There were other birds, too, far too many to catalog here—red-browed firetails shining in the sun, six kinds of honeyeater, two species of dove, a darter drying its unfurled wings, a blue-winged kookaburra, an azure kingfisher, a sacred kingfisher, a white-bellied cuckoo-shrike, a rufous whistler, rainbow bee-eaters, a satin flycatcher darting after insects, red-winged parrots, rainbow lorikeets, and, perhaps most eye-pleasing of all, a lovely fairy-wren. (Lovely is part of the bird's name, as well as a fitting adjective.) The fairy-wren was a male. Its cobalt head contrasted so sharply with a black throat and drab body that the bird looked like a creature out of myth, half animal, half god. By the time we made our way back to the car and tent, nine new species graced a cumulative list that now exceeded three hundred species.

In the middle of the walk, we had a crocodile encounter. Debbie and I were standing near an arm of the water hole, focusing binoculars on shelducks, when I spied something low in the water, a hundred feet away and moving left to right at great speed. Our lenses revealed it to be a crocodile. American naturalists employ a formula for making quick estimates of alligator length; the number of inches between the eyes and the nostrils approximates the number of feet the alligator is long. If the formula applied to the estuarine crocodile, the animal we were seeing in Catfish Waterhole measured about twelve feet in length. "Look!" I cried to Debbie, pointing. As she raised her glasses, the crocodile sank from view.

That wasn't the end of it. The arm of the lagoon was thick with water lilies, their pads nearly covering the surface. After the croc vanished, lilies in the distance began to quiver. Then pads closer to us were jarred, and then pads closer still. A large object was brushing against their submerged stems, no doubt, and it was making a beeline toward us. Egad! We backed away. The lilies ceased to shake, and the pool lay as calm and benign as a bathtub.

After breakfast we packed up the tent and drove a few miles to a picnic area beside Sandy Creek. Virginia said a goanna had chased her there recently, and, desperate for contact with one of the lizards, we would do our best to invite a repeat performance. We sat. We ate. We wafted the scents of peanut butter, jelly, and sardines on the hot breeze. While waiting, we watched crimson, star, and double-barred finches flit among shrubs that grew along the dry creek and envied them as they cooled off in a puddle.

Although the calendar asserted it was winter, the air was scorching, nearly a hundred degrees Fahrenheit. Patience wears thin in such conditions, and we soon lost ours with the goanna. Seeking shade, we drove away, bound for a campground called Kalpowar.

Shuddering along corrugated roads, searching fruitlessly for a speed at which the Toyota's springs might find harmony with the jolting, we pushed northward. Hundreds of mosque- and castle-shaped termite mounds along the route stood higher than the car, making the drive seem like an architect's tour of Lilliput. At one point something large and yellow streaked across the road. We stopped where it had vanished. A dingo looked back at us over its muscular shoulders, blinking in the sunshine.

Something was wrong with the car. Its motor stalled a half-dozen times, and each time it died, we prayed to the gods that the problem would not evolve into something big. We finally rattled into Kalpowar, much relieved. Before us spread all the comforts—picnic tables, tent sites marked out on an irrigated lawn, sinks, cold running water, and toilets that flushed with a roar.

After the tent went up, we picked our way down to shallow pools in rocks along the river. The water was blue, the stone red, the gorge shaded by massive eucalypts. After taking in the scene, we set off upstream, following the bank. Virginia said a sixteen-foot crocodile ruled a nearby pool, and with luck we might catch it basking.

To keep the water in view, we had to navigate carefully along a steep, muddy bank. The footing was dicey, and it would have been easy to slip and skid into deep water. There is nothing like danger to summon ancestral talents. Soon we were brachiating branch-to-branch like apes, advancing one cautious step at a time.

A half hour later we stood by the pool Virginia had described. Birds sang, and dragonflies darted over the water. Someone unfamiliar with crocodiles might have seen the place as an ideal swimming hole, shucked his clothes, and leaped to his doom. By this point we were dizzy from the heat and drenched with perspiration. "Care for a swim?" I asked.

"You go," Debbie said.

"Ladies first." Beneath the joking, we were edgy. We had read enough stories about crocodiles seizing, thrashing, drowning, and disassembling humans to make our stomachs churn like washing machines. With relief as well as disappointment, we turned our backs and walked into the bush. The croc had refused to appear.

The hike to camp brought us through a savanna of scattered eucalypts and tall grass. Pushing through the blades, sometimes on a footpath, often not, we inhaled the scent of wild mint and scanned the trees for birds. All was still.

Hot and tired, we were staggering along when I walked into a spider's web. The thing was enormous! I backed off to the point where eyes could focus. Strands of white silk interwove to form a net about six feet across, six feet high, a dozen inches thick. Who made it, I wondered—the volleyball spider? A search of the web revealed the weaver. It was an arachnid of modest proportions, with long, thin legs radiating out like spokes. The body was straw-colored and about the size of a grape. The spider was likely a member of the genus *Nephila,* a group that includes Australia's champion web-builders. *Nephila* catch and eat insects, for the most part, but are also known to ensnare and sometimes devour frogs, lizards, small birds, and bats. Their webs have a yellowish cast and are sturdy and elastic. Hats caught in them are plucked from their wearers' heads, and Aborigines once collected the silk and spun it into fishing line.

Night came on swiftly, and stars glittered overhead. For hours we sat reading and writing, capitalizing on the luxury of a picnic table. Interruptions came frequently. At one point a troupe of black flying foxes winged in, settling with a noisy whooshing in a tree near our tent. Coming from eastern North America, where bats are small and insectivorous, we were always astounded by flying foxes. Black, leathery wings joined to form Dracula-like capes when the animals came to rest, but in flight vampirish associations no longer applied; the bats looked like Dachshunds that had somehow learned to fly. The black flying foxes of Kalpowar had big eyes, snouts that tapered handsomely, and reddish brown mantles draped handsomely over ebony backs. Remove the wings and you could pass the animal off as a dog.

The bats left us shortly after their arrival, perhaps bound for a tree with tastier fruit. They fled as they had arrived, awkwardly, with a crashing of leather against foliage and a noisy stirring of air.

From that point on, all our visitors were frogs. First came cane toads, one first, then another. They hopped into the pool of light cast by our lantern and came to rest nearly nose-to-nose at the base of a tree. Cane, or marine, toads were brought to Australia from Hawaii (where they had been introduced from the West Indies). Agricultural experts imported them to control insect infestations in Queensland's cane fields. Unfortunately the toads controlled nothing, not even themselves. More fecund than rabbits, they spread far and wide, and their range continues to expand. Many Australians despise cane toads, and for reasons easily understood. Cane toads devour not only insects and spiders, but also birds, lizards, and native frogs. They are themselves eaten by goannas, which may later sicken and die. Glands behind the toads' eyes produce toxins that kill or torment would-be predators.

Ignoring the toads, we welcomed the next arrival. It was a Roth's tree frog, a drab little amphibian with eyes whose upper halves appeared to be filled with blood. Jim, as we named him, looked the victim of a long, hard night on the town.

Cogger's herpetology said that Roth's tree frog had bright yellow markings on its thighs. This was hard to believe. Two inches long and gray-green, Jim was the picture of plainness. To settle the matter, I caught him. I teased his legs away from his pulsating body, and on the insides of the thighs, shocking yellow appeared against a black background. Cogger was right—Jim was wearing women's underwear. The book said nothing of the purpose of the markings, but we guessed that our friend used them to catch the attention of lovers, enemies, or both.

A few minutes later a cousin of Jim's flopped down from a branch above. Too rambunctious for its own good, the second frog leaped straight for the lantern. Wet toes struck hot metal. We heard a ghastly hiss. The webbed feet stuck fast for a moment, then pulled away. We groaned in sympathy. The frog sat still for a moment, palpitating its throat, and then wriggled into a crevice. On the spot, we swore off the gas lantern and went back to using candles.

Among the several species of frog we encountered that night, the most impressive came last. It was a green tree frog, and I found it in a toilet bowl in the campground "Gents." Even if I had found the frog in a pond, I would have laughed at the sight of it. The creature was monstrous, about the size of a man's fist, and it had a meaty, overhanging brow that imparted a touch of the Neanderthal. The skin was bright, pale green, and if you looked closely you could see that it was spattered with tiny white dots. The toes culminated in wide, round suction cups. Green tree frogs, we had learned, are serious predators. In addition to insects, they eat birds and bats.

By the time we crawled into sleeping bags a half hour after midnight, we had explored both the "Gents" and the "Ladies" and found a frog in every bowl. And why not? The water was fresh and cool, the human traffic light, and insects swarmed in great number.

A half moon glowed in the sky, casting the silhouette of a gum tree on our tent. We slept soundly, not waking until the sun was bright and hot.

At about noon, having dismantled the tent and hauled in a load of sun-dried laundry, we climbed into the car and headed south. Our plan was to leave Lakefield and drive to Cooktown, the northernmost city on the Queensland coast. For several reasons we felt glum. The drive would be long and bumpy, and having gotten a late start, we might not reach Cooktown until well past nightfall. Nor had we had our fill of Lakefield. And leaving the Northeast meant that our affair with Australia's Circe was drawing to a close.

We paused several times during the drive to watch agile wallabies. The animals hopped away from the roadsides where they were feeding, then stopped to gauge whether we posed a threat. Termite mounds rose up everywhere, some of them eight feet high. Together they gave touches of interest to a landscape otherwise dull and monotonous.

Termites loom large in northern Queensland's ecology, perhaps because earthworms are nonexistent or scarce. The monsoonal rains of the wet season make the soil intolerable for worms, which take poorly to long-term inundation. Termites, by contrast, build homes that rise well above the flood zone. This leaves them dry during the wet season and thus able to monopolize the recycling of leaves, wood, and bark.

After stopping to admire a wallaby, we were gaining speed when I noticed a dark shape lumbering across the road ahead. I saw, or thought I saw, the low, long shape of an immense lizard, crossing from right to left. The thing was so far away I couldn't be sure what I was seeing. Could it be the reptilian grail for which we had long searched? There was no time to waste. The animal was moving swiftly. I pressed the accelerator to the floor.

Soon we were rocketing south at nearly seventy miles per hour, skimming the road's corrugations. Dear Zeus! The ambiguous shape transformed itself into a goanna. When we were near, I hammered the brakes, swung to the shoulder, and leaped out.

About five feet long from the tip of its nose to the point of its banded tail, the goanna mounted a berm of soil at the road's edge and made for the bush. Debbie rolled down her window and cried, "Hey!" The lizard froze. It was massive, the most dinosaurlike creature we had ever seen. The legs were heavily muscled, the torso ready to burst through the skin. Dark streaks ran above and below the eyes, and on the back, circles of dirty white appeared, too randomly distributed to form a pattern.

The lizard started to move again. It was a sand monitor, or Gould's goanna, the most widely distributed monitor in Australia. Its speed was slow at first. It threw its body from side to side like a snake. Then, in apparent fear, the goanna rose up on its limbs and bolted. It ran with assurance, the torso swinging easily back and forth in coordination with the legs, the clawed feet tearing into the ground. When the sprint was over, the goanna planted itself in the grass, turned its neck toward me, and thrust out a blue-black tongue. The tongue waved back and forth hypnotically, like a snake-charmer's cobra.

I was raising a camera to take a photo when the lizard hissed. Again it lurched into motion. Striding deliberately for a dozen feet, it stopped with its snout poised over an eight-inch hole in the ground. The lizard's head swung back and forth, as if options were being weighed. I froze. Suddenly it shot for the hole. To my astonishment, the entire reptile vanished into the ground.

Standing there, we reevaluated our plan. Why leave Lakefield? We crossed Cooktown off the itinerary, returned to the car, and turned toward the ranger station. Another night at Catfish Waterhole would provide a few more hours of excitement.

The office where Virginia Mini had issued our camping permit was deserted. We looked to the cluster of sheds and houses that made up the ranger station; no one there. We shouted; no answer. One of the buildings looked like a residence, and we were walking toward it when a door banged shut and a man stepped toward us. He was dressed in well-worn khaki and wore a thick five o'clock shadow. Spying us, his eyes narrowed to slits. At a distance we took the ranger to be middle-aged, but as he drew near we could see a face that wrinkles had only begun to etch.

Introductions followed. The man was Tim Logue, the district ranger. What did we want? He sounded wary, although I couldn't imagine why. Thinking it might break the ice, I mentioned that Debbie and I sometimes worked for the United States National Park Service. A dam broke. Professional courtesy rushed out, and Tim proved eager to do whatever he could to help us.

We wanted a campsite. "No worries," he said with a wry smile. In the ensuing conversation, it came out that we had not been able to reach a particular chain of wetlands because our car had low clearance and lacked four-wheel drive. The somber face cracked another smile. "I need to run that loop this afternoon whether you come or not," Tim said. "You might as well join me."

And so we spent the afternoon with the district ranger, lurching through gullies and streambeds. The wetlands teemed with birds. We saw great flocks of shelducks and waders, and there was a waterhole so crowded with blooming lotuses that the surface was obscured. Tiptoeing over the lotus pads, comb-crested jacanas walked on attenuated toes, their red combs glowing in the sunshine. Green pygmy-geese circled the jacanas, forcing their way through the lotuses. They looked like ducks, which may have been no coincidence. According to geneticists, pygmy-geese *are* ducks.

The last wetland we came to was vast. It measured more than a mile across, and the tall eucalypts on the far shore melded into a frieze of gray-green foliage and stout white trunks. Tim frowned, pointing to the shallows. Plants had been ripped up, the mud churned. Lotuses and water lilies were conspicuously absent, and in their place grew exotic weeds.

"Livestock?" I asked.

Tim scowled. "Pigs," he said. "Bloody mobs of them. Look." He pointed to an enormous sow, charging out of the forest in the distance, advancing toward the shore. "She's pregnant, by the look of her. More work for me." Tim explained that the least favorite part of his job was pig-shooting. It was a necessary evil in a part of Australia where feral hogs, descended from ancestors put ashore by Captain Cook, inflicted terrible damage on wetlands.

Driving back through country luminous in the day's last sunshine, we arrived back at the ranger compound as deep shadows deepened. "You can't leave without a cuppa," said Tim. Indeed, to do so would have been to violate an Australian custom. So we trudged inside Tim's one-story house for tea.

The cuppa led to "fish burgers" made from a fish called red emperor. A camper had given his catch to Tim, and he said he needed help finishing the meat before it spoiled. It was glorious stuff, sweet and tender, a splendid contrast to beans and rice. A second round of tea followed, and when the cups were drained, Tim produced a bottle of Scotch. When we finally stood to leave, the sun had been down for hours.

"I have an idea you might like the sound of," said Tim with another of his cryptic smiles. "Tomorrow morning I have to drive out to Old Faithful Waterhole and check on a problem crocodile. He's a big brute, about sixteen feet, and very aggressive. When he started rising out of the water and snapping his jaws as people got out of their cars, we closed off the place to visitors. We need to check on him now and again. Maybe you'd like to come along. I can put you up in a workman's cottage so we can get an early start in the morning."

A rogue crocodile that clacked its teeth at cars? The offer sounded too good to refuse.

In the morning we awoke to the rumble of a truck. After a cuppa, "breakie," and a short delay, we rumbled down the road and turned into a pair of wheel ruts. Tim followed the faint track for a mile or two. Trees and termite mounds rose on either side, and tall grass swept against our undercarriage, hissing.

Only 9,000 visitors find their way to Lakefield National Park in an average year, and most of them come to fish. Old Faithful Waterhole, wet even in the dry season, was a popular destination until its dominant bull croc decided he was tired of company. Tim told us the Park Service was uncertain how to handle the situation.

"Has any visitor to the park ever been eaten by a crocodile?" I asked. As I spoke, we were out of the truck and creeping toward the shore.

"Not yet," said Tim. Sinewy, sturdy, and square of jaw, our companion cut a figure like John Wayne in his salad days.

Communicating with hand gestures, we advanced to a break in the trees. Water lay ahead, and along its far shore we saw a sandbar. "There," whispered Tim. On the sand, baking in the tropical heat, lay a dark, knobby object that could have been a truck tire, cut and stretched out flat. It was a crocodile. Gauging the length was tricky, but I guessed the animal measured about twelve feet.

Backing off, we advanced behind a shield of vegetation to a second opening. This one was closer to the sandbar, and we now looked at the shore straight on. Thirty feet to the left of the first crocodile, a second basked, this one a third shorter and much less massive. I smelled smoke. Tim had rolled a cigarette and was drawing on it ceremoniously. "I don't think that's the rogue," he said, disappointment in his voice.

"Where do you think the big one is?" asked Debbie.

The corners of Tim's mouth twitched. "Wish I knew," he said.

Later we learned that Tim was mistaken about the crocodile's length. The problem animal was a dozen feet long, not sixteen. We had almost certainly seen the monster.

A few months after our visit, on the twelfth of December, park rangers and volunteers came to Old Faithful Waterhole and built a trap of nets and counterweights. Baited with a hog carcass, the trap caught the big croc on the second morning. The rangers next employed a promising new technique in the management of problem crocs—scaring the living daylights out of the beast. The idea was to teach the croc that people and boats were terrors to be avoided, while allowing it to remain lord of its domain. It has been found that when an aggressive male is removed from a water hole, another male assumes the dominant position, and problems arise anew.

All through the day and night, the crocodile was harassed. Boats roared back and forth, and after dark, lights were flashed in its eyes.

At last report, more than a year after its capture and torment, Old Faithful's big crocodile was behaving like a pussycat. Confident that the situation was resolved, rangers reopened the campsites beside the water hole in 1997. Since then, no crocodile problems have been reported.

Back at Tim's place, we enjoyed a final round of kindness. Corned-beef "sangers," or sandwiches, were pressed on us, preceded and followed by tea. We easily could have lingered on, yet a long drive lay ahead.

Leaving Lakefield and Tim Logue required great resolve. The fact of the matter was that Queensland had bewitched us. Like Odysseus, who lingered a year with Circe, we had stayed far beyond our original intent. July was nearly over, and we wanted to reach Western Australia by early September. Between Lakefield and the W.A. border lay several thousand miles of driving, first across interior Queensland, then through the Northern Territory.

With tears in our eyes, we turned the car southward, bound for the road that would lead us over the Dividing Range toward the vast, arid West.

7

Hot in Hades

HEAT. CAR. ROAD. Flat. Trucks. Glare. Heat. Drink. Grass. Trees. Dirt. Dust. Death. Tired. Sleep. Slogging across Queensland's interior, crossing into the Northern Territory, and prodding ourselves northward to the Timor Sea and Darwin, we moved through a sun-scorched hell. At times my journal entries, written during cool evenings that followed infernal days, degenerated into strings of words, monosyllables that rattled against one another like bones in a skeleton. Road. Heat. Death. Death. Death.

Whereas Odysseus crossed a river to get to Hades, we traversed the Great Dividing Range. One day, on Magnetic Island near Townsville, we climbed trees, photographed koalas, and snorkeled in cool ocean water. The next we were climbing a series of ridges and dropping into Australia's interior. The change was shocking. It was like driving west from the rainy, forested coast of Maine, cresting a hill, and finding oneself in Arizona. Ahead the landscape stretched flat, hot, and arid to the Indian Ocean, more than two thousand miles away.

If any doubt lingered about the uncanny parallels between our run for the Northern Territory and Odysseus's descent into hell, the corpses erased it. Death presented its hideous, shriveled face everywhere. Along the shoulders were dead kangaroos, dead birds, and dead echidnas in such numbers that it was hard to believe an animal in the Territory remained alive. Drag and drive, drag and drive. We were back to our routine of hauling kangaroo corpses off the highway to save the lives of scavengers.

Odysseus went to the Underworld seeking advice from Teiresias of Thebes, a dead, blind prophet. According to Circe, Teiresias was the only person who could provide the Greeks the directions they would need to reach Ithaca safely. To speak with the dead man, Odysseus would have to cross the Styx, find the confluence of two particular rivers, dig a hole nearby, and fill it with drinks: first milk and honey, then sweet wine, then water, then the blood of a ram and a black sheep Circe had supplied as parting gifts.

Reaching the fatal shore, Odysseus followed the directions carefully. Teiresias appeared in due course. He warned that the journey would not be easy, that Poseidon had it in for the Greeks as a result of their blinding his Cyclopean son. Odysseus must sail homeward via the island of Thrinacea. There he and his men should abstain from harming oxen and sheep they would find. Helios owned the animals, and he would slay anyone who meddled with them.

After the consultation, Odysseus spoke with his dead mother and a host of other women—Epicaste, Leda, Ariadne, in short, a virtual Who's Who of the Greek female dead. Then came the men: Agamemnon, Achilles, Heracles, and Orion. Tantalus appeared, too, standing thirsty in a pool from which he couldn't drink, and Sisyphus, struggling to push a rock uphill. In the end, the sight of the dead people sickened Odysseus, and he fled back across the Styx.

For us, flight was not an option. It took five days to drive from the Queensland coast to Katherine Gorge, our first important stop in the Territory. Passing through country so flat and barren that only the curvature of the earth limited our perspective, we amused ourselves by reading aloud from an Arthur Upfield mystery, *Bushranger of the Skies.* Throats grew scratchy in the dry air, no matter how much water we drank, so we alternated sessions of reading with music. We had two working tapes: Bing Crosby's *Country Style* ("When the Bloom Is on the Sage," "Take Me Back to My Boots and My Saddle," etc.) and a collection of ballads by the Australian folksinger John Williamson, which included "Send Down the Rain" and "Longreach Is Waiting for Rain." They captured the poignancy of the landscape, and we listened over and over until we knew the words by heart.

The empty miles gave plenty of time for contemplating our motivations. Why were we here? We had been on the road for six months, long enough to forget the reasons for coming Down Under in the first place. Yet our surroundings reminded us of the answer every time we looked up and saw a wedge-tailed eagle floating in the sky, watched a kangaroo bounding across a plain, or won the trust of a lizard. This business of ours was pure biophilia, to use a term coined by the biologist Edward O. Wilson. We were drawn to wild places and the life that inhabited them. In Australia, Debbie and I were happiest, most fulfilled, when surrounded by the objects of our fascination. Ours was a mission not only of learning but of being—we wanted to really *be* in Australia, and doing so meant avoiding the artifice of cities and towns, which merely represented Australianized versions of Northern Hemisphere counterparts. We aimed to linger long and well in the real Australia, the place that English-speaking denizens of the island continent call "the Bush." It is an ancient world, far older even than the Aborigines, who are often called mankind's oldest race. We made an effort to see not only the pretty places where tourists flocked, but also the wastelands, the places of desolation, the "utter loneliness" and "manlessness" that D. H. Lawrence recoiled from. We hungered for it all—the sights, sounds, scents, tastes, and textures of a place unlike any other.

There were birds. Hundreds of little corellas, white parrots that moved in immense flocks, screeched at us from trees that popped up occasionally along the roadsides, and mobs of cockatiels and budgerigars whirled past like windblown leaves. Cranes called brolgas looked up from their feeding when we passed, their gray, gaunt shapes perfectly suited to the harsh world in which they eked out a living.

A few sights were pathetic. Once I dragged a big male red kangaroo out of the road. It had died without losing a drop of blood, and its penis, thin, red, and pointed, extruded from its sheath in a sad, final erection. In another place we saw an echidna, swollen, belly up, a black kite hunched over the carcass, the monotreme's insides trailing out like spaghetti. There were cattle, too, a few alive, a few freshly dead, but most reduced to lumpy, deflated pancakes of skin and bones. The air was heavy with the stench of decay. Lacking air conditioning, we had no choice but to drive with windows rolled down and embrace the full experience.

It was in country much like this that the explorers Robert O'Hara Burke and William Wills ran low on food and died in 1861. Then, as now, surface water was rare and edible plants practically nonexistent. Recent studies by the Australian biochemist John Earl show that Burke and Wills probably died from eating freshwater mussels and the spores of a fern called nardoo. Both foods were abundant at the explorers' final campsite at Cooper's Creek. Local Aborigines ate mussels and nardoo routinely, but only after neutralizing their toxins by roasting the mussels and grinding the nardoo in water. Burke and Wills, too pigheaded to seek advice from "savages," downed the stuff raw, or so Earl theorizes. The toxins destroyed the Vitamin B_1 in their bodies, and slowly, painfully, the men succumbed to beri-beri.

Nights brought surprises. Just before the second sunset of this leg of the journey, we were refused entry to a campground that catered only to caravans. Other options being few, we checked into a twenty-five dollar room in the Mud Hut Hotel. It was a two-story, wooden edifice straight out of the Old West. Perched above the bar, our room was unheated, and its lone window was stuck half open. A herd of swine had tracked mud and toilet paper through the men's washroom, and our bed sagged like a hammock.

Through much of the night, shouts, laughter, television jabber, country and heavy metal music, and cigarette smoke rose through the floorboards. I tossed and turned for hours, shivering inside my sleeping bag as blast after blast of Antarctic air thundered into town, driving out the heat. The last thing I remember hearing was a drunken conversation outside on the street. Midway, both participants vomited, but they worked around that obstacle and kept on talking.

The following night we slept in a campground outside Mount Isa. The place was crawling with people and birds, and we hobnobbed with both until an early nightfall. Darkness sent us fluttering into town like moths, seeking a bright nook in which to read and write. We found it in a clean, well-lighted place—a McDonald's hamburger restaurant. For hours we sat in plastic chairs, nursing cups of coffee, scribbling letters and journal entries. The banality of the setting soothed nerves frazzled the night before.

Despite the landscape's bleakness and the endless parade of carrion, life of some kind flourished everywhere. We saw no wandering Aborigines, as Burke and Wills had a century earlier, and settlements were spaced about as widely as our fuel tank would tolerate. Yet just when boredom threatened to set in, a couple of emus would loom in the distance, bustards would trot into view, or a clump of trees would be filthy with parrots—little corellas as white as bleached handkerchiefs, or pink-and-gray galahs. In Mount Isa, we awoke to find the trees around our tent hosting a congress of ring-necked parrots, varied lorikeets, red-browed pardalotes, and galahs.

We spent the last night of our marathon at Three Ways Roadhouse. Three Ways is the point where the Stuart Highway, running between

Darwin and Port Augusta, meets the Flinders Highway, which had just carried us west from Townsville. West of Three Ways lie Aboriginal lands through which there is no paved road. Between Three Ways and the Western Australia border is a stretch of 350 miles, beyond which one would have to trek another 530 miles, across the Great Sandy Desert, to taste the brine of the Indian Ocean.

No matter which way you turn, Three Ways is in the middle of nowhere. Yet the night we arrived, the campground behind the fuel pumps bustled with people. There were old folks towing caravans, parents stuffing children into tents, a few odd foreigners such as ourselves, and a husband and wife who told us they were missionaries. The missionaries and their five children were bound for Arnhem Land in the far North to "witness to the Aborigines." The irony floored me. Fresh from the showers, coiffed, perfumed, and dressed in Sunday-school clothes, the pair saw nothing awry in their plan to tell a people whose ancestors had been birthing and dying in Arnhem Land for 100,000 years the rules by which they should live.

We hurried away, as others might from serpents.

Right at dark, after we had enjoyed a stroll in the last orangey light of day, a convoy of trucks smeared with gray and brown paint roared into the campground. It was an invasion. Dozens of soldiers in camouflage uniforms piled out, gathered stiffly, and awaited orders. Most of the mob were men, but longer hair and softer facial contours revealed a few hardy females. Could it be that a unit of the Royal Australian Army was planning a bivouac among us? The answer came promptly. Headlights switched off, engines ceased to rumble, and leather boots marched toward doors labeled "Gents" and "Ladies." It all seemed surreal.

As if through a blast furnace, we drove 414 miles the next day through Renner Springs, Newcastle Waters, Daly Waters, and Mataranka. The temperature climbed to one hundred degrees Fahrenheit. Radiating a blue of such intensity that it stung our retinas even through sunglasses, the sky was barren of clouds.

There were no green mountains or muddy rivers to cross, no amber waves of grain. At first glance, this country was simply rock and sky, garnished in places by sun-seared grass and scattered groves of eucalyptus and casuarina. But in the middle of it all, something miraculous happened. Imperceptibly at first, monotony yielded to interest. The land buckled. Ridges of ancient sandstone pushed above the plain, widely spaced at first, then multiplying. After days of driving on a treadmill, looking at a foreground that rarely changed, I suddenly understood why geographers call elevation changes "relief."

For a couple of days we lingered near Katherine, a town of about 4,000 on the banks of that Australian rarity, a riverbed with water in it. The Katherine River was named by the explorer John MacDouall Stuart, honoring the daughter of one of his sponsors. Later the watercourse gave its name to the town. Katherine was an oasis, a place where travelers replenished supplies of water and beer, bought provisions, focused weary eyes on irrigated and cultivated greenery, and rubbed elbows with fellow nomads. The land around it was cattle country, and the people we saw in town were cattlemen and cowboys, black and white, dispirited Aborigines trading dole checks for alcohol, sober Aborigines trying to help the misguided, government officials, and passersby.

It wasn't Katherine that we came to see, but Katherine Gorge, or Nitmiluk, a national park a half hour's drive from town. Endowed with cool water and riparian forest, the gorge sounded like a promising place to find wildlife. We aimed to locate water, too. The heat was relentless and draining, and nothing, not even freshwater crocodiles, would keep us away from a swim.

At a supermarket, we stepped out of the car and were greeted by a gaunt Aboriginal man. His eyes were bloodshot, and his clothes draped loosely over his bones. His voice rose dry and croaking, like the call of a desert frog. "G'day, mates," said the man, whose ancestors may have frequented this oasis for tens of thousands of years. He launched into a meandering and halfhearted story of being stranded in town without transportation. He had saved money to buy a car, he said, and now was only $2.20 short of the sum needed to complete the purchase. Could we help him? His breath, even at a distance, reeked of beer. We listened politely. We wanted to help, but not by underwriting a drink. "Sorry," I said, intending to follow up the refusal with an offer to buy the man a meal. Before I could say more, he muttered "Okay, okay," and shuffled away, conversing softly with himself in words we could not understand.

Aboriginal contact continued to prove elusive. There were opportunities, of course, to pay a fee and attend "authentic" Aboriginal gatherings, and more costly chances to hire Aboriginal guides to lead us places. Our bank balance, however, precluded such luxuries. Paying for anything but food, fuel, and camping was out of the question. At the same time, we found little appeal in the experiences money might have brought us. If contact would come at all, it would have to come serendipitously.

On we drove. The forest grew lush and forested as we moved toward the gorge. Many of the trees had gorgeous salmon-colored bark, and we soon learned to identify them as northern salmon gums, *Eucalyptus bigalerita*. Among the trees, birds moved, but we were too hot and tired to pursue them until a flock of finches inspired us to stop. We looked them over and found some with black masks, brown backs, and white-and-black underparts. These were masked finches, a common seed-eating bird of Australia's North. Others had blue-gray heads, ebony throats and chins, and long tails that came to points like quill pens. Slightly larger than their flock mates, these were long-tailed finches. Both species nest in colonies and are thought to mate for life.

The first thing we did after parking under a shade tree in the Katherine Gorge campground was brew a pot of tea. It was madness. We were coated with salt and perspiration, and the temperature in late afternoon still hung in the nineties. Yet more than a few Australians had told us that no drink proved quite as refreshing on a hot day as a steaming cup of tea.

"The hotter the tea, and the more you sweat while drinking it, the cooler and fresher you feel afterwards," wrote Ludwig Leichhardt in a letter dated February 6, 1844. It's an interesting theory. We downed our cups, fell into a vicious fever, and nearly expired on the spot. No wonder Leichhardt perished during his third expedition to the interior. It wasn't hostile natives or the desert that got him, but the tea.

Restored by cold showers, we set about identifying kangaroos that peered at us from the bush. The animals were as tall, and as long of tail and limb, as eastern grey kangaroos, yet their color, a rusty tan, was wrong. Thumbing through Strahan's *Complete Book of Australian Mammals,* we came upon them quickly. The kangaroos were antilopine wallaroos, a tropical species that ranges across the northern portions of Queensland, the Northern Territory, and Western Australia. The book's description of habitat matched the country around us—an open forest of eucalypts with grasses growing among the trunks.

Sweating profusely when I fell asleep that night, and still marinating in my own juices when I awoke in the morning, I suggested to Debbie that we spend the day estivating like desert frogs. She scoffed, bolting into the sunshine. A minute later came the inevitable summons. "Birds!"

I staggered to my feet. Birds were everywhere—great bowerbirds, red-shouldered parrots, little friarbirds, silver-headed friarbirds, blue-faced honeyeaters, and red-collared lorikeets. Color variants of the rainbow lorikeet, these jockeyed for position on a limb drenched every thirty seconds by a lawn sprinkler. Magpie-larks ran along the ground, and as we ate breakfast, a blue-faced honeyeater, the most glamorous of its tribe, perched on our picnic table and gave us an imperious stare.

Despite heat and lethargy, we managed two walks that day. The first brought us to the Katherine River. There we found a blue-winged kookaburra gazing down its massive bill at tourists climbing into tour boats. Near the launching area, there was a tall tree in which it appeared someone had hung black napkins to dry. Out came binoculars. The "napkins" were black flying foxes, roosting peacefully. Had we arrived during the March–April breeding season, the picture might have been different. At that time the bats spend long hours "grooming and displaying their external genitalia" like humans at a nudist camp. In the full swing of things, they engage in sexual intercourse at a rate of eight times per hour. This may explain their fecundity. Black flying foxes form colonies containing hundreds of thousands of individuals.

We gazed in awe. In our country, bats the size of hawks appear only in vampire films. Occasionally one of the animals, perhaps dissatisfied with its perch or offended by the odor of a neighbor, would flap off with noisy sweeps of its wings, circle, and settle on another branch.

The second walk brought us up a ravine between high sandstone cliffs. Palms grew along the bottom, casting welcome fans of shade. The path led to an overlook from which we looked over treetops to the emerald waters of the river and had our first panoramic look at the gorge. While grand, the view meant little to us. The heat was dizzying, heads throbbed, and it was all we could do to stumble back to camp.

The following morning we set off for Butterfly Gorge, a ravine that drains into the Katherine. According to park literature, the walk would take four hours. In the end it took six, partly because of heat, partly because we found objects of interest along the way, and partly because of a glorious swim.

There were birds in the eucalypt and casuarina trees, and more fine specimens of the palm, *Livistona enermis,* we had seen the day before. The palms brought welcome touches of green to the landscape, and the occasional salmon gum added a fetching dab of rouge.

Descending into Butterfly Gorge, we left the sun and slipped into the shade. We looked for butterflies, but found none. Nearing the mouth of the ravine, we heard something rustle in dry leaves. A search produced the source, an eastern blue-tongued lizard that looked like a bratwurst with legs. Dementia brought on by dehydration probably accounts for my naming him, or it, "Skippy."

Skippy captivated us from the moment we first saw him. His head represented merely an extension of his blue-gray torso, and it culminated in a blunt snout. The tail was fat, not quite as thick as the body, but almost, and it held its girth nearly to the end. The eyes gleamed a warm light brown, and despite their owner's outward calm, they tracked our moves with concern. From end to end, Skippy measured about twelve inches.

I picked up the lizard, which made no attempt to escape. He felt neither hot nor cool but neutral, and his scales were wonderfully smooth. Returned to the ground, Skippy performed a trick. He opened his mouth and stuck out a broad, fleshy tongue, a tongue the color of a child's after eating a grape popsicle. We laughed, which probably wasn't the reaction the lizard was hoping for. He flattened his body, doubling his apparent size.

Not wanting to put our new acquaintance through further stress, especially on such a hot day, I placed him on a rock in deep shade. He lay there blinking for a minute, smacked his lips, and plodded off into a crevice.

Eastern blue-tongued lizards range in a crescent from the Kimberley region of Western Australia, east to the Pacific coast, south through the eastern states, and west into South Australia. No more able to climb trees than the sausages they resemble, blue-tongues roam the ground in search of sun, shade, snails, bugs, dead things, flowers, fruit, and each other. Females deliver as many as two dozen live-born young.

From Skippy's retreat it was only a hundred paces to the river. Peeling off boots and socks, we leaped in. The water enveloped us in bliss. As Leichhardt knew, nothing works like misery to make the relief that follows euphoric.

The river was deep. We did little but paddle in place for a while, laughing like children. Then we swam out to the mouth of the cove, where we could see up and down the channel. A tour boat cruised by with a load of hot-looking passengers, and we counted ourselves lucky not to be on it. Far better to enjoy Katherine Gorge as Emerson and Thoreau would have advised us, backstroking across a cove frequented by pythons and freshwater crocodiles.

The prospect of encountering a freshwater croc, or "freshie," appealed to us even though we knew our hearts might flutter at the sight. The smaller of Australia's two crocodiles grows no longer than the average sofa, feeds mainly on fish, and attacks humans only when assaulted.

The pattern we established during our hike to the gorge proved a template for nearly every day we wandered in the Territory. Moderate activity in the morning, followed by swimming in the afternoon; by midday it was too hot for us to think of anything but immersion in cool, clear water.

In the morning we set off with the intention of driving to Darwin, the only city of note on Australia's northern coast. Yet it was not to be. Under the cruel tropical sun, the road became a bed of coals, the car a sauna, the people in it overheated and ornery. When a road forked off toward Edith Falls, we took it. We knew nothing of the place, but "falls" had the right ring to it just then.

Five minutes after parking, we were up to our necks in blessed water. A river poured through a notch in the sandstone bedrock and spilled into the pool. It was gorgeous. In the middle of our reverie, Debbie began to shout. "Snake! Snake!" Her finger pointed to a shape in the water.

Jolted back to reality, I looked to see a large, leathery reptile swim past me. The head appeared oddly angular for a snake's. It was unusually large, too, and poked from the water like the face of a novice swimmer. Then I saw the legs. This was no snake! Greenish, faintly dotted with white, and three feet from bow to stern, it was a type of goanna, the Mertens' water monitor.

I swam after the goanna, and Debbie joined me. The long tail sliced through the water, and we followed close behind it. Soon the shore was reached. The reptile hauled itself out on a boulder and sprawled in the sun. We stayed close by, treading water, admiring our discovery. Then Debbie spoke again.

"A crocodile," she whispered. "A freshie."

To our left, ten feet away and in the water with us, a freshwater crocodile pointed its toothy snout at us from a patch of water mostly concealed by overhanging plants. Yellow-green eyes bulged from a scaly head, and they watched us. The length of the animal was a bit over five feet—nearly double the size of the water monitor. I swam closer, halving the distance. The croc held its place, its expression wooden. We turned from the pool's scaly guardian after a minute or two and swam and swam all over until goosebumps covered our skin. Back on the rock, the monitor still basked, and the croc floated in its leafy boathouse. All was well at Edith Falls.

As we climbed out on the shore, a pale yellow bird with a black bill and a dark streak across its cheek peered down at us from a limb. It was a new species for us, number 354 on our list, the yellow-tinted honeyeater.

At dinner that night, we joined forces with Arnold and Pat Grodski, neighbors in the campground. The Grodskis had recently sold a restaurant near Melbourne and, to celebrate their new-found freedom, were camping their way around Australia. It was a wonder we hadn't met earlier. Outside the Grodskis' pop-up trailer, we sat until midnight, eating, sipping wine, trading stories, and finding common ground in politics, Terry Lane, and Philip Adams. Lane is a cerebral radio journalist with the Australian Broadcast Corporation. Adams, a curmudgeonly newspaper columnist, pens a weekly rant for the *Weekend Australian*. Six months in Australia was long enough for us to adopt a few heroes, and Lane and Adams were among them.

The following dawn launched the weirdest day of our odyssey. Things began innocently. We awoke to a chorus of birds, wriggled out of the tent, and found the trees and bushes alive with birds—yellow-tinted honeyeaters, crimson finches, double-barred finches, great bowerbirds, pied butcherbirds, and more. We might have run off to hunt for new species had not the strangest-looking reptile either of us had ever seen crawled into view, dragging a prodigious tail.

It was Frilly Willy. The campground manager had told us about him. *Chlamydosaurus kingii*, the king of lizards, measured a mere two feet from his blunt, scaly nose to the tip of his long, tapering tail. His color was gray-brown, and his limbs, although muscular, were puny compared to a monitor's. The frill was the thing—a leathery shield, sawtoothed along the edges, that fell behind the lizard's head like a bridal veil. Willy could have unfurled it if he'd wanted to, transforming himself into a convincing, albeit miniaturized, facsimile of a *Triceratops*. Yet the frill remained down. This lizard had lost his fear of humans.

We walked up to Willy, and he honored us with a momentary unfurling. As we gasped in admiration, the frill collapsed like a tent whose poles had been removed. Willy then marched over to a small tree and climbed it.

Later in the day, after we enjoyed a farewell swim in the green-gold pool, we found the lizard again and witnessed something remarkable. He stood up on his hind legs and sprinted like a track star. Debbie and I had arrived at Edith Falls knowing that frilled lizards lived in New Guinea as well as Australia, were classified as agamids or dragons, ate insects, lizards, and an occasional small mammal, and unfurled their frills to intimidate predators and rivals. But this business of running like a human on two legs came as a revelation.

Looking into Willy's yellow eyes, I had a sense that our tender interest in him might not be returned if our sizes were reversed. We humans berate ourselves for mistreating wildlife, yet our behavior toward animals smaller than ourselves often approaches the saintly. Consider the present example. Roasted over a fire, Willy might have provided a toothsome lunch and helped to stretch our budget. Eating him, however, would have violated our sensibilities, not to mention Australian conservation law. No, Willy would run free, beguiling others. But if the tables were turned? I suspect he would have swallowed us and not felt a moment's guilt.

We met one more interesting animal before leaving Edith Falls. I was diving with mask and snorkel, trying to retrieve car keys I had lost during a swim, when a small fish appeared amid the fat, hump-backed barramundi that circled the pool like carousel horses. It was an archerfish, *Toxotes jaculator*. The archer employs an extraordinary means of catching prey. It rises to the surface and scans overhanging limbs until it finds a promising bug or spider. Then, with a target in view and a mouth modified for the job, the fish spits. If it hits the bull's-eye, the target tumbles in the water and the archer gulps it down. Archerfish have been known to down targets three feet off the water.

The day grew curiouser and curiouser. For four hours we traced a vein of sizzling asphalt until Darwin took shape around us. We had expected to find Australia's northernmost city a sleepy, tropical paradise. Instead we found traffic and ugly strip development everywhere. Most of the buildings looked as if they had been erected in a hurry, perhaps the year before.

Darwin had some reason to look new and hastily assembled. Twice in recent memory the city had been flattened. In 1942, 180 Japanese warplanes flew bombing raids over the rooftops, killing 243 people, wounding more, sinking eight ships, and reducing much of the metropolis to rubble. The raid was one of ninety-six by Japanese Imperial forces on the Australian mainland. The second cataclysm came in 1974. On Christmas Day, as the city's Protestants and Catholics gave praise to a benevolent deity, Cyclone Tracy shrieked into town. Winds up to 170 miles per hour destroyed more than half of Darwin's houses, and by the time the storm abated, sixty-six humans and countless plants and animals lay dead. Knowing the history, I could forgive Darwin some of its fast-buck thinking. When tomorrow may bring apocalypse, it makes a certain amount of sense to make hay while you can.

And make hay we did, our first night in town. Our hosts were Jack and Joyce Edmunds. When we arrived at their house in a leafy suburb, they were dressing for a dinner and dance at Darwin's Royal Australian Air Force base. We were immediately invited to join them.

At the Officer's Club, Jack produced a wallet and "shouted" us the buffet of meats, seafood, vegetables, and desserts. We felt as though we were back at O'Reilly's. After the meal, Joyce led us to a courtyard. There, courtesy of the Australian taxpayer, we swilled complimentary booze, took in a tropical breeze, and tried to ignore a rock band hired for the apparent purpose of drowning out all conversation. At our table the day's strange denouement began.

An English medical researcher I'll call Robert, about forty-five and so wildly hairy we might have taken him for a werewolf, took a shine to Debbie. Quite drunk, he regaled her with tales of his days as a medical examiner. Would we all like to come back to his place and watch forensic videos? "You're kidding," said Debbie. "Do you mean *autopsies?*" Robert took another swig of Heineken and nodded grandly. *Odyssey* parallels weighing heavily, we set off in the Edmunds' chariot for the Underworld.

"Most of the people I cut up deserved to die," said Robert, leading us inside after a moment's genuflection before his Harley-Davidson. Beer and whiskey were served. As we settled down in a comfortable living room, our host, leering at Debbie with eyes enlarged grotesquely by thick glasses, told us that the people we would see dissected had gotten what was coming to them. "They did stupid things and got what they asked for," said a man who had just rocketed home at the wheel of a car, his belly brimming with liquor.

Thus began the weirdest, most unsettling end to a night on the town I have ever experienced. On video, we watched Robert slice open an Aboriginal man. He had died, the police believed, by drowning. In stereo, Robert-on-tape and Robert-in-the-flesh described the dead man's heart and lungs. Scrutiny proved that the deceased had succumbed to a heart attack. In a second tape, Robert hacked into a charred, twisted thing that had lately been a human being. It was the corpse of a man killed and incinerated in a car wreck. Revolted less by the sight of the body than by the callous narrative delivered by our host, we stood and cried, "Enough!"

Robert downed two more drinks, then fired up the Harley. "Would you like to ride?" he said to Debbie with a courtly wave of the arm. She declined. With a roar of pistons, Robert, wearing no helmet, shot down the drive and raced ahead. When we reached the highway, he was waiting, grinning ghoulishly. I felt relieved when we drove away into the night.

Riding home, we were passing an auto parts store when its glass façade exploded. A fireball burst into the parking lot, a hellish tumult of flame. Just then, a dark sedan parked on the shoulder raced off without turning on its lights. Jack said it was the third time that year the shop had been torched. The videos, Robert's cruel humor, and the fireball haunted us.

We awoke in the morning craving air and sunshine. Joyce and Jack took us sailing. There was little wind on the Beagle Gulf. Leaden clouds hung low, suggesting the roof of a circus tent about to collapse, and the air felt like the exhaust of a clothes dryer. Even with Joyce's skillful hand at the tiller, the voyage proved less a sail than a slow, languorous drift.

Three of the Edmunds' friends had come along: an English doctor who considered himself Canadian but lived in Darwin, a woman who taught in a local Montessori school, and her husband, an electrical engineer. We spent half a day with them, gazing back at a green coastline fringed with mangroves and mud. Conversation ranged from where we'd been and where we intended to go to the ups and downs of Darwin. The company was affable, but our hearts weren't in it. All we could think of was the Bush.

Before leaving Darwin, we picked up mail at the Central Post Office. One envelope brought cheers. Our Melbourne friends Peg and Keith MacLeod, overdue for a holiday, had decided to fly to Broome, a port city on the coast of Western Australia. The timing was perfect. When our travels in the Territory ended, we would cross the Kimberley plateau, enter W.A., and, without much bending of a malleable schedule, roll into Broome the same day. A telephone call clinched the plan. In a generous act typical of them, Peg and Keith had rented a two-bedroom motel unit, offering one of the rooms to us.

For two weeks we zigged and zagged around a part of the continent Australians call the Top End. Birds abounded, and many of them were new to us. At a place known as Fogg Dam, an hour's drive from Darwin, we found six new species—the rufous banded honeyeater, the pied heron, the white-browed crake, the whiskered tern, an owlish-looking hawk called the letter-winged kite, and the Australian pratincole. Vaguely tern-like, the pratincole had a golden back, a chestnut cummerbund, and demonic black eyes. It nests on the dry plains of Australia's interior, and winters on the Top End coast. The origin of pratincoles has long been debated. Recent genetic work suggests they belong in the same family as gulls, auks, and puffins.

Reptiles and amphibians inhabit the Northern Territory's monsoonal rain forests in formidable numbers, and it wasn't long before we were up to our necks in them. Our first night after leaving Darwin, we camped behind a pub at a place called Corroboree. Hundreds of Roth's tree frogs inhabited the men's room, the majority crowded into a decrepit ventilation unit. When I used a toilet, sixty or more bloodshot eyes gazed down at me. This was no place for the self-conscious.

At Fogg Dam, snakes slithered out on the roads as the sun fell. We eased close enough to identify two of them. The first was a keelback, a slender, mud-colored serpent that reminded us of an American garter snake. Keelbacks are nonvenomous and feed chiefly on frogs. I was about to reach down and pick it up when prudence stopped me. What if I was wrong, and this was not a keelback but a gwardar? Cogger labeled the gwardar, a common snake in this part of the country, DANGEROUS in capital letters.

Identifying serpents is serious business in the Top End. The herpetologist Richard Shine, a professor of evolutionary biology at the University of Sydney, writes of a snake lover who traveled to the Northern Territory aiming to photograph an olive python. Before long he found one nine feet long. The snake was slithering across the Arnhem Highway not far from Fogg Dam, and the man hurried out of his car to photograph it.

As the reptile enthusiast shot pictures, the snake eased off the road. The man reached down and hauled the snake back. The reptile looked inert in the camera's viewfinder, as animals often do after being handled and posed. To get a better image, the man poked his subject on the nose. The snake perked up, and the photographic session ended successfully. Back in Sydney, the man developed the film and brought his prints to Shine's office. "They proved to be excellent photographs," Shine writes, "of a very large and somewhat surprised king brown snake." The king brown is among the world's deadliest reptiles.

A few minutes after the keelback crawled off the road and onto the floodplain, an antilopine wallaroo, a tropical species of kangaroo, bounded into view, cast us a quizzical glance with upturned ears, and disappeared into the bush. Beset by hordes of mosquitoes, we motored on. We were halfway back to the main road in thickening darkness when another snake appeared in the road.

I stepped out for a look, and the reptile looped to form a pyramid of coils. It was a water python, a powerful constrictor that occurs in great numbers in Top End wetlands. Shine estimates that tropical floodplains such as the one at Fogg Dam support more predators per square mile than the vaunted plains of the Serengeti. Each acre provides home to hundreds of water pythons.

Like other pythons, the water python possesses hind limbs. All that one can see of them are spurs, barely the length of a human thumbnail. Each spur ends in a claw. Legless lizards, by contrast, have no legs at all, proving the futility of differentiating snakes from lizards by the presence or absence of limbs.

I was certain enough of the python's identity to approach it. As I was moving in, a Land Cruiser sped toward us from the opposing direction, headlights blazing. It squealed to a stop a few feet from the snake. From an open door bounded a man in khaki. "Water python, *Liasis fuscus,* one of mine," he announced briskly, too busy for pleasantries. With the pronouncement, the man snatched the snake, thrust it in a cloth sack, and sped away. I stood dumbfounded by the rudeness.

In the morning we returned to Fogg Dam, cooked a breakfast of French toast beside the car, and sipped coffee while watching day break over the floodplain. We saw no snakes, but gulls, terns, pratincoles, and letter-winged kites sailed across the sky. Feeling nourished, we climbed in the car, returned to Darwin, and drove three hours south to Litchfield National Park.

At Wangi Falls we found a site in a busy campground, pegged our tent under the watchful eye of a great bowerbird, and hurled ourselves into cool water beneath twin waterfalls. This first day at Litchfield, we hiked along a footpath that carried us up a ridge behind Wangi Falls. Halfway up the slope, we stopped in our tracks. A dove cooed in the treetops. Might it be a rose-crowned fruit dove, one of the most colorful birds in Australia, a species for which we had searched widely but unsuccessfully in Queensland? Debbie checked a range map. Yes, the rose-crowned fruit dove, a bird of the Wet Tropics, had jumped the Gulf of Carpenteria and landed squarely in the Northern Territory.

Peering through palm fronds and a gray-green curtain of eucalyptus leaves, we managed to find the bird. First we glimpsed its orange underside, then its jade-green wings and blue-gray breast brushed lightly with green. "Is the tail tip yellow?" asked Debbie. It was. "Can you see the head?" I couldn't. Then the plump, compactly built creature reached out to snatch a berry. Catching sunlight, its forehead and crown flashed rosy red. We cheered. A second later the bird was gone. This was the only rose-crowned fruit dove we saw in Australia.

Our most important discovery that day, dove aside, was a man. He maintained an open-air office at the campground's snack bar. After being told by several people that he led the finest natural-history tours in the Northern Territory, we made it our business to visit him. His name was Greg Wallis.

Hair thinning on his crown and thickening on his upper lip and jaw, Greg met us with a warm "G'day." About thirty-three, he stood over six feet tall in bare feet, feet that never wore shoes or sandals in the three days we spent in his company. Greg had been born in Cairns, raised in Sydney, and educated in biology at Sydney University. For five years he'd run a tour company that operated in Kakadu National Park. Recently he had taken a job with the American-born cattle rancher who owned Welltree Station, a grazing property adjoining Litchfield. The Reynolds River ran through the place, and there were lots of birds, lizards, and crocodiles. Greg served as business manager, boat captain, tour guide, naturalist, and bus driver for a company that led trips to a croc-infested water hole inside the Welltree boundary.

After talking with Greg and discovering his intimate knowledge of the flora and fauna, we longed to go on one of his trips. Unfortunately, there was a hitch. For the moment we were broke. Debbie was juggling funds between two accounts, a high-interest reserve and the low-interest stash from which we drew our daily bread. We had spent the last of the low-interest money on camping fees, and wouldn't have more until a new month began.

We told Greg our dilemma. "No worries," he replied with a smile. "Come along. When you get back to Darwin, send me what you owe."

Trust was one of Greg's many virtues. Another was an extraordinary knowledge of Australia's reptiles and amphibians. A third was a willingness to share information. "If it's big goannas you want to see," he said,

"I suggest you start by visiting the picnic area down by the plunge pool. Have you seen *Varanus panoptes,* the floodplain monitor? They're pests around here. Yesterday two of them were working the picnic tables, hoping to scare up a bit of tucker."

When Greg bustled off to start a tour, we hurried to the picnic area. There we found two miniature Godzillas, each about five feet long. Their torsos were massive. One of the monitors snooped around a vacant picnic table, darting out a long tongue. The other swung its body back and forth while retreating slowly to the Bush. I followed the second animal. It looked dirty and dry, its hide a dull blackish green. Beneath the grime, rows of yellowish spots appeared at one-inch intervals. The skin had a beaded look, like that of a Gila monster, especially on the legs.

Nearing the goanna, I caught long looks at its prodigious tongue. It shot out several inches, exploring the air and ground. The divided tongues of lizards and snakes are thought to help them follow scent trails. If one tine of the fork receives a stronger odor of food than the other, a two-parted vomeronasal organ in the mouth perceives the difference, and the reptile adjusts its course.

When I had moved near enough to touch its broad, scaly back—had I been foolish enough to try—the monitor rose up on its legs, angled its head toward me, and hissed. I backed off quickly. Goanna attacks are rare, but the reptile was equipped to teach me a lesson with teeth and claws if I invaded its personal space.

Early the following morning, Greg stepped out of an ancient Land Cruiser and strolled over to our campsite, grinning. Something was up. His belly bulged as if he were eight months pregnant. "Have a look at this. She's cool, and I'm keeping her warm." Greg pulled a cloth sack from inside his shirt. In went an arm, and out came a snake. It was colored so dark a brown that I first mistook the skin for black. An iridescent sheen on the scales reflected morning sunshine. "A water python," I said. Greg nodded affirmatively.

The snake was five feet long and as thick around as Greg's wrist. It wrapped around itself and his arm like an enormous pretzel. Where the coils looped up and over each other, we glimpsed a smooth, mustard-colored belly.

As other campers approached timidly, Greg delivered an impromptu lecture. The snake was nonvenomous. It fed mainly on rats during the dry season, and when the monsoon arrived and flooded rodents out of their burrows, it devoted its energies to hunting birds and eggs. As pythons go, the water python was a midget. The maximum length, Greg said, was about three meters (nine and a half feet), a modest figure compared to the twenty feet and more attained by the amethystine pythons of Queensland.

After the snake went back in the bag, we were off. At a bend in a rough dirt road, Greg parked beside an orange van to which someone had taken a blowtorch and removed the vehicle's back and most of the roof. Inside, padded benches were bolted to the floor. "Climb in," he said. We sat beside another couple who had been waiting when we arrived.

For nearly an hour, we rattled and shook our way across Welltree. The station covered 145 square kilometers (fifty-six square miles), said Greg, and ran between 5,000 and 6,500 cattle. Much of the grazing country looked raw, as if it had been hacked out of the monsoonal forest a few years earlier.

When a plume of smoke appeared on the horizon, Greg told us to watch for hawks. "We'll run the edge of the burn," he said, "and kites will be working the periphery, too, going after rodents, small marsupials, lizards, snakes, and insects fleeing the blaze." He was right. As we neared the fire, which had been set to dispose of brush and promote the sprouting of grass, dark, ominous shapes cut circles in the sky. They were black kites, busy transforming a bad day for displaced creatures into a nightmare. The scene suggested an Ingmar Bergman film—white smoke, black earth, blackened tree trunks, and angels of death descending from heaven to slay the wounded.

At a low place where the road crossed a swamp, trees crowded in on either side. Greg stopped here to liberate the python. Quickly we were rolling again. He told us to watch for frilled lizards clinging to trunks blackened by a recent fire. A mile ahead I spotted one, as immobile as a statue. Greg coaxed the lizard gently from its perch. On the ground, it bared its teeth and spread an orange frill. Pictures were taken, and then we returned the king of lizards to its char-broiled tree.

At the end of the journey, a boat waited in glassy water dotted with lotus pads. Taking the controls in the stern, Greg backed us into the channel. We sat on benches, shaded by a canopy, while he stood, scrutinizing the river ahead.

For an hour and more we cruised the billabong. Sacred lotuses with leaves the size of dinner plates fringed the shorelines, their pink whorls of petals punctuated by yellow centers. Reptiles loomed in every direction:

estuarine crocodiles basking openmouthed on the banks, freshwater crocs lurking in dappled light beneath palm trees, a Mertens' water monitor sprawled along a limb, and floodplain monitors stalking ponderously along the shore like dinosaurs of old.

Greg pointed out birds. There were Nankeen night herons roosting in a tree, and below them in the water were green pygmy-geese and magpie-geese. Comb-crested jacanas walked the lotus pads, darters dove for fish, and herons and egrets stalked frogs and fish in the shallows. High in a tree, we saw a pair of white-bellied sea eagles guarding a nest. At one point we rounded a bend and surprised several hundred wandering whistling ducks. They stood flatfooted, shoulder to shoulder, watching nervously as we passed. Through it all, Greg kept up a smooth, erudite commentary.

When the tour was over and we were back at the campground, Greg took us aside. "I was disappointed we didn't see more crocs this morning," he said, knowing I was eager to photograph them. "No one has signed on for the afternoon trip. If a few people do, please be my guests and come along for the ride."

As luck had it, people did sign up, and the end of the day found us back on the water. This time crocs appeared by the dozen—in the water, on the banks, among the lotuses with only eyes and nostrils revealing their presence. Evening light cast the place in sepia, and lotus leaves, lily pads, and reeds radiated soft shades of green. Minus the crocodiles, the bill-abong would have made a splendid place for a swim.

On the way home, Greg asked for reactions. We praised the scenery, wildlife, and commentary, but I confessed disappointment in the crocodiles. I wanted to see really big ones, and at close range. "A photographer in Queensland told us to go to Shady Camp," I said. "Have you heard of it?"

Greg paused. "Right. Shady Camp. Yes, it's a great place for big crocs, all right. Filthy with them." Greg was choosing his words deliberately. "Be careful. I used to lead tours there, but gave it up. Too risky. We went in small boats. I could handle my own, but never be sure about the others."

And so it came to pass that, forty-eight hours later, we arrived at Shady Camp. As the Australian love of irony had led us to suspect, the camp wasn't shady. Three or four elephantine trees loomed over a patch of dirt designated for tenting, but the limbs were light on leaves. The few present hung limply, providing an ineffectual shield against the sun. A young couple, also tenting, ignored our greetings.

A mile up the road we made arrangements with a man to deliver us a boat at seven the following morning. Now it was late afternoon. Eager to explore a little before dark, we walked from the campground to the low, grassy riverbank. The place looked like a country club for reptiles. Estuarine crocodiles appeared everywhere, in the water, on the banks, more than twenty all told. We saw white pelicans and pied cormorants, too, and a brave or foolish jabiru wading in the shallows.

We spied an observation platform rising above tall grass. "Let's have a look," I said to Debbie. She looked as if I had suggested we jump from the Empire State Building. We were halfway there when we heard a crocodile charging through the grass, the blades brushing against belly armor and producing a loud hiss. What to do? We reminded ourselves that crocodiles hunt in the water, not on land, and continued. *Cautiously.*

There was more hissing, and, farther along, more still. Three big crocs slipped through the grass and into the river before we reached the lookout.

From the tower the peaceable kingdom spread before us: lotuses abloom, green water shimmering in the evening light, pandanus palms making the place look like a resort in Hawaii. The river, the St. Mary's, winds across flat land to the sea, making it a virtual commuter route for crocs moving between the interior and the coast. A quick guess suggested that adult crocodiles outnumbered the humans in the area by ten to one.

We tried cooking dinner, but gave it up in a cloud of mosquitoes. Inside the tent, a sauna in the tropical heat, perspiration glued us to our sleeping bags. We tried to sleep, but turned anxiously. It would be hard to say which caused more torment, the vampires that whined by the millions outside, prodding their syringes through the tent netting, or thoughts of the terror we would face at dawn. At some feverish moment in the middle of the night, we conferred. Should we call the whole thing off? Should we leave a scribbled last will and testament in the car? When dawn came, could we find the nerve?

Time proved our mettle. With sunrise we shed the worst of our forebodings and walked bravely, if not boldly, to the boat ramp. The sun by this time hung like a ripe orange in a Dresden blue sky. The mosquitoes were gone, banished by a breeze. Only when the boat started sliding backward with us in it did we run the risk of fainting.

The motor started; thank heaven for that. Soon fifteen horses of power were pushing us upstream. The St. Mary's was no river out of Conrad, no passage toward the heart of darkness. The world was afire with morning sunshine.

We cruised along briskly at first, noting a crocodile capable of swallowing us here, and another there, meanwhile keeping a watch on any reptile that showed interest in us or surpassed the length of the boat. We saw a darter, or snake-bird, perched on the shaggy crown of a palm, hanging wings out to dry in the manner of its close relation, the anhinga of the Americas. A jabiru with a broadsword for a bill and a glossy purple head stalked the shallows, stepping deliberately on legs of cherry red. Comb-crested jacanas trotted along the lotus leaves, looking like Frenchmen in crimson berets.

I asked Debbie if she wanted to try her hand at piloting. Game for the challenge, she crept toward the stern along one gunwale while I followed the other into the bow. It was a delicate procedure, especially in the middle of a river filled with crocodiles. Debbie took the motor's control arm and had her first try at running an outboard. She performed beautifully for a first-timer, but after a few jerky starts and turns, we agreed that it might be in both our best interests to resume our original positions.

We spent five hours on the river. As the time passed, we grew confident enough to approach the biggest of the crocs. Earlier, I had asked the rental agent if there was anything stupid we could do to put ourselves in peril. "Aw, they're all right, mate," he replied. "But don't be silly and come at one of the big fellows directly if he's sunning on the bank. Approach from upstream or down, but never straight on. Out of the water, crocs are easily frightened, even the big ones. If you head straight at him, he has no choice but to run for the only safe place he knows—the water. He'll take the shortest route possible. Now, if you're sitting there in his line of travel, and he accidentally knocks over the boat"—the man broke into one of his piano-keyboard smiles—"then you've got a problem. In the water the crocodile loses his fear, and you become interesting to him."

Eager to engage as little crocodilian interest as possible, we motored close to the monsters on the downstream side and drifted in from above. We scared only one croc into the water. As luck had it, it was the biggest we saw in Australia, a massive, heavily armored reptile with a tail that alone must have weighed several hundred pounds. Estimating length was difficult, for the tail and trunk formed an arc. I have no doubt the snout-to-tail measure was several feet longer than the boat.

The croc rose on its feet, walked on its pudgy legs to the shore, and eased itself into the water. I shuddered. It is one thing to stand on dry land and be told that crocs show no interest in boats, and another to be drifting among them, watching a particularly large specimen submerge before your eyes.

Greg had warned us not to visit Shady Camp in the wet season. "In the Dry [season], the place is safe enough," he said. "But as the Wet [season] approaches, the male crocodiles get a bit territorial, particularly the big, dominant ones. It's rare, but boats can be attacked, maybe because big males see them as rival crocodiles." We had seen photos of aluminum boats whose hulls had been chewed and mangled.

The only idiotic thing we—I—did at Shady Camp was very foolish indeed. Feeling bold after my initial trepidation, I let enthusiasm get the better of me and tried to catch a baby croc. It might have proved my undoing.

Drifting downstream through sacred lotuses, we were admiring the pink flowers when a hatchling crocodile, barely a foot long, appeared amid the floating leaves. It was too good an opportunity for a herpetophile to resist. I swung the boat around, then extended a tender, fleshy arm out over the side. On the shore a ten-foot croc lay basking, eyes angled in our direction.

My first lunge missed. I was about to attempt a second when sanity dawned. Female crocs, like mother alligators, will defend their recently hatched young. It was entirely possible that the mother of this hatchling lay beneath us, gazing up with baleful, hooded eyes. Suddenly feeling nauseous, I pulled back my hand. My heart pounded in my chest. We all make stupid mistakes, and sometimes we pay for them. On this occasion I had been lucky. But what if—? Neither Debbie nor I had the stomach to speak of alternative outcomes.

In the afternoon, more than usually glad to be alive, we drove east toward Kakadu. Kakadu National Park covers a vast area about a third the size of Tasmania. Among Australia's parks, only Uluru is better known.

Rolling over roads scorched by the sun, our interests narrowed to a cool swim and cold beer. To our dismay, we found neither. The river near our campsite was full of crocodiles, and looking at it longingly, we sympathized with Tantalus. We could look but not leap. Adding insult to injury, other campers were swilling beer, and the nearest place to buy a cold drink was miles away.

We found refreshment in cool showers, then passed the evening reading about the park. Two groups of Northern Territory Aborigines own Kakadu, we learned, and they manage it under a cooperative agreement with the Australian Nature Conservation Agency. Many of the rangers are Aborigines. So are ten out of fourteen people on the Board of Management. Perhaps this was why, more than in any other Australian park, we felt we were visiting a home, an inhabited landscape, rather than passing through a refuge from which humans had been forcibly removed.

Centered on the drainage of the South Alligator River, Kakadu stretches more than 150 miles from Field Island in the Van Diemen Gulf to the park's southern boundary, near Mount Lambell. The boundaries enclose nearly 8,000 square miles. There are twenty-five species of frog in the park, almost one hundred different reptiles, nearly a third of the continent's bird species, and, at last count, sixty kinds of mammal.

What visitors see in Kakadu, we were told, depends entirely on the season. Traditionally the Aborigines of the sandstone escarpments and crocodile-infested floodplains recognize six divisions of the year. There is *Gurrung,* the time in which we visited. Spanning August, September, and early October, *Gurrung* brings heat and drought and concentrates waterbirds in shrinking wetlands. For locals, this was and is the time to hunt file snakes and turtles.

Next comes *Gunumeleng,* lasting from October into early January. This is a time of rising heat and thickening air. Thunderstorms boom and pummel, the land turns green, and birds spread out as water holes multiply and creeks begin to flow. Toward the end of *Gunumeleng,* the several hundred Aboriginal people who still live in Kakadu move, as their ancestors did, to temporary homes in nearby sandstone ridges.

After *Gunumeleng* comes *Gudjewg,* bringing monsoonal rains that last through most of March. Getting around Kakadu and the entire Top End is difficult at this time, except by airplane. Roads flood, rivers rage, waterfalls thunder, and goannas and snakes take to the trees. Magpie geese nest during *Gudjewg,* and Aborigines feast on their eggs.

Late March or early April ushers in the brief interval of *Banggerreng,* a period of vicious thunderstorms and declining rain. Fruits ripen and waters recede.

Yegge arrives in late April and lasts a little more than a month. The drying of the landscape continues, water lilies flower, and Aborigines set fire to the lowlands. Ash from the burns promotes the growth of grasses, which in turn fatten the antilopine wallaroos and wallabies that the natives hunt with spears.

Rounding out the Kakadu year is *Wurrgeng*. This season runs from June through most of July. *Wurrgeng* brings the coolest, driest weather of the year. Days are warm but not hot, nights are cool, and the Aborigines hunt magpie geese and kangaroos and continue burning the lowlands. We arrived when *Wurrgeng* had ended and *Gurrung* rolled around again, turning the park into an open-air sauna.

What to do at Kakadu? We felt bewildered by the options. There were wetlands to scan for waterbirds, warm roads to cruise on cool nights for reptiles, visitor centers crammed with exhibits, boat cruises, interpretive programs, and, tucked in nooks in sandstone more than a billion years old, the largest assemblage of rock art in the world. A few corners of Kakadu were off limits, either to protect Aboriginal privacy or to keep prying eyes away from controversial uranium mines within the park. By and large, however, we faced a hundred things to do and see.

We started with the art. Bringing only a passing familiarity with Aboriginal painting to Ubirr, a bluff pocked by shallow caves, we found that the people who had daubed ochre and other pigments on the sandstone had interests similar to ours—food, wildlife, and people, the first two often overlapping. There were images of kangaroos, fish, birds, lizards, generously endowed men, and anatomically correct women. Animal art often highlighted places where fat, a rare item in the Aboriginal diet, could be found. Some of the paintings may have been 15,000 or 20,000 years old, but many of them looked new. The paradox was clarified by a ranger. Aborigines made the art to use, again and again, in ceremonies and schooling. A painting 10,000 years old might contain pigment daubed on last week.

On top of Ubirr, a crowd gathered to watch the sunset. We fell in, sat on ancient stone, and found ourselves in a cosmopolitan crowd that included Japanese, Germans, French, Indonesians, Africans, Indians from India, Argentines, Canadians, and Americans from places as diverse as Anchorage, Montreal, and Buenos Aires.

Below, water holes, floodplains, and winding river channels turned yellow, then orange, then pink, red, and blue. Surrounded by a United Nations of companions, we watched the sun melt on the steamy horizon and felt—corny as it may sound—part of a tribe, a brother-and-sisterhood embracing all nations. It was good to sit together in a place where countless generations of Aborigines before us had undoubtedly paused, looked, and contemplated. Sunrise and sunset, growth and decay, living and dying—all played on the stage before us, timeless and good.

The next day's adventures began on a trail near Meil, where we had spent the night. At first all went well. We gazed at termite mounds that towered above the track, saw green-ant nests in the trees, and spotted a chestnut-quilled rock pigeon, a signature bird of the Top End. But when we returned to the car, something was wrong. The glove box gaped open, its contents scattered. Without thinking, Debbie snapped at me. "Did you leave the glove compartment open?"

I circled around to the driver's door. The keyhole was damaged, and I realized at once that the lock had been forced. Panic set in. Nearly ten thousand dollars worth of uninsured photographic gear was squirreled away inside, along with clothes, camping gear, and our traveling library. If the thief had cleaned us out, our odyssey was over. A search of the car ensued. To our relief, nothing was missing except for a small flashlight, a few papers, and a screwdriver.

A visit to the nearest ranger station produced disappointing results. The man in charge wouldn't look away from his computer long enough to hear our story. Fortunately a sympathetic maintenance woman lurched in the door. The police were coming, she said, and we should meet them at the campground grocery.

When the officers finally arrived, they explained that the thief had robbed a dozen cars in a short, swift spree. "Happens all the time," they said, no more interested in the crime than the ranger at the computer. "Be happy you didn't lose more." One couple from Berlin were missing their camera, airline tickets, and cash.

Having seen enough of crime and punishment for one day, we cruised off in search of a positive experience. At Nourlangie we found it. Among the hundreds of rock art galleries in Kakadu, these are the most cele-brated. We were fortunate to visit them in the company of an Aboriginal ranger named Jeff Lee. He was slight of build, of moderate height, and had skin the color of dark coffee. His eyes were dark too, and, shaded by a green baseball cap, they could be seen only when he looked sideways, exposing the whites.

Jeff's voice was as soft as a dove's, and we had to strain to hear him. He spoke with pride of ancestors who had lived near Nourlangie since the Dreamtime, a formative period central in Aboriginal lore, during which great spirit-beings roamed the country, sculpting the landscape. In one of the rock shelters, Jeff pointed to human stick figures. His grandfather had painted them. Having loved and looked up to my own grandfathers, I understood this young Aborigine's connection to the art and the rock. His voice resonated with awe.

On our way back to the car, which sat unlocked in the parking area, we looked closely at other rock paintings. Most of the Ubirr art we had seen was rendered in a stick-figure style known as Mimi. Named for ancestral spirits the Aborigines believe created the images, Mimi works are extremely old, some of them dating back 20,000 years. Only the rock engravings at Jinmium, near the Western Australia border, may be older. Some authorities believe the Jinmium art is more than 100,000 years old. If correct, this would make it 70,000 years older than the earliest cave art of Europe. At Nourlangie, the majority of paintings were executed in a more recently evolved style called "X-ray." The figures were fleshy and full, and inside them we could usually find bones. Unlike the monochrome red ochre of the Mimi, the X-ray paintings combined reds, whites, and browns.

The painting that impressed us most at Nourlangie appeared at the base of a cliff. It presented a man, white with red bones. His arms stuck out, powerful legs spread open, and a prodigious penis dangled toward the earth. According to a nearby plaque, he was Nabulwinjbulwinj, "a dangerous spirit who eats females after striking them with a yam." X-ray art of this type first appeared in the Northern Territory around 9,000 years ago. Local Aborigines, the Gagudju and the Djablukgu, still employ the ancient techniques.

That night we pitched our tent at Jim Jim Billabong, a quiet water hole frequented by crocs. After dinner and nightfall, we drove over to Yellow Waters, the starting point for Kakadu's most popular boat cruises. Greg Wallis had told us that if we poked around the boat ramp after dark, we might find a file snake. Of course, we might find a crocodile, too, so caution was advised.

The file snake, na-warndak or gedjebe to the Aborigines, is arguably the weirdest of all reptiles. There are three species, two of which occur in Australia. Aside from a close kinship to each other, file snakes have no near relations.

The Arafura file snake, a reptile not described in scientific literature until 1980, flourishes in Kakadu's rivers and billabongs. Big and floppy, like a sort of reptilian bloodhound, it seems to be a medium-sized snake living in an extra-large skin. Aside from its distinctive looseness, the epidermis is rough, like a file. The texture helps the snake grip the slippery skin of fish. Entirely aquatic, file snakes hunt, sleep, make love, and give birth without leaving the water.

Greg had said that if we failed to discover a file snake at Yellow Waters—and this proved the case—we would have to finesse our way down a four-wheel-drive-only road to a water hole called Maguk, or Barramundi Gorge. There, he said, we could don masks and snorkels and pull the snakes out of underwater lairs.

The next morning, around nine, we were roused by a blue-faced honeyeater singing above our tent. The trademark smells of an Australian campground sifted through the mosquito netting—sausages frying, bacon crackling, potatoes sizzling on hot metal. What to do? Free of commitments, we proclaimed the day a holiday.

I cooked a breakfast lavish by our standards: French toast with maple syrup, fried potatoes, orange slices on the side, and a pot of Atherton Tableland coffee. Quietly we idled away the morning and early afternoon, tasting, chewing, sipping, writing letters, scribbling notes in our journals, and often just gazing over the placid surface of the billabong. The opening lines of Banjo Paterson's "Waltzing Matilda" came to mind:

> Once a jolly swagman
> Sat beside a billabong,
> Under the shade of a coolibah tree.
> And he sang as he sat,
> Waiting while his billy boiled,
> Who'll come a-waltzing Matilda with me?

As it happened, our jollity lasted only until the air heated up. Every bush fly in the Northern Territory arrived to explore our ear canals, perform gymnastic feats on our nose hairs, skinny dip in the corners of ours eyes, and dance between our lips.

Fleeing to a pub at Cooinda, we spent an hour chatting with David Scott and Leslie Dell from Scotland. They were architects who had married, thrown off their careers, and set off to bicycle around Australia. They covered long distances by airplane, then hopped on their bikes and pedaled around regions that interested them. A plane had dropped them in Darwin.

Before the bartender could lose patience with our thirst for ice water, we set off for Maguk. The first thirty miles carried us over asphalt to the four-wheel-drive turnoff. The road ahead looked sound enough, so we kept on going. The ruts were shallow, and there were no raging rivers to ford. The greatest surprise was a twenty-foot-high tower of earth, saliva, and termites that loomed over the road like the Tower of Babel.

Once the tent was up, we tried driving to the end of the road, where a path led through monsoonal forest to the water hole Greg had described. Alas, between the campground and the walking track we nearly found ourselves in a Sisyphean jam. The problem was a stream crossing. There was no water in the bottom, but the high water of Gudjewg and Bangger-reng had cut a deep channel and banked it with drifting sand. This was no place for a conventional automobile, especially one that was overloaded. Still, the extra weight might give us traction, and we had not come so far to give up without a fight.

Reckoning that a Land Cruiser with a winch and a friendly driver would come along if we needed rescuing, I took aim, put the car in low gear, and pressed the accelerator. The car nosed into the gully. At the bottom we hung up, an axle catching and our drive wheels starting to spin. For a moment it seemed as if we might spend the evening like Sisyphus, trying to push our way out of the ditch with no hope of success. Then the tires grabbed. With the dead weight of books, cameras, tripods, and dusty clothes working to our advantage, we bucked forward. Up we went, out of the ditch and onto hard ground. How would we get back? Just like Odysseus, one hurdle at a time.

Reached by a twenty-minute walk up a leafy valley, the water hole presented a paradisiacal scene. Maguk was like something from a dream. Through a notch in a high-rimmed sandstone basin, water poured like frothy cream. The falls emptied into the far end of the pool, and between the spray and us lay several hundred feet of malachite-green water. Along the near shore grew pandanus palms, skinny-trunked things with over-sized crowns. Root masses bulged over the water, and it was underneath them that Greg insisted we grope for snakes.

"Now, Greg," I had said. "This is Australia. How do I know I've got a file snake by the tail? What if I grab something poisonous?"

"No, no, mate. Perfectly safe. No other snake hides under pandanus roots, their heads in air pockets, bodies in the water."

"What if it tries to bite? These snakes are big."

"No worries. File snakes are pussycats. They never bite, never even try. I promise."

I must confess. After we dove into the cool water, I pulled on a mask, slipped the business end of a snorkel into my mouth, and clamped my teeth on the rubber. The water was not quite clear, nor entirely murky. I kicked frog-style toward the undercut bank. The root mass of each palm looked like a nest of serpents, and among them, if Greg was right, lurked the snakes. Could I summon the nerve to grab one? Perhaps. In my mind, visions of successful conquest wrestled with images from Hollywood. I recalled nerve-racking scenes in which burly actors struggled with monsters of the deep in games of do-or-die-before-the-air-gives-out. In the end, I searched halfheartedly and never found my quarry.

Yet in the morning, having muscled the car through the sandy gully two more times, I returned to the pool with greater nerve. I swam, snorkeled, searched, failed, and persisted. After peering and groping among hundreds of slimy roots, I finally spied what I both dreaded and hungered for: a bulge of reptile, gray-brown, blotchy, and as thick as my arm just below the elbow. Would I? Maybe. First I swam to the surface and called Debbie.

Three young men from England meanwhile splashed through the same corner of the pool. I dove down to confirm the snake's location, and when I couldn't find the reptile at first, I thought the swimmers had scared it off. But no, there it was, a dark coil looped among roots blackened with algae.

Debbie went under. Sputtering back to the surface, she looked pale. "Are you really going to do it?" she asked.

Thinking of John Wayne before he wrestled the giant octopus in *Wake of the Red Witch,* I decided to be brave. Sucking a deep breath into my snorkel, I dove and headed for the snake. Truth to tell, I was petrified. I grabbed. The snake pulled away and was gone. Or was it? Greg's words came back to me. I should reach in with my arm and feel around. Could I? I could not. Oh hell, yes. I stuck my arm into the hole. Nothing. The monster of the deep was gone.

Relieved and disappointed in equal measure, I continued the hunt. A little farther down the shore, I found a loop of snake of narrower diameter. This one looked manageable—about as thick around as a rake handle, at least the six inches of it I could see. Beaded skin identified the reptile as a file snake beyond reasonable doubt.

Why not? I grabbed it. The body of the animal felt soft and flabby, like a piece of wet foam rubber covered by rough cloth. Slowly, carefully, making sure not to harm it, I worked the snake free of the roots.

Out of the water, the reptile was comely, at least to a couple of reptile lovers. From snout to tail it measured about a yard. The head was bulbous and broad, like a python's, with small round eyes covered by translucent scales. At the front of the face, nostrils opened like the barrels of a double-barreled shotgun. The tongue was extraordinary. Forked all the way to the base, it looked like two rather than one. The captive struggled halfheartedly, abrading my skin with its rough hide. It never attempted to bite.

Hidden by distance from other swimmers, Debbie, the snake, and I caused little stir. Yet things went differently when we returned in the afternoon. This time I caught the big snake, the one I had missed. It was back in its lair, and now I grabbed it with something like confidence. Out it came, inch by inch, like a worm pulled from the ground by a robin.

Aboriginal women catch file snakes in a similar manner late in the dry season. Reptiles in hand, they do something I didn't do—put the animals' heads in their mouths and yank, snapping their necks. The herpetologist Richard Shine reports that two or three women, working in a team, can catch and kill one hundred file snakes in a day. Aborigines value the flesh, says Shine, and children relish the oviducts of female snakes, organs that Shine likens to "a string of large pearls."

The second snake, only a little longer than the first but far more massive, was likely a female. Females dwarf their scrawny mates and take longer to mature sexually, about nine years to the male's six. Both are sluggish by day but show enormous vigor at night, swimming through rivers and pools in pursuit of the fish that sustain them. The home range of a file snake may cover a dozen acres.

Delighted by the reptile and admittedly pleased with myself, I held the rough coils and waded toward the bank. I had a camera in a day pack and wanted to shoot a few photos. Unfortunately, I had not counted on the reaction of the crowd.

A four-wheel-drive minibus had dumped a load of tourists at the trailhead, and by midafternoon our private retreat swarmed with people. It became apparent that the general attitude toward reptiles differed from ours. One moment the shallows were crowded with smiling faces, and the next a stampede was clawing up the bank. Clutching the snake,

I continued to advance. Only when several people retreated down the track as I fumbled for a camera did I realize the trouble.

Not wanting to ruin anyone's day, I retreated to the shallows. I felt a bit like David Attenborough as I delivered an impromptu talk about the snake and its habits. Flashes popped and video cameras whirred. Before long, my comments would be playing on television screens in Tokyo, London, Paris, and New Delhi. "Here's a red-blooded Australian," I imagined people saying, "a real-life Crocodile Dundee." After I released the snake back into the water, most people lost interest in swimming.

During our return to the car, a plump bird stepped out of the undergrowth and paused on the path ahead of us. It was about the size of a pigeon and looked as if someone had snipped off its tail. Walking, the bird hunched forward as if carrying too much weight. Mother of Zeus! It was a rainbow pitta, the most colorful bird in the Territory.

Like the noisy pitta we had seen in Queensland, the rainbow had a black face, luminous green back, pale blue across the shoulders, and flamboyant orange underwear. The difference between the species lay in the breast. Where the noisy pitta wears orange-yellow on its chest, the rainbow clothes that portion of its body in black. Ironically, this absence of color in one place intensifies the radiance of hue in the rest. Even someone who cared little for birds would have waxed poetic over this one.

We built a campfire that night, drained the dregs from a jug of wine, and drifted to sleep beneath a bone-white moon.

The next day was our last in Kakadu. Debbie was feeling a bit worse for wear, so we passed the hours quietly, meeting Leslie and David in the Cooinda pub for another round of ice water, then driving on to a campground called Kakadu Holiday Village. That night we enjoyed electric lights and hot showers for the first time in many days. And Debbie revived sufficiently to enjoy a final bit of adventure.

Our quarry was the northern death adder. Greg said we might find one near the campground, soaking up heat from the pavement after the sun went down. The road he advised us to cruise traversed the floodplain of the South Alligator River. How common were death adders in the area? "There are *heaps*," said Greg with a smile.

"Death adders have relatively large fangs and very toxic venom, and are among the most dangerous snakes in Australia and the world," writes Harold Cogger in *Reptiles and Amphibians of Australia*. Yet we were not afraid—at least not much. Specialists at ambush, death adders look and act

a lot like rattlesnakes. Having experience with the latter, we felt confident
we would be safe in the company of the former as long as we knew where
they were. In the bush, where camouflage makes a snake all but impossible
to see, the death adder constitutes the herpetological equivalent of a land
mine. Step on one, and you're in deep fecal matter. Asphalt would be different. On blacktop a snake would stand out. It would see us, and we it,
and both parties would have a stake in ending the encounter peacefully.
Back home we had photographed big rattlesnakes on highways at night,
and we planned to approach the death adder as we had them—cautiously,
keeping well outside striking range.

We cruised and cruised some more. Most sane human beings would
have been relieved to find the road barren of adders, but we were sorely
disappointed. Two hours produced nothing, not even a lizard. When all
seemed lost, we spied a little brown snake along the shoulder.

We got out of the car for a look. It was a peculiar snake, striped, about
eight inches long, with an oversized snout. Behind the eyes there were ear
openings—features that no snake possesses. Here lay *Lialis burtoni,* Burton's snake-lizard.

Unlike a python, which has tiny external hind limbs, the snake-lizard
has no visible limbs. It belongs to a family, the pygopods or "flap-foots,"
that herpetologists consider closely related to geckos. Most legless lizards,
including the glass lizards of the United States, have movable eyelids.
Snakes do not, and neither does the snake-lizard. As I held the thing in my
hand, it stared it me, but only because it had no other choice.

We were quite taken with Mr. Burton. He was small, docile, easy to handle, and his nose reminded us of the comedian Jimmy Durante, who made
a career out of poking fun at his own formidable proboscis. Rather than
attempt to bite or wriggle away, he accepted his predicament with dignity.

After a brief look, I lowered the reptile to the ground. It lay there a
moment, then crawled into the bush. If it was hungry, the reptile might
have spent the rest of the night poking under fallen logs and leaf litter,
looking for skinks. Every other legless lizard settles for a diet of bugs, but
not the Burton's. More ambitious than its cousins, it preys on skinks,
which are among the slipperiest of reptiles. Hinged teeth, possibly unique
among lizards, slip under the victims' smooth scales, giving the snake-
lizard an iron grip.

On the home stretch, we found a bird floundering on the side of the
road. It was a barn owl with a broken wing. A sorry sight, the bird leaped

from the ground in hopeless attempts to fly, and, failing, hopped away from us, dragging the limb behind it. What to do? It was midnight. If we left the bird to fend for itself, it might be ripped apart by a fox. The solution we came up with was to catch the bird in a towel, keep it overnight in a box, and give it to a ranger in the morning.

Although the circumstances could have been cheerier, we were excited to see the barn owl. It is one of a scant few Australian birds that is an American bird, too. The most wide-ranging land bird of all, the barn owl hunts mice from Eurasia to India and Africa, throughout the three Americas, across Tasmania, and over much of continental Australia.

In the morning we drove out of Kakadu, bound by way of Darwin and Katherine for Western Australia. The owl came with us. The campground ranger had asked us to ferry it to a veterinarian near Darwin. The receptionist at the veterinary clinic proved to be the doctor himself, a friendly Chinese man named Ulrick Wong. He spoke softly, and his face wrinkled in compassion as he lifted the bird from the box. As fingers worked their way into feathers, the vet's mouth sank. "It's a magnificent creature," he said. "But the wing is badly broken. There's only one thing I can do."

And he did, with tenderness and reverence. Feeling gloomy, we thanked the doctor and fled for Darwin. Only the following night, when we slept under the blazing Australian stars along a lonesome highway, did our spirits lift. We could hear the movements of kangaroos in the bush, and wondered about brown snakes and death adders. Except for the occasional stirrings of animals, the silence was profound. No planes, no cars, no sounds of machines or voices—all we could hear was our own placid breathing. Lying there, a few miles from the Western Australia border, I made a philosophical descent toward sleep, thinking that the world was, if nothing else, a marvelous place to be sad.

8

Sirens

ELSPETH HUXLEY FOUND Australia's Northwest "a strange mixture of the immemorial and the bud-new." She was more right than we knew. The morning we crossed into Western Australia, we awoke before sunrise under a veil of blue light. The air was deliciously cool, the ancient, worn-out landscape flat and serene. In a tree behind us, a pied butcherbird announced the birth of the day in rich, bell-like tones, just as pied butcherbirds have done for tens of thousands of years. We had arrived at the place after dark. Only when I staggered to my feet in early morning did I notice the bud-new—human excrement and toilet paper strewn far and wide over the red dirt on which we slept. By dumb luck, we had missed the tainted ground by a dozen feet.

Breakfast could wait. We raced on, passed through a fruit inspection station at the border, and entered Australia's largest state. Immense is too mild a word for Western Australia. It covers more territory than the United States east of the Mississippi River, and supports a population smaller than Milwaukee's. "W.A.," as the natives call it, abounds in minerals and natural beauty and might be hailed as a paradise were it not unsparing of human lives and dreams.

Like the Sirens that Odysseus faced, Western Australia presented powerful allurements—uncrowded coastlines, vast stretches of open land, picturesque red-rock mountains, grand forests, a spring wildflower display unsurpassed in the world, waves of amber grain, and enough frogs, lizards, snakes, turtles, birds, and mammals to keep a pair of naturalists happy for years. Yet beneath the surface, like a sword behind the cape of a bull-fighter, death hovered always near.

In T. E. Lawrence's translation of the *Odyssey*, the Sirens "sit singing in their plashet between high banks of mouldering skeletons which flutter with the rays of skin rotting upon the bones." Had the Greeks attempted to sail past the Sirens with open ears, their bones and skin would have been added to the heap. As it was, Circe warned them. The crewmen plugged their ears with beeswax and Odysseus, curious to hear the voices that had wrecked a thousand ships, ordered himself bound to the mast. There he heard the Sirens' sweet, deadly singing while the sailors ignored his cries to turn the ship toward shore.

We employed a similar strategy. Traversing lethal desert and unforgiving prairies in a two-wheel-drive car, we kept watch on each other's tendency to breach the margin of safety during the enthusiastic pursuit of reptiles, birds, and marsupials. Villages were few, doctors fewer, and death adders all too common. Across the parched landscape, food, fuel, and auto mechanics were thinly spread. The Sirens of adventure called, but if the voices beckoned one of us toward peril, the other would bind him to the passenger seat and drive on.

Our introduction to W.A. came in the region known as the Kimberley, short for Kimberley Plateau. Three times the size of Nevada and crossed by two paved roads, this was four-wheel-drive country, poorly suited for a car.

The Gibb River Road, the most picturesque and direct route across the Kimberley, cuts 415 miles through no-man's-land from Kununurra, near the Northern Territory border, to Derby in the West. Rough and rocky, the route crawls up and over mountain passes, fords rivers swirling with crocodiles, and twists and turns over a million shuddering corrugations. For us, the route's foremost attraction was Windjana Gorge, a place renowned for razor-edged cliffs and freshwater crocodiles. Some of the rocks at Windjana are all that remain of a barrier reef that flourished during the Devonian Era, when the plateau lay under warm seas. Unfortunately, we never reached the place.

Although it was tempting to pit our car against the Gibb River Road's dangers, the lessons of the *Odyssey* commanded us to do otherwise. In the interest of safety, we chose the prosaic option, a paved road called the Great Northern Highway. It led south and west from Kununurra to Hall's Creek, west to Fitzroy Crossing, and 245 miles farther westward through empty country to Broome and the Indian Ocean.

Happily, the road-more-traveled had merits. We moved swiftly, a welcome advantage in blistering heat in a car without air conditioning. On pavement, without corrugations to bounce our eyes like Ping-Pong balls, we could focus on the sights. Most interesting among them were baobab trees, called "boabs" here, which gave the landscape an African look.

Baobab seeds drifted from Africa to Australia about 75 million years ago, give or take a few million. Inside pods that resemble baseballs, the seeds survived the long journey across salt water, perhaps high and dry on a raft of flotsam. One day the sea lifted a baobab pod, curled into a wind-up, and heaved the thing up on a Kimberley beach. The pod burst, seeds germinated, and Australia gained a tree distinguished from all others by the magnificent corpulence of its trunk.

By and large, Australian trees hold their stringy, drought-adapted leaves throughout the year, so the leaflessness of the boabs we saw stood out. At first glance we took them for dead. Only after we parked and examined a grossly inflated specimen did we see that the gray, pebble-grained bark was tight, like a child's skin, and the limbs, tapering abruptly, appeared healthy and unbroken.

Someone had carved "DRAC" in foot-high letters in the bark, yet the tree appeared to suffer little from the indignity. Dozens of pods lay on the ground, most of them cracked into slivers. I picked up an intact one. It was a baseball covered with peach fuzz, and at one end was a short, stout stem, like that of an apple. Plucking out the stem, I pulled back my right arm, raised my left leg, and threw. The pod sailed through the air erratically like a knuckleball, struck a rock, and shattered. This was seed distribution, boab-style; I was glad to be of service.

All day long we saw boabs, one here, one there. Each rose starkly against a sky so blue and dry it frightened us, a sky that would shrink and mummify us if given half a chance. D. H. Lawrence wrote of the "untouched blue sky overhead" he found in Australia's East. I wondered what he would have said of Kimberley skies, even more empty, lovely, and cruel. It was amazing to us that the boabs could stand up to them. They do so by storing immense volumes of water in their trunks, and by shedding leaves at the onset of the Dry Season. To endure the terrible conditions of the Northwest, a plant or animal needs all the help it can get. The longest heat wave in the world was recorded at Marble Bar, just south of the Kimberley, between October 23, 1923, and April 7, 1924. On 162 days, the temperature climbed above 100 degrees Fahrenheit. By Kimberley standards, Debbie and I were lucky. The thermometer never topped ninety-five, although our glass-sided, black-seated automobile pushed the number higher.

Although the landscape appeared barren, there were mummified cattle from time to time that revealed the presence of a grazing industry. Until recently, cattle ranching accounted for nearly all the economic activity in the region. Now a giant diamond mine chews up the country nearby, and a $100-million dam blocks the course of the Ord River. Lake Argyle, behind the dam, is the second largest reservoir in Australia. Its waters nourish agriculture, and the agriculture gave rise to a town, Kununurra, where we passed the night.

The next morning we bustled off, driving four hundred dizzy, dusty miles under a blistering sun to Fitzroy Crossing. We arrived with high hopes of visiting Geike Gorge, the only one of the region's deep gorges we had a chance of seeing. As it happened, we found a sign along the narrow road leading from town to the park, saying that camping at Geike was no longer permitted. Continuing anyway, we passed three tour buses speeding in the opposite direction. Powdered earth fogged the air. At the park entrance came more bad news. The only way to visit Geike Gorge was to lay out twenty dollars apiece for a guided boat tour. Spending the money was out of the question. Forty dollars would feed us for several days.

Disappointed and angry, we growled. We had traveled hard and far to reach this place and see—nothing. The park's managers had chosen to shut out swagmen and hoboes, people scratching around Australia on a shoestring, in favor of the well-fed, well-coddled, well-heeled, so-called eco-tourist. In principle I applauded the concept of eco-tours, partly because they help people in places such as Fitzroy Crossing earn livings with a lighter environmental impact than ranching or mining. In practice, however, I often cringe. Eco-tours swarmed over Uluru and Kakadu like locusts, and here they monopolized Geike, selling access to the place's beauty like a souvenir. Call me a curmudgeon, especially on a hot afternoon, yet I insist that the selling of beauty, and of access to beauty, cheapens it, even though the monetary price rises. And I ask: Is an adventure really adventurous if you pay someone to lead you through it by the hand?

Debbie interrupted my complaining. These were the best as well as the worst of times, she said. Without a tourist industry in the Kimberley, we might be back in Darwin, crying in our beer that the highway to the West was impassable. I conceded the point. A few minutes later we drove away and pitched our tent in a caravan park mobbed with retirees and fruit pickers.

Having accepted the unacceptable, we rose the following morning in sunshine. I shuffled to the ablution block to brush my teeth and found myself standing beside a bald man in front of a wall of mirrors. He was fussing with what little remained of his hair. Gazing into the looking glass, I chuckled at the sight of my own mop, bushy, tousled, uncombed for nearly a week. We appreciate a resource, it seems, only after it becomes scarce.

On we charged, out of Fitzroy Crossing into a landscape of red rock, blue sky, and gray-and-pink parrots. The birds were galahs, and we saw them by the hundreds, flapping over overgrazed pastures, the fine details of their feathers blurred by rising heat, and then, turning suddenly, wheeling overhead in explosions of lurid pink, and ebbing back to gray. Much of the country was blackened by fire, and in the burned areas, birds abounded. Besides galahs we saw diamond doves, tiny things with gray heads, mud-colored backs, and a liberal overlay of white speckles, and in the air, black-breasted buzzards that soared against the blue with dark wings daubed toward the tips with silver.

Pushing westward, ticking off the miles, we found our conversation drifting back to Hall's Creek, a frontier town between Kununurra and Fitzroy Crossing. The tension in the place made us edgy. A few weeks before we arrived, Aborigines from Hall's Creek and the surrounding country had gone on a rampage, smashing shop windows and threatening merchants. While misguided, the riot made a certain amount of sense in a region where white Australians own nearly all the wealth and Aborigines provide most of the labor.

Coasting into Hall's Creek from the scrub, we found about twenty dusty, tired-looked Aboriginal men shuffling around the center of town, looking dazed, staring at us. They wore blue jeans and T-shirts mostly, and floppy hats that hid their eyes in shadow. Children, a conspicuous presence in most Aboriginal groups, were nowhere to be seen. About a dozen of the men gathered under a tree, its tattered crown giving little shade. Several of the party stood. The rest sat. It was a peculiar scene—no apparent talking was going on, just sitting and milling and enduring. The clothes of the men hung loosely on their frames, and their faces wore blank expressions, as did ours. The heat was oppressive. We sensed explosive tension beneath the surface calm.

The Mobil station where we bought fuel offered a stark contrast. The proprietor was white, neatly dressed, and well-spoken. He processed our purchase on a bank machine, its electronic brain communicating with a computer back at the main office in Melbourne. Out at the pumps, a man towing a caravan spoke to us. Seeing our license plates, he asked if we were Tasmanians. The man was white. His car and caravan were white. The pumps and the petrol station were white. Only the shattered housing of the fuel pump, shattered by a rock or club, suggested the proximity of another world, another color.

In Hall's Creek, volatility is literally as old as the hills. Just outside of town, in 1.7-billion-year-old dolomite brushed by the wind, paleontologists found evidence of one of evolution's great revolutions. Minute specks in the rock proved to be the fossils of single-celled organisms, some of which included pyramid-shaped clusters of microscopic spheres. Each cluster was enclosed within a membrane. What were they? Experts believe the clusters represent cell nuclei caught in the act of asexual reproduction, or mitosis. While the process of mitosis is old-hat to high-school biology students, its appearance around 1.7 billion years ago marked perhaps the most important fork in the road of life. Bacteria and other nonnucleated organisms turned down one half of the divide, while cells with DNA organized inside nuclei veered down the other. Without mitosis, there would be no boabs, no diamond doves, no you and me.

The country grew flatter and more monotonous the closer we drew to Broome. It was with joy and relief that we at long last saw the city rise into view. When we ran out of asphalt, the luminous turquoise of the Indian Ocean spread out before us. We abandoned the car and ran for the water and felt the sea cool our oven-baked feet. "Are there crocodiles here?" Debbie wanted to know. As far as I knew, the cold-blooded misanthrope's range ended at Derby, well to the north and east, but there's nothing more comforting than certainty. We retreated to the sand.

Ten minutes later we were driving down a palm-lined street when a Land Cruiser slowed ahead of us and the driver waved his arms. It was Keith MacLeod.

Again we found ourselves in the high-spirited, protective custody of two of our favorite Australians. Keith led us in convoy to the motel and poured celebratory glasses of wine. Peg—"Mopsy," Keith calls her—appeared a few minutes later, carrying groceries. "Oh, oh!" she cried, speechless while delivering hugs. Shortly thereafter, we were ordered to the shower. When we emerged, scrubbed of Kimberley dirt, Peg had spread snacks on the table.

For four nights we stayed with the MacLeods in their extra bedroom. We wined, dined, slept in soft comfort, showered, soaked up goodwill, and told stories of our adventures. Four months had passed since we'd parted company, and there was much to tell.

By day we explored the countryside in the MacLeods' four-wheel-drive. One morning we drove to the Broome Bird Observatory, a nature reserve a few miles south of town. At the peak of the spring and autumn migrations, the beaches at the observatory teem with millions of shore-birds. Some of them come from Siberia and North America, making long flights over the ocean twice every year. Alas, we arrived at a quiet time.

During a couple of hours of walking, we saw a great bowerbird tending its bachelor pad, and several thousand black-tailed godwits taking wing along the beach. The godwits flooded the sky with black and white and brown, slowly fading into blue. There were huge flocks of common sand-pipers, too, and in the scrub, rainbow bee-eaters and red-headed hon-eyeaters. With the addition of the new birds, our list grew to 382 species. It was a respectable total for a couple of generalists who followed their whims.

Talk of pearls and pearl-diving left us confused until Keith sorted out the problem. The so-called "pearl" boom that put Broome on the map in the nineteenth century involved mother-of-pearl, a material that develops inside certain clams, not the pearls that grow by accretion within oysters. Immigrants came from afar to seek fortunes in pearl, the majority from China, Japan, the Philippines, the Middle East, and the islands that today constitute Indonesia. The chief demand for mother-of-pearl came from the button industry. Eventually plastics caught on and the pearl divers lost their livelihood.

Today, Broome is known for the other kind of pearl. After World War II, local entrepreneurs took up oyster farming and pearl cultivation. Suc-cess followed. Broome's fortunes rebounded, and today the city numbers 9,000 year-round residents.

On our third and final day with Peg and Keith, we loaded the Land Cruiser and set off to the north. Keith drove, following pavement that soon degenerated into dust. We rattled on for more than two hours, stop-ping occasionally to botanize or chase a bird. Eventually a consensus was reached. Going farther might result in getting stuck miles from help, so we would turn back toward Broome.

A few minutes later we pulled off the track into the shade of a tree. An old beach umbrella leaned against the trunk, an ancient thing with a

hardwood center post, brass fittings, and a canopy of rotting but still effec-
tive canvas. We took this as a sign. Peg broke out the victuals, Keith
uncorked the Chardonnay, and for an hour we relapsed into lotos-eating.

To my eyes the grandest scene of the day came when we were nearly
home. At the summit of a ridge we stopped at a place where bedrock was
exposed over large areas. Blazing red, it rolled down to the sea and met
milky blue water in a gorgeous juxtaposition of color. Keith fossicked.
Soon he was handing us fossils—a perfect, if fragmented, imprint of a
fern, a leaf like that of a eucalypt, and a three-inch-long shard of bone
from an ancient vertebrate.

The day ended as they all did in Broome. We gathered in the shade of
the motel patio, sipped South Australian wine, caught up on adventures,
and enjoyed visits from eastern blue-tongued lizards. A second kind of
lizard also appeared, and it waved good-bye to us: a species known as
Lophognathus longirostris, or "ta-ta." The ta-ta lizard was dark, striped, and
slender, and it hauled around a tail of preposterous length. From time to
time the reptile raised one of its front feet and waved it back and forth in
the air. Was it really bidding us farewell? Perhaps not. The behavior probably frightens insects into moving, and so gives the lizard a better chance
to catch them.

Early the next day, having made a pact to reunite at our journey's end
in Melbourne, we bade the MacLeods farewell and set off down the highway. For several hundred miles we would skirt the edge of one of the
world's harshest deserts, the Great Sandy. The road paralleled the coast,
the sea out of view.

South of Broome, we entered the range of one of the two Australian
lizards I most wanted to see: the thorny devil, *Moloch horridus,* an agamid
covered in spikes as if it has walked straight from a punk rocker's day-
dream. The other I longed to see was the perentie, *Varanus giganteus.* The
perentie is the world's third-largest lizard and the most formidable of Australia's goannas. Another day of driving would put us in its range.

Fellow travelers had warned us that the highway from Broome to Port
Hedland offered little more than monotony and heat. There was truth to
the reports. Yet in the morning, before the heat slammed into us like a
railway locomotive, and in the afternoon, after it broke, we found much
along the route to enjoy. There was no scenery. Flat land extended to the
horizons, covered with little more than spinifex grass and scrub. Motion
was provided by miniature tornadoes that whipped dust into swirling

columns, and color by masses of purple wildflowers blooming along the shoulders. There were lizards, too. To keep ourselves amused and to save lives, we stopped to identify each of them and carried the reptiles afterward to safety. There were three varieties: ta-ta lizards, central netted dragons (we had seen one of these in the Center), and a species new to us, the dwarf bearded dragon.

We saw birds as well, sailing across the sky and perched in bushes. Among them were zebra finches, brown falcons, black-faced cuckooshrikes, and—new to us—spotted harriers. Harriers are hawks, a lowcruising kind that hunt at dawn and dusk and have evolved owl-like faces adapted for gathering sound.

The date was the seventh of September. Spring had come to Western Australia, bringing flowers that grew more showy with every mile. Nearly all of them were mulla-mullas, tall, purple things that grew in racemes like goldenrod. They represented the first trickle of a botanical torrent that would astound us for weeks to come.

After spending the day traversing flat scrublands that run between the Indian Ocean and a virtually trackless desert ten times the size of North America's Mojave, we pitched our tent at Pardoo Roadhouse. It was one of those watering stops that spring up magically in the outback right about the time a driver starts glancing nervously at his fuel gauge. Despite the harshness of its landscapes, Australia is forgiving to motorists. Nearly every time we left a town, there was a sign telling us exactly how far we would have to drive to reach the next source of fuel. We carried a jerry can to fill with extra petrol, but so far we hadn't needed it. Without fail, we followed the Australian practice of topping off the tank at every opportunity. It had kept us out of trouble for 15,000 miles.

Driving into Port Hedland the next day, we were jolted into the twentieth century. Signs of industry confronted us everywhere—derricks lugging high-tension power lines from place to place, toxic-looking evaporation ponds and glittering white dunes at a salt works, grim-faced men in trucks roaring to and fro, and, converging on the harbor, railroad tracks. One train came and another went, the departing train empty, the arriving one loaded from one end of its mile-long string of cars to the other with red rock. The rock was red because it was heavy with iron oxide.

South and east of Port Hedland lies the Hamersley Range, in a region known as the Pilbara. It is a country of low, ancient mountains and deep gorges, all made of rock so red, so rich in iron oxide, that a stone hefted in the hand feels like a chunk of steel. As naturalists, we were fascinated to learn that the Pilbara iron deposits, the largest known concentration of iron ore on the earth's surface and the stuff from which Toyotas, Hondas, and Mazdas are made, were created not by inanimate geologic forces, but by living organisms.

Pilbara iron commemorates a great leap forward in evolution. Two and a half billion years ago, cyanobacteria—many of us knew them in our school days as blue-green algae—began harnessing the sun's energy with the help of a magnesium-based molecule called chlorophyll. Until this epochal change, the oceans of the world were rich in dissolved iron.

Armed with chlorophyll, cyanobacteria multiplied in unprecedented numbers and flooded the seas with a waste product called oxygen. Oxygen reacted with iron, the oceans literally rusted, and billions of tons of iron oxide precipitated to the bottom. This went on for some 700 million years. The results were a global ocean nearly barren of iron and seabeds piled high with iron oxide. In most parts of the world, geologic upheavals dispersed the iron. Meanwhile the sea beds that eventually bulged up to form the Pilbara remained geologically serene.

Today, in a state proclaimed by a former Western Australia premier as "the land of movable mountains," Pilbara ore makes its way from great open-pit mines gouged out of Western Australian mountains to freighters waiting at Port Hedland. The ships swallow the stuff in cavernous holds, then set off northward. Up through Indonesian waters they churn, through the Sunda Strait between Sumatra and Java, past Borneo and Singapore, up the South China Sea, and on to the great industrial cities of Japan, Taiwan, and Korea. Purified in titanic smelters, the by-products of ancient life are transformed into cars, trains, ships, waffle irons, and toasters.

An industrial outpost in a far corner of nowhere, Port Hedland seemed noisy, busy, and caught up in its own importance. Debbie and I recoiled from its grime and clamor, even as we acknowledged the city's service as midwife to our Toyota. We arrived, we looked, we left. Firing up the Pilbara-born contraption that had carried us more than halfway around Australia, we aimed for the mountains of ore.

At an unnamed junction south and west of Port Hedland, we turned onto a road that would lead us southward into Millstream-Chichester National Park. Asphalt gave way to dirt, a change we had gotten used to in Australia's backcountry, and the winding route carried us up into low, eroded hills. The country here reminded us of the Dakota Badlands. The climate was too dry to support a forest but wet enough for grassland, and the hills came in pastel colors ranging from gray to green to brown. Some looked like enormous dirt heaps, lightly garnished with grass.

As we climbed higher and the light grew soft, colorful wildflowers crowded up to the road. There were the pale, blue-purple spikes of mulla-mulla, familiar to us now, and a gaudy new apparition called Sturt's desert pea. Brilliant crimson blossoms covered the peas by the dozen, the flowers big and many-pointed like the hat of a medieval jester. Sturt's desert pea suggested a grossly enlarged version of the wild columbine of eastern North America.

Driving became perilous. There were so many flowers to enjoy that I often lost my concentration at the wheel, a risky development on a mountain road without guard rails. The fading light brought spinifex pigeons out on the road, birds that were as diffident and pig-headed around cars as kangaroos. We crept along at twenty miles per hour, waving arms, shouting, clapping, and honking.

As glamorous as fashion models, the pigeons had orange breasts, red and white faces, an array of black and gray bands, and heads decorated with prodigious topknots. The birds were utterly trusting, and it made me sick to my stomach when we hit one. All I could do was lay the corpse in a patch of wildflowers, mutter a sincere but meaningless apology, and drive on even more slowly than before.

After finding no pythons in residence at a place called Python Pool, we continued through the dusk as color drained from the landscape. Night descended. There were no lights, no lines along the roadsides, no reflectors to keep us from sailing off cliff edges, no other cars to give us comfort, just a pervasive blackness. Creeping forward, we reached a camping area an hour after sundown. Three lanterns burned in the distance, telling us we had neighbors.

Morning brought birdsong. Spring had arrived, and the trills, whistles, and chiming notes that shook the air told of romance and battles for territory. It was wonderful to lie back on sleeping bags, close our eyes, and listen, not to a cacophony of cars and buses, or to the roar of central heat or air conditioning, or to the cruel buzzing of an alarm clock, but to symphonic music finer and sweeter than any heard in a concert hall.

When we crawled into the light of day, we found the tent shaded by gum trees. A canal full of green water flowed nearby, and the air was cool

and moist. Looking up, we saw the piccoloists and the flutists—tree martins, singing honeyeaters, crested bellbirds, and budgerigars.

The day's drive was barely under way when Debbie shouted to pull
over for a bird. I obliged, groaning. A succession of long, hot days in the
car, jammed into tight quarters for hours on end, had created an explosive
atmosphere. We are both thickheaded. We know what we want to do and
how and when we want to do it. Clashes were inevitable, and both of us
struggled to prevent them from exploding, fearing the worst. A collapse of
our relationship would have ended the odyssey. We struggled on, by turns
sad, seething, and confused. That afternoon Debbie lost the wedding ring
I had carved for her out of mountain laurel heartwood, and quietly we
both took the event as a bad omen. Odysseus and Penelope pined for each
other during their long separation; absence made their hearts grow
fonder. We, on the other hand, were learning that togetherness can exact a
terrible cost.

We stopped. We looked. I was glad that we did, although I kept my
pleasure to myself. The bushes along one side of the road flashed sema-
phores of color. The branches shook with painted finches—stunning
creatures with gray-green backs, flaming red rumps, ebony bellies spotted
handsomely with white, and, on the cheeks and bellies of the males, dazzling patches of crimson.

Morale slightly improved, we drove on to the park's visitor center. It
was an old farmhouse, built on the site of an earlier structure that was
assembled from timber cut in England, shipped halfway around the world,
and muscled from the coast to the site by bullocks. The new place dated to
the 1920s. A plain, one-story ranch house, it was ringed by verandas to
keep the heat down, and situated near a water hole planted with three
kinds of palm. At one time the homestead served as nerve center for a station covering a million acres and running 55,000 sheep.

The place was deserted, except for a tame kangaroo grazing on the lawn.
Inside we found exhibits. There were rusty tools left over from the ranching
days, murals depicting prehistory, history, natural lore, and buttons that,
when pressed, spurred gritty Aboriginal and English voices to speak of earlier times. My favorite exhibit was a map of the ranch in its heyday, painted
in large scale in 1932 by a twelve-year-old boy. In pictographs of guileless
charm, we learned of happenings big and small. An upside-down black bird
was captioned, "Grandfather shot crow here." Other sketches bore the
words "Stuart found two queer birds here," "Two boys had a fight here,"

"meat house," "fowl yard," "blacksmith shop," and "native camp." The last was accompanied by the figure of a black man, naked, holding a boomerang in one hand and a brightly colored shield in the other.

It was after we left the homestead that Debbie's ring vanished. We were fording a shallow river shaded by paperbark trees when Debbie stepped out to shoot a photo. After she returned and we had driven several miles, we discovered that the ring was missing. The situation presented a problem. The likely site of the loss was several miles back along a one-way dirt road, and we had barely enough fuel to get us through rugged country to the next source of petrol. Going back would require a long detour, one that might leave us stranded far from help. Symbolism hung heavy in the air. Would we give up on the ring, or take a chance to find it? Give up on our marriage, or work to regain what we had lost? We took a chance, driving slowly to conserve fuel. We never found the ring.

At this point, Debbie wanted to leave the interior and head for the more civilized coast. I argued for sticking with the plan that had brought us here: to continue south and east to Karijini National Park in the Hamersley Range, and strike for the coast several days later. Risk came with the second course. We had about 125 miles of rugged, empty country to cross before we could purchase fuel. Our gauge registered less than half. At our usual rate of consumption, we would reach the petrol depot with room to spare, but estimating fuel use on rough outback roads is an uncertain science. And there was another consideration: the day was windy. The only feasible route to Karijini took us through Wittenoom, once the center of a lucrative asbestos-mining industry, now a ghost town. Road maps warned of windblown asbestos from old tailings. If we chose the Wittenoom route, we would follow advice, roll up the windows despite the heat, close off the vents, and stay in the car. One point worried us. The rubber gaskets that sealed our doors against the outside world were in tatters.

We discussed, debated, and argued. Eventually the case for Wittenoom and Karijini prevailed, and we lurched ahead in hostile silence.

Wetting handkerchiefs and tying them over our mouths and noses, we crept into town on a radiant spring afternoon. The place looked deserted, although we noted a few camper vans in the Wittenoom Caravan Park, and laundry hanging behind a house on a side-street. There were houses and restaurants, a petrol station, and tree-lined streets, all devoid of people, as if some plague had descended and struck down the populace.

On a windy day, walking down Wittenoom's main street would invite death. Asbestos fibers taint the air, and they cause mesothelioma, sometimes decades after exposure. The disease is an aggressive cancer of lung tissue or the abdomen. According to the Western Australia Department of Health, Safety, and Welfare, blue asbestos, the kind mined and milled around Wittenoom, was "the most hazardous type of asbestos known."

Poor old Wittenoom. Its picturesque setting, rising against a backdrop of red hills, made the abandonment of the settlement seem all the more tragic. This was indeed a place of Sirens—golden and alluring in the last hour of daylight, yet cruel and lethal.

A few miles down the road, the Sirens sang loudly. We came upon the photographic opportunity of a lifetime. A bearded Aboriginal man, his chest, legs, and feet bare, dressed only in ragged shorts, was staggering out of the bush. In a hand held higher than his shoulder, he clutched the tail of an enormous lizard, its lifeless, bloody head dangling near the ground. In the other hand he held a wooden club. The scene was remarkable enough, but adding to its novelty, the man, who seemed straight out of the Stone Age, was marching toward a shiny automobile. Beside the car stood a pair of Aboriginal women, perhaps in their twenties. Smiling and laughing, they called out greetings to the man. The women were dressed in blouses, skirts, and shoes, neat and clean, as if the two were bound for an office party. O temptation! I wanted nothing more than to leap from the car, introduce myself, and shoot photographs. The situation also offered the opportunity we had long hoped for—a chance to meet Aboriginal people on casual terms. Last, the temptation was three-headed because the lizard bludgeoned by the man was a perentie, perhaps the only one I would ever see.

In the moment of decision, the wind freshened. It pushed the man's hair to one side and inflated the blouses of the women. O cruel fate! We lashed ourselves to the mast of our own resolve, gave friendly waves to the people on the shoulder, and rumbled on toward Karijini.

Just before sunset, we found the petrol station. Prices were exorbitant. Then we raced as darkness fell. The road brought us through Yampire Gorge, a menacing name for a beautiful place that could be viewed safely only with a gas mask or from the safety of a sealed automobile. We drove the dusty road slowly, stirring up as little asbestos as possible, breathing through our moistened handkerchiefs. Every time another car approached, which was often, we pulled to the shoulder and waited for the dust to settle. Where were the people coming from? There was no town nearby. The cars rode high on their springs, unburdened by camping gear. Employees getting off the day shift at a mine? That must be it.

For two nights we slept at a campground in Karijini National Park, above the Fortescue River. The car sat empty, and we stayed well away from it, letting the winds carry away its fine coat of dust.

Near the campground yawned Dales Gorge, a much-reduced but equally beautiful Grand Canyon. By a steep, rough track, we descended into the ravine until after fifteen minutes we reached the bottom. Flat slabs of red rock lay akilter, as if the marble floor of some ancient ballroom had been heaved up and scattered by an earthquake. A cool, dry wind blew in gusts, and for the first time in months, we pulled on sweaters.

The Fortescue River flowed not evenly and continuously, but in fits and spurts from one rocky pool to another. The first basin we found was stunning. Bordered on three sides by an amphitheater of stone terraces, it looked uncannily like a Roman bath. The water lay as flat as glass, and the terraces were spruced up with clumps of fern and grass. It looked as if an interior decorator had come along and primped the place for *Architectural Digest*.

From the first pool we made a gentle ascent over plates of loose stone to a second waterhole, far less grand. Clotted with dark algae, the water looked like spinach soup. A third pool was warmed by the sun, its algae a cheery green. Underfoot, frogs squawked. We hunted for them to no avail.

Along a ledge dripping with seepage and bristling with ferns, we crept through cool shadows until we could go no farther. Below the ledge lay a jumble of boulders, and beyond them a fourth water hole known as Circular Pool.

A stone's throw from one side to the other, the water hole was nearly perfectly round. A quarter of its circumference was bordered by a wall of rock that served as a showcase for ferns and miniature waterfalls. Far from the range of crocodiles, the water looked inviting. Stripping down to shorts, I leapt in.

The instant I hit the water, I howled. The pool was icy! As my testicles beat a hasty retreat for their place of origin, I clawed at the offending substance and hauled myself out on a rock. I stood there, covered with goose-bumps, knees knocking, while Debbie laughed and laughed.

Working our way back down the gorge, I relished the warmth of the rocks. In them we began to notice blue veins, some of them fuzzy, like bits of tattered cloth. This was the dreaded blue asbestos, the boom and bane of Wittenoom. Fortunately the mineral is harmless in its natural state.

After passing the track that carried us into the ravine, we veered to the right when the valley bottom diverged. The trail was sparsely marked. At one point we sidestepped along a narrow ledge until the shelf petered out to nothing, and below lay a twenty-foot drop. Retracing our route, we found footprints in mud, followed them into tall grass, crossed a channel on steppingstones, and rediscovered the marked trail on the far side of the creek.

Three-quarters of an hour later we reached Fortescue Falls, a narrow plume of water that cut diagonally across a broad staircase formed from natural terraces. At the bottom lay a Y-shaped pool, in the middle of which bobbed a very white, very well fed, very naked woman talking to her husband on the shore in an English accent. We gazed idly at the falls for a while, taking a few photos, then circled to the far side. Only then, passing the woman's husband with clothes draped over his arm, did we comprehend the situation. The woman had been treading water for fifteen minutes, waiting for us to go away so she could flop out on a warm rock and wriggle into her trousers.

Radiating a splendid jade green in the sunshine, the pool looked far warmer than the other. We threw down our packs and stepped in. The water was pleasingly cool, a perfect balm for hot skin. As I swam toward the falls, my peripheral vision took in the sight of the Englishwoman lumbering into the shallows. She struggled to slide a fleshy thigh into the underpants her husband handed her, and, just when the job was nearly done, fell back into the pool. Poor soul. European modesty about nakedness seemed a silly thing in the vastness of Western Australia.

Near the gorge rim during our hike out, we met an Australian couple who had climbed to the top of Fortescue Falls. There was a python sunning there, they said, a big, fat one. Did we have the energy to climb back to the bottom, then pick our way up the falls to the reptile? Alas, the answer was no.

Feeling more at peace with each other than we had in days, Debbie and I loaded the car on Wednesday, September 11, and made for the coast. The drive took two days. On the first we passed through Tom Price, a bustling and surprisingly attractive mining town named for a vice-president of Kaiser Steel. At sundown we camped at the Nanutarra Roadhouse on the North West Coastal Highway. The second day brought us through country memorable for dunes of brilliant red sand. The road, a dirt track, required slow driving and thus made for good lizard hunting. Hour by hour we scanned the shoulders for thorny devils without success. Yet one discovery pleased us nearly as much, a delicate red dragon, *Ctenophorus femoralis,* whose ruddy skin matched the hue of the sand on which it lived.

In midafternoon the second day after leaving Karijini, we reached a paved road leading north. It led sixty-four miles through a town called Exmouth to Northwest Cape, and then hooked south into Cape Range National Park.

Moving swiftly, we reached the Cape Range visitor center, secured a site at a campground called Ned's Beach, threw up our tent, and set off on a cruise along the road. Mountains were not our quarry. There weren't any, really, but just low, rumpled hills creeping to within a mile of the sea. A ranger named Les had greeted our interest in reptiles with enthusiasm and suggested that we run the roads looking for perenties. We had enough time for a quick pass before a Ned's Beach ritual—a BYOB daily happy hour, organized by the campground hosts, Gwen and Norm Cole.

The American herpetologist Eric Pianka has spent much of his career studying Australia's goannas. He describes the perentie as "exceedingly unapproachable." Our chances of finding one were poor. "During 207 days in the field over sixteen months in 1966–1968," Pianka writes in the *Australian Journal of Ecology,* "I encountered only two live perenties . . . and found no evidence of perentie tracks in the sandy desert." Debbie and I would have been justified in giving up the chase before it began, and taking our warm beer straight to happy hour. Yet good luck had followed us all the way around Australia. Athena, it seemed, was looking after us as she had Odysseus. Inspired by our successes, we decided to "give it a go."

The gods smiled on us that golden afternoon. Hardly had we turned onto the main thoroughfare, our progress monitored by a dozen curious kangaroos grazing along the roadside, than I spied a large, scaly head peering at us from a clump of mulla-mulla. *No, it couldn't be. This was too easy.* I brought the car to a halt. Debbie's window was directly opposite the lizard, their noses six feet apart. There was no mistaking it. Here was *Varanus giganteus,* the elusive perentie, before us in the flesh.

We drove ahead fifty feet, shut off the engine, and crept back quietly. The lizard, spotted so densely and broadly on its forward half that its black background color was reduced to a netting, stood motionless in the exact place where we had left it. The length of the beast was somewhere between five and six feet, making the perentie slightly longer and heftier than the largest floodplain monitor we had seen in the Northern Territory.

The grandest lizard either of us had ever seen, the perentie was a dwarf compared to the giant monitor, *Megalania prisca,* that roamed Australia during the last ice age. Crocodile-sized, the giant monitor grew to twenty feet in length, had inch-long cutting teeth, and probably fed on large Pleistocene mammals, including humans.

The giant monitor died out, and until Aborigines and dingoes came along, the perentie reigned as the top predator in Australia's western deserts. It was, and is, fast and powerful. Employing a hide-and-go-seek hunting style, it lies in ambush much of the time, waiting for unsuspecting rabbits, rodents, and marsupials to happen along. If patience fails, the perentie stalks. Was I imagining it, or was the lizard before us sizing us up? If we were smaller, and the perentie larger, we might have run for our lives.

Pianka relates an Aboriginal story of how the perentie gained its coloration. Long ago, a perentie and another desert monitor, *Varanus tristis,* decided to paint each other. Wielding the brush first, the perentie decorated its cousin handsomely. Then came the smaller monitor's turn. It started off well, the brush creating a netlike pattern from the perentie's snout to midsection, but then, frustrated by how long the job was taking, the artist picked up the paint and dumped it over the perentie's hindquarters. According to the legend, the perentie continues to seek revenge, and its cousin lives an arboreal life for fear of retribution.

We watched the live perentie dart out its tongue, wave it in the air, and suck the thing back in like a piece of spaghetti. The tongue was forked and delicate, and the lizard was using it to gather smells.

Suddenly the perentie began to move. Rising on muscular legs, the front higher than the rear, the lizard emerged from its hiding place with confident strides. Out on the pavement it padded, its head swaying from side to side. We enjoyed a marvelous look at its exterior, the intricate netting of the head, neck, and shoulders grading into a haphazard, polka-dotted paint job in the rear. Any thought I might have entertained of capturing the animal for close examination vanished immediately. I saw the sharp claws and the long, powerful tail that would have bludgeoned me savagely if I made an aggressive move.

Its body swinging back and forth with each stride, the perentie moved quickly across the pavement. At a safe distance, a mother kangaroo watched the lizard go, and so did a mule-eared joey hanging its head and forelegs out of the pouch. I followed, shooting photos, until the last inches of the perentie's tail vanished like a snake into a thicket of mulla-mulla.

Debbie and I would soon have the pleasure of warm beer at the camp-ground happy hour, but the perentie had to satisfy its own need for drink by devouring succulent food. Opportunities to lap up surface water come rarely in the desert. Moisture is conserved in the perentie by dehydrating urine in the cloaca, recycling the water, and excreting not a liquid urine but pellets composed chiefly of uric acid, a solid.

I am not overly fond of afternoon drinks. They sink me into a languor from which escape comes only after Herculean effort. At the big table outside Gwen and Norm Cole's caravan, however, I sat elbow-to-elbow with fellow travelers and felt only joy. Things were going beautifully for us. We were running out of days, but we had made it nearly three-quarters of the way around Australia, seen most of the sights we had come to see, rubbed noses with the platypus, stood eye-to-eye with the peren-tie, and hopped far and wide among more than a dozen species of kanga-roo. Our marriage had cracks in it, but what union doesn't? Ours could probably be mended, and here on the continent's splendid western coast, I looked forward to the challenge.

At happy hour, engaging in conversation on several fronts, we learned several things. Len and Jen Kenna, nature enthusiasts from New South Wales, promised us that thorny devils, the last lizard on our must-see list, abounded along the roads south of the Cape. Someone else told us about whale sharks that came in great number every March or April to the Ningaloo Reef, lying just off the Cape Range coast. A connoisseur of plankton, the whale shark is the largest of living fish, growing to fifty feet and more in length. It patrols the reef, slurping up the microscopic larvae of coral that spawn in a single, wild orgy on a moonlit night in autumn.

We also gained a tip that proved valuable the following day. There were dozens of fine snorkeling places at Cape Range National Park, and we were feeling bewildered by the options. Where to go? Our companions took up the matter, then reached a consensus. Turquoise Bay was the place. It would give us live coral, myriad fish, sea turtles, and an outside chance of running into a creature of myth made flesh, the dugong. Mem-bers of a group of mammals known as sirens, dugongs are close cousins and virtual look-alikes of the West Indian manatees that enthrall nature lovers in the southeastern United States.

Before turning in that night, we couldn't resist a cruise along the road
in search of reptiles. Les, the herpetophilic ranger, had informed us that
death adders abounded at Cape Range. A little night driving, he said,
would give us a chance of seeing one.

We had no choice but to drive slowly. The roads were mobbed with
kangaroos, all of the species known in W.A. as the euro. We had seen
euros months earlier, in South Australia. Now, as we eased forward, eyes
scanning the warm ground for reptiles, euros did what opossums do when
cars approach them on North American roads—stood and gawked, doing
everything but moving out of the way. There were hundreds of them. We
might have imagined that every kangaroo in Western Australia was heading to the beach for a swim.

It had been a long day, and fatigue quickly sent us home. We never saw
a death adder. But we did, somewhere along the way, happen upon a serpent whose midsection looked like a green rubber hose. It measured about
two feet long. The head and tail were cream-and-coffee brown, and the
eyes were set in white circles. Out came Cogger. Before us lay a yellow-
faced whipsnake, a lizard-eating, egg-laying reptile whose venom is considered only mildly toxic to humans.

Morning began with a side trip to watch euros and emus drinking at a
water hole. Then we donned bathing suits and drove to Turquoise Bay.
The water was colored as advertised, and so was the sky. In the distance,
perhaps a quarter-mile out, we could see breakers foaming over the reef.
The sun was hot, the air indifferent, the water cool and bracing. It was
Friday the thirteenth of September.

"Certain tribes of Western Australia believe that a man swims well or
ill, according as his mother at his birth threw the navel-string into water or
not," writes Sir James George Frazer in *The Golden Bough*. My umbilical
cord, I believe, was conceded to a doctor, who turned it over to a nurse,
who dropped it in a trash bin. No wonder my aquatic skills were shaky.

We swam, we snorkeled, we saw. Floundering around as best I could in
a surging, sloshing basin that tested my courage far more than had the
snake-infested freshwater pools of the Top End, I peered through an ever-
fogging mask at a Who's Who of the piscine tribe. We had no book for
identifying fish, so I apologize to the ichthyologically astute reader for my
vagueness. There were colorful fish and plain fish, blue-spotted rays and
parrotfish, and, most impressive of all, a rugby-ball-sized triggerfish that
nudged loose chunks of coral aside with its snout, searching beneath them

for breakfast. We saw green sea turtles, too, scooting gracefully along like water beetles, bobbing to the surface for air, and diving into the depths in a dazzling explosion of bubbles.

Debbie and I were standing on hot sand, taking a breather and a warm-up, when we spied an enormous brown form in the water. It appeared shapeless, perhaps a plastic bag that ebbed and flowed with the current. Yet it was an awfully large bag. Could it be the shadow of a cloud? The sky was clear. A siren? I pulled on a mask and flopped in the cove to investigate.

A few kicks and pulls brought me nearly broadside to the thing's formidable bulk. At first all I could see was a great wall of brown. Closer examination revealed skin, tough and leathery and the color of strong tea. To gain perspective, I backed away. Now I could see what appeared to be a geriatric walrus, toothless and overly thick around the middle. There was a small dark eye near the whiskered head, and I could see it move to focus on me.

The dugong was perturbed by my presence not in the slightest. Waving its flipperlike front limbs and swishing its tail, which was broad and fleshy, the animal angled its muzzle to the ocean bottom and snatched up a mouthful of sea grass. I watched as the green strands disappeared inside cheeks that were bulbous and jowly.

To touch or not to touch? I was tempted. Even brave Odysseus had not petted a Siren and lived to tell the tale. Yet I resisted. The animal had trusted me to get close, and I had no wish to violate its confidence with a move that might be perceived as an assault.

Trusting creatures, dugongs and manatees have been hunted, polluted, and otherwise driven to extinction or near-extinction across most of their range. Among surviving populations, Australia's are the most numerous. Hunting them has been banned. In earlier times, Aborigines and Europeans killed dugongs for fat and flesh. The fat, according to Carl Lumholtz, who hunted dugongs with Queensland natives, provided an "excellent remedy for consumption and nervous prostration." As for the meat, Lumholtz reported "an exceedingly delicate flavour, . . . something midway between veal and pork, but better than either."

After I had traded places with Debbie, and she had enjoyed a swim with our blubbery companion, we stood on the shore and watched the dugong surface and dive. It gulped air delicately, barely ruffling the surface, and remained submerged between breaths for a little more than a minute.

In the water we had looked for teats or sexual organs, but hadn't seen any. If the dugong was a typical female, it gave birth every few years after thirteen- or fourteen-month gestations. Young come one at a time and keep close to the mother for eighteen months. Barring murder or mayhem, dugongs become sexually mature at about the same age humans do, and they live up to seventy years.

I was curious to see if the dugong would break wind. A friend of mine, a National Park superintendent who ran a coastal refuge in Florida, once asked a manatee researcher how she managed to locate the animals in a watery labyrinth of rivers and backwaters. The answer: by watching, listening, and sniffing for their farts. Here I tried the process in reverse, starting with the animal, then waiting for telltale bubbles. Alas, however, the dugong and its seventy-five-foot intestine refused to demonstrate their prowess.

After the dugong, Cape Range memories accelerate into a blur. We lingered two more nights and, on the afternoons that preceded them, partook in campground happy hours. We swam again in Turquoise Bay, but the siren was absent this time, bewitching someone else. Evenings and mornings, we crept into a wooden observation blind near a water hole and watched emus and kangaroos socialize and drink. The emus came first, many of them gawky fathers looking like drag queens with their faces painted blue and midriffs swathed in feathers that looked like grass skirts. We knew they were fathers because they ambled in with young in tow, the little ones striped and handsome and a little bigger than chickens. Mother emus end their maternal chores with the laying of monstrous eggs.

When the kangaroos appeared, they rose as if by magic out of tall grass. They came in force, but none drank until a powerful male appeared, probably the dominant bull. The big roo would sit, testicles dangling between his legs on a hairy stalk, and sip and lick his paws and flutter his eyelids with the boredom that attends life at the top. When he had swallowed his fill and asserted his primacy to his satisfaction, he would lumber off, leaving the water to his companions. In would come younger, less muscular males, young females, and mothers with bulging pouches, some with heads sticking out of them, some not. We found it comical to watch mothers lean over to drink while their babies nosed out of the rumble seat, stuck their muzzles into the water, and lapped up refreshment simultaneously.

The emus and euros had all the time in the world, but for Debbie and me, the calendar was pressing. The feeling we had long had of time stretching before us without limit was gone. On the first of November, scarcely a month and a half away, we would board a flight for New Zealand. By our reckoning, we needed a month to sell our car in Melbourne, wrap up affairs, and enjoy an encore jaunt with our lotos-eating friends to the Grampians. This meant that in two weeks we would have to race through the remainder of Western Australia and hurry back to the point of our beginning.

Slowly, dolefully, on a cool, breezy morning, we packed up the car, made good-byes to campground friends, and drove away from Ned's Beach. We were tempted to stay at Cape Range forever, to cast our fates among sirens and sea turtles. Yet adventures still loomed ahead.

9

Scylla and Charybdis

AFTER SLIPPING PAST the Sirens, Odysseus faced three immediate hazards. First there were the Skurries, a set of rocks notorious for sinking ships. The Greeks navigated around them without incident, then sailed toward the ugliest misanthropes in literature: Scylla and Charybdis.

In T. E. Lawrence's rendering of Homer, Charybdis is a lethal swallower of ships that "sucks down the sea" three times daily. Nearby, in a cave, dwells "dread, yelping Scylla," who has "twelve splay feet and six scrawny necks," each neck holding up "an obscene head, toothy with three rows of thick-set crowded fangs blackly charged with death." Scylla had reason to be vicious. Once beautiful, she had captured the heart of Poseidon, but, in doing so, had run afoul of Amphitrite, the sea-god's jealous wife. With magical herbs, Amphitrite turned Scylla into a hideous beast that neither man nor god could love, then banished her to a remote place. Monstrously frustrated by her inability to exact revenge, Scylla took out her fury on ships and sailors.

Losing six good men but escaping with his life, Odysseus put Scylla and Charybdis behind him. Driving south toward Shark Bay, we hoped for similar luck. There were reasons to be fearful. The tumbler in our car's ignition switch was broken, and each time we shut off the engine, we never knew if the key would turn again. Sometimes it took more than an hour of persistent fiddling to succeed, and during the struggle worry crept in. The prospect of being marooned in dry, hostile country with no town, mechanic, or drinking water for hundreds of miles was ugly and fearsome.

Breakdown was not the only hazard we faced. There were road trains that thundered past, nearly flattening us from time to time, and, reminding us of the risk, there were roadside memorials that included crosses, flowers, photos of accident victims, and fragments of wrecked automobiles. Safe passage was by no means assured. As always, snakes were worth thinking about, too. Western Australia is renowned among herpetologists for its death adders and bardicks, its western brown snakes and king browns, and black tiger snakes that lurked in the swamps where we planned to search for pitcher-plants. Of all threats to life and limb, the one that concerned us most was the drunken driver. I had read *One for the Road,* Tony Horwitz's entertaining 1987 chronicle of a hitchhiking journey around Australia. "In Australia," Horwitz found, ". . . discipline doesn't exist. Drinking is done at all times, for no specific purpose." Drivers taught Horwitz that distances in the bush were measured not in miles or kilometers, but in the number of beers one consumed while traveling from place to place. We didn't need Circe to tell us how to minimize this hazard. By driving only during daylight hours, we would reduce our chances of meeting inebriates (so went the theory, anyhow) and also help to preserve the health of night-active kangaroos.

Our first stop was Carnarvon, one of the largest settlements (which isn't saying much) on Australia's Indian Ocean coast. We tried to buy a new ignition tumbler, but the result was a lesson in the remoteness of the region. Both a Toyota dealer and an auto parts store came up empty, and clerks in both establishments advised us to limp the rest of the way to Perth, 565 miles to the south, through sparsely settled country. The only alternative was to wait a week for the part to be delivered.

To the north and south of Carnarvon, we had the pleasure of meeting the Lilliputian monster called the thorny devil. I invoke *Gulliver's Travels* for two good reasons. Wearing a crown of thorns that would repulse a *Tyrannosaurus* if it were large enough, the devil, a *Triceratops* in miniature, fits in the palm of a hand. Looking down on one, you feel like Lemuel Gulliver towering over a dinosaur. The other link to Jonathan Swift was geographical: coordinates given by Gulliver place Lilliput on or just off the Western Australia coast.

The thorny devil—*Moloch horridus* to scientists—is kin to the dragons or agamids we had seen elsewhere. Yellowish below and red-brown of back, the lizard takes its name from the spikes that cover it from snout to tip of tail. The devil eats insects and is so particular that most of its diet consists of ants of a single genus. North American horned "toads" look a good deal like thorny devils, but the similarities between the two lizards are only skin-deep.

Like windup toys, the devils moved in slow jerks, their tails held high. If you approached one, it lowered its tail, which made for a disappointing photograph. Our Ned's Beach friend Jen Kenna had given us the solution: lift the tail of a thorny devil into an upright position, and it stays exactly as you leave it.

Close examination showed that the valleys between the lizard's epidermal Matterhorns connected to form a network of vales. Scientists investigating the devil's ability to survive in landscapes where years may pass between rainfalls examined these valleys and found something astounding. By capillary action, the gaps between the peaks take dew that forms on the devil's skin and channel it to absorbent pads at the corners of the mouth. The devil ratchets itself along, drinking the moisture that collects on its back. The thorny skin also deters predators and helps to dissipate heat.

Along the road, in one of the shrubs that added interest to a flat and monotonous landscape, a songbird caught our attention. The head was black, the underside white, and at close range we noted a crescent of blue beneath each of the bird's eyes. Our list stood at 391 species, and the possibility of reaching four hundred looked more realistic every day. Out came the books, then the pronouncement. Before us perched bird number 392, the pied honeyeater.

South of Carnarvon, we crossed the track that in the 1970s brought Robyn Davidson and a caravan of camels from the center of Australia to the Indian Ocean. Davidson's account of the journey, *Tracks,* is a classic of Australian exploration and an inspiring tale of bravery and endurance.

At dusk we reached the Overlander Roadhouse, topped off our fuel, and turned down a secondary road toward Shark Bay. Night had fallen and the black velvet sky was sprinkled with glitter when we pulled into a caravan park at Hamelin Pool. The place was all but deserted. Beside an old telegraph station we set up camp, cooked a perfunctory meal, and retreated to sleeping bags. The time was nine o'clock. In the morning we would rise an hour before first light.

A night owl requires a compelling reason to stir before the rooster. Mine needs explaining. At Hamelin Pool, a cove nearly cut off from Shark Bay proper, rapid evaporation produces water of unusually high salinity. In the brine, cyanobacteria (organisms once known as blue-green algae) build pillars of stony material that can stand several feet high. Biologists call the structures stromatolites. Such formations are exceedingly rare, confined in the world's oceans chiefly to Hamelin Pool and a patch of seabed off the Bahamas. In less salty water, mollusks graze on cyanobacteria, and stromatolites never have a chance to form.

We were determined to visit the pool's stromatolites because they offered a glimpse into life's evolutionary past. In the Pilbara, in rocks estimated to be 3.5 billion years old, paleontologists discovered fossil stromatolites uncannily similar to the living, growing pillars in Hamelin Pool. The Earth itself is only 4.5 billion years old. Too remote for us to visit, the Pilbara fossils represent one of the earliest irrefutable proofs of life on the planet.

Which brings me to our motive for rising before dawn. A romantic at heart, I wanted to arrive at the pool before first light. There we would sit, wait, and watch the day dawn on the dawn of life itself.

Debbie and I hauled our carcasses out of warm sleeping bags into the chill, black air before the stars had dimmed. I had risen at a similar hour on other occasions to witness a bird carol in the dawn, but this was the first time I had stirred so early to view single-celled organisms. Biologists once classified so-called blue-green algae and bacteria as plants. No longer; today the organisms, whose cells contain no nuclei, are placed in the kingdom Protista. Few people have heard of protists, yet they are the distant forebears of us all.

The vigil began. Lo and behold, the stars in the east began to fade. The sky faded, too, changing from the indigo of new blue denim to the cerulean of jeans after a hundred washings. Meanwhile the horizon, the bay, and the submerged stromatolites materialized before our eyes.

The stromatolites looked like pillow-sized blobs of concrete, crudely smeared with roofing tar. As biological wonders go, the mounds of slime, silt, and limey cyanobacterial excrement could not compare with honeyeaters, bowerbirds, and eagles. We were on the verge of leaving disappointed when Debbie gasped in surprise. "Look at this one," she cried. "Doesn't it look like the Venus de Milo?"

I took a look and was dumbfounded. Amid the jigsaw-puzzle-piece-shaped stromatolites, one stood out, and Debbie was pointing to it. To me the thing suggested not the famous amputated Venus but something more stupendous. The upswept hair, the strong chin, and the gyrating pelvis left no possibility of mistake. It was Elvis! No kidding! In a hypersaline arm of the Indian Ocean, 10,000 miles and twelve time zones from Graceland, 3.5 billion-year-old life-forms had sculpted an irrefutable likeness of the King.

After shooting photographs that would later plant looks of concern on the faces of our friends, we bade the blue-green Elvis farewell and spent the day watching birds. The coastal scrub was alive with species: chiming wedgebills, pied honeyeaters, masked woodswallows, and a cherry-red apparition called the crimson chat. Australia's chats are closely related to honeyeaters. Brush-tipped tongues allow them to lap nectar from flowers. We saw more than a dozen crimson chats, and the colorful males glowed in the bushes like Christmas ornaments. Appropriately, they spent a great deal of time chatting, their whistling representing a musical rivalry for willing females and territory.

We enjoyed a sunset audience with Elvis, crawled into the tent shortly thereafter, and set off in the morning for Monkey Mia. To the east lay half of Shark Bay, to the west the other half, the road running up a peninsula that divided them. Soon we crossed into François Peron National Park, named for the French zoologist who visited the area in 1801 and 1803.

Shark Bay was named by the English explorer William Dampier on August 6, 1699. "The Sea-fish that we saw here," wrote Dampier, ". . . are chiefly Sharks. There are [an] abundance of them in this particular Sound, and I therefore give it the name of Shark's Bay."

Seventy-three years after Dampier, Shark Bay was visited by Comte Louis-François Alesne de Saint-Allouarn, commanding the ship *Gros Ventre*. Saint-Allouarn was second in command of a French expedition under the leadership of Yves-Joseph de Kerguelen-Tremarec, whose commission was to find the mythical Great Southern Continent and claim it for Louis XV. Kerguelen-Tremarec failed to reach Australia, despite his claims to the contrary, but Saint Allouarn had better luck. *Gros Ventre* put a landing party ashore at the mouth of Shark Bay in March 1772. Up went the Tricolor, and out came a parchment claiming the continent for France. After a ceremonial reading, the parchment was sealed in a container and buried.

Had Saint-Allouarn lived to tell the tale, Australians might today be speaking French. He perished on the return voyage, however, leaving his claim unpublished for nearly two centuries. In the mid-twentieth century, France's assertion of sovereignty over Australia came to light, but by then the southern land had asserted its independence from colonial powers, and the French were out of luck.

Even today, Shark Bay teems with life. An estimated 10,000 dugongs loll and spout methane in its warm waters, attacked occasionally by the sharks that Dampier found abundant. Lacking a boat, we had little chance of seeing either dugongs or sharks. Our hopes for a close encounter with marine life rested on a place called Monkey Mia. There, guidebooks promised, wild dolphins swam out of the Indian Ocean for the sole purpose of interacting with humans. At a place called Disappointment Reach, for ten dollars a head, we could wade into the shallows and meet the cetaceans ourselves.

Natural-born skeptics, Debbie and I had planned to give Monkey Mia a wide berth. Sane people we met in campgrounds insisted that the dolphin interaction was genuine and exciting, however, and our resolve weakened. Suddenly here we were, ready to inflame cynicism or swallow mouthfuls of crow.

The fur on the back of my neck rose when our wallets were lightened at a slick, no-expenses-spared Dolphin Information Centre. Nearby, rather than the lonely stretch of beach the dolphins had been frequenting since the 1960s, we found a caravan park, chalets, tennis courts, and a boat launch. A sign pointed to the "Dolphin Meeting Place."

We waddled down to the water, joining about one hundred other people doing the same. Someone called our names. It was Mary, as in Richard and Mary, a Melbourne couple whose company we had enjoyed in a Northern Territory campground. "Ghastly," said Mary, nodding to the crowd. I had to agree.

Soon a well-fed park ranger appeared in chest waders. Orders were barked. "I want everyone in a line," she shouted, her voice amplified by a bullhorn. Then came the reading of rules. "Dolphins are to be fed only in the Dolphin Interaction Area under the supervision of a ranger," we were told. I stopped listening and started marveling at the crowd. Americans, Japanese, Germans, and a few token Australians had found their way to this spot in the middle of nowhere. The nearest city, Perth, lay five hundred miles and more by bleak, empty highway to the south. Later we found tour buses idling in the parking lot and realized how the miracle was performed.

A fin broke the water's choppy surface. People cheered. A dolphin swam toward the beach, one cetacean to entertain a hundred camera-flashing observers. The ranger selected four children and handed each of them a fish. Fifty feet away, the rest of us watched. It was better than television, at least marginally. We could smell the fish and the sunscreen. On the beach, a bearded man caught my eye. He was shaking his head.

"Yes, it's pathetic," he said later. "This place used to be magic. There were plenty of dolphins and very few people. The dolphins really did come to be with you. I think they were curious. But I tell you, mate, the tourists have wrecked it. Bloody businessmen built the caravan park"—he waved a red, scabby arm battered by the sun—"and the parks service brought in the rangers. Now hardly any dolphins come at all, and the ones that do are bribed with fish." We chatted about sharks and other matters, then parted on a philosophical note. "People are lovely," said my companion, "but there are just too bloody many of them."

Turned off by the commercialism of Monkey Mia, we retreated down the peninsula. Back on the main north-south highway, we crossed a line on the map marked "Vermin Proof Fence" and shortly thereafter spied two shapes crawling across the road. They looked like dog feces that had sprouted legs and were determinedly heading east. Ah, this was our cup of tea—a spontaneous discovery, tending toward the bizarre.

A close look revealed the plodders to be stumpytail lizards, also known as shinglebacks. One walked hard on the heels of the other. Dampier's description of the beast in *A Voyage to New Holland* provides the right touch of comedy. The lizards were, he said,

> a sort of Guano's [sic], of the same Shape and Size with other Guano's . . . but differing from them in 3 Particulars: For these had a larger and uglier Head, and had no Tail: And at the Rump, instead of the Tail there, they had the Stump of a Tail, which appear'd like another Head; but not really such, being without Mouth or Eyes: Yet this Creature seem'd by this Means to have a Head at each End; and, which may be reckon'd a fourth Difference, the Legs also seemed all 4 of them to be Fore-legs, being all alike in Shape and Length, and seeming by the Joints and Bending to be made as if they were to go indifferently either Head or Tail foremost. They were speckled black and yellow like Toads, and had Scales or Knobs on their Backs like those of Crocodiles, plated on to the skin, or stuck into it, as part of the Skin. They are very slow in Motion; and when a Man comes nigh them they will stand and hiss, not endeavouring to get away. Their Livers are also spotted black and yellow:

And the Body when opened hath a very unsavoury Smell. I did
never see such ugly Creatures anywhere but here. The Guano's
I have observ'd to be very good Meat: And I have often eaten
of Snakes, Crocodiles, and Allegators [*sic*] and many Creatures
that look frightfully enough, and there are but few I should
have been afraid to eat of, if prest [*sic*] by Hunger, yet I think
my Stomach would scarce have serv'd to venture upon these
N. Holland Guano's, both the Looks and Smell of them being
so offensive.

Dampier's account of the stumpytail might have been lifted from the
pages of *Gulliver's Travels.*

In one regard Dampier's portrait falls short. He describes the stumpytail's hiss, but leaves out the most impressive part of its greeting. Walk up
to one of the lizards, as we did, and it turns to confront you, opens its
mouth with an audible gasp, and sticks out a purple tongue.

The stumpytail is a kind of skink. In Australia, skinks diverge into hundreds of species, the majority of which are brown and striped and in all
but subtle particulars look identical. Once you've seen one Australian
skink, it's tempting to conclude you have seen them all. The stumpytail,
however, resembles a dingo or emu dropping.

Its behavior is singular, too. The Australian herpetologist Michael Bull
has studied a population of South Australian stumpytails for more than
fourteen years. Almost from the start, he noticed that males and females
stuck together like glue during the spring breeding season. "They fed on
the flowering roadside weeds together," Bull writes, "they sheltered under
bluebushes from the hot midday sun together and, when moving from
one place to another, they wandered in tandem formation, with his nose
closely following her tail." The train of two we saw was no anomaly.

Bull's findings grew more interesting when he found that about eighty
percent of males tailed the same females they had followed the preceding
year. Long-term pair bonds are the exception rather than the rule in the
wild. In fact, no reptile anywhere was known to give its mate a second
look after copulation. Yet Bull found that most stumpytail couples
reunited every spring. One pair of lizards in the study group remained an
item for fourteen years running. How does a male know which female is
the love of his life after months of separation? The answer is unknown.
Noting that stumpytails see poorly, Bull speculates that pheromones play a

part. Males find upwind partners faster than ones that lie downwind, and at the onset of the lovemaking season, they spend a good deal of time tasting the air with their tongues.

Stumpytail courtship is a rough business. Like most liaisons, it starts innocently. The male nibbles the female's flanks, starting near the tail and slowly edging toward her head. Then, in a burst of passion, he spreads his mouth wide and clamps down on her head. The female responds, if the male's attentions are received favorably, by elevating her knobby tail. With a twist of his torso matched by a complementary pivot of hers, the male inflates his two-parted cloaca, turning it into a penis, and enters her from the side. A calm ensues. Several minutes later the pair divide. They remain close, however, plodding one after the other until summertime.

In the weeks to come, we would see dozens of stumpytails. Usually they were crossing a road in morning or afternoon, before or after the heat of the day. We always stopped when one lizard scurried onto the pavement, knowing its mate would follow like a lovesick dog.

When the lizards vanished into tall grass, we climbed into the car and resumed the journey. The farther south we drove, the more impressive grew the wildflowers. More than 7,000 species of plants live in Western Australia, the majority unique to the region. Separated today from Australia's east by a vast desert, and divided in the past by shallow seas, the western third of the continent evolved a flora unlike that of the rest of the country.

In the afternoon we left the highway to enter Kalbarri National Park, a half-day's drive from Shark Bay. The entire landscape had erupted in bloom. There were mulla-mullas by the thousands, mauve and feathery, and, towering over them (and us), a shrub called white-plume grevillea, its branches festooned with masses of cream-colored flowers. We saw grass trees, or *Xanthorrhea,* topped with six-foot flower spikes; masses of pink *Parakeelya* creeping along the ground; banksias; wattles; fringed lilies; and a shrub called smokebush, or *Conospermum.* Smokebush engulfed the roadsides in a milky haze. Livestock had obliterated wildflowers along the highway, but in Kalbarri, protected from ravenous ruminants, plants staged the finest flower show either of us had ever seen.

We camped on the coast, just outside the park boundary, at a place called Red Bluff. A hundred feet below, enormous swells from the Indian Ocean crashed against a stony shore. We had been warned to tread carefully here. Erratic, oversized waves called "sleepers" rise out of nowhere, and a person caught at the base of a cliff may be dashed against the rocks.

The evening was chilly. Each day brought us farther below the Tropic of Capricorn, which we had crossed between Cape Range and Carnarvon. We were back in temperate Australia. Days were warm, not hot, and nights had turned cool.

Our day at Kalbarri delivered the best and worst of times. The ignition switch of the car grew increasingly recalcitrant, and at a remote trailhead, miles down a dirt road, the tumbler stopped working altogether. While we struggled to revive the car, flies descended. "We . . . found such multitudes of flies here, which perched on our mouths and crept into our eyes, that we could not keep them off our persons," wrote François Pelsaert, a Dutch explorer who visited the coast in 1629. Flies were as numerous as ever. They probed every accessible orifice, blackened skin like a pox, and kept us twitching and dancing and swatting.

On the positive side, the wildflowers were glorious. We saw every blossom of the day before, with the addition of a plant called the red-and-green kangaroo paw. The kangaroo paws stood a foot high, and at the summit of each leafless stem a gaudy assemblage of red and green blossoms demanded attention. The flower cluster was as fuzzy as its namesake. It comprised more than a dozen fleshy spikes, red at the base, green at the tip. One by one, each spike unfolds. Inside lurk a stigma, a fan of stamens, and a glistening pool of nectar.

If hummingbirds visited Western Australia, they would go mad for kangaroo paws. The tubular flowers, smeared with rouge and seducing pollinators with sweet and copious nectar, are the stuff of hummingbird dreams. In the absence of hummers, honeyeaters fall under the spell. The bird thrusts its bill and tongue into a flower to drink, and comes away with head and neck dusted with pollen. It then flies on to the next plant, holding up its end of a bargain that has served the interests of both organisms for millions of years. The coating of golden pollen on some of the birds we saw at Kalbarri was so heavy that we at first mistook them for new species.

A morning that began with car trouble gave way to an afternoon of happy reunions. In a parking area where we took turns swatting flies and wrestling with the ignition switch, we were greeted by a couple we knew only as Lynne and Peter. They were circling Australia on a journey much like ours, and moved in a similar rhythm. Since the Kimberley, we had seen them on and off a dozen times, always stopping to check on each other and exchange greetings when one of our cars was stopped along the road. Lynne and Peter promised to return to the parking area later in the day. If we were still marooned, they would give us a ride to a place where we could telephone for help.

Soon after Lynne and Peter clattered away, the Toyota started. Relieved, we set off down the road. We had only covered a few miles when a dark sedan pulled close to our rear bumper, honking its horn. We looked back. The people in the front seat were waving for us to stop.

Coming from the United States, where some people make livings persuading other cars to stop, and then rob and shoot the occupants, we ignored the gestures and kept driving. We looked back from time to time, and at one point when sunlight illuminated our followers clearly, we saw that they were laughing. Something about them looked familiar.

We pulled over. Incredible! Our pursuers were Leslie and David from Kakadu. We had made loose plans for a rendezvous in Perth, hundreds of miles to the south, yet here they were, as surprised to spy a familiar car as we were to discover them behind us. David had an aunt who lived in Perth, and they had chauffeured her to Kalbarri to see the wildflowers.

Just before sunset, we hiked along bluffs above the sea. Debbie saw whales breaching and spouting, but I looked repeatedly, seeing nothing. Yet I did find something of interest—a striped snake, about a foot long, gliding into the heath. Something was odd about the reptile. Rather than slithering in the usual S-curve, it moved in a straight line.

I ran back to the car, a hundred yards away, and hauled out Cogger. To my surprise, I found the apparition not among the snakes, but among legless lizards called pygopods. The pygopod we had seen was a common scaly-foot, a hunter of spiders and insects. Scaly flaps, the remains of rear legs, help the lizard move across the ground. Like snakes, pygopods see the world through permanent goggles rather than lidded eyes. A few species blur the distinction between snakes and lizards almost completely by eliminating external ears.

During the two days that followed, we roamed inland, following secondary roads and marveling at the flowers. Entire landscapes from horizon to horizon lay under carpets of yellow everlastings. At times the color was almost too much to bear—the gold of the plains and the blue of the sky, amplified by brilliant antipodean sunshine. We had traveled in the North American Southwest when cacti, ocotillo, and other desert plants were blooming, yet this was grander. It seemed as if the land itself, the rocks and the dirt, had exploded in cosmic yellow.

So dazzled were we, in fact, that I nearly ran the car off a cliff. We had stopped in Coal Seam National Park, a place recommended for the splendor of its flowers. Yellow everlastings of the genus *Cephalipterum* dominated the place as they had elsewhere, yet Coal Seam's hills and valleys gave them a chance to rise and fall in a way they never enjoyed on the plain. Out of the everlastings, wattles rose in great masses of yellow bloom, drenching the air with perfume.

On top of a hill that afforded a view over a valley, we parked and walked to the edge of a hundred-foot cliff. We were standing there, taking in the blue and gold, when I heard a crunching of gravel. It was the Toyota. Our parking brake worked poorly, if at all, and I had absentmindedly left the transmission in Drive. Gravity was pulling the vehicle and everything in it toward disaster.

I would like to claim that I sensed what needed to be done and leaped into action. In fact, I stood gawking in disbelief. Meanwhile the car, about twenty feet from the edge, gained momentum. "Oh, shit!" said Debbie, who was now watching, too. The car, the nearest point on the brink of the cliff, and I formed an equilateral triangle. Could I reach the brake in time? I ran, hoping a decrepit wooden guardrail would halt the drama before I risked my neck.

The car met the rail when I was a stride away. Moving about five miles per hour, its front bumper made contact, and I heard a groan of wood and metal. The railing begin to give. Then the car stopped. I opened the driver's door, put a foot on the brake, and trembled.

Thoughts of the car and our belongings plummeting onto the rocks at the base of the cliff monopolized my consciousness only for a moment. Almost at once I was distracted by a bird. It was something new, green of back, striped on the underside. Could it be Horsfield's bronze cuckoo, a species we were eager to find? We looked for a white crescent circling the cheek and running through a red eye. There it was. According to our reckoning at the time, this was the four hundredth species of bird we identified in Australia. Only when reviewing our tally at journey's end did we find that Horsfield's bronze cuckoo was actually number 399. By then, however, the issue was academic. The real number 400, a western gerygone, flitted into view a few days later.

The cuckoo appeared on the twenty-first of September, the Southern Hemisphere's vernal equinox. Spring had officially arrived. Although birds engaged our interest all over Australia, I had not contemplated how little courtship and territorial behavior we witnessed until, on our way out of Coal Seam, we ran into a mob of flirting, fighting galahs.

The galahs we had seen up to this point appeared in flocks. They staged great shows of pink and white, and we relished their presence in the dry country. At Coal Seam, the situation was different. Galahs occurred in twos and threes.

We walked over to a dead tree to get a look at a trio, and found one galah poking its red-eyed face out of a hole in the trunk, another with brown eyes unfurling its crest at the top of the snag, and a third, also brown of eye, circling the other two, squawking. The bird in the hole was a female, the other two males. As a rule, galahs mate for life. We guessed that the bird perched on the apex of the tree was the female's mate, and the squawker an aspiring home-wrecker.

Galahs, like woodpeckers in other parts of the world, nest in tree hollows. Year after year, a pair comes back to the same cavity. Ornithologists speculate that permanent pair-bonding reduces the energy galahs expend in courtship, providing a significant advantage to birds inhabiting ecosystems low in energy. Juvenile galahs associate with each other in nursery trees, playing, grooming, screeching, and practicing gymnastic tricks with their feet and bills. From time to time the parent birds wing in, single their progeny out of the mob, and feed them by regurgitation.

For several days after leaving Coal Seam, my notebook entries tailed off. We drove, we marveled, we pushed on. At sunset one afternoon, we took a walk in Nambung National Park among pillars of rock, most barely taller than we were, standing by the hundreds on a slope of sand. The place looked like an Australian Stonehenge. Geologists attribute the formation to erosion rather than to Druids, but the atmosphere of the place, hard by the sea with great black clouds massing overhead, suggested the work of Titans.

A storm descended shortly after we pitched our tent in a seaside town called Cervantes. Rain, the first we had seen in months, slanted down in sheets, and thunderbolts spread like tree roots across a sky so black we could see nothing between flashes, not even the hands at the ends of our arms.

Next came Perth. The city was the size of San Diego, but so remote from other population centers that it might as well have been on the moon. We stayed with a friend, kept an appointed rendezvous with Leslie and David, and collected mail. A wildflower show was being held at the city's famous botanic garden, but we decided to skip it. After wandering among Sturt's desert peas, mulla-mullas, everlastings, and kangaroo paws in the outback, we had little interest in seeing plants that had been kidnapped and tamed. I felt sorry for John Muir. On December 16, 1903, he stopped in Perth after crossing the Indian Ocean on a steamer, but could only tarry a day. He found the city park "fine" and the "scarlet-flowered eucalyptus a glorious show." Back on the boat before midnight, Muir scribbled: "Never were strangers more royally and kindly entertained."

We fled Perth after two nights, much as we had run from Sydney. The place was clean, friendly, and exciting as cities go, but the commotion of cars and people bruised ears attuned to the subtle music of the bush. Indians brought from Stone Age lives in the Amazon to testify at hearings in modern cities have found the end-of-millennium world most of us live in appalling—the noise, the bustle, the impoverishment of nature, and the tainted air are more than they care to bear. We knew the feeling. The citizens of Perth may be ignorant of what they give up to live amid steel and concrete, but we had come straight from the wilds and knew their sacrifice all too well.

For us, it was back to everlastings and wattles, to kangaroo paws and grevilleas, back to, as D. H. Lawrence described them in *Kangaroo,* "the most delicate feathery yellow of plumes and plumes and plumes and trees and bushes of wattle, as if angels had flown right down out of the softest gold regions of heaven to settle here, in the Australian bush." After the city, the bush felt more congenial than ever.

North of Perth we drove through fields of wheat, planted in broad bands of tillable soil. South of the metropolis, we edged into the cool Southwest. This corner of Australia enjoys a Mediterranean climate, typified by mild, rainy winters and dry, hot summers. Green paddocks dotted with sheep and dairy cows sprang up, and as if by sleight of hand, the yellow of native everlastings yielded to the gold of cultivated rape, the plant whose seeds yield canola oil. We drove all day, heading south and east, bound for a place called Dryandra.

None of our guidebooks listed Dryandra State Forest. *The Penguin Touring Atlas of Australia* failed to assign it a spot on the map. Yet the place was famous, at least among naturalists. An extraordinary diversity of woody plants of the genus *Dryandra* flourish there, all honoring Jonas Dryander, a Swedish botanist and friend of Joseph Banks. Dryandras are classified as Proteaceae, making them close kin of banksias, grevilleas, and hakeas. They tend to be shrubby and prickly, and to produce showy, fist-sized clusters of flowers. Honeyeaters pollinate dryandras, attracted by their bright colors and abundant nectar. Aside from its distinctive flora, Dryandra National Forest gains fame as one of the last strongholds of the numbat.

Numbats are gorgeous creatures that look something like cat-sized chipmunks, except that their stripes run across the back, rather than down. They have gray heads, cinnamon-colored backs, and a black line running through each eye. Although marsupials, numbats have no close relation. Ecologically, they function somewhat like echidnas. With long snouts and longer tongues, numbats probe decaying logs and leaf litter, lapping up termites.

Rangers at the Conservation and Land Management Agency (CALM) in Perth provided little encouragement when we told them we wanted to see a numbat. The animals were rare, they said, and our chances of catching a glimpse of one were poor. Given our luck in tracking down other elusive animals, however, we arrived in Dryandra hopeful. Numbats were elusive, but we were patient, persistent, and had sharp eyes.

After miles of sunny pastoral country, the forests of Dryandra, crowded with gaunt, tattered eucalypts, appeared somber and dark. The road was paved with coarse gravel, and it wound through groves of trees called wandoo and jarrah. The land rolled gently and was rarely steep. Crunching along at an easy pace, we stepped out from time to time to admire a patch of golden cowslip orchids or gush over a thicket of blooming dryandra. The light was dim in the forest, even though sunset was hours away. All was quiet, save for the occasional twittering of an unseen bird or the screech of a passing parrot.

Among hundreds of gray, sun-bleached trunks that lay scattered on the ground, we strained for glimpses of numbats. On several occasions one of us spied one, then had the discovery deconstruct into a twist of moribund branch or a clod of sun-dried earth.

The naturalist's curse, and blessing, is that while searching for one thing, he always finds another. As the afternoon wore on, while finding no numbats, we discovered a western brush wallaby, a kangaroo that was new to us. The medium-sized bounder was colored a rich, glossy gray, except for a touch of black at the end of the tail and a bold white stripe that ran handsomely across each cheek. We found the animal grazing in a patch of grass. A few months earlier, kangaroos had seemed so commonplace that we'd almost taken them for granted. But not now. We savored the view.

More than a week had passed since our last sighting. The lengthening gaps between kangaroos foreshadowed an event we dreaded—the day not far off when we would board an airplane and leave kangaroos behind.

There were birds in the bush, too. We enjoyed our first bonafide look at a malleefowl, a mound-building cousin of the brush-turkey and the scrub fowl. The malleefowl had the cryptic coloration of a quail, but stood as long and tall as an American turkey. Lemuel Gulliver might have seen one and mistaken it for a Brobdignagian partridge. The malleefowl burst into the road, jogged ahead of us for a dozen yards, ducked its head, and slipped into the undergrowth.

Nearby, the bird probably had a mound built of sand and leaves. If a female, it would show up at the heap only long enough to lay an egg from time to time, averaging around nineteen or twenty eggs a year. Each takes a week to form inside the female's reproductive tract, and the last may be laid as long as five months after the first. During the interval, the male tends the mound, a compost pile perhaps a dozen feet across and three feet deep in the middle. When the weather is cool, he adds to the pile, and when things turn warm, he subtracts. Heat generated by the decomposition of leaves incubates the eggs. In summer, when excess warmth becomes a problem, the male covers the mound with sand. Mornings, he sweeps off the top, allows the mound and the sand to cool, and kicks the sand back into place. If he does his job, the interior remains a constant 91 degrees Fahrenheit.

Seven weeks after a malleefowl egg is laid, give or take a day, a chick kicks its way through the eggshell, only to find itself buried alive. Now the big, scaly feet that typify birds of the Megapode family prove their utility. Kick by kick, the hatchling digs its way to freedom. The bird is precocious. Trotting off alone into the scrub, it fattens itself on bugs, berries, and seeds with no help from its parents.

After the malleefowl, we ran into a flock of rufous tree creepers and, after the treecreepers, a yellow-plumed honeyeater and, after the honeyeater, an inland thornbill. I must credit Debbie with figuring out the thornbill. Long ago I had given up trying to sort out this drab, look-alike group of birds, but my Penelope kept after them. On this day she scrutinized a golf-ball-sized sphere of feathers that resembled every other thornbill we had seen. "Aha," she cried. "A reddish brown rump and a striped breast—it must be something new." Out came the book. Before us, plucking insects off a branch, appeared the inland thornbill, number 404 on our list.

We saw more birds, too, everything but a numbat. Seeking clues that might aid in our sleuthing, I conducted an archaeological dig in the back of the car and unearthed our mammal book. It confirmed that numbats are day-active, so we were looking for them at a sensible time of day, and that they represent a living oxymoron, a marsupial without a pouch. Female numbats have woolly underbellies, and it is there that newborns cling, nursing on their mothers' teats.

Although numbats once flourished from the vicinity of Dryandra, east across Western Australia and South Australia, to the westernmost parts of Victoria and New South Wales, they survive today only in the far South-west, and there only in two tracts of forest totaling a few hundred square miles. Lumbering and the introduction of predators such as the red fox account for the animal's decline. Today numbats face a serious risk of extinction.

Just before nightfall, we gave up the search. The air turned cold, about 40 degrees Fahrenheit, and we shivered for the first time in months. As we drove on, a group of rustic buildings materialized around a bend in the road. Smoke trailed from a chimney. We made inquiries. The place was an old Boy Scout camp, and cabins were available for rental. A few minutes later we were unrolling sleeping bags in a room littered with mouse droppings.

A lawn sloped away from the cabin's front door, and as the light failed, dark shapes the size of housecats began to gather. Numbats? Not likely. A numbat walks on four legs, rather than hops, and these things were bounding. We moved closer for a look. The animals were brush-tailed bettongs, an endangered species of kangaroo known locally as the woylie.

"Woylie" is a homely name, befitting the animal. Colored a mousy gray-brown from snout to tip of tail and touched with a rufous tinge on the feet, as if they had stepped in cinnamon, the woylies had short ears and blunt muzzles. Yet the drab exterior of the animal belies an interesting life. The woylie almost never drinks—a rare claim in Australia. Moisture comes from its diet, which consists of subterranean fungi half of the year, and from seeds, tubers, bulbs, resins, and insects the rest of the time. Biologists studying the woylie's diet find that it lacks important nutrients. Where does it get them? By hosting millions of bacteria in the foregut, apparently. The bacteria dismantle fungi into components the woylie can assimilate, and also in themselves provide a nourishing protoplasmic soup. By day, woylies sleep in nests of grass, bark, or both. They carry building materials in much the same manner as the musky rat-kangaroos of Queensland, hauling the stuff with their tails.

Woylies once ranged across most of Australia. By 1980 they had dwindled to three relict breeding populations, including one at Dryandra. The fact that both woylies and numbats died out nearly everywhere else while continuing to flourish at Dryandra suggests more than coincidence. The most interesting and likely theory explaining the survival of the animals in this corner of the Southwest involves shrubs of the genus *Gastrolobium,* which abound at Dryandra. *Gastrolobium* is the natural and original source of the poison sodium monofluoroacetate, known around the world as Compound 1080. In the United States the use of 1080 by sheep ranchers to control coyotes is controversial because the stuff also kills golden eagles and the rare, highly endangered black-footed ferret. As noted in an earlier chapter in reference to the western grey kangaroo, animals native to Western Australia, where the poison occurs naturally, are resistant or immune to its effects. European foxes and rabbits are not. Biologists speculate that when foxes prey on small mammals that have fed on *Gastrolobium,* they die, leaving fewer predators to trouble numbats and woylies.

The woylies hopped over the grass on delicate feet, stopping from time to time to pick up tidbits—bugs, perhaps, and earthworms. As wildlife watching goes, this was pretty low-key. There were no lions gorging on zebra, no hippos belching in mudholes, no herds of wildebeest or lakes crowded with flamingos. Most people would have gladly traded the experience for a night in front of a television. Not we; every day Debbie and I saw a kangaroo, we lived out a dream.

We watched the woylies, all five or six of them, until their dark shapes melted into the gloom.

Morning brought a second round of numbat hunting. We saw perfect numbat habitat, strewn with rotting logs, and when we rummaged in the leaf litter, we found hordes of termites. Nevertheless, the pouchless marsupial refused to appear. We did bump into an echidna. As round and spiny as a sea urchin, the cousin of the platypus poked its leathery bill into cracks in logs, lapping up insects by the dozen.

At four in the afternoon we gave up. By six we had left Dryandra, navigated a series of serpentine roads bordered by fields of golden rape, nearly plowed into a mob of sheep, and arrived at the dairy farm of Terry and Judyth Salom. There we passed two nights in a warm bed while a dangerous chill fell on our marriage.

After nearly eight months squeezed into a car without air conditioning, sleeping nights on lumpy ground in a tent without conveniences, aggravations with each other had come to a head. Debbie was at her wits' end. One morning at the Saloms', she slipped me a letter. It was full of anger and sadness, anger at the ire she felt I directed toward her, and sadness at the state to which our partnership had sunk. In fact I *was* angry, mad that *she* was mad, the sort of self-righteous irritation that spins around in a vicious cycle from one person to the next and back again. I was sad, too, sad that for days on end, Debbie seemed to speak of nothing but birds—of the plumage differences among honeyeaters, of the subtleties of thornbills, of beaks and bellies and little else. It was a mess. Our anger and blame and dissatisfactions had become self-perpetuating. Just as wave compounds wave, producing a grotesque and twisted amplification, when a microphone is held close to a loudspeaker, our annoyances, unresolved differences, and personality quirks had reached explosive alignment. The next twenty-four hours, I sensed, were critical. We would either start down the road to a better, more three-dimensional relationship, or break up in shouts and wails.

My own feelings were such that I couldn't discuss Debbie's note without a bitterness too strong to control. So I chose the indirect approach, to go east by sailing west. I tried to put my grievances aside for a while, no matter how justified they might be, and see things from Debbie's point of view. It would only work if she did the same. Neither of us wanted our marriage and odyssey to end. We held too much in common, not material things, not a house or children, but a love of wild places, wild animals, freedom, beauty, and kindness. Perhaps the Saloms' sturdy marriage, a union of a strong-willed feminist and a thoughtful but iron-willed dairyman, acted upon us positively. We spoke little to each other until the morning we drove off, bound for no place in particular. Yet something had changed. A new respect took the tension out of our dialogue. We were two tigers who, when confined to the same cage, finally thrash out an understanding.

On we drove, subdued but on the rebound. Impulses led us deep into the forested Southwest. From Bunbury we followed the coast road, skirting the edge of Geographe Bay. After Busselton, the highway veered inland, taking us away from Cape Naturaliste and south to Margaret River. Margaret River is a resort town generously endowed with boutiques and restaurants. There, sitting in a café overlooking the main street, we found ourselves on the edge of tragedy.

An ambulance screamed down the road, then another. Police cars raced by, wailing. Faces along the street wrinkled in concern. A few minutes later we were turning off the busy highway onto a side road when we saw two cars lurch to a halt, partially blocking the intersection. A woman emerged from one of the vehicles, a man from the other. I will never forget the look on the woman's face as she ran to meet the man. Tears poured down her cheeks, her mouth twisted unnaturally, and her eyes gaped in utter, convulsive horror.

Later we learned the story. A group of teachers and schoolchildren, enjoying a field trip to the beach, had retreated during a driving rain to a shallow cave carved by erosion in a bank of crumbling limestone. Heavy rain had been falling for days at Margaret River. It was cruel luck that on the afternoon of the outing, the cave's roof, saturated with moisture, collapsed. Rescuers were still digging out bodies when we caught the news. At least nine—and perhaps more—had died in the cave-in.

Sobered by the tragedy, we kept moving. There were all sorts of things we might have done in the Southwest, such as backpacking along the coast through Leeuwin-Naturaliste National Park, or dropping in on manta rays that crowd a bay near Karridale. But time pressed. We drove on, south and then east to Nannup. Cool gray weather and towering forests gave us a feeling of being in the Adirondacks, the Maine woods, or coastal Oregon, not hot, dry Australia. Appearances were partly deceptive. This corner of the country is more lush and moist than many, yet dry, warm weather would arrive in a week or two and linger for months. We had caught the last showers of the wet season.

Elsewhere on the planet, the same climatic regime would support a forest much less grand, if any forest at all. In Australia, however, trees excel in making much of little—little moisture unevenly distributed, and soils nearly barren of nutrients vital to the growth of most plants. Three species stood out in these southwestern forests, all members of the genus *Eucalyptus*.

Karri, *E. diversicolor,* approaches three hundred feet in height, placing it in an exclusive club of the world's tallest trees. Fellow titans include Tasmania's swamp gum (*E. regnans*) and stringybark (*E. delegatensis*) and

California's redwoods (*Sequoia sempervirens* and *Sequoiadendron giganteum*). A twenty-year-old tree may stand eighty feet from earth to crown. Jarrah, *E. marginata,* commonly grows to a hundred feet and more, the largest specimens reaching 165 feet. Both karri and jarrah produce hard red wood with a handsome grain. Red tingle, *E. jacksoni,* may top two hundred feet, yet its girth is more impressive than its height. Trunks may swell to thirty or forty feet around, and grain-silo-sized individuals sixty-five feet in circumference have been recorded.

The health of the karri and jarrah forests are the subject of violent debate. Western Australia's land management agency, CALM, mocks environmentalists in name and deed. Advertising itself as a voice of dispassionate reason in slick flyers, "fact" sheets, and a magazine published ostensibly for the education of locals and tourists, CALM claims to regulate logging of the big trees in a manner that ensures their long-term survival. Peter Foss, W.A.'s Minister for the Environment, writes in CALM's eight-page "Facts About W.A. Forests" that "the management of Western Australia's native hardwood forests is firmly based on balanced and ecologically sustainable use." Later in the publication, Foss dismisses critics. "Some interest groups," he asserts, "will never be satisfied with the balance of ecologically sustainable uses we reach."

The story has another side. Our copy of *Australia: The Rough Guide* alleges that CALM's "primary goal is securing the interests of the Southwest's $300 million logging industry." Fifteen percent of the native trees are cut for timber, the book asserts, while the remaining eighty-five percent go to wood chips, a practice the authors compare to "shooting elephants for dog food." Only half of the original forest remains, and the surviving portion is going fast. Why did the karri and jarrah forests we drove through seem to stretch on forever? *The Rough Guide* suggests that the impression is created by loggers mindful of public relations. Corridors of giant trees are left along highways, yet behind these "beauty strips" lurk erosion-gouged clear-cuts.

After a night in Nannup, home of the largest jarrah mill in Western Australia, we pushed on to the Perup Forest, another numbat stronghold. We had time only for a quick pass through the refuge, but hoped for dumb luck. It never came. Night found us at a grassy clearing called Fonty's Pool. We erected the tent in a downpour, then spent the evening huddled in a tin-roofed cooking shelter, sipping tea, shivering, and scribbling in our journals.

The following day carried us over narrow, winding gravel roads. We drove through stands of colossal karri, the trunks tattered and gray like those of so many Australian trees. At Pemberton, another mill town, we visited a gallery featuring local wood crafts. Here we grasped firsthand why Western Australians speak of karri and jarrah as if they were royalty. Tables, chairs, clocks, and all manner of odds and ends revealed the ruddy colors and fine, sweeping grain of the wood.

Rain poured down as night fell. When we saw a sign for a bed-and-breakfast along an empty stretch of road, our hunger for comfort got the best of our frugality. We also felt a need to linger. For the past couple of hours we had traversed some of the grandest country in Australia. The roads ran straight for the most part, but there was no monotony. The pavement climbed up and down like a roller coaster. Most of the forest was gone, cleared for pasture, although towering occasionally above cows and sheep stood a titanic karri. There were several patches of old-growth woods. Driving through them felt like passing up the nave of a cathedral. Afternoon sunshine filtered through the canopy as if slanting through clerestory windows.

When we reached the bed-and-breakfast by way of a dirt track, it didn't look like much. The establishment consisted of a one-story wooden farmhouse, squat and plain, painted white and separated from the lane by hedge and gate. A woman named Anna, about seventy, answered our knock. The price for a bed and cooked breakfast, she said, was fifty dollars. We had forty, plus a few coins. Debbie stalled, giving the woman a chance to lower her price. At this hour the innkeeper could hardly afford to be choosy. Meanwhile I stepped from the car and mined my pockets. Now we had $43.50. Anna frowned. Could we give her forty dollars, and mail the balance from Albany? A brow wrinkled, lips quivered. "All right," she said without enthusiasm.

Inside we trod. The house was warm, thanks to a woodburning stove. Anna proved warm, too. She gave us the run of the kitchen and introduced us to an old man named Bob Prew, who was sitting by the fire. We brewed tea and coffee, tossed together a pot of stew and noodles, and enjoyed a talk with Bob about sustainable agriculture, the future (if any) of the human race, and the importance of living close to the land. I could have spoken with this thoughtful man for weeks and never tired of him. Anna sat quietly, soaking up the talk.

After Bob limped home, Anna puttered off to bed. Realizing I had left my toothbrush in the car, I laced on boots and stepped out into the sparkling night air.

My eyes were first drawn to a moon just past full. Cream-colored, luminous, and just beginning to rise, the great orb sat like a giant egg on the sward of a paddock. The night was cool and damp. Frog song shook the air, and I enjoyed a wave of pleasant feelings about life and the universe. For perhaps half a minute I gazed at the moon, listened to the amphibians, and drank in the fecund scent of wet grass and cow shit.

Then I remembered the toothbrush. Turning toward the car, my eyes overshot the mark, drawn to an extraordinary sight. Light from the moon danced across mist in the western sky. The full spectrum of light, red to yellow, yellow to blue, and blue to violet, spread in a perfect arc. I was awestruck. I had never heard of, let alone seen, a rainbow caused by the moon. *A moonbow!* Quietly, I ran to fetch Debbie. Together we watched the moonbow for several minutes until clouds blotted out the moon and the colored light faded from view.

Expectations are funny things. High hopes have a way of leading to disappointment, and modest wishes are often exceeded. So it was the day we left Brook Farm bed-and-breakfast. We drove through Walpole-Nornalup National Park, best known for a treetop walkway that runs through a section of forest canopy. The walkway struck us as an anticlimax and an eyesore. It was a monstrous fretwork of shiny steel, a chrome-plated Eiffel Tower hung sideways, high above the ground. Intruding on an otherwise green and appealing forest, the structure seemed less a useful means for exploring its surroundings than a monument to bureaucratic excess and the edifice complex. We walked across the thing to get our money's worth. There were no signs to point out one species of tree from another, no exhibits to get the visitor excited about the complex ecosystem through which he was passing, just girders and cables and the cheap thrill of plodding high among the trees. Birds boycotted the area as if they had examined the addition to their world and flapped away in disgust.

Happily, the day's end provided a counterpoint. Leaving the forest behind us, we broke into agricultural country, zigged and zagged between sheep paddocks and fields planted with rape, crawled through country towns, and chugged into a range of low mountains known as the Stirling Range. Immediately we felt our spirits lift. As the sun fell below dark, forest-clad peaks, we pulled into the Stirling Range Caravan Park for a one-night stay.

One night stretched into three. Much of the countryside had recently been scorched by a controlled burn run amok, and the plant kingdom had responded with an outpouring of leaves, stems, and blossoms. Orchids were everywhere. More than one hundred species occur in the Stirling Range, a subset of some 1,500 flowering plants in total, and everywhere we looked, we seemed to spy a new one. A local farmer who introduced himself as Gary showed up at midmorning to lead a wildflower walk. Within a ten-minute stroll of our tent, he had shown us orchids of twenty species: spider orchids of two or three kinds, jug orchids, purple enamel orchids, candy orchids, dragon orchids, bird orchids, rabbit orchids, donkey orchids, bee orchids, vanilla orchids, cowslip orchids, blue china orchids, and more. All the plants were low and delicate, none standing more than shin-high. Later in the day, Debbie and I ventured out on our own. In an area no larger than the average living room, we found scarlet banksias, mountain bells, and a dozen different orchids.

The flower we most wanted to see, the hammer orchid, eluded us. At day's end we confessed our failure to Tony Sands, the campground manager. Tony had greeted us warmly the night of our arrival, and he seemed to know a good deal about everything. Could he tell us where hammer orchids were found?

Tony could not. But he knew someone who could, an old, retired sheep shearer named Jack Ryall. Jack and his part-Aborigine wife came to the caravan park every year at this time and stayed for several weeks. Jack loved orchids, Tony said, and while his wife enjoyed domestic comforts in a trailer, the old man set off every day in search of plants common and rare. If anyone could lead us to a hammer orchid, it was Jack Ryall.

The following morning we knocked on the door of Jack's weather-beaten caravan. We were greeted by a plump, sixtyish woman with bronze skin and a broad smile. As we stood explaining our business, a man's wrinkled face poked out from behind her.

Jack was older than his wife, perhaps seventy-five. He had big, fleshy hands that looked as if he had recently scoured them with steel wool. His eyes were thin slits, and his cheeks were folded with creases. "Yes," he said, pleased by our interest. "I can show you hammer orchids. Would you like to see them now? I'll take you to them."

Jack drove his car, and we, intending to leave the Stirling Range as soon as the expedition was over, trailed in ours. We clattered up a steep gravel road bordered on both sides by low shrubs and grass-trees. Jack's arm poked out from time to time, gesturing toward a particularly fine spider orchid or banksia. A mile or two after the start, he pulled onto the shoulder.

Jack's trousers hung low on his hips, as old men's pants often do. He walked quickly, showing us only his back. We marched into the bush, ascended a low knoll, and dropped into a gully. Jack went into a crouch. "Have you seen the flying duck orchid?" he asked. We had not. The tiny blossom was extraordinary. Take a duck in flight, turn it green, shrink it to the size of a table grape, and mount it on a thin stem, and you have something like the flower we knelt to examine.

A little farther on, Jack dropped to his knees. Several drab, inconspicuous orchids rose from the ground before him. They had single, delicate stems about ten inches high, each topped with a flesh-colored thing that looked less like a flower than a diminutive catapult. The similarity was no coincidence.

The hammer orchid, genus *Drakea,* plays a cruel practical joke on wasps. In size, shape, even in the scent it gives off, the hammer orchid mimics a female thynid wasp well enough to draw the attention of males. A male thynid is driven by lust. If all goes well for him, he finds a flightless female displaying her allurements on the top of a plant stem, snatches her up, and hauls her away for a binge of sex and feeding that may last several days.

When a male wasp attempts to abduct a hammer orchid, however, things go wrong. The "female" refuses to let go of the stem. He tugs; she holds on. Eventually he pulls hard enough that the false temptress, hinged to the pollen-bearing part of the flower, flips over. He goes with her, and in the process hammers himself on organs coated with pollen. He may attempt to fly off with her several more times before giving up the elopement. In the end he flies off and falls for the same trick elsewhere. The plant's reproductive needs are satisfied, and the wasp tries again.

After waiting several minutes for a wasp to appear, and not seeing one, we teased the little orchid with a finger to see how it worked. The mechanism showed evolution at its mischievous best. The false female was firmly connected to the rest of the plant, yet a twitch of the finger easily swung it into position for pollinating.

Jack left us soon thereafter. Before leaving the mountains, Debbie and I decided to visit the trailhead at the end of the road. A wildflower called the southern cross was blooming there, Jack said, and we wouldn't want to miss it. October was in its second day. We had to get going. Yet we drove to the place Jack described, took brief, dutiful looks at the flower, and started for the car. We were crunching across a gravel parking area when someone shouted, "Debbie and Ed!"

To be greeted by name in a remote corner of Australia was always a shock. This time the shouts came from Jen and Len Kenna, friends from the Ned's Beach campground at Cape Range. Jen and Len were keen naturalists. Immediately began a whirlwind of tale-telling, the conversation shifting to the Kennas' caravan for a pot of tea and buttered bread. Before we knew it, we had decided to camp another night. The Kennas, Debbie, and I would undertake a joint nocturnal expedition in search of the honeypossum, a rare, elusive marsupial that occurs only in Australia's Southwest.

Honey-possums are not possums, nor do they often taste honey. Biologists consider them the lone survivor of an ancient marsupial family. Having neither close relations nor visible teeth, honey-possums are mouse-sized, striped in the manner of chipmunks, and narrow of snout. They sleep by day and spend nights climbing among the nearly 4,000 species of flowering plants in Australia's southwestern heath lands, poking into blossoms and lapping up nectar and pollen. A few bats subsist on such a diet, but the only terrestrial mammal in the world to get by exclusively on nectar and pollen is the honey-possum. The beast is well adapted to its lifestyle. A marvelous sense of balance, strong legs, and grasping feet make the honey-possum a consummate high-wire artist, and its delicate, brushtipped tongue is just the thing for spiriting out sweet drinks from nectaries inside flowers. Every time the tongue is retracted, the honey-possum scrapes it clean with a washboardlike palate and the vestiges of canine teeth. As one would expect, the animal moonlights as a pollen delivery agent. Its movements are vital to the reproduction of certain banksias, and it was to an extensive patch of these shrubs that Jen, Len, Debbie, and I were headed after nightfall.

Together we enjoyed a twilight dinner at a picnic table in a lonely corner of the park. Dishes stowed, we piled into the Kennas' car and began the search. For three hours we crept back and forth along a stretch of road where Debbie and I had seen scarlet banksias covered with dozens of blooms. Taking turns, one of us would climb out of the warm car and walk ahead with a light, breath condensing in the cool night air, scanning the shoulders for flowers. I walked more than a mile, the car creeping along behind me. Debbie and I felt embarrassed. We couldn't find the banksias. A few stray blossoms but nothing more, and none had honey-possums lapping up their nectar. Fortunately, Len and Jen were good sports. We laughed, complained, and finally gave up the chase, arriving back at the campground a little after midnight.

In the morning, after a round of good-byes, we set off for the coast. The Stirling Range gave us a rousing send-off in the form of parrots. Four species dropped from the sky shortly after we left the caravan park—red-capped and ring-necked parrots, which we had seen before, and two that were new to us, the elegant parrot, which was blue, yellow, green, and nearly as tiny as a budgerigar, and the regent parrot, a distinguished look-ing apparition with a long black tail. The male regents were lemon yellow, the females lime green. Both had orange bills, and their wings were edged in black and daubed with crimson.

Down from the mountains we rolled, down through Kamballup and King River to Albany (the first syllable is pronounced like the diminutive for Alfred), on the southern coast. The city occupied a bulge of land where Princess Royal Harbour met King George Sound. Albany sounded English, looked English with its narrow streets lined with shops and pub-lic buildings made of stone, and, on the cool, drizzly day of our arrival, felt English. We would gladly have stayed a week, but the urgency of our schedule allowed only a night.

Following signs, we drove to a tourist information center housed in an old railway station. There we posed two questions to a handsome woman in a floral dress, her fingers crowded with rings. Where was Two Peoples Bay? And where could we find, not in a garden but in some wild and stinking swamp, the famous Albany pitcher plant? "The first is easy," said the woman, proceeding to scratch out directions on a piece of paper. A dozen miles east of Albany, Two Peoples Bay Nature Reserve is the sole home of one of the world's rarest birds. Our second query proved nettle-some. After conferring with her colleagues, the woman came back to us, frowning. If seeing pitcher plants in a garden wasn't acceptable to us, she said with an undertone of reproach, we should try two locations she would mark for us on a map.

Thus began a race against darkness. Muttering thanks, we bustled off to the car and punched the accelerator. The first location, merely a wet spot beside a highway, yielded no sign of *Cephalotus follicularis,* a plant unique to the swamps and marshes of Albany. No more than an inch or two high, the Albany pitcher plant, according to the biologist Allen Keast, "can be found only by the most resolute hunting." Its claim to botanical fame is a fleshy, modified leaf that fills with rainwater. Into the cup, or pitcher, the plant secretes digestive enzymes. Insects and spiders are attracted to the leaf, which is tinged with the color of raw beef, and as they clamber around the rim, the would-be scavengers trip on downward-facing hairs and tumble into the liquid. Hungry for nutrients difficult or impossible to obtain from local soil, the plant digests its victims. Look up "convergent evolution" in a biology text, and you may well find a photo of the Albany pitcher plant. Although unrelated to the pitcher plants of the Northern Hemisphere, this carnivorous plant of Western Australia has evolved an identical means of survival in nitrogen-poor environments.

Hunting with the resolve that Keast said was needed, we drove to the second location. It was a vast, swampy moor, covered by a clammy mist and just inland from the sea. A light rain fell, and wisps of fog drifted by like tattered ghosts. The Hound of the Baskervilles would have felt at home here. As it was, we worried not about demonic dogs, but about snakes and quicksand.

The woman at the tourist office had mentioned snakes. These coastal bogs were full of reptiles, including deadly tiger snakes. Owing to the weather, the prospect of blundering upon unreceptive reptiles didn't worry us. The weather was too cool, or so we assured ourselves. Yet we had not counted on quicksand. Beside the road, a sign warned of shifting, supersaturated ground that could engulf the unwary walker.

For an hour we picked our way carefully—*very* carefully—around the marsh. We watched for snakes and quicksand and at all times stayed "within cooee" (Australian for shouting distance) of each other. In the end we received a thorough drenching, returned to the car studded with goosebumps, and found precisely nothing.

As we continued toward Two Peoples Bay, the light grew dim and our spirits slumped. The charmed life we had been leading for eight months, in which the animals and plants of our fervid dreams appeared magically before us, seemed to have reached an inglorious end. We had failed to find a honey-possum, failed to find a pitcher plant, and now, in the ebbing light, we were almost sure to fail in our hunt for the noisy scrubbird.

We rattled into a gravel parking area just before dark. Two Peoples Bay, the watery part, was hidden from view by thick vegetation. This coastal scrub, blackened by shadows, was the last stronghold of the bird we had come to find.

We listened. That's what one does when searching for a noisy scrubbird. Although secretive and notoriously difficult to get a look at, the bird is garrulous, hence "noisy." The "richness of its vocabulary," writes the ornithologist Tim Halliday, is "an adaptive response to the denseness of its habitat." This made sense. The vegetation along the road and bordering the parking area formed a wall of stems and leaves so thick and impenetrable it might as well have been made of brick. A bird living here and wanting to discover, or be discovered by, prospective mates would find noise a useful tool.

We strained to hear the trills and whistles the noisy scrubbird is said to make, and we listened for mimicry. Instead we heard nothing—not the crashing of waves, not the drone of an airplane, not the twittering of a swift or the warbling of a honeyeater. *Nothing.* A footpath beckoned, looping through a cut in the scrub. We took it on the run, the night closing in around us. *Nothing.* We shared the discouragement of the ornithologists who searched for the noisy scrubbird between 1889 and 1961, finding nothing. The bird was presumed extinct until H. O. Webster blundered on the relict population at Two Peoples Bay. The rediscovery caused great excitement among ornithologists and bird lovers. The scrubbird, a bug and seed eater, represents an ancient line of birds that evolved in Gondwana.

Defeated again, we drove back to Albany. Along the way we found one of the consolation prizes that Australia was always good at providing, a fat, puffy frog singing in a puddle by the roadside. It proved to be a humming frog, *Neobatrachus pelobatoides,* a look-alike of the spadefoot toads that live in North America and Eurasia. The skin was warty, the eyes dark and pained-looking, as if the animal were straining to recall an important telephone number. The humming frog is closely related to the peculiar marsupial frog and gastric-brooding frogs of Queensland.

When I picked up the frog to pose it for a photograph, it began to turn white. What was going on? I looked closely and saw a milky latex oozing from the bumpy skin and sliding onto my hand. I tried to rinse the stuff off, but it refused to budge. The material had the gluey consistency of eel slime.

Nearing the caravan park where we would camp, we rounded a bend in the road and saw dozens of frogs congregating in a puddle. They were green-and-golden bell frogs, far more pleasing to the eye, truth be told, than the drab and homely scrubbird. The frogs had round suction cups at the tips of their fingerlike toes, and their golden skin was handsomely flecked with green. Bell frogs utter sounds that remind hearers more imaginative than I of bells. There are several species in a genus restricted to Australia and New Guinea.

Early the next morning we made an encore visit to Albany's tourist office. This time we begged. Couldn't some local plant lover tell us where to find pitcher plants? The staff huddled behind the counter. A hand reached for a phone. "Yes, yes, I see. I'll tell them. Thank you very much." The news was good.

Before the hour was out, we had circled much of Princess Royal Harbour, ventured well out on the Flinders Peninsula, and reached an unmarked trailhead. Ahead, down a muddy track, lay Torndirrup National Park. The advice we had been given called for walking a quarter mile to a marsh haunted by tiger snakes. There we were to bend over, step carefully, and scour the ground for pitcher plants.

This time we had daylight on our side. The marsh appeared where our informant said it would. There were no signs warning of quicksand, but this was Australia, where a traveler must rely on his wits, not on posted warnings. We proceeded cautiously. No devilish swirls of mud appeared, eager to swallow us, nor did any snake rear up to strike. At the base of a clump of red bottle-brush, we at last spied our quarry.

The pitcher plants grew short and squat, hugging the mud, their green leaves touched with reddish purple and seeming to sprout directly from the roots. Each leaf was shaped liked a pitcher in which one might serve milk or water. Fringing the openings, white, vertical ridges gave the impression that someone had shored up the rims with loops of thread. I peered inside. Each pitcher held an ounce or so of fluid. The stuff was thick with bugs and spiders, most of them dead, a few still writhing.

We might have lingered, but this was the fourth of October. If we were going to reach Melbourne in time to sell our car and enjoy a farewell round of lotos-eating, we had to get going.

That night, at the end of an all-day drive, we pulled into Fitzgerald River National Park. We arrived after sunset, pitched our tent in inky blackness to the sound of crashing surf, and were up and rolling the following morning by nine. We would have seen nothing at Fitzgerald River, which covers nearly a million acres and provides home to rare birds, endangered mammals, and more than 1,700 species of plants, had I not turned the car down a side road as we started toward the highway. Soon we lurched to a halt on a rocky terrace above the sea, and Debbie was shouting like Ahab. "Whales!" she cried.

Indeed there were, one immense, one merely big, lolling in the bay side by side. Although we had four hundred miles to drive that day, we found an hour to sit on a windy headland and watch a mother southern right whale nurse its calf.

The mother seemed the size of a railroad car, its baby a quarter that size. Both floated just beneath the surface of a turquoise sea, drifting with the water's ebb and flow as if they had no more to worry about than taking an occasional breath from their dark, puckered blowholes. Whalers hunted southern right whales nearly to extinction along this coast, and they might have finished the job around 1980, had not a 1978 statute banned the use of harpoons. Since the law took effect, the cetaceans have made a modest recovery. Again right whales gather in Antarctic waters to fatten themselves on krill, then cruise to Australia's southern coast to deliver and nurse their young. The whales have no need to feed after their Antarctic binge, so they sport about the bays, drifting along like hybrids of dirigible and submarine, reveling in the good life.

Slowly the whales drifted close to shore. They looked dark, fleshy, and shapeless, and to be frank, I found them ugly, garden slugs magnified to hideous proportions. On their heads were chancrous lumps. My Penelope knows a great deal more than I do about whales, and she named the lumps "callosities." She also pointed out that the whales' backs lacked dorsal fins, something I hadn't noticed. Why, I asked, is the species known as the "right" whale? Surely if a young female brought one of these brutes home to her mother, the old krill-eater would pronounce him Mr. Wrong. The name was given by whalers, Debbie said. The right whale was easy to catch, floated even after you'd killed it, and yielded enormous amounts of oil.

The whales began to cavort. The young one blasted spray from its blowhole, and the mother followed suit. A few seconds later the two of them breached and splashed back into the brine like dolphins.

"Where are you going?" asked Debbie. "We have a long way to drive."

"Call me Ishmael," I said, a tripod slung harpoonlike over my shoulder. I had never photographed a whale, but the deficit was soon remedied.

We did not cover four hundred miles that day. Two hundred was more like it. Yet the shortfall brought a happy result. Rather than spending the night at some godforsaken roadhouse in the middle of nowhere, we camped at Cape Le Grand National Park, a refuge that protects one of the finest stretches of coastline in all of Australia. We were excited about the locale, for the heath around the campground offered one last chance to search for the honey-possum.

The night was cold, chilly enough to send us straight from supper to sleeping bags. Yet the lure of the honey-possum called for sacrifice. Bundled up in sweaters and windbreakers, we picked our way along a walking track, scrutinizing every bush with a flashlight.

In a shrubby eucalypt called marlock, *Eucalyptus conferruminata,* Debbie's peripheral vision caught movement. She was certain that she had seen a small mammal, even though a close look at the place revealed nothing.

Round, frilly blossoms covered the marlock, each suggestive of a yellow-green pom-pom, and nectar glistened at the base of the stamens. We waited in the dark, switching on the light from time to time in hopes of seeing the creature Debbie had glimpsed. It failed to reappear. What to do? Calculating that tiger snakes lay snug in underground lairs this chilly night, we left the path, got down on our hands and knees, and nosed under the bush like a couple of wombats. There we sat like statues, listening to the crash of distant surf and the whispers of our own breathing.

Four or five minutes passed. Then we heard a rustling, coming from a point just above and ahead of us. I switched on the light. Down a twig climbed a mouse-sized animal. Stripes ran down its back, and there were tiny toes that looked like human fingers. The snout was conical, nearly as pointed as an ice cream cone. In a flash the creature was embracing a flower and poking its nose into the depths. Cramped and uncomfortable, yet bursting with excitement, we sat and watched the honey-possum transact its business.

When the little apparition eventually darted away, its belly laden with nectar and pollen, its snout dusted with gold, we laughed and embraced to celebrate our good fortune—not only our luck at Cape Le Grand, but the magic that had followed us nearly everywhere in Australia. At every turn, it seemed, the animals of our wildest imaginings had hopped, crawled, flapped, slithered, and climbed into view, with little effort required on our part to find them. In finding a honey-possum, we had met a marsupial whose sperm are longer than any other mammal's—the reproductive equivalent, perhaps, of speaking softly and carrying a big stick.

In keeping to a schedule, we proved as hopeless as ever. We lingered a second night at Cape Le Grand, hoping for another honey-possum. Unfortunately, a change in the weather defeated us. Cold, bitter winds descended on the coast, creating conditions in which honey-possums are rarely active.

On the morning of our departure, we awoke to loud thumps. Immediately outside our tent, it seemed, two campers were starting the day with a fistfight. Aside from the thumping, the battle was oddly silent. Poking our heads outside, we found not angry men, but three western gray kangaroos. Boxing and rising up on stiff tails to deliver fierce kicks to the groin, the dark, camel-faced males were hammering out a pecking order much like a pack of farm boys.

We bade the pugilists farewell, struck camp, and, with a blend of fear and excitement, sailed for the Island of the Sun.

IO

Island of the Sun

OUR LAST GREAT hurdle was to haul weary bodies, gear, and the out-back dust that covered our car and everything in it across the vast, sun-scorched plain that stretches between Cape Le Grand and Adelaide. By this time the Toyota had nearly 186,000 miles (nearly 300,000 kilometers) on its "clock." Tires were worn, the starter was complaining, the transmission oozed fluid, and having reached an advanced age, the car was generally on the verge of being overtaken by entropy. We were by no means certain the chariot was up to the job ahead.

The region we proposed to traverse—the Nullarbor, meaning "no trees"—threatens the traveler with peril. One of the broadest expanses of flat land on the planet, the region is alternately scorched by sun, blasted by wind, drilled by rain, and pounded by hail. It is a formidable obstacle to man, beast, and plant, a zone of death and emptiness that divides Western Australia from the settled lands of the East.

The first *Homo sapiens* heroic or foolish enough to cross the Nullarbor on foot in a single assault may well have been the explorer Edward John Eyre. Aborigines maintained a sparse, erratic presence on the plain, and if one of them was mad or ambitious enough to attempt an unbroken crossing, we have no record of it. According to Alan Moorehead, Aborigines considered the dusty wastes of the Nullarbor the realm of demons and "would not chase a kangaroo there." Eyre, a Yorkshireman, had commercial aims. He wanted to pioneer a stock route between King George Sound, near Albany, and Adelaide.

For nine grueling months in 1840 and 1841, Eyre plodded westward. Along the way he experienced the worst and best of luck. The worst came when two young Aborigines accompanying the expedition killed his last surviving English companion and stole much of the remaining food and water. Improbably, however, good luck loomed just ahead. At wits' end and crippled by thirst and starvation, Eyre and a faithful native companion named Wylie spied a French whaling ship. It was anchored just offshore and captained by an Englishman named Rossiter. When Rossiter saw Eyre and Wylie's predicament, he outfitted them with new clothes, gave them food, drink, and soft bunks on the ship, and sent them away with flour, biscuits, rice, beef, pork, sugar, tea, cheese, butter, salt, brandy, saucepans, tobacco, pipes, treacle, wine, sardines, and water. Eyre and Wylie took their movable feast and completed the journey.

Confronting the Nullarbor's cruel sun and vastness, we thought again of Odysseus. Perhaps considering himself home free after slipping past Scylla and Charybdis, the intrepid Greek had one last crisis in store. Circe had warned about Thrinacia, the island where her father, Helios, the Sun God, kept sacred cattle. The animals would look plump and appetizing to the sailors, Circe said, but it was vital that the livestock not be touched. If the Greeks harmed even a single cow, Circe predicted the loss of Odysseus's ship and death of his crew.

As a story of adventure and derring-do, the *Odyssey* has its virtues. Unpredictability is not among them. Odysseus and Co. landed on Thrinacia, and while their leader slept, the crew knocked off a few of Helios's favorite ruminants. When the fearless leader awoke to the smell of beef roasting on the barbie, he knew the party was done for. The Greeks fled to the ship and nearly escaped, but a violent storm appeared and fulfilled Circe's predictions. Only Odysseus survived, holding on to fragments of mast and keel.

In our attempt to "sail the Nullarbor," as John Williamson puts it in song, we would stick to beans and rice and lay off the cattle, just in case. The gambit worked. The day we left Cape Le Grand, we covered 430 miles of dry, stony country without incident. This represented our longest day's journey thus far in Australia, and we would better it the following day.

Approaching the plain, we found the land hilly and handsomely garnished with trees and shrubs. Flatness quickly set in, however, and before long our eyes were straining to come to terms with it. North, south, east, and west, the world lay as flat as the surface of a lake. The rocks beneath the scabrous surface were ancient, some of them dating back more than a billion years to the Archeozoic. Above, the sky loomed empty and blue, broken only by the malevolent yellow eye of Helios. "The country is unbelievably flat and uninteresting," wrote Herbert Hoover, who worked as a mining engineer in this corner of Australia from 1897 to 1899, long before he became thirty-first president of the United States in 1929. "There is not a fish in a stretch of a thousand miles."

The road across the Nullarbor was a virtual drag strip. There were no bends for dozens of miles, and no policemen to monitor the velocity of the few cars that passed. We cruised along at a steady 100 kilometers per hour (62 mph). Every other car—there weren't many—shrieked past us and grew smaller and smaller until it vanished over the rim of the earth. Along the shoulders were the usual corpses. Among the ones fresh enough to identify, we saw shinglebacks, western blue-tongued lizards, wedge-tailed eagles, emus, and kangaroos.

That evening I nearly joined the roadside dead. At a remote petrol depot called Cocklebiddy, we paid for a campsite and were told to "pitch the tent out back, wherever you like." We drove far enough from the compound to escape bright lights and the chugging of diesel generators, switched off the engine, unloaded gear, and erected our shelter. While dinner was cooking, I walked about fifty feet away and set up a camera on a tripod. The night sky was perfectly black, and the stars glittered brightly. Aiming the lens at the Southern Cross, I fixed the shutter in an open position. A long exposure would leave stars tracing arcs around the southern celestial pole.

A half hour later the lens was still open and Debbie and I were forking gruel from our bowls, when I noticed a set of headlights far out in the bush, making for the roadhouse. As the lights grew bright and near, it became clear they were headed for my camera and tripod. I ran. Charging across the desert, I reached the photographic equipment a half-second before the car did, and snatched it out of the way. Debbie screamed. I stood blinking and bewildered in the glare of lights and roar of engine noise. Missing me by inches, the vehicle sped on, passed the petrol depot, and accelerated down the highway.

In the morning we pressed on. Pleased to be still among the vertical, I gazed out at the horizontal, two-dimensional Nullarbor and reckoned us lucky to have come so far without serious threat to life and limb.

There had been a sign at the western edge of the plain, delivering a message in pictographs. It showed three silhouettes: a camel, a kangaroo, and a wombat. By this time we had seen a few of Australia's feral camels and thousands of kangaroos, but a southern hairy-nosed wombat, a rare species found only in the Southwest, would have been something new. All day we kept up a vigil, scanning the featureless country for round, hairy rumps and broad, koala-like faces. Mile gave way to mile. Every plant that might have been green was blanched of color by sun and drought. Alas, no wombats waddled out of their burrows.

Southern hairy-nosed wombats endure on the Nullarbor, but only barely. To reproduce, and for females to manufacture a sufficient quantity of milk for nursing, the bulldog-shaped marsupials must have three consecutive years of green feed. In this dehydrated world, green feed appears only after rains, and rains come erratically. Biologists estimate that the wombats breed no more than twenty or thirty times a century, which may explain why individuals live long if they survive the perils of youth. In captivity, southern hairy-nosed wombats have lived twenty years.

The only wildlife sighting of note on our second Nullarbor day was a Major Mitchell cockatoo that flapped into view at a roadhouse. We were standing by the petrol pumps, slaking our engine's thirst, when the Major Mitchell darted in for a look at us. It approached, veered, and perched on a rusty barrel. Something was not quite right. Major Mitchells have alabaster backs, and their cheeks and undersides are rose-colored. This specimen was smudged with black. Out came binoculars. It seemed that the parrot had supervised an auto repair job, or visited a grubby corner somewhere, and its feathers were smeared with grease. We groaned. Seeing the Major Mitchell in such a state was akin to looking at a fine portrait and finding that a vandal has added a mustache.

On we sped, on and on. Pausing near Eucla, just south of the South Australia border, we gazed over a cliff toward the sea. Beyond lay the Great Australian Bight, aquamarine and whipped white in places by gusting wind. Over the horizon, across 2,400 miles of icewater teeming with krill, whales, seals, and penguins, lay the part of Antarctica known as Wilkes Land. Below us, perhaps 150 feet straight down, surf pounded the Kangaroo Continent with spray and thunder.

The cliffs that run six hundred miles along the edge of the Great Australian Bight look like a raw wound. Something was ripped away from them a few tens of millions of years ago, a thing called Antarctica. The two coastlines no longer match exactly, but geologists studying drainage channels have mapped ancient river valleys on Antarctica and found corresponding courses on the Nullarbor.

As the day wore on, our reluctance to leave the West gave way to its antithesis, a desire to have the journey over with and to reach as far as possible toward Melbourne. We traversed, when all was done that day, 609 miles. Long past sunset, hours after a red glow had ignited the bottoms of low, fleecy clouds and the flames had burned and died, we braked to a stop in Wudinna, South Australia.

The following day, rising at dawn, we drove for hours until a sign announced Port Augusta. Debbie leaped out of the car. We had seen this place before. I parked and ran over, and we danced a jig. Cars and trucks raced by on three sides, bound for Alice Springs and Adelaide and the Nullarbor, their drivers staring as if we were lunatics. Yet this was a moment for celebration. We had driven our trusty car all the way around Australia.

II

Calypso, Alcinous, and Arete

AFTER THRINACIA, ODYSSEUS'S long and hazardous journey was nearly done. The obstacles had been run, and only one hurdle of consequence remained to delay the hero's return.

The final hazard for Odysseus was Calypso. When the wanderer was all but home free, this beautiful and lusty nymph held him captive on a remote island—not for a week or a month, but for seven trying years. "In every other way except in giving him his freedom," Edith Hamilton writes in a sanitized synopsis, "she overwhelmed him with kindness. All that she had was at his disposal." No kidding. A less delicate reading of the *Odyssey* suggests that while the Greek pined for his wife by day, every night Calypso screwed his brains out.

As for my own Penelope and me, we were nearly at journey's end when we slipped once more into the clutches of Beris Caine. For thirteen nights this fair goddess seduced us with kindness. Had we not fallen under her spell already, we would have done so now. She gave us soft beds, plied us with sweet delicacies and fine wines, listened to our tales of Sirens, Cyclopes, and the Underworld, and invited the neighbors over for a succession of dinner parties. That was only the beginning. She loaned us her washing machine, provided free use of her telephone, and after our beloved car was sold to young men from Switzerland, handed us the keys to her Land Cruiser.

One by one and two by two, we made good-byes: to Beris's friends Elaine and Di, to Max and Eva Redlich who lived next door, to Beris's handyman, Jeff Lacy, and his dogs, to the rainbow lorikeets and the red wattlebirds that lapped from Beris's bird feeders, to Bill the blackbird, who appeared at Beris's kitchen door every day, looking for currants. One of the most tearful of partings came with a horse we had met in South Australia six months earlier.

After making a farewell visit to Wendy Willow in Adelaide, we detoured south to the Coorong with the idea of finding Duke in his paddock. If we found him, would he know us? We located the paddock. It appeared to be empty, but a scan with binoculars revealed horses in the distance. One towered grandly above the others like an equine god.

Letting ourselves through the gate, we advanced slowly, calling the horse by the name we had given him. At first there was no response. Then the head turned. Recognition was instant, or seemed to be, because at once the beast began to canter, his mane flying in the breeze, his dappled flanks shimmering in the last glint of sunshine. As massive, bell-bottomed legs thundered toward us, uncertainty struck. Had we done the right thing by entering the paddock? Neither of us knew the first thing about horses. For all we knew, this one was about to flatten us.

Before panic could set in, Duke was upon us. He walked up and buried his head in our sweaters, and we hugged and stroked him. Debbie pulled out a carrot. To our surprise, Duke showed no interest in the food. Affection seemed his only interest, which was just fine with us. We drank in his horsey smell and warmth. Great clumps of hair came off and stuck to our clothes. Such joy, such sadness! We had imagined the reunion for months. For us, Duke had come to represent the things we loved about Australia—beauty, power, warmth, gentleness, and the bracing tonic of danger.

A final excursion in Victoria provided the last bird for our list. Beris and the MacLeods spirited us away to the Grampians for an encore round of botanizing, bird-watching, and lotos-eating. It was Old Home Week. We rented the same farmhouse that had served us so well the last time. Again we socialized with the owners, a bright, generous farming family, the Beveridges. Beris's friend Elaine Nagy came along, and so did Althea Pollock, a cohort of the MacLeods. Tom Quigley joined us, too. He had telephoned Beris to inquire about us while we were crossing the Nullarbor, and she had persuaded him to come along.

The bird materialized the third day. Great, screeching flocks of corellas gathered around the house that morning, as they did every dawn at the farmhouse. It was our last day in the mountains, and we weren't looking at birds at all, when parrots dropped onto the road ahead of us like falling leaves. They were slender birds, green for the most part, with bellies as yellow as lemons and indigo wings touched with turquoise. Zeus be praised! These were blue-winged parrots, the 419th species for our list. Collectively the birds produced strange chirps and rattles that seemed to come not from individual parrots but in a single voice from the flock. Graham Pizzey, perhaps with tongue in cheek, renders the complex of sounds as "chappy-chappy-brrt-chippy-chippy-brrt."

When we pulled into Beris's driveway, safely home from the mountains, our driving in Australia was all but over. We had driven 25,000 miles, all told, about 40,000 kilometers. The distance approximates the earth's circumference at the equator.

Beris released us, much as Calypso eventually liberated Odysseus, so we could spend a few last days with the MacLeods. Little did I know that a surprise fortieth birthday party was in the works, and I was the guest of honor.

At a similar point in the *Odyssey,* the hero sails away from Ogygia, Calypso "having washed him and adorned him," in T. E. Lawrence's words, "with sweet-smelling clothes." In similar fashion we departed Beris. Having enjoyed free use of her soap and hot water, and having rendered our clothes, if not sweet-smelling, then at least fresher than they had been in months, we drove away fit for human company.

After leaving Calypso, Odysseus washed up naked on Scheria, land of the Phaeacians. We arrived at the MacLeods' fully clothed. Odysseus was taken in by Alcinous the Generous, a good and kind king cut from the same cloth as Keith MacLeod. Alcinous's queen, Arete, "gifted in qualities of mind," "revere[d] . . . as divine," and able to "resolve the disputes of those for whom she has countenance, even when the affair is an affair of men," was a match for the intelligent, quietly diplomatic, and divine Peg MacLeod. Under the pretext of organizing a dinner for a few friends, these royal hosts conspired with Beris and my Penelope to stage a party celebrating my fortieth birthday.

In the meantime we told the MacLeods stories, just as Odysseus regaled Alcinous and Arete in their palace of gold and silver. We reminisced about Tasmania, trumpeted the glories of South Australia, waxed poetic about Queensland, enthused over Victoria, reflected on New South Wales, boasted of our exploits among man-eating crocs in the Territory, and recounted meetings with perenties, dugongs, honey-possums, and Elvis in Western Australia.

When my birthday arrived, October 28, Debbie led me out on a walk. We found our last echidna. When the four-footed ball of thorns dug itself into red soil, daring us to dislodge it, I felt like scratching a hole and doing the same. After nine months in this wonderful country, surrounded by captivating wildlife and lion-hearted people, I hated to leave. Australia felt like home. My diction bristled with Australianisms such as "Good on you" and "G'day." I hurried to a newsagent every Saturday to buy *The Weekend Australian*. Each week the paper ran a column by Philip Adams, a crusty, incisive commentator on current affairs. I would miss my weekly encounter with Adams's original thinking—and so much more.

Back at the house, a glass of wine was forced into my hand as the festivities began. All the usual suspects were there—Beris, Elaine, Max and Eva Redlich, the MacLeods' daughter Anne, Anne's husband Terry, Anne's daughter Emma Popplewell, and the MacLeods' nearest neighbors, Peter and Edda Padovan and Peter and Sue Carson. I cried when they sang "Happy Birthday," and I grew teary again when gifts piled up beside my plate. It was the grandest party anyone could have asked for.

Our last day in Australia was Halloween. The car was sold, bags were packed, and six heavy boxes of extras had been sealed and ferried to the post office for shipping. Feeling sentimental, we recruited Beris to retrace the steps we'd taken with her the day we arrived, and walked along Port Philip Bay. The afternoon was warm and sunny, although a cool wind blew over the Bass Strait from Tasmania. We rambled, reminisced, watched a Nankeen kestrel hover on the breeze. I felt like a patient the night before heart surgery.

In the evening we enjoyed a last supper of pizza at Elaine's, then walked home to Beris's. The ticking of an old clock nearly drove me mad. The sounds that marked the passing of seconds seemed grotesquely amplified. It was odd; I hadn't noticed them before. Each tick struck like a hammer on an anvil. I was the anvil.

That night I had no stomach for writing. In fact, over the past two weeks my journal entries had dwindled to nothing. Like a man on death row, I wanted to relish every moment, to soak up every lumen of sunshine, to drink in the air and feast on the water. I wanted to feel the voices of lorikeets, wattlebirds, kookaburras, and Australian voices reverberate on my incus, malleus, and stapes.

After a champagne-and-omelet breakfast, Beris, Peg, and Keith drove us to the airport. Saying good-bye was awful. A woman at the gate stopped us, hefted my carry-on bag, which was stuffed to excess with photographic gear, and opened her mouth to protest. Then she saw Debbie's tears. I was speechless, feeling as if Ayers Rock had lodged in my throat. "Go ahead," said the official, and we staggered up the ramp.

O Australia! Silently I made farewells—to the kangaroos and wombats, the koalas and kookaburras, the snakes in the grass, the crocodiles in the estuaries, the bowerbirds in their bowers, the platypuses in quiet pools, and to the most generous and good-humored of hosts.

As the jet lifted off the runway, I felt as if part of me remained behind on the ground, and it was being ripped not very gently away from the part of me hurtling toward the stratosphere. For a half hour we craned our necks to gain our last views of the continent.

Hardly had we left Tullamarine Airport than I said, "Gum trees." Below lay a patch of bush, the shaggy gray-green crowns of eucalypts discernible even from great height. On we flew, on over rolling country quilted with farms, until the dark, forested mountains of the Great Dividing Range bulked up beneath us. Then we followed the coast. We looked down on an inlet, round and blue with a village beside it, and tried to convince ourselves it was Wonboyn Lake, a place we knew.

Suddenly the coast made a ninety-degree turn northward, toward Sydney and Brisbane, and we knew that the inlet was not Wonboyn, but Malacoota. Somewhere along its shores, Peter Kurz and Margaret Inman were enjoying breakfast in a room full of doves.

The jet swung eastward, heading over the Tasman Sea. For a moment we glimpsed the real Wonboyn Lake off to the north. Then Australia slid away behind us and vanished into the mist.

12

Home to Ithaca

ALTHOUGH DEBBIE AND I had left home with smooth chins, one of us now sprouted a beard, returning home like Odysseus, a stranger to family and friends.

A touching moment comes late in the *Odyssey* when the wanderer's dog, a puppy when the man of the house left home and now an ancient thing pining for the return of its master, recognizes Odysseus when others fail to do so. The dog feebly wags its tail, then dies. Sadly, Debbie and I had a similar experience. My parents' dog, a beloved basset hound named Ben, developed cancer shortly after our return. He wagged his tail wildly at the sight of us, and succumbed not long thereafter.

In the final analysis, the decision to bring my Penelope along on the journey proved wise. Admittedly, there had been hours and days when the opposite seemed true, when our his-and-hers adventure seemed a nightmare. Yet we had slogged through the quicksand and tiger snakes together, and emerged with a stronger marriage.

By traveling as a team, we avoided all the problems Odysseus faced on returning home, as well as the troubles Penelope endured in his absence. There was no house to reclaim, no suitors to drive out and hack into quarters and loins. In fact, there was no house at all. Our possessions, few as they were, lay tucked in the attics, barns, and cellars of friends and family. Not having a home proved to be a sword with two edges. The unkind cut came when we needed a place to live, to begin again where we had left off a year earlier.

We tried Mississippi for a while. Although our friends there welcomed us home with fanfare and a deluge of goodwill, we had run out the clock on the Gulf's sweltering shores. We longed for mountains and hills. The journey had reminded us how much we missed the varied topography of our native Northeast, and our old friends and families. For several months we tried Tennessee. Debbie took a temporary job as a park ranger in Great Smoky Mountains National Park. I launched into work on this book. As the end of Debbie's contract neared, however, we felt unsettled. Eastern Tennessee was agreeable in a hundred ways, yet for us some *je ne sais quoi* was missing.

Inspiration struck soon thereafter. We would move back to our native Northeast. We longed to live on the fringe of a university town—not Yale's New Haven or Harvard's Cambridge, but a rural hotbed of knowledge and culture, surrounded by fields and woods. There we could have the best of all worlds—the intellectual and cultural life of the campus, the community spirit of a small town, wild places, and the pastoral realm of the farm. Ithaca was good enough for Odysseus. Why not for us?

A year after our return from Australia, we moved to upstate New York, to the city of Ithaca, home of Cornell University and Ithaca College. Ovid is just up the road, and thirty miles away, over a series of ridges and swales, beyond a hundred fields of corn, lies Homer.

The kangaroo dreams continue.

Acknowledgments

WITHOUT THE ASSISTANCE and forbearance of a great many people, our journey and the writing of this account of it would never have survived the metamorphosis from vaporous dream to concrete reality.

At Sierra Club Books, Beth Gibson, editor and human being extraordinaire, discovered, critiqued, and gently but firmly helped me cajole this book into its final form. I also want to thank all the gang at Sierra Club Books for believing in the project and helping it find its way to you, the reader. Special thanks go to Lauren Karten and David Wade Smith.

In Australia, I'm grateful to the following individuals, in alphabetical order by surname: Philip Adams, Jo Aldridge, Roger Aldrige, Alvaro Ascuii, Suzanne Ascuii, Colleen Bakker, Herman Bakker, Norman Barnes, Algernon Beveridge, Alister Beveridge, Andrew Beveridge, Chris Beveridge, Lachlan Beveridge, Megan Beveridge, Andy Bishop, Warren Blinman, Michael Boyny, Sabina Boyny, Trevor Burslem, Beris Caine, John Carey, Maggie Carey, Peter Carson, Sue Carson, Densey Clyne, Gwen Cole, Norm Cole, Jeannette Conway, Ina Dallas, Leslie Dell, Jack Edmonds, Joyce Edmonds, Len Elson, Solange Etienne, Jim Frazier, Kerry Gordon, Peter Grant, Arnold Grodski, Pat Grodski, Colin Harmon, Matt Hartridge, Cathy Herbert, Ian Herbert, Dorothy Hicks, David Hopkins, Margaret Itman, Gwen Johnson, Bill Jolly, Jen Kenna, Len Kenna, Tess Kloot, Peter Kurz, Jeff Lacey, Duncan Lambourne, Terry Lane, Ruth Lathlean, Beth Lennep, Annette Lenton, Colin Lenton, Tim Logue, Keith MacLeod, Peg MacLeod, Mary MacNeill, Richard Mac-Neill, Max Mapleson, Pat Mapleson, Virginia Mini, Colleen Morgan, Elaine Nagy, Betty Nicholson, Lloyd Nielson, Michael O'Reilly, Peter O'Reilly, Tim O'Reilly, Jenny Osborne, Edda Padavan, Peter Padavan, Althea Pollock, Emma Popplewell, Tom Quigley, Eva Redlich, Max Redlich, Di Rex, Steve Robertson, Paul Rodwell, Jane Rodwell, Jack Ryall, Judith Salom, Terry Salom, Aileen Sands, Tony Sands, David Scott, Stephen Simmons, Barbara Smith, David Smith, Rob South, Eric

Strautins, Anne Sullivan, Terry Sullivan, Margie Taylor, Martin Taylor, Gwen Thelander, Ian Thelander, Alex Thomas, Glen Threlfo, Frank Trezise, Jo Trezise, Mark Trezise, Vincent Turler, Bev Vance, Mike Vance, Sammy Vance, Greg Wallis, Rachel Wallis, John Wamsely, Amy Wardlaw, Matthew Wardlaw, Peter Wardlaw, Ros Wardlaw, John Williamson, Wendy Willow, Helen Winter, John Winter, Ulrick Wong, John Young, and Junell Young. A few others are equally deserving of gratitude, even though we failed to catch the full names: Bill the Blackbird, Duke the Horse, Graeme of Tasmania's Royal Automobile Club, Harry and Marie (Tasmanians who helped us replace a water pump near Alice Springs), Lynne, Peter, Marianne, Oliver, Paul, Sammy, Zita, Sandra, Wayne, and Yarlee.

In the United States of America, friends, relations, and neighbors stored our belongings, propped up our morale, fed us, housed us, paid our bills, and handled all of our correspondence. Among those due thanks are Cecilia Alsina, James P. Alsina, Joan Armstrong, Joan Belson, David Berry, Saradel Berry, Gail Bishop, Linda Boyd, Anne Bradburn, Donald Bradburn, Cara Chapman, Dianne Chapman, Jerry Chapman, Charlie Clark, Gayle Clark, Liz Cox, Ron Cox, Patrick Dugan, Frank Dulany, Vilma Dulany, Bill Fischer, Tish Galbraith, Joan Gilley, Joan Gordon, Beth Herr, Joan Hirsch, Peter Hirsch, Bill Hodge, June Hodge, Betty Hopkins, Gary Hopkins, Michael Hurrell, Alfred Johnson, Geraldine Johnson, Noah Johnson, Victor Johnson, Hal Junker, James Junker, Jeff Junker, John Junker, Mary Junker, Ben Kanze, Edward Kanze Jr., Joyce Kanze, Jackie Kingston, Emily Koester, Henry Koester, Emily Kowach, John Kowach, Dirk Leach, Jett Leake, Lawrence Leake, Jeanne Lebow, Pat Ledden, Betty Lennep, Ken Lewis, Suzanne Lewis, Vi Lewis, Berna Lincoln, Stan Lincoln, Larry Lisco, Marilyn Lunceford, Wayne Machado, Jeff Main, Nora Manuele, Glenn Miller, Margaret Miller, Ken Morgan, Tom Nash, Wally Page, Jeff Parsons, Mary Anderson Pickard, John Porco, Laurie Porco, Barbara Richardson, Mitch Richardson, Bill Ross, Nancy Ross, Jack Sanders, Sally Sanders, John Sheckter, Madeline Sheckter, Mortecai Sheckter, Steve Shepard, Adoree Shortle, Andy Silton, Maggie Silton, Bobby Davidson Smith, Neil Soderstrom, Ken Soltesz, Rick Strout, Steve Sundlof, Julio de la Torre, Chris Vinsonhaler, Larry Walther, Marianne Walther, JoLynn Williams, Rob Williams, Marion Wingo, Jeff Woods, Sharon Woods, Elaine Zika, Frank Zika, and Shirley Zimmerman.

At the Blount County Library in Maryville, Tennessee, Kim Radford secured the use of rare books and microfilm copies of John Muir's

Australia log. At the University of the Pacific in Stockton, California, Daryl Morrison of the Holt-Atherton Department of Special Collections arranged for me to examine the Muir microfilm. To these, and to the staffs of the public libraries of Ocean Springs, Mississippi, and Trumansburg and Saranac Lake, New York, I wish to express thanks. I also owe appreciation to Mary LeCroy of the American Museum of Natural History for information on Wallace's Line, cassowaries, and bowerbirds; to Michael Klemens of the New York Zoological Society, Charlie Daugherty of Victoria University of Wellington (New Zealand), and Michael Thompson of the University of Sydney for information on Australian reptiles; and to John Wamsley of Earth Sanctuaries Ltd. for our discussion of his work in rescuing endangered Australian mammals. To these people, and to all the other Good Samaritans whose names I failed to catch or list, I wish to express good wishes and gratitude.

The Muir-Hanna Trust's permission to reprint extracts from John Muir's Australia notebooks is gratefully acknowledged.

Among our Australian friends and hosts, it seems unfair to single out any for special thanks. Yet Beris Caine, Peg MacLeod, Keith MacLeod, and their friends and neighbors must be acknowledged for kindnesses and support far beyond those demanded by ancient Greek laws of hospitality.

In Ithaca, Lang Elliott, and in Townsend, Daniel and Scott Drake provided friendship at crucial points during the research and writing of this book. Other friends in Ithaca and the Great Smokies provided moral support, too, especially Susan Hurwitz, Betsy Darlington, Greg Budney, and all the good people of the Rongovian Embassy and the Finger Lakes Land Trust.

Finally, I want to thank my Penelope for sticking with me through the thick and thin, for courage in the presence of spiders, snakes, and crocodiles, for tending my wounds and for suffering a few at the hands of an Odysseus who was at times a less-than-ideal traveling companion, and for being, nearly all of the time, an enthusiastic, loving, lovable, talented companion. It is testimony to Debbie's skill as a navigator that we drove a distance around Australia equal to the circumference of the earth, yet found our way back to Melbourne in time to catch our homebound flight. Debbie also contributed in numerous ways to the production and polishing of the manuscript that became this book. For her faith, love, and comradeship, I'm deeply grateful.

Bibliography

THE FOLLOWING BOOKS provided ideas, information, and inspiration, and are recommended for further reading.

HOMER AND EMERSON

Emerson, Ralph Waldo. *The Portable Emerson.* Edited by Mark Van Doren. New York: Viking, 1976.

Hamilton, Edith. *Mythology.* Boston: Little, Brown and Co., 1942.

Homer. *The Odyssey.* Translated by T. E. Lawrence. Ware, Hertfordshire: Wordsworth Editions, 1992.

Homer. *The Odyssey.* Translated by E. V. Rieu, with revisions by D. C. H. Rieu. London: Penguin Books, 1991.

Homer. *The Odyssey of Homer.* Translated by Samuel Butler. Roslyn, New York: Walter J. Black, Inc., 1944.

Richardson, Robert D., Jr. *Emerson: The Mind on Fire.* Berkeley: University of California Press, 1995.

AUSTRALIA, GENERAL

Abbey, Edward. *Abbey's Road.* New York: Dutton, 1979.

————. *Confessions of a Barbarian.* Edited by David Peterson. Boston: Little, Brown, and Co., 1994.

Arden, Harvey. *Dreamkeepers.* New York: HarperCollins, 1994.

Australia State of the Environment, 1996. State of the Environment Advisory Council, editors. Collingwood, Australia: CSIRO Publishing, 1996.

Bassett, Jan, ed. *Great Southern Landings: An Anthology of Antipodean Travels.* Melbourne: Oxford University Press, 1995.

Blackburn, Julia. *Daisy Bates in the Desert.* New York: Vintage Books, 1994.

Blainey, Geoffrey. *Triumph of the Nomads: A History of Aboriginal Australia.* Woodstock, New York: Overlook Press, 1976.

Chatwin, Bruce. *The Songlines.* New York: Penguin Books, 1987.

Collins, David. *An Account of the English Colony in New South Wales.* 2 volumes. London: Cadell and Davies, 1798.

Conrad, Joseph. *Mirror of the Sea.* Oxford, England: Oxford University Press, 1981. Original edition published in 1906.

Conway, Jill Ker. *The Road From Coorain.* New York: Alfred A. Knopf, 1989.

Cook, James. *Captain Cook: Voyages of Discovery.* Edited by John Barrow. Chicago: Academy Chicago Publishers, 1993.

———. *The Journals of Captain James Cook on His Voyages of Discovery.* Edited by J. C. Beaglehole. Vol. 1, *The Voyage of the* Endeavour, *1768–1771.* Cambridge, England: Cambridge University Press, 1955.

Daly, Margo, et al. *Australia: The Rough Guide.* London: Rough Guides, 1995.

Dampier, William. *A Voyage to New Holland.* Original edition published in London in 1729. Gloucester, England: Alan Dutton, 1981.

Davidson, Robyn. *Tracks.* New York: Vintage Books, 1995.

Durack, Mary. *Kings in Grass Castles.* London: Corgi Books, 1976.

Facey, A. B. *A Fortunate Life.* Ringwood, Victoria: Penguin Books, 1981.

Finlay, Hugh, et al. *Australia: The Lonely Planet Guide.* San Francisco: Lonely Planet Publications, 1994.

Flannery, Tim, ed. *The Explorers.* Melbourne: The Text Publishing Company, 1998.

Flinders, Matthew. *A Voyage to Terra Australis.* London: G. and W. Nicol, 1814.

Flynn, Errol. *My Wicked, Wicked Ways.* New York: Buccaneer Books, 1959.

Frazer, Sir James G. *The Golden Bough.* Abridged edition. New York: Macmillan, 1951.

Hanbury-Tenison, ed. Robin, *Oxford Book of Exploration*. New York: Oxford University Press, 1994.

Hoover, Herbert. *The Memoirs of Herbert Hoover: Years of Adventure 1874–1920*. London: Hollis and Carter, 1952.

Horner, Frank. *The French Reconnaissance: Baudin in Australia, 1801–1803*. Melbourne: Melbourne University Press, 1987.

Horwitz, Tony. *One for the Road*. New York: Vintage Books, 1987.

Hughes, Robert. *The Art of Australia*. Ringwood, Victoria: Penguin, 1970.

————. *The Fatal Shore*. New York: Vintage Books, 1986.

Huxley, Elspeth. *Their Shining Eldorado: A Journey Through Australia*. New York: William Morrow, 1967.

James, Lawrence. *The Rise and Fall of the British Empire*. New York: St. Martin's Press, 1994.

Keay, John, ed. *Permanent Book of Exploration*. New York: Carroll and Graf, 1993.

Kenny, John. *Before the First Fleet: The European Discovery of Australia, 1606–1777*. New South Wales: Kangaroo Press, 1995.

Kohen, James. *Aboriginal Environmental Impacts*. Sydney: University of New South Wales Press, 1995.

Lawrence, D. H. *Kangaroo*. Mitcham, Victoria: Penguin Books, 1950.

Layton, Robert. *Uluru: An Aboriginal History of Ayers Rock*. Canberra: Australian Institute of Aboriginal Studies, 1986.

Leichhardt, F. W. Ludwig. *The Letters of F. W. Ludwig Leichhardt*. 3 volumes. Cambridge: Cambridge University Press, 1968.

Lines, William J. *Taming the Great South Land: A History of the Conquest of Nature in Australia*. Berkeley: University of California Press, 1991.

Lumholtz, Carl. *Among Cannibals*. New York: Charles Scribner's Sons, 1908.

Mackaness, George, ed. *Book of the 'Bounty.'* London: J. M. Dent and Sons, 1938.

Mitchell, Major T. L. *Three Expeditions into the Interior of Eastern Australia*. London: T. and W. Boone, 1838.

Moore, T. Inglis, ed. *Book of Australia*. ed. London: Collins, 1961.

Moorehead, Alan. *Cooper's Creek*. New York: Harper & Row, 1963.

———. *The Fatal Impact*. Honolulu: Mutual Publishing, 1966.

Morris, Jan. *Pleasures of a Tangled Life*. London: Arrow Books, 1990.

Mountford, Charles. *Brown Men and Red Sand*. Melbourne: Sun Books, 1967.

Moyal, Ann. *A Bright and Savage Land*. Sydney: Collins, 1986.

Muir, John. Unpublished journals, included in the John Muir Papers, Holt-Atherton Center for Western Studies, University of the Pacific, Stockton, California. Microfilm edition, reels 29 and 30.

Nordhoff, Charles, and James Norman Hall. *Mutiny on the Bounty*. Boston: Little, Brown and Co., 1932.

Norman, Don. *Errol Flynn: The Tasmanian Story*. Hobart: W. N. Hurst and E. L. Metcalf, 1981.

O'Reilly, Bernard. *Green Mountains, Cullenbenbong, and Over the Hills*. Sydney: Envirobook, n.d.

Penguin *Touring Atlas of Australia*. Ringwood, Victoria: Penguin Books Australia Ltd., 1995.

Pilger, John. *A Secret Country*. New York: Alfred A. Knopf, 1991.

Polmar, Norman, and Thomas B. Allen. *World War II: The Encyclopedia of the War Years, 1941–1945*. New York: Random House, 1996.

Sale, Kirkpatrick. *Rebels Against the Future*. New York: Addison-Wesley, 1995.

Sharp, Andrew. *The Discovery of Australia*. Oxford: Clarendon Press, 1963.

Shillingsburg, Miriam Jones. *At Home Abroad: Mark Twain in Australasia*. Jackson, Miss.: University Press of Senate, 1996.

Shreeve, James. *The Neanderthal Enigma*. New York: Avon Books, 1996.

Swift, Jonathan. *Gulliver's Travels and Other Writings*. Edited by Louis A. Landa. Boston: Houghton Mifflin, 1960.

Theroux, Paul. *The Happy Isles of Oceania*. New York: G. P. Putnam's Sons, 1992.

Thomas, Tony. *Errol Flynn: The Spy Who Never Was*. New York: Citadel Press, 1990.

Tindale, N. B. *Aboriginal Tribes of Australia.* Berkeley: University of California Press, 1974.

Trollope, Anthony. *Australia.* St. Lucia, Queensland: University of Queensland Press, 1967.

Twain, Mark. *More Tramps Abroad.* London: Chatto and Windus, 1907.

Ward, Russell. *Australia Since the Coming of Man.* New York: St. Martins Press, 1987.

White, Patrick. *A Fringe of Leaves.* London: Penguin, 1976.

———. *The Tree of Man.* London: Penguin, 1955.

———. *Voss.* Middlesex, England: Penguin, 1957.

AUSTRALIA, GENERAL NATURAL HISTORY

Archer, M., S. J. Hand, and H. Godthelp. *Riversleigh: The Story of Animals in Ancient Rainforests of Inland Australia.* Balgowlah, New South Wales: Reed Books, 1991.

Attenborough, David. *Life on Earth.* Boston: Little, Brown, 1979.

———. *The Living Planet.* London: Collins, 1984.

———. *The Private Life of Plants.* Princeton: Princeton University Press, 1995.

Balderstone, Simon. *Kakadu: A Heritage for the Future.* McMahons Point, New South Wales: Weldons Pty. Ltd., 1987.

Banks, Sir Joseph. *Journal of the Right Hon. Sir Joseph Banks.* Edited by Sir Joseph D. Hooker. London: Macmillan and Co., 1896.

Breeden, Stanley, and Belinda Wright. *Kakadu: Looking After the Country—The Gagudju Way.* Brookvale, New South Wales: Simon and Schuster, 1989.

Buchmann, Stephen L., and Gary Paul Nabhan. *The Forgotten Pollinators.* Washington, D.C.: Island Books, 1996.

Clyne, Densey. *The Best of Wildlife in the Suburbs.* Melbourne: Oxford University Press, 1993.

———. *The Garden Jungle.* Kenthurst, New South Wales: Kangaroo Press, 1996.

Darwin, Charles. *The Descent of Man.* New York: Modern Library, n.d. (First published in 1871.)

―――. *The Origin of Species by Means of Natural Selection.* New York: Modern Library, n.d. (First published in 1859.)

―――. *The Voyage of the 'Beagle'.* New York: Doubleday, 1962.

Diamond, Jared. *The Third Chimpanzee.* New York: HarperCollins, 1992.

Evans, Howard Ensign, and Mary Alice Evans. *Australia: A Natural History.* Washington, D.C.: Smithsonian Institution Press, 1995.

Flannery, Tim. *The Future Eaters: An Ecological History of the Australasian Lands and People.* New York: George Braziller, 1994.

George, Wilma. *Biologist Philosopher: A Study of the Life and Writings of Alfred Russell Wallace.* London: Abelard-Schuman, 1964.

Grzimek, Bernard, ed. *Grzimek's Animal Life Encyclopedia.* 13 vols. New York: Van Nostrand Reinhold, 1984.

Kanze, Edward. *Notes from New Zealand: A Book of Travel and Natural History.* New York: Henry Holt, 1992.

Keast, Allen. *Australia and the Pacific Islands: A Natural History.* New York: Random House, 1966.

Martin, Paul S., and Richard G. Klein, eds. *Quarternary Extinctions: A Prehistoric Revolution.* Tucson: University of Arizona Press, 1984.

Morrison, Reg. *Australia: The Four Billion Year Journey of a Continent.* New York: Facts on File, 1990.

Pyne, Stephen J. *Burning Bush: A Fire History of Australia.* New York: Henry Holt, 1991.

Ratcliffe, Francis. *Flying Fox and Drifting Sand.* Sydney: Angus and Robertson, 1947.

Sadleir, Richard. *Animals of Australia and New Zealand.* London: Hamlyn Publishing Company, 1970.

Serventy, Vincent. *Australia's National Parks.* Sydney: Angus and Robertson, 1969.

Vandenbeld, John. *Nature of Australia.* New York: Facts on File, 1988.

Wallace, Alfred Russell. *The Geographical Distribution of Animals.* 2 vols. New York: Harper and Brothers, 1876.

Whitmore, T. C., ed. *Biogeographical Evolution of the Malay Archipelago.* Oxford: Clarendon Press, 1987.

————. *Wallace's Line and Plate Tectonics.* Oxford, England: Clarendon Press, 1981.

FLORA

Brooker, Ian, and David Kleineg. *Eucalyptus: An Illustrated Guide to Identification.* Melbourne: Reed Books, 1996.

Costermans, Leon. *Native Trees and Shrubs of Southeastern Australia.* Adelaide: Rigby Publishers Ltd., 1981.

————. *Trees of Victoria and Adjoining Areas.* Frankston, Victoria: Costermans Publishing, 1994.

Jones, David L. *Cycads of the World.* Washington, D.C.: Smithsonian Institution Press, 1993.

Naughton, Peter, ed. *Forest Trees of Tasmania.* Longreach, Tasmania: Forest Resources, 1995.

White, Mary. *The Greening of Gondwana.* Frenchs Forest, New South Wales: Reed Books, 1986.

Wildflowers of the Western State. Albany, Western Australia: Rolsh Productions, 1994.

INVERTEBRATES

Holldobler, Bert, and Edward O. Wilson. *The Ants.* Cambridge: Harvard University Press, 1990.

McKeown, Keith. *Australian Spiders.* Sydney: Sirius Books, 1963.

Preston-Mafham, Rod. *The Book of Spiders and Scorpions.* New York: Barnes & Noble, 1996.

AMPHIBIANS AND REPTILES

Bennett, Ross. *Reptiles and Frogs of the Australian Capital Territory.* Woden, Australian Capital Territory: National Parks Association of the ACT Inc., 1997.

Bull, Michael. "Sleepy Lizards: Paired For Life." In *Australia Nature* 25, no. 6, 35–39.

Cogger, Harold G. *Reptiles and Amphibians of Australia.* Chatswood, New South Wales: Reed Books, 1994.

Coventry, A. John, and Peter Robertson. *The Snakes of Victoria.* Melbourne: Department of Conservation and Environment, 1991.

Greer, Allen E., ed. *Biology and Evolution of Australian Lizards.* New South Wales: Surrey, Beatty and Sons, 1989.

King, Dennis, and Brian Green. *Goanna: The Biology of the Varanid Lizards.* Sydney: University of New South Wales Press, 1993.

Neill, Wilfred T. *The Last of The Ruling Reptiles: Alligators, Crocodiles, and Their Kin.* New York: Columbia University Press, 1971.

Pianka, Eric R. *The Lizard Man Speaks.* Austin: University of Texas Press, 1994.

Shine, Richard. *Australian Snakes: A Natural History.* Chatswood, New South Wales: Reed Books, 1991.

Tyler, Michael J. *Frogs.* Sydney: Collins, 1976.

White, J., et al. "A perspective on the problems of snakebite in Australia," in *Biology of Australasian Frogs and Reptiles.* Edited by Gordon Grigg et al. Sydney: Royal Zoological Society of New South Wales, 1985.

BIRDS

Attenborough, David. *The Life of Birds.* London: BBC Books, 1998.

del Hoyo, J., et al., eds. *Handbook of the Birds of the World.* Barcelona: Lynx Edicions, 1992.

Feduccia, Alan. *The Origin and Evolution of Birds.* New Haven: Yale University Press, 1996.

Halliday, Tim. *Vanishing Birds.* London: Sidgwick and Jackson, 1978.

Johnsgard, Paul. *Arena Birds.* Washington: Smithsonian Institution Press, 1994.

Perrins, Christopher. M., and Alex L. A. Middleton, eds. *Encyclopedia of Birds.* New York: Facts on File, 1985.

Pizzey, Graham. *A Field Guide to the Birds of Australia.* Princeton: Princeton University Press, 1980.

———. *The Graham Pizzey and Graham Knight Field Guide to the Birds of Australia.* Sydney: Angus and Robertson, 1997.

Reader's Digest Services, eds. *Reader's Digest Complete Book of Australian Birds.* Sydney: Reader's Digest, 1977.

Rowley, Ian. *Bird Life.* New York: Taplinger Publishing Co., 1974.

Simpson, Ken. *Field Guide to the Birds of Australia.* Ringwood, Victoria: Viking, 1996.

Skutch, Alexander F. *The Minds of Birds.* College Station: Texas A&M University Press, 1996.

MAMMALS

Augee, Michael, and Brett Gooden. *Echidnas of Australia and New Guinea.* Sydney: University of New South Wales Press, 1993.

Dawson, Terence J. *Kangaroos: Biology of the Largest Marsupials.* Sydney: University of New South Wales Press, 1995.

Fleay, David. *Paradoxical Platypus.* Melbourne: Jacaranda Press, 1980.

Gould, John. *Australian Marsupials and Monotremes.* Facsimile edition, with an introduction by Joan M. Dixon. New York: Doubleday, 1975.

Grant, Tom. *The Platypus.* Sydney: University of New South Wales Press, 1995.

Lee, Anthony and Roger Martin. *The Koala.* Sydney: University of New South Wales Press, 1988.

Macdonald, David, ed. *Encyclopedia of Mammals.* New York: Facts on File, 1984.

Nowak, Ronald M., ed. *Walker's Mammals of the World.* Fifth edition. Baltimore: Johns Hopkins University Press, 1991.

Russell, Eleanor, and Marilyn B. Renfree. "Tarsipedidae." In *Fauna of Australia: Mammalia,* edited by D. W. Walton and B. J. Richardson. Canberra: Australian Government Publishing Service, 1989.

Savage, R. J. G. and M. R. Long. *Mammal Evolution: An Illustrated Guide.* Oxford, England: Facts on File, 1986.

Strahan, Ronald, ed. *Complete Book of Australian Mammals.* North Ryde, New South Wales: Angus and Robertson, 1983.

Sutcliffe, Antony J. *On the Track of Ice Age Mammals.* Cambridge, Mass.: Harvard University Press, 1985.

Triggs, Barbara. *The Wombat.* Sydney: University of New South Wales Press, 1996.

Index

About the Author

EDWARD KANZE, writer, photographer, and naturalist, is also the author of *Notes from New Zealand: A Book of Travel and Natural History, Wild Life: The Remarkable Lives of Ordinary Animals,* and *The World of John Burroughs,* published in paperback by Sierra Club Books. He travels and lectures widely, writes a weekly natural history column for the Hersam Acorn Newspapers, and lives with his wife, Debbie, in the Adirondack Mountains.